Reframing Diversity and Inclusive Leadership

Reframing Diversity and Inclusive Leadership

Race, Gender, and Institutional Change

SETH N. ASUMAH
and
MECHTHILD NAGEL

Published by State University of New York Press, Albany

© 2024 State University of New York

All rights reserved

Printed in the United States of America

No part of this book may be used or reproduced in any manner whatsoever without written permission. No part of this book may be stored in a retrieval system or transmitted in any form or by any means including electronic, electrostatic, magnetic tape, mechanical, photocopying, recording, or otherwise without the prior permission in writing of the publisher.

For information, contact State University of New York Press, Albany, NY
www.sunypress.edu

Library of Congress Cataloging-in-Publication Data

Names: Asumah, Seth Nii, 1954– author. | Nagel, Mechthild, author.
Title: Reframing diversity and inclusive leadership : race, gender, and
  institutional change / Seth Nii Asumah and Mechthild Nagel.
Description: Albany : State University of New York Press, [2024] | Includes
  bibliographical references and index.
Identifiers: LCCN 2023015600 | ISBN 9781438495828 (hardcover : alk. paper) |
  ISBN 9781438495842 (ebook) | ISBN 9781438495835 (pbk. : alk. paper)
Subjects: LCSH: Universities and colleges—Administration. | Educational
  leadership. | Educational equalization. | Education, Higher—Social aspects.
Classification: LCC LB2806 .A77 20247 | DDC 378.1/01—dc23/eng/20231017
LC record available at https://lccn.loc.gov/2023015600

10 9 8 7 6 5 4 3 2 1

To
Lorraine Y. Brathwaite
&

Dr. Tosha Abiana Asumah
&

Sariah Asumah Brown
S. N. A.
To
Philip Otieno
M. N.
&

To
All those who have died so that we can live,
all those who are made for loving freedom and justice,
lovers of the oppressed, and those who have sacrificed their lives
for diversity, equity, inclusion, liberation,
and social justice all over the world.

Contents

List of Illustrations — xi

Acknowledgments — xiii

Foreword — xv
    Elizabeth Davis-Russell

Preface — xix

Introduction: Providing a Context for Diversity, Equity, and Inclusive Leadership in the American Polity and in a Culture of Discontent — 1

Part 1.
How Do Diversity and Inclusion Leadership Matter Today?

Chapter 1   Diversity Studies and Managing Differences: Unpacking SUNY Cortland's Case and National Trends — 25

Chapter 2   The Illusion of Inclusion: Risk Management's Co-optation of Diversity and Inclusion Leadership at Whitehill University — 51

Chapter 3   New Trends in Diversity Leadership and Inclusive Excellence — 79

| Chapter 4 | Risk Management, Hegemony, and the Pitfalls of Diversity within the Academy | 97 |

Part 2.
Anti-oppression Traditions and Oppressive Practices: Searching for Interlocking Systems

Chapter 5	Race, Questioning Immigrant Bodies, and Heteropatriarchal Masculinity: Rethinking the Obama Presidency	123
Chapter 6	The Politics of Racial Exclusion in the Era of Inclusion: Seeing More Than an African Immigrant in US Immigration Policy	151
Chapter 7	Black Lives Matter, All Lives Matter?	171
Chapter 8	The Color of COVID-19 and the Knee-Lynching of George Floyd: Interrogating Systemic Racism and Inclusive Leadership	193
Chapter 9	Me Too, Me Two, and Misogynoir	217
Chapter 10	An American Kaleidoscope: Rethinking Diversity and Inclusion Leadership through the Prism of Gender and Race	237

Part 3.
Visions/Second Sight

| Chapter 11 | Racial Identity, the Danger of Being Too Comfortable, and Antiracist Decision/Policy-Making: Rethinking Whiteness | 259 |
| Chapter 12 | Ubuntu Ethics: I Am Because We Are | 289 |

Conclusion: Sustaining an Inclusive Community of Learners—
Recognition, Reconciliation, Accountability, and the Pedagogy
of Healing   311

References   325

Index   355

Illustrations

Figures

Figure 3.1	The Funnel for Diversity Leadership for Change and Inclusive Excellence.	84
Figure 5.1	"I Can't Breathe! A Better America," by Cartoonist Arend van Dam.	129
Figure 5.2	"The Color of Justice," by Cartoonist Mark Wuerker.	138
Figure 5.3	The Beer Summit.	139
Figure 6.1	Black African Immigrant Population in the United States, 1970–2015.	162
Figure 6.2	Where Do African Immigrants Come From?	162
Figure 6.3	Age Distribution: Youth, 2015.	164
Figure 6.4	Education Levels.	166

Tables

Table 5.1	A Typology of the American President—Samples of Presidents and Categories for Racial Attitude/Behavior and Policy Action.	135
Table 10.1	Gender Stereotypes.	241
Table 10.2	Model of Transactional and Transformational Leadership.	252

Acknowledgments

Many people have supported us in this journey of undulating and crucial terrain for the global human condition and our educational endeavors. Our research activities were challenged by the global pandemic of COVID-19 and protests for racial justice after the death of George Floyd in May 2020, yet we overcame those struggles and challenges to complete this task. Words are powerful, but we are not certain that the weight of our words would convey the totality of our gratitude. Many friends and colleagues in making the writing of this book a possibility have assisted us. This journey would have not been possible without the patience and support of our families and loved ones. Over the years, our colleagues, students, and participants of the SUNY Cortland Summer Institute for Diversity, Equity, Inclusion, and Social Justice and international and state-wide diversity and inclusion projects have enabled us to sharpen our ideas in the areas of diversity and inclusive leadership.

We would like to extend our appreciation to Erik Bitterbaum, president of SUNY Cortland, for his generous and continuing financial support for our research and intellectual endeavors, to former provost Mark Prus, for funding the annual Summer Institutes for Diversity, Equity, and Inclusion (DEI) that brought sweet inspiration to us for writing another book in the area of DEI, and to Elizabeth Davis-Russell, former provost of SUNY Cortland and former president of William Tubman University, Liberia, for reading the manuscript and writing a foreword to this book. To SUNY Cortland's chief diversity and inclusion officer, Lorraine Janove-Lopez, we have a friend in you for the struggle for justice, and we thank you for your continuing support for our diversity, equity, and inclusion undertakings. Very few people are more central to what we do than our friend and colleague Ibipo Johnston-Anumonwo, who has been a coauthor, coeditor and a sweet inspiration to many of our projects, including this one. We extend our sincere thanks to Eunice G. Miller for proofreading and formatting the final manuscript.

Our special appreciation goes to James Peltz, associate director and editor in chief, and Rebecca Colesworthy, education editor for the State University of New York (SUNY) Press for their collegiality, patience, and crucial roles in working with us on our second book with SUNY Press. To the manuscript reviewers who provided valuable comments to enable us to sharpen our thoughts, please accept our thanks.

For all those that we have forgotten to extend our appreciation, please take it on our heads and not on our hearts, we humbly apologize. This book project represents the product of collaborative and challenging coauthorship, and, ultimately, we take full responsibility for its contents.

Foreword

Elizabeth Davis-Russell

As America and the rest of the world struggle with white supremacist and autocratic leaders, higher education should be in the forefront to present models of education to combat this trend. Asumah and Nagel offer a "blueprint for change." Are academic leaders and executives ready to cooperate and implement this blueprint for change? I must confess that, after forty-five years of a career in higher education as a faculty member and administrator, I am skeptical about how many institutions of higher education will accept this blueprint for change.

Using the American Association of Colleges and Universities' definition of diversity allows the authors more latitude to look at intersectionality, which is critical to any discussion of diversity. Therefore, leaders in higher education can no longer be simplistic in their approaches.

By talking about building social justice in "our beloved community," the authors' approach blunts the often-flung criticism that advocacy for social justice or any criticism of America's inequitable system means that one does not love this country. Asumah and Nagel remind us that, while white America would want us to believe that its policies for governance are race neutral, they fail to acknowledge that systemic racism is the foundation of this society. White America wants us to continue to make them comfortable. White supremacist and autocratic leaders are threatened by any effort at inclusion. Even an examination of racism is seen as a device to indoctrinate and divide. Therefore, several states are rushing to ban teaching of subjects such as slavery, systemic racism, and critical race theory (CRT) because those make their children uncomfortable. And Blacks and other people of color are expected to continue to make accommodations that result in comfort for white America. Forget the reality of slavery and systemic racism and pretend that those are figments of overactive imaginations. Let white America continue its delusions, which give them comfort and continue to subjugate Blacks and other people of color.

The authors set out to make the case for the "symbiotic relationship between diversity and democracy" and expose the contradictions between the founding ideals of democracy and the actions of leaders who espoused those ideals. I contend that those leaders did not have people of color and women in mind when they crafted those ideals. If they had, would not the Preamble read "All people are created equal," rather than "All men are created equal"?

The authors make a valid case that the models and practices of the corporate world are not always applicable to higher education. Risk management is one of those that require closer examination. Organizations and institutions employ risk management plans to protect their reputation, finances, operations, and those they consider their customers/clients/members. If higher education institutions adopt this model and use it to silence the voices clamoring for inclusion and diversity, one questions the applicability of the use of such a model. I contend that higher education should be developing the models/frameworks that are best for it and give direction to the corporate world that can augment them for its use. Higher education educates and trains the leaders of the corporate world. Higher education has decades of teaching and research to inform models of human diversity, yet getting higher education to embrace this role has been difficult. As Asumah and Nagel point out, "higher education can sustain richer forms of learning, dynamic pedagogy and epistemology with integrity only if institutions of higher learning that profess moral and inclusive excellence are committed to diverse perspectives and people of multicultural orientation." Yet too many institutions have rushed to model the corporate world or have engaged in surface and superficial changes that look at number of students of color as their commitment to diversity. While representation is essential, if critical issues such as oppression and systemic racism are not addressed in meaningful ways, the responses are hollow and lead to disillusionment.

While the authors point to Mitch McConnell's "legislative obstructive/destructive behavior" that "emasculated" President's Obama's policies, this pattern has been evident in this society since its inception. When Blacks bought their freedom, America had to get rid of them. So, the American

Colonization Society took Blacks to Africa. When Blacks got power during Reconstruction, the Ku Klux Klan rose to decimate Blacks and what progress they had made. When Black Wall Street in Tulsa prospered, whites burned it to the ground. White America finds ways to punish Blacks and other people of color when they get out of their assigned roles. This contempt for Black people and this fear of their ascendancy to power is evident in every facet of life in America.

Blacks and people of color are here to stay. Therefore, white supremacists and autocrats want unilateral power to control every aspect of the lives of those who are different from them. When one examines the circle of power, Black women are outside of that circle. While white women may not be at the center where white men are, they are within the circle and have often used their access to power against Black women. This has resulted in a division that is historical.

In this country, that division began during slavery, where most white women upheld the institution of slavery and even participated and benefitted from it. Plantation rapes exacerbated this division. Instead of confronting their husbands, the white women blamed the enslaved women, even the children who were raped.

It continued during the abolitionist and suffragette movements. Even the white women involved in antislavery movements, while they worked with Black men such as Frederick Douglas, did not embrace Black women into those movements. This angered Sojourner Truth, who gave several scathing speeches protesting Black women exclusion.

In 1868 when Congress ratified the Fourteenth Amendment, which was passed in 1866, granting full citizenship to former enslaved people and free Blacks, it introduced the word *male* into the Constitution, thereby giving states the right to determine which male citizens could or could not vote. Female suffragettes were frightened by what they saw as the implications for the proposed Fifteenth Amendment. They disagreed on how to respond, and this division pitted the likes of Susan B. Anthony and Elizabeth Cady Stanton against Frederick Douglas, Sojourner Truth, and other abolitionists who wanted freedom. These white women chose their gender over freedom for enslaved persons (Wilson and Russell, 1996).

The division was evident in the twentieth century when the likes of Mary McCloud Bethune and other prominent Black women were forbidden to march in marches for equal rights for women, leading to the formation of parallel associations and organizations. Even though there have been some crossovers, by and large, these continue today.

In their book *Divided Sisters*, Midge Wilson and Kathy Russell (1996) identify a number of issues that account for, exacerbate, and continue this division. Among these are power, privilege (skin-color privilege, that is a fact of being white in this society), competition (vying for the small piece of pie given to women by men), and standards of beauty—white women as the standard of beauty by which Black women are judged.

As far back as colonial times, we see a definite distinction between white women and Black women. "On plantations in the antebellum South and throughout a good part of the twentieth century, many While middle-class and upper-class families across America could count on the service of Black women to cook their food, clean their homes, and raise their children" (Wilson and Russell, 1996, p. 5). This was not a reciprocal situation. "And to this day, in female-dominated, pink-collar occupations, where as many as 70 percent of women are employed, far more White women supervise Black women than vice versa" (p. 5).

Wilson and Russell point out that beneath the surface of relations lie often unspoken feelings of guilt on the part of white women, and resentment on the part of Black women who feel that "even the poorest white women seem to have a better chance of experiencing upward social mobility than many middle-class Black women" (p. 5).

For white and Black women, we must recognize that we have the same struggles, and instead of guilt and resentment, we must get to know one another on a non-superficial level. Our history must not be neglected, and when it's presented, it must be an integrated one.

As we look at our beloved community, what is needed is a transformation, deep structural change. We must go beyond our comfort zone and our sense of "us" and "them" to dismantle systemic racism and embrace models of diversity that exemplify integrity, civility, ethics, civic virtue, dependability, and trustworthiness.

Asumah and Nagel offer a hopeful note amid the clamor of white supremacy. However, they recognize that that hope can only be realized when "all stakeholders for diversity and inclusion are engaged in an enterprise that fulfills the expectation of the human condition—for who we are and the affirmation of social justice would be secured as the guiding principle for each other's existence."

Preface

Much is at stake in today's society like never before. More than ever, Americans face division even in our own families over ideology, the rise of extremism, weaponization of legislative instruments for the racialization of the American society, the threat to democracy, immigration and migration policy quagmire, rising levels of racism, women's reproductive rights issues, trans justice, political and educational leadership problems, economic downturns, and major pandemics. Moreover, community neotribalism, increases in mental health problems, high rates of psychic disequilibrium, mass delusional disorders about electoral politics, the reimagination of dystopia, and persistent questions about diversity, equity, and inclusion (DEI) continue to define the American polity. Colleges and universities are microcosms of the American society, and all of them are not relieved from many of the problems and issues above, including the recent irrepressible societal divisiveness and the adverse effects of inclusive leadership lacunae. Our book speaks to the pressing need for inclusive leadership in all its facets, as a question once urgently asked by Dr. Martin Luther King, Jr., "Where do we go from here?" We write this book in times of profound uncertainty, but the evolving work of diversity, equity, and inclusion is hope-affirming.

Five years ago, when our award-winning anthology *Diversity, Social Justice, and Inclusive Excellence* (Asumah & Nagel, 2014) became a popular book for teaching diversity and inclusion classes and professional development institutes, our students, colleagues, and popular readers tickled our consciousness through discussions and personal notes to us that the field of diversity, equity, and inclusion could be confusing. Even more mystifying are the recent debates over inclusive curriculums, politicization of intellectual discourse, the contumacy over science, research, and the literature of diversity, equity, and inclusion, critical race theory (CRT), critical whiteness studies (CWS), inclusive leadership, and identity politics. We realized that, with all the different diversity categories, theoretical frameworks for analyzing race, gender, identity politics, and a remarkable proliferation of antiracism work and programs on university and college campuses, a distinctive work on inclusive leadership and social justice paradigms was needed to appreciate the American higher education system and the American polity.

We recognized that whiteness and white institutional presence (WIP) in higher education and the American polity have irrepressible and omnipresent properties, yet critical whiteness studies is missing in most DEI leadership endeavors. Critical whiteness studies interrogates color neutrality (colorblindness), comfortability, ontological aggrandizement and contested spaces, the epistemologies of holy innocence/ignorance in diversity leadership, racism, and sexism. The fundamental questions of who is included in the American polity, and what American colleges and university campuses—a microcosm of the United States of America—are becoming or unbecoming in recent times have been rampant. We set out to answer some of the questions about oppression, injustice, microaggressions, and the reemergence of white supremacy and misogynoir on American college campuses and the society by changing our focus from "sensitivity" and risk management paradigms in a diverse community to inclusive leadership and rethinking what can be done to mitigate the perils of our racialized American society.

We realize that America's diversity, equity, and inclusion problems and issues are more complex than "sensitivity" trainings, taking one class on DEI, tolerance, allyship, and risk management traditions, and we must transcend those boundaries in order to reach a society defined by the qualities of inclusion, equity, and social justice. Nevertheless, the more diversity and inclusion classes and institutes we offer, the more we realize that persistent gender and racial disparities on our campuses and in the American polity are not epiphenomenal or an aberration. Higher education leadership, institutional leadership, and sociopolitical leadership have contributed to the building and sustenance of gender and racial inequity and oppression through policy, practice, and leadership that were not inclusive for almost two hundred years since the end of the American Civil War in 1865, through the Reconstruction era, and the civil rights movement of the 1960s.

In keeping with the theme of sustainable diversity and inclusion endeavors in communities where respect, cultural competence, and inclusive excellence are collaborative and necessary tools for citizenship and community interdependence, we approach this project with a mindset of letting our vision for the beloved and equity-minded community—America—be America again, as Langston Hughes and Martin Luther King, Jr., would affirm. Another civil rights leader and historian, Vincent Harding did not miss the chance to pose the question in his seminal essay *Is America Possible?* All three civil rights leaders above had concerns about the democratic experiment and DEI issues in the United States. Yet, like Harding, we are hopeful, affirmative, and provide testimony through this work that, "yes, yes, yes, America is possible. It *will* be. It *must* be" (Harding, 2007, p. vii). It is this possibility and hope-affirming vision that motivate us to continue our work in diversity, equity, and inclusive leadership.

Our research, teaching of DEI courses, and facilitating of professional development institutes, for a combined experience of over fifty years, have informed us that risk management strategies are assessed for their potential for success or failure in sustaining long-term viable changes in academic and corporate contexts. Yet they are full of political maneuvering, instrumentalization, and business modalities that do not always work for higher education and society, where human work and value-added considerations must be applied—placing emphasis on the essence that diversity work must be intentional to achieve the best practices and results. In this volume, we have eclectically grappled with diversity and inclusion problems and issues, with special emphasis on inclusive leadership, race, and gender, given the unstable nature of the diversity concepts of race and gender and how they persistently shape society in ways that increase the value of some groups while marginalizing others. Furthermore, race and gender maintain an interlocking connection to the system of oppression and matrix of domination and yet their indispensability in inclusive leadership cannot be overemphasized.

From our intellectual space in building the anthology *Diversity, Social Justice, and Inclusive Excellence* (Asumah & Nagel, 2014), classes on diversity and inclusion, and our Summer Institute for Diversity, Equity, Inclusion, and Social Justice at SUNY Cortland and other SUNY institutions, colleges, and schools for the past twenty-five years, the scaffolding for constructing this book project for the past three years has been unshakable and solid. Yet the conspiracy of events such as COVID-19, popular protests during the George Floyd murder case, student protests on college campuses for social justice, and the presidency of Donald Trump affected the original foundation and the superstructure of this intellectual building. Nevertheless, the rooms and the facilities within this building are equipped with the accoutrements to enable us to address some of the pressing issues and find solutions to build our future fortress and structures of social justice in the American society.

Part 1 tackles the importance of diversity and inclusion leadership. The introduction serves as an overview of the book, providing a context for diversity and inclusion leadership in a culture of discontent, anti-wokeness, cancel culture, and divisiveness in America today. We make the case for the symbiotic connection between diversity and democracy. As the United States continued to expand in the era of settler colonialism and cultural imperialism, the founding ideals of democracy would conflict with the actions of most of its own leaders and those who cherished the ideals of freedom, liberty, justice, equality, diversity, equity, and inclusion. We attempted to answer the following questions: What happened along the way in maintaining the founding qualities of the United States of America? Why should a country with such a foundation and leaders who were imbibed with the fluids of freedom and justice continue to find no tangible reasoning for granting all people, regardless of race, ethnicity, sex, gender, class, disability, religion, region, and other diversity categories, the same things the leaders and power holders will argue is American—reconciliation, respect, equity, and fairness? In this introduction, we point readers to how to tackle race and gender politics, utilizing the prism of an intersectional analysis. Yet, we note that we may not quite succeed with troubling heteronormativity effectively. Audre Lorde's warning, "The master's tools will never dismantle the master's house," continues to haunt us. There are some small steps that we think are hope-affirming in the totality of the work.

Chapter 1 enables us to juxtapose diversity studies and diversity management and examine how SUNY Cortland, the institution where we work, like other colleges and universities, has responded to trends in the United States to mitigate the effects of social alexithymia and injustices through diversity and inclusion professional-development programs and institutes. We begin with reviewing the transition from multicultural studies and women's studies at the State University of New York at Cortland to the expanded attention on diversity studies, antiracism projects, inclusion and equity-minded policies, and the challenges ahead for SUNY Cortland.

We highlight some pitfalls and benefits of diversity management, the concept of "managing diversity," and hope we will contribute to a richer understanding of these concepts and implementation of policies and procedures at universities elsewhere. Considerable endeavors and actions of civil rights and social justice movements have global implications, as most recently seen with Occupy Wall Street, which was started by New York City College students. So, our hope is that we may also contribute to a global discourse at the praxiological level—the intertwining of theory and practice and human action, attitude, behavior, and policy. Yet, the process of managing differences, campus climate, and campus culture has a history of its own at SUNY Cortland.

"The Illusion of Inclusion: Risk Management's Co-optation of Diversity and Inclusion Leadership at Whitehill University," chapter 2, is an innovative approach to combining ethnographic research, teaching, and creative narrative in reporting the contumacy of diversity imposters and educational establishmentarians, who continue to resist faculty and students demands for change. This chapter is a result of over fifty years of our combined experience of teaching, research, presentations, workshops, visiting scholarships, observations, and external reviews, and is an attempt to capture some of the critical lessons that we have learned at many universities and colleges in the United States, Europe, Africa, and Central America. Whitehill University (WU) is a microcosm of the United States. This Research 1 (R1) institution is in trouble with diversity and inclusion, just as the US has been in trouble even before the knee-lynching of George Floyd and the global uprising against systemic racism of the 2020s. Furthermore, there has been an immense increase in the hegemonic powers of university administrators, especially in predominantly white institutions (PWIs), and, ironically, this power differential enables these administrators to maintain the hegemony of whiteness to boost their claim of urgency to protecting students, especially whites, in the academy, while the lived experiences and concerns of students of color are mostly ignored.

In chapter 3, "New Trends in Diversity Leadership and Inclusive Excellence," we argue that diversity is a fact of life, and it is here to stay, even though not everyone is excited about diversity and inclusion, including Florida's Governor Ron DeSantis and many other leaders who have successfully secured anti-DEI laws and policies in their states. Democratic pluralism has not been appropriately designed to deal with the issues of history, geography, and number of people that contribute to the strengthening of the United States' national ethos, identity, and culture. Today's increasingly diverse student body, faculty, staff, services, curricula, and infrastructures are among the major challenges facing administrators and faculty of higher education. As we elaborated in our previous anthology on diversity, higher education can sustain richer forms of learning, dynamic pedagogy, and epistemology with integrity only if institutions of higher learning that profess moral and inclusive excellence are committed to diverse perspective and people of multicultural orientation. Yet, we cannot forget that the historical legacy of higher education as a space/place for exclusionary socialization and not for populist learning continues to prevail today despite the endeavors in public educational systems such as the State University of New York, the California State University system, or other public university systems in the United States. In this chapter, we intend to interrogate the complexity involved in diversity management, recruitment, retention, hiring practices, and the process of inclusion. We analyze the agency of difficult dialogue that emerges in diversity management, educational leadership, and associated benefits and pitfalls. We provide examples of some best practices and models for infusing diversity and inclusion institutes, and inclusive professional development programs into higher learning.

Chapter 4, "Risk Management, Hegemony, and the Pitfalls of Diversity within the Academy," highlights conflict-laden approaches of managing diverse voices, identities, and discourses within the US academy. Furthermore, we demonstrate in our discussion that diversity risk management has been rampant in the academy, and we provide evidence to collaborate with our concerns for the conflict-laden, contentious approaches of managing diverse voices, spaces, identities, and discourses within a risk-averse, increasingly corporate academy. Historically, calls for a paradigm shift in general education began with the new disciplines of Black studies and ethnic studies, followed by women's studies. Importantly, these demands came from below, engendered by militant student protests, and were not a diversity management decision from above in the 1960s. These interdisciplinary studies programs were granted by besieged administrators (e.g., from San Francisco State University, Cornell University, and the City University of New York) as a concession to a revolutionary student body that protested US imperialist wars and racist state repression within its territory, especially on reservations and in cities.

Part 2 is dedicated to intersectional analysis of systemic oppression. In chapter 5, "Race, Questioning Immigrant Bodies, and Heteropatriarchal Masculinity: Rethinking the Obama Presidency," we connect the analysis of diversity and inclusive leadership to the American presidency to demonstrate that the politics of antipolitics, whiteness, and hegemonic masculinity are not only present in the ivory towers—universities and colleges—but they are prevalent even at the highest office in the nation—the American presidency, because of the agency of gender and race. We argue that the macroscopic nature and complexity of the concept of race, heteropatriarchal masculinity, microaggression, and immigration issues put President Obama in a double-bind situation during his presidency in any attempt for productive decision/policy-making involving especially race and immigration. Double-bind situations produce limited options and exposure to penalties no matter what approaches President Obama took in confronting racial issues, immigration reform, and a challenge to heteropatriarchal masculinity in the United States. Furthermore, racial and heteropatriarchal hegemonic masculinity, which shape the policy-making process asphyxiated most of Obama's attempts for effective decision-making and policy reforms. This asphyxiation emasculated President Obama in his policy confrontations with lawmakers who are/were predominantly white heteropatriarchal hegemonic establishmentarians, and protectors of whiteness, such as the current Republican Senate Minority Leader, Mitch McConnell, whose interest in producing gridlocks and policy myopia, was/is paramount to their ego-maintenance, self-preservation, and whiteness, instead of the country's interest. As a heteropatriarchal hegemon, McConnell's legislative obstructive/destructive behavior has continued even during the Biden-Harris administration. In Obama's case, the position of discontent for a Black president was so obvious that the election of one of America's worst and most racist and sexist presidents, Donald Trump, was a direct reaction and response to the apparent disapproval and backlash associated with putting a Black man in the White House.

Chapter 6, "The Politics of Racial Exclusion in the Era of Inclusion: Seeing More Than an African Immigrant in US Immigration Policy," contends that, despite the claim by the United States as the "land of the free," US immigration policy always has included the politics of exclusion. Whiteness structures both university campuses and the American society in a state of convenient harmony for the dominant culture. As a normative structure, whiteness emerges constantly in US immigration policy. Notably, the macroscopic nature and complexity of immigration issues concomitant with recent increases in African immigrants in the US with higher educational levels and their rate of employability have contributed to the labeling and scapegoating of Black Africans in the immigration debate. Furthermore, the neo-racial structural model, neonationalism, patriotism, and heteropatriarchal hegemony, which tend shape the contemporary policy-making apparatus, asphyxiated immigration policy initiatives but increased conservatives and former President Trump's policy myopia, fueling the attacks on African immigrants, which derailed US policy initiatives in Africa. In the balance of this chapter, we provide some historical trajectories of African migration to the US, the politics of exclusion in US immigration policy, the characteristics and qualities of African immigrants in recent times, failures of US policy goals, the reasons for scapegoating Black Africans, the agency of the racial despotic state in immigration policy, and the urgency for demystification of the Black African "self" in the American psyche.

In chapter 7, "Black Lives Matter, All Lives Matter?," we discuss antiracist activism in the streets and on college campuses during the times of the Black Lives Matter movement. We also show how pedagogical and epistemological efforts fall short when faculty use a white racial frame even when they teach about social justice and diversity. In this context, we mention Todd Pittinsky's positive psychology neologism of "allophilia," that is, developing a friendship, liking, or love with those who are different from me. We note that this kind of love is not agape love, but it includes the sense of white goodness, niceness, whiteness as epistemologies of ignorance—racially blissful, as philosopher Charles Mills notes, and the friendship that constantly echoes, "I am too nice to be a racist." Yet allophilia for many reasons sustains systemic racism, whiteness as property, and white supremacy. Are college intergroup dialogues the answer to raise awareness about anti-Black racism? We contrast Pittinsky's approach with Frantz Fanon, who focuses on "disalienation of the Black man." Fanon gives a foundational account for white reasoning for anti-Black racism. He analyses how Black bodies are organized to survive a social world that is designed for white enterprises.

In "The Color of COVID-19 and the Knee-Lynching of George Floyd: Interrogating Systemic Racism and Inclusive Leadership," chapter 8, we argue that even during crises and catastrophes, when most people and institutions must demonstrate compassion, systemic racism exacerbates the levels of prejudice, discrimination, white hegemonic power, and white supremacy, resulting in disregard for Black lives and the rise of policy myopia, which presents new challenges to inclusive leadership and moral consciousness. Furthermore, we offer this chapter as testimony to America and the world that even though many white Americans are becoming more racially conscious and reawakening (woke), our work in justice and racial equity has many miles and years to travel. Contrariwise, despite a plethora of multiracial demonstrations and denunciation against police brutality after the killing of George Floyd in Minneapolis, Minnesota, by a white police officer, Derek Chauvin, most non-BIPOC folx in "comfortable" spaces/positions in the United States are still in denial about systemic racism. The omnipresence of systemic racism has obscured and obliterated our objective racial lenses so much that this country's educational and political leaders have settled for the status quo since the civil rights movement (1960s), until the global pandemic and the videotaped murder of George Floyd on May 25, 2020, provided yet another wake-up call to America for racial justice.

"Me Too, Me Two, and Misogynoir," chapter 9, engages in a comparative analysis of recent social movements, inspired by specific hashtags on twitter and social media in general. Many college and university students found a new space for confronting racial and gender-based oppression and challenging hegemonic leadership through these movements. We analyze the logic of misogynoir and cultural appropriations and instrumentalization of race, looking at current and historical examples. In a way, Me Too was the rallying cry of white upper class US women who participated in abolitionist circles, condemning the practice of chattel slavery. By instrumentalizing race, too often Black women disappear from view. Kristie Dotson's analysis of epistemic oppression shines a light on what exactly is detrimental to Black women's agency and how Black women and organizations are resisting testimonial quieting. In the balance of this chapter, we draw on contemporary examples that are indicative of the assaultive microaggression of "misogynoir," a term coined by Moya Bailey in 2008, which then went viral, again without proper attributions to its originator, a Black feminist queer scholar. Bailey uses the term misogynoir specifically in highlighting misogynist and racist media representations of Black women. We conclude the chapter with an analysis of the Black Lives Matter movement in Europe, specifically Germany, which was dubbed Me Two by antiracist activists.

In chapter 10, "An American Kaleidoscope: Rethinking Diversity and Inclusion Leadership through the Prism of Gender and Race," we offer a pathway out of the traditional and heteropatriarchal hegemonic deficit model of leadership prevalent in corporate America and institutions of higher learning by interrogating some of the traditional leadership models through the prism of gender and race and analyze two different leadership paradigms. One is concerned with gendered and racialized patterns of leadership styles and the other deals with a broader diversity and inclusion process of leadership, as the process of leadership is more important in a relational democracy than a position, per se. We argue that these different approaches and processes ought to be subjected to an intersectional analysis, which foregrounds gender and racial equity, inclusive excellence, and social justice considerations. Furthermore, it is our contention that, in the American polity, gender and race have structured our lives with deeper implications and impacts on women and people of color because of the historical contradictions of American life and the enduring agency of heteropatriarchal leadership in these changing times. Gender and racial stratifications, formations, and oppression continue to shape our leadership approaches and models. We interrogate diversity management that undervalue gender and race, and emphasize how inclusive leadership, intentionality, diversity, equity, and social justice are important to our work.

Part 3, titled "Visions/Second Sight," is the last section of the book, and it examines identity politics, Ubuntu ethics, soul searching, accountability, and the nature of the beloved community. In chapter 11, "Racial Identity, the Danger of Being Too Comfortable, and Antiracist Decision/Policy-Making: Rethinking Whiteness," our primary argument is that in heterogeneous, multiracial societies, such as the United States, where major decisions on our college campuses and in the polity are made predominantly by white folx, the dominant group's acknowledgment of their whiteness as power instruments and group-phenomenologically sustained variables, could enhance race relations and facilitate the decision-making and policy process. By consciously accepting race as an agency and discounting colorblindness or color neutrality in every political activity, whites in America could use their white privilege positively in race relations and in the policy-making sphere. Furthermore, we argue that the essentialization and episteme of "comfort" in racial conversations, discursive consciousness, difficult dialogues, and racialized decision-making are concomitant with dangers of illusion of resolve, solution, and closure, while racial identity issues and problems remain unresolved.

"Ubuntu Ethics—I Am Because We Are," chapter 12, examines Ubuntu ethics as a vision for everyday business of the academy. As we have noted in this book, diversity management has been treated like risk management with a sharp increase in funding for such offices in the academy during the Obama administration. Today, at the federal level, support for marginalized citizens and immigrants of color is at a low point. Any feeble attempt to diversify the universities is counteracted with restrictive executive orders that smack of transphobia, xenophobia, and racism. It remains to be seen how historically Black colleges and universities (HBCUs) and Tribal Colleges continue to survive amid bomb threats, the onslaught of white supremacists in the previous administration, and over thirty states—including Florida, Arizona, Idaho, Oklahoma, Texas, Iowa, North Dakota, Tennessee—engaging in policies against inclusion, critical race theory (CRT), diversity, and transgender politics can explain themselves to those who are opposed. At the same time, carceral feminist politics have ushered in punitive policies that again disadvantage Black male students. We argue that a healing process has to occur for those who have been historically traumatized and their perpetrators. Restorative justice practice should be advocated much more vigorously than currently happens on college campuses.

The conclusion brings us full circle. The human soul wants to be connected and appreciated for the value it contributes to the community. It does not want to be fabricated, exploited, stigmatized, acculturalized, or fixed because of the comfort of others. Our work is still evolving as new questions are being asked about how to teach American history, critical race theory (CRT), the contumacy over assaults on democracy and diversity, new anti-Black voting laws to deny the sacred right and universal adult suffrage for, especially, BIPOC folx in the states of Georgia, Arizona, Florida, Texas, North Carolina, Mississippi, and Alabama. The beloved community, as realized by a liberated people during the brief era of Black Reconstruction, will rise again when all stakeholders for diversity and inclusion are engaged in an enterprise that fulfills the expectation of the human condition—for who we are and the affirmation of social justice would be secured as the guiding principle for each other's existence. The ignoble practices of injustice, prejudice, and discrimination would be nailed in the coffin of oppression as we continue to confront our historical contradictions and rediscover our future possibilities by maintaining the centrality of our lives through the halls of social justice.

This book's strength lies in our ability to give academic leaders and executives of corporate America a blueprint for change. They must begin in earnest to prepare for a new epoch. A veritable renaissance of the hope-inspired epoch of Radical Reconstruction has begun: diverse, marginalized group organizations, and individuals singled out for ostracism are no longer politely retreating to the margins. A case in point: prize-winning journalist Nikole Hannah-Jones was at first willing to agree to accept the Knight

Chair without receiving tenure, so as to not tarnish her alma mater, the University of North Carolina at Chapel Hill. In the end, emboldened by tremendous national and legal support, she turned away from UNC and joined Howard University with great purpose: establishing a Knight Center for Journalism with an initial twenty million dollars. Campus leaders also need to pay attention to the power of a tweet (e.g., Me Too tenure denial), as they know very well that nothing less than their college ranking and reputation are at stake. A telling headline indicates what is at stake for the image and reputation of premier institutions: "Leaders Settled for Less and Wound Up with Nothing" (Stripling, 2021). In addition, most public and private institutions are racing for making enrollment numbers or are facing the threat of closure given a declining traditional cohort of teenagers. Certainly, national demographic projections show that the white cohort is declining, especially, white male college-bound students. Beginning with the Trump era, Black students are intentionally heading for HBCUs, and HWCUs (i.e., white institutions) must take note that BIPOC tenure-track faculty are exiting these spaces in large numbers, as it is predictably happening at UNC.

With this book, we caution against the short-term gain of "resolving to stay silent" in the face of public scrutiny, because this tactic will have the potential to backfire tremendously. A campus climate that is ripe with misogynoir hostility and suspect tenure decisions drives junior and senior BIPOC and LGBTQ scholars away. Repairing relations in a racially charged, arctic climate will take another generation. Nevertheless, surveys about campus climate and performative antiracism projects are not sufficient to eradicate the system of oppression. Campus culture and university ecology must be interrogated and reimagined differently. The stakes are high and the moral imperative to do good and stand up for what is right should be heeded. We also note that policy conversations about diversity, inclusion, and equity do not amount to the tangible goal of social justice. If Black lives truly matter, we must ask with Randall Robinson (2000) what is owed to Black Americans. Repairing without reparations and without a reckoning with racial capitalism will not bring about abolition democracy.

Introduction

Providing a Context for Diversity, Equity, and Inclusive Leadership in the American Polity and in a Culture of Discontent

This primer on diversity and inclusive leadership mainly highlights equity and inclusion challenges for democracy and diversity for the nation state and in US academia, and provides a framework for interrogating whiteness in our racialized society and higher education. We review how institutions have been impacted by global social justice movements with a focus on racial and gender injustices—highlighting the Movement for Black Lives and the Me Too movement, which originated in the US and quickly spread across the globe.

We are uniquely qualified to champion the cause of diversity and inclusive leadership, as we have dedicated our academic work to this field, emerging several decades ago. This book is a result of over fifty years of our combined experience of teaching, research, presentations, workshop facilitating for professional development, visiting scholarships, classroom observations, and external reviews, and it is an attempt to capture some of the critical lessons that we have learned at many universities and colleges in the United States, Europe, Africa, and Central America. Among these universities and colleges that we have engaged are the University of Oxford, University of Westminster, and University of Surrey in England; University of Hamburg and Fulda University of Applied Sciences in Germany; McGill University, Canada; University of the West Indies, Jamaica; University of Ghana, University of Cape Coast, Kwame Nkrumah University of Science and Technology, and Valley View University in Ghana; United States International University in Kenya; University of Cape Town in South

Africa; University of Calabar and the University of Ibadan in Nigeria. In the United States, our work and engagements have brought us to Xavier University, University of Wisconsin–Madison, University of Oklahoma, Harvard University, Yale University, Cornell University, Lehigh University, Ithaca College, Syracuse University, Princeton University, Massachusetts Institute of Technology, University of Massachusetts Amherst, University of Tennessee-Knoxville, Seton Hall University, Fairleigh Dickenson University, Roberts Wesleyan College, the University at Albany (SUNY), Binghamton University (SUNY), the University at Buffalo, SUNY Brockport, Empire State College (SUNY), SUNY Cortland, SUNY Oneonta, SUNY Morrisville, SUNY Delhi, SUNY New Paltz, SUNY Purchase, and SUNY Plattsburg. Nagel also had fellowships and residencies at the Max Planck Institute for the Study of Religious and Ethnic Diversity, Göttingen, Germany and the Czech Academy of Sciences, Prague. Asumah was a Carnegie-African Diaspora Fellow at the University of Ghana, Legon, where he collaborated with African educators on diversity, equity, and inclusion (DEI) leadership projects and political change.

We made casual contacts with many other institutions that are not on this list. Importantly, we have led multiday diversity, equity, and inclusion institutes for faculty, administrators, schoolteachers, and principals in various institutions. In addition, we are called upon to assist with crises situations between faculty and students or other stakeholders in institutions of higher learning. At this point in our professional lives and after publishing several articles and books on diversity, equity, inclusion, and social justice, we have realized that DEI work is human work, and it has become our modus vivendi—a way of life. Making the personal political and advancing inclusion, equity, and antiracism strategies, not only in our student bodies, but in the administrative ranks in the academy and leadership in the American polity, especially in times of discontent and grievance culture, are paramount to our mission.

Perhaps aside from former President Trump and his compatriots, like Florida's governor, Ron DeSantis, who do not believe in diversity training and leadership, most academics, politicians, and corporate executives would affirm that diversity and inclusive leadership is not an option anymore and it is concomitant with modern-day organizational leadership. Diversity and inclusive leadership transcends the boundaries of transactional leadership, which dwells on the environment of exchange of services and rewards to maintain the status quo of an organization. The genesis of diversity and inclusive leadership is therefore ingrained in the genuine relational ability to reach the mind and soul of all organizational members, faculty, and students and to bring them to their fullest potential and capacity to produce, contribute, and perform with a diversity, inclusion, and equity mindset. Furthermore, we advocate a diversity and inclusive leadership model, which examines problems and find solutions based on a racial and gender equity framework.

As we have mentioned in our previous work in *The Routledge Companion to Inclusive Leadership*, edited by Joan Marques (2020), dean of the School of Business and professor of management at Woodbury University, many national leaders, college and university presidents, provosts, and deans are mostly "white heteropatriarchal leaders, who have accumulated and consolidated power for years despite this era of diversity and inclusion. Many of these leaders are mostly removed from their students and faculty, depending strictly on a transactional style, which, like the Great Man model, is linear, hegemonic, risk-abating, masculinist, rational, practical and unidirectional" (Asumah & Nagel, 2020, p. 178). Given the symbiotic relationship between democracy and diversity, organizations and institutions of higher learning that continue to follow the leadership model only drag their institutions to organizational leadership implosion and wakefulness deficiency. Our experiences in the United States, Europe, and Africa, unfortunately, confirm our fear that wakefulness, as an important diversity leadership ingredient for inclusive college campuses, is completely absent in the modus operandi of these leaders. Wakefulness in diversity and inclusive leadership provides an impetus for mindful listening to diversity entities, meaningful interconnectedness, and well-being of all stakeholders—students, faculty, and administrators. Marques asserts, "Wakefulness requires a leader's ability to take a hard look at his or her own values and beliefs and finding out whether they align with the collective" (2020, p. 7). We have found out in our work and commitments in diversity and inclusion that the wakefulness lacuna, misalignment of values, microinvalidation, barriers to inclusion, cultural incompetence, and risk management paradigms have all contributed to the recent discontents in our community of learners and the nation state.

Theories about diversity and inclusion leadership have become necessary tools for organizational development. Diversity and inclusion leadership for companies and institutions of higher learning are not luxury anymore; they are a necessity for the proper functioning of any organization. During the Obama administration, some palpable gains had been made, which were then walked back during four years of the Trump regime. Nevertheless, every major multinational company, every public and private college and university has had to prioritize diversity initiatives, including hiring diversity managers who report to the CEO or presidents of these organizations. Employees and, increasingly, students enrolled in the academy go through diversity and implicit bias training for onboarding and orientations. What is the value of these institutional efforts? Do they provide a less chilly campus climate for those who have been historically marginalized? Do they help to change institutional (DEI) cultures for the better? Do they enable us to understand whiteness (beyond personhood, but in systems and policies), white privilege, the complexities of gender, race, space, and inclusive leadership in the academy? Do they embolden a backlash that recasts those who are yesterday's bullies as today's victims?

We are sympathetic to critical perspectives that analyze institutionalized oppression and in general adopt a broader, macroscopic perspective in social injustice. In their article "Who Benefits? A Critical Race Analysis of the (D)Evolving Language of Inclusion in Higher Education," Harris et al. (2015) tackle the elephant in the room: white supremacy in academia that flourishes unabated even though many diversity initiatives are poured into efforts to stem the tide of institutional racism. Their diagnosis reveals an excessive focus on process (of inclusivity) and performative events instead of outcomes. Such superficial "diversity talk" will not guarantee that the increasingly diverse student body will ever work with a professoriate that matches their demographics. A case in point: the State University of New York (SUNY) recently launched a faculty fellow initiative, Promoting Recruitment, Opportunity, Diversity, Inclusion, and Growth (PRODiG), that would address racial mismatch in science, technology, engineering, and math (STEM) and other fields. Its own analysis showed a paucity of Black and Latino faculty. In the end, the initial class of some ninety fellows hired on many of the sixty-four SUNY campuses were predominately white women. We had the opportunity to do a presentation on diversity and inclusion mentoring during the statewide orientation process for the first PRODiG cohorts, and it was not a surprise that the white women in attendance took advantage of this orientation to expand their networking and privilege by requesting a separate consortium for empowerment—redefining space and privilege.

Of course, white women are also underrepresented in STEM fields, especially at university centers. However, by focusing on a fair process rather than on goals, Black, indigenous, and people of color (BIPOC) students find themselves again shortchanged. Meanwhile, the BIPOC PRODiG colleagues who joined SUNY had to quickly learn how to navigate another form of STEM—space, time, energy, and motion, which are controlled by the hegemony, whiteness, and white institutional presence (WIP) as noted by one scholar in his work on people of color and environmental stress in institutions of higher learning (Pierce, 1975). White women again are benefiting from "inclusion strategies" as they have since the "death" of affirmative action in *Regents University of California v. Bakke* (1978) and *Gratz v. Bollinger* (2003). For most white men, affirmative action policies are all about inflating their egos to make reference to "quotas," which even though illegal, based on the *Regents University of California vs Bakke* (1978) decision, still occupies a place in the minds of white men as a major problem in diversity and inclusion. The conservative majority of the US Supreme Court struck a final blow to affirmative action and race-based admissions in the recent cases of *Students for Fair Admission, Inc. v. President & Fellows of Harvard College* (2023) and *Students for Fair Admissions, Inc. v. University of North Carolina* (2023), and most non-veteran, white men, who are not a protected class under affirmative action welcomed the SCOTUS decisions with a sigh-of-relief.

With reference to white women, as demonstrated by the research of Unzueta et al. (2010), this is how most white professional women perceive affirmative action—to be beneficiaries of the policies or not. If they view affirmative action as a "quota" system, then they are in the same ego-maintenance cahoots with white men. However, if white women find themselves to be beneficiaries of affirmative action, they do not engage in the ego-maintenance assumptions that "undeserving" BIPOC folx were hired for a particular position or college admission (Unzueta et al., 2010). In the end, we see that, again, despite good intentions, it is mostly whites who benefit from "diversity and inclusion" strategies.

We depart from Harris et al.'s (2015) insightful critique with respect to the term "inclusive excellence," first promulgated by the Association for American Colleges and Universities (AAC&U). These authors worry about co-optation of funders like the Ford Foundation, which has had specific interests in quelling radical demands for social justice and undermined democracies in the Global South (p. 30). We are sympathetic to their claim that AAC&U freeze-frames inclusive excellence by appealing to demographic shifts in the professoriate, asking BIPOC faculty to do more than their fair share of antiracist pedagogy, critical whiteness studies (CWS), critical race theory (CRT), and building an awards structure, which "quantifies and commodifies inclusive excellence" (p. 31). These authors charge that AAC&U ignore interlocking systems of oppression, specifically any concern about social justice. Thus, the organization caters to the neoliberal ideology of the Ford Foundation that funds it, rather than providing a meaningful progressive blueprint for social-justice oriented scholars and teachers. We concur with Cabrera et al. (2017) that higher education and diversity studies are missing an important link in addressing social justice issues because of the hegemony of whiteness, color neutrality (colorblindness), epistemologies of ignorance, prevalence of comfortability to sustain whiteness, especially on predominantly white institutions (PWIs), and the ontological aggrandizement of whiteness in higher education (pp. 7–9). Diversity endeavors on college and university campuses have succumbed to the practice of "niceness," submission to white fragility, white leadership, white institutional presence—overwhelming white leadership and authority on college campuses, contribute to high levels of performative DEI activities, and lip service to diversity rather than concrete policy and institutional change. Yet, we argue that inclusive excellence still has a place and should be cultivated by all stakeholders on the twenty-first-century campus. We think that the term can be used to effectively incorporate anti-oppressive education that includes the entire professoriate, not just the chosen few BIPOC faculty. It is a good concept, which we use to move away from the meritocratic-laden ideology of "academic excellence." In the following section, we provide a brief genealogy of the promises and contradictions of the social and political ideologies that characterize the American polity and the drama of democracy and diversity to structure the context for the continuing struggle for inclusive spaces and places in higher education. In this context, we stand with scholars and researchers who remind us that the term "higher education" was coined to separate and describe learning that was designed for the elite in society and not for commoners (Geiger, 2005). Our current structures and systems of higher education contain elements of inequity and elitism. The irony of popular higher education is that its origins were not what present public educational institutions were designed to promote. Historically, higher education, like the American society, was structured and influenced by individualism and meritocracy, which processes and values could be counterproductive to the principles of inclusion, diversity and democracy, so far as minoritized groups and women are concerned.

Democracy and Diversity: The Origins

At the inception of this country, interlocutors of nation building, democracy, and the new American Constitution vigorously engaged in debates in the Federalists Papers about the American political experiment with a republic, homogeneity, and the size of government and the nation state—the anti-federalist advocated for a smaller central government and more power to the states within the union. The federalists, on the other hand, argued for a larger republic with politics of difference, heterogeneity, and diversity, which would provide strength to the new republic. Hamilton, Madison, and Jay saw the power of diverging viewpoints. Or did they? Hamilton was clear about how differences in opinions should not be seen as deficiencies but would provide sociopolitical vitality for the new nation state. The federalists were victorious in their quest for a republic whose foundation will comprise of a complex, continual experimentation with both democracy and diversity (Sunstein, 1992). Hitherto, democracy and diversity had a symbiotic relationship and that ideal was fully demonstrated in the debates by both opponents and proponents of the nature of the United States and multicultural democracy. Madison in Federalist 10 warns the republic about factions, but he emphasized the essence of equality, liberty, and difference (Sunstein, 1992). Our work on these noble ideals continuous to evolve even today.

Diversity and inclusive leadership demand particular attention during these times of discontent, internet information frenzy, political divisiveness, and the effects of the global pandemic, and the fight for racial justice. As diversity and inclusion have become indispensable and irrepressible, diversity and inclusive leadership is a sine qua non. Nevertheless, there are very few institutions that offer doctoral degrees in diversity leadership, and, ironically, most organizational leaders who preach the gospel of diversity and inclusion do not attend professional development institutes for diversity and inclusion. In over twenty years of leading diversity and inclusion institutes around the world, we can count with the fingers on one hand presidents, provosts, deans, and directors who have taken time out to attend some of our colloquiums or professional development institutes.

Making the Case for Diversity and Inclusive Leadership

A critical exploration of diversity leadership has never been more important than in our times of discontents, global pandemics, political insurgency, and racial injustice. We began this work over six years ago, and our analysis since then has been shaped by social and political upheaval during the Obama administration, Trump era, and its remnant Trumpism. We braced ourselves when Trump was elected by a minority of voters, thanks to the Electoral College system, as we knew it would only be a matter of time that some of the liberal reforms made under the Obama administration would be dismantled. It is interesting and ironic to note from our discussion above that the same Electoral College victory in 2016 that gave the Trumpublicans the power to rule would be attacked by Trump insurgents on January 6, 2021, because the political tide did not flow his way. Is this recent event at the Capitol with predominantly white males in our times of discontent the irony of democracy and diversity?

What happened to the United States' security apparatus and leadership during the insurgency is still under investigation. As ardent observers and researchers for politics of inclusion and social justice, we were not disappointed with our prediction, when billionaire Betsy DeVos was confirmed to a cabinet post in charge of the Education Department. She had no prior experience in education administration, but unions and education administrators alike worried that she would dismantle public education as we knew it. When DeVos finally resigned in early January after an attempted coup, or what Latin American observers label *autogolpe* (Call, 2021), incited by the outgoing president, unions had two words: "good riddance." Her parting "gift" was yet another transphobic policy memorandum, which outlined that Title IX does not apply to transgender students (Padgett, 2021).

Nonetheless, the historical contradictions surrounding the American nation state, whose origins rest on the principles of democracy and diversity as defining qualities and characteristics but whose actions and deeds have suffered from institutional anemia in activating the principles of equity and inclusion, demand deeper explanations. Indubitably, at the infancy of the nation state, those who shepherded its development and historic undertakings restricted themselves to a polity organized around white heteropatriarchal hegemonic male political culture. As the United States continued to expand, the founding ideals would conflict with the actions of most of its own leaders and those who cherished the ideals of freedom, liberty, justice, equality, diversity, equity, and inclusion. What happened along the way in maintaining the founding qualities of the United States? Why should a country with such a foundation and leaders who were imbibed with the fluids of freedom and justice continue to find no tangible reasoning for granting all people, regardless of race, ethnicity, sex, gender, class, disability, religion, region, and other diversity categories the same things the leaders and powerholders will argue is American—reconciliation, respect, equity, and fairness?

Perhaps most of us are blinded by the abstract and legal constraints that were propounded in the writings of the founders to prevent the general populace (whites) from the tyranny of the majority and to make sure that democracy and diversity prevailed. However, we cannot succumb to historical amnesia by forgetting that the founding of this country was violent, including looting, pillaging, raping, dehumanization, disenfranchisement, injustice, and betrayal by some of our leaders. The "We" in "We the People" in the Declaration of Independence has not maintained its real meaning. It has never represented the totality of the American polity. Black bodies were stolen from Africa to build this nation—the holocaust of enslavement. Black folx must fight back to retrieve their bodies from the American body politic. Indigenous people's lands were looted, and it is ironic when some political commentators associate "looting" with, especially, Black bodies in Black Lives Matter demonstrations. Have Americans quickly forgotten the statecraft, leadership, soldiery, and yet deception of Benedict Arnold, whose battlefield engagement was second to none but defected to the British side of the war? Are President Trump and his seventy-four million followers, some of whom staged an abortive coup d'état against the United States Congress and the nation's sacred temple of democracy and diversity, the Capitol, on January 6, 2021, modern day Benedict Arnolds?

Our experimentation with democratic and diversity projects has not taken a productive shape, because the American political culture has not been properly healed from the past atrocities and calamities. The body politic is not healed sufficiently for reconciliation to ensue. Those in leadership positions are not bold enough to make social justice, racial equity, and inclusive democracy a campaign promise. The Biden-Harris administration is one of the few to make racial justice an agenda, something that has been delayed by too many leaders, but now it cannot be deferred anymore. However, as we wait for President Biden to put his "whole soul" in this race project, leaders at our various social institutions must genuinely make racial justice a priority. Race, in the politics of inclusion and equity, is the elephant in the American room. The *longue durée* of race as sociopolitical foundation and superstructure of the American political culture makes us vulnerable in placing the racial body only in historical terms, but history is not dead, we live history.

Race and Racism

The concept of race, a crucial diversity category that signifies and symbolizes socioeconomic and political conflicts and interests by making references to different phenotypes, is a "master category" of our lives. Race, as we understand it today, is a social construct. As Omi and Winant inform our cognitive structures in this work, "Race is a way of 'making up people.' The very act of defining racial groups is a process fraught with confusion, contradiction, and unintended consequences. . . . We assert that in the United States, race is a master category—a fundamental concept that has profoundly shaped, and continues to shape the history, polity, economic structure, and culture of the United States" (2015, pp. 105–106). However, race intersects with gender, sex, religion, geography, class, sexual orientation, and other diversity categories that dominate our lives and make any sociopolitical analysis meaningful. It is impossible to comprehend and appreciate diversity leadership without organizing our thinking process around the intersectionality of race and the other matrices of domination above.

Our cultural and racial interdependence is inevitable; nonetheless, the race project in the United States received its impetus from European racist pseudoscientists and explorers who made contacts with Africa and the "new world." Even over two hundred years before the founders sustained the holocaust of slavery in the New England area and the rest of the United States, the Portuguese, as chronicled in the work of Gomes Eanes de Zurara, the biographer of Prince Henry, anti-Black racism would serve as strong justification for African slavery (Kendi, 2016, p. 23). As soccer enthusiasts and social justice advocates, we lament the horrible and racist slavery roots of many of the English Premier League clubs, whose establishments sustained their wealth and fame through the blood, sweat, and free labor of enslaved Black people. Ironically, the English Premier League has made kneeling to the ground, before any match starts, a symbol for racial justice after the killing of George Floyd by a white police officer in Minneapolis on May 25, 2020.

What happens in the American polity and on our college campuses concerning race, gender, and white hegemony may be localized but does not consist of isolated cases. We can make strong connections and linkages of oppression, marginalized groups, cultural imperialism, and exploitation across the Atlantic Ocean. English aristocracy and owners of wealthy English Football Association League organizations, such as Liverpool Football Club and Manchester United, have created their wealth on the backs of enslaved Black people from Africa and the Caribbean. These owners and leaders, whose ancestors exploited Black folx, and the English Premier League, are just making efforts to weed out racism after

George Floyd's murder (Bona, 2020). Major English banks such as Lloyds and Barclays are culprits of the enterprises that exploited Black bodies and the Black race for their enormous wealth and power. These banks, still today, continue to sponsor the most prestigious English Premier League, La Liga in Spain, and the Ligue de Football Professionnel in France. Even though both Lloyds and Barclays have denounced racism and embraced diversity and inclusion, history is not dead.

Besides, the over seventy-year reign of Queen Elizabeth II of the United Kingdom ended on September 8, 2022, in Balmoral Castle, Scotland. The queen died peacefully, but the constitutional monarchy of the United Kingdom is not dead. Soccer fans and supporters of the English Premier League missed the opportunity to sing the national anthem, "God Save the Queen" during the time of national/global mourning. A minute of silence for the Queen preceded every match when the league resumed. The lyrics of the national anthem changed slightly to "God Save the King"—King Charles III. For her seventy years of reign, at the seventh minute of every football match in the English Premier Leagues, there was a pause and a loud applause by the fans and supporters. Yet many former colonized people and the British Commonwealth are not afraid to associate those seventy years of her reign with British imperialism, colonialism, exploitation, and cultural imperialism. During the ten days of mourning for the death of the Queen of England, the English Premier League was suspended briefly and resumed after a few days. The world missed the symbolism of the kneeling by the players before each game started—an action against institutional and global racism—a gift of protest gesture to the world from Colin Kaepernick, an American civil rights activist and football quarterback who played in the National Football League. For some time, no one knew whether the Kaepernick kneeling against racism would ever return to the Premier League, because it was stopped to introduce new antics associated with the English monarchy to the beautiful game. This is how quickly the world forgets about the pain of marginalized and colonized people. Alas, the Kaepernick kneeling against racism has returned to some football stadiums in the United Kingdom, but it is fading away slowly, nevertheless, because racism is still alive and kicking.

In the European football leagues, colonized Black bodies play for their former colonizers. Black bodies are usually highly anointed with the holy water and legacy of assimilation and cultural imperialism to remain competitive with their European teammates. In fact, we do not have to go too far in history to realize how France won the 2018 World Cup in

Russia with predominantly Black talented African bodies. Talented Black bodies are still traded in these leagues like the times of Maafa, the holocaust of slavery, plantation agriculture, and the system of sharecropping. Most soccer players in the United States have the aspiration of playing in the English Premier League, a business-leisure system whose origins in exploiting Black folx and women are unpardonable.

In the United States, the higher education system is the training ground for professional football, soccer, and other sports. Most talented student of color athletes find their way into the National Football League (NFL) and, in soccer, Major League Soccer (MLS), with the hope of playing in the English Premier League, La Liga in Spain, or Ligue de Football Professionnel in France. So, from the higher educational systems that were not designed to grant success for colonized Black bodies to leagues that continue to utilize Black bodies for profit, the plantation mentality still prevails—mostly Black players doing the hard manual labor, and exclusively white managers, administrators, and leaders doing all the "thinking"—something Iris Marion Young characterized as the reasoning/body dichotomy: "The work of abstract rationality is coded as appropriate for white men, while the work that involves caring for the body or emotions is coded for women and the 'menial' work of serving and being servile is coded for nonwhites" (1990, p. 222). Other studies have provided similar evidence. Kovel maintains that modern capitalism and social arrangements have always structured functions of society and labor partly based on race and gender. Whiteness has been exclusively associated with reason, while Blackness is relegated to the body (1984, pp. 141–148).

Many profit-making Division I (D-I) colleges and universities in the United States whose wealth and endowments were derived from the system of slavery and enslaved Black people are not just in the business of knowledge production. Rather, they are in the business of wealth creation through sports, leisure, and pleasure with strong foundation of systemic racism, sexism, and white heteropatriarchy. However, in the United States, the most profitable college sport is American football, generating about $31.9 million per annum, per school on the average, followed by basketball, and a majority of the players are Black. Two top Texas schools, Texas A&M University, and the University of Texas at Austin each had projected annual value of $147 million for 2022 (Crawford, 2021). The context remains the same, exploitation, marginalization, and cultural imperialism are tools of whiteness. White heteropatriarchy, and hegemonic leadership are prevalent in the institutions of higher learning and society at large, where Black bodies are used and confined. Inclusive leadership approaches could facilitate the mitigation of systemic racism, sexism, and institutional change.

No matter how it is analyzed, European and white American leaders used three reasonings to continue their anti-Black race projects in America: (a) profitability—the fact that Maafa, that is, the African holocaust, provided an economic system of merchants, plantation agriculture, and free laborers to start infant industries in America based on the exploitation of Black Africans; (b) practicability—Indigenous people and white indentured servants were not good slaves, they failed the system, so Black Africans (physically strong, performed manual labor, and locationally displaced, low escape possibilities) were the practical choice for enslavement; (c) justifiability—European and white American racist mentality, religious absurdity, false biological assumptions of race, white cultural "superiority," and social Darwinism, survival of the white "fittest" race, all provided justifications for the treatment of the powerless and voiceless (Karenga, 2010). White kings, explorers, founders, and political leaders engaged and continue to engage in the politics of anti-Black racism and racial despotism.

Racial Despotism and Anocracy in a Democracy

From the inception of this nation state, therefore, white racial hegemony and racial despotism have shaped the body politic of United States. In racial despotism, the endeavors to fully understand the agency and authority of race and to restructure the country into an antiracist nation state are extremely slow—from the end of slavery, Emancipation Proclamation, Radical Reconstruction, the Great Migration, Jim Crow, the civil rights and Black Power movements, to Black Lives Matter. In the process of racial despotism, diversity leadership is highly challenged by various white heteropatriarchal leaders, whether it is Jefferson, who struggled with the political morality of owning slaves and writing "All men are created equal" or the Trump administration's policy that targeted Blacks, Latino, Muslims, immigrants of color, and favored white immigrants.

Trump displayed his preference for Norwegians—"We should have more people from places like Norway"—and not immigrants from "shithole" countries, like Haiti, El Salvador, and Nigeria (Aizenman, 2018). Is American democracy becoming an anocracy because of lack of inclusive leadership? Are so many states and local governments becoming an anocracy—political entities with mixed authoritarian and democratic structures and powers? President Biden might have a case for campaigning for the midterm elections of 2022 with a theme that emphasizes the "battle for the soul of the nation" ("Biden Addresses Threats," 2022). The picture is clear, there are questions involving the leadership style projected within the Trump administration and Make America Great Again (MAGA) followers that continue to make policies in states and local governments that threaten the "soul of democracy."

The Irony of Democracy and Diversity

The irony of democracy is that it can produce space for an inevitable tension with diversity. When the general populace or competing constituents engage in the politics of difference for their perceived rights and sacred constitutional demands, there is an obscured and yet a legitimate call for inclusivity—diversity and democracy. Structural and systemic paralysis can easily emerge if the tensions between diversity and democracy are not reconciled at the proper time and with due diligence. Diversity and inclusive leadership are very essential at this point. Former President Trump, in his leadership role as an American president, was a quintessential example of a leader who represented what we see as irreconcilable differences in diversity and democracy. Trump talks about democracy even after his presidency, but his actions were/are autocratic and very much against diversity. Many examples of his demonstration of the tension between democracy and diversity include his rejection of the democratic process of the US Congress meeting to ratify president-elect Joe Biden's Electoral College victory and his incitement of a coup d'état and insurgency at the United States Capitol, the sacred temple of democracy. In addition to many immigration policies by Trump against immigrants of color and his attack on, especially, Black female reporters such as Abby Phillip and April Ryan, he propounded an executive order banning racial sensitivity trainings and critical race theory, calling them "efforts to indoctrinate government employees with divisive and harmful sex-and-race-based ideologies" (Cineas, 2020).

Lacking diversity and inclusion leadership in our times of call out culture and a culture of discontent could adversely affect democracy. In a recent prime-time address to the nation from Philadelphia, President Biden gave us a premonition that MAGA Republicans and former President Donald Trump represent extremism, a threat to democracy and the "Soul of the Nation" (MSNBC, 2022). In this work, democracy "refers to the ideal that all human beings have equal value, deserve equal respect, and should be given the equal opportunity to fully participate in the direction of the society" (AAC&U, 1998, p. 9). This definition is more meaningful to our work in that it also strengthens the pillars of diversity—people are respected for who they are. Their differences are not seen as deficiencies, they maintain added value to the beloved community, and they have the equal opportunity to participate in issues that affect their lives. Therefore, we find in Lincoln's Gettysburg Address in 1863, which provided a formidable architecture to the building of our democracy, the following: ". . . and that government of the people, by the people, for the people. . . ." This vision might be sufficient at Lincoln's time, but we have reached a point in time of a multicultural democracy.

Participatory democracy that relies on liberal theory has the ability to engage in the suppression of Black, Indigenous, people of color (BIPOC) folx, as we have experienced in recent times—difficulty to register, purging voter rolls, disenfranchising returnees from prison, rigid voter identification requirements, and restricting early voting (American Civil Liberties Union, 2020). The multicultural and inclusive democracy model that we propose would "correct" the inadequacy of traditional participatory democracy by ascertaining that representation is genuine and reflective of the diversity of the general populace through devising a system that would recognize the disenfranchised and BIPOC folx. Multicultural and inclusive democracy is relational, not only procedural in context (Asumah and Johnston-Anumonwo, 2002, p. 422).

Diversity

In this work, we apply the American Association of Colleges and Universities characterization of diversity. Here, in our modified definition, diversity refers to the "variety created in any society (and within any individual) by the presence of different points of view and ways of making meaning [in discussions and actions] which generally flow from [references to different races, ethnicities,] cultures, and religious heritages, from the differences in the socialization processes of women, men, and [gender non-binary people], and from differences that emerge from class, age, and developed ability" (AAC&U, 1998, pp. 9–10). Before inclusion and equity attracted attention in the past fifteen years, diversity enjoyed the monopoly of attention in both individual and institutional spheres. Consequently, diversity is sustained through individual and institutional endeavors and dynamics, and, because power and human agency are involved, it is susceptible to "-isms"—racism, sexism, classism, ageism, and multiplicities of "-isms"—intergroup dynamics of superordinates and subordinates seeking power, resources, equity, recognition, justice, and respect. Since the civil right movements, diversity has become a hallmark for institutional and community interaction and engagement.

As with everything else, implementation of diversity in our institutions can be complex. America's diversity project is becoming even more complicated because of different generations, recent gender nonbinary categories, geography, changes in immigrant populations, and transdisciplinary and multiperspectival approaches in identifying diversity categories. Leaders at state and national levels and at institutions of higher learning must devise new and effective measures in dealing with diversity projects. Furthermore, it is not unusual to learn from historically marginalized groups that diversity programs are not addressing the real issues of oppression and systemic racism. Many institutions are so caught up in the game of increasing representation—numerical diversity—that they fail to pay attention to problems associated with the "numbers game."

Organizations and institutions that are in the business of just "showing" how diverse their workforce or student population is, based on race, ethnicity, age, gender, and developed ability may do well in the areas of touristic diversity and on their websites; one may be surprised to learn about the institutional climate and what their equity score card indicates. These same organizations may demonstrate strong diversity categories at the entry levels, mostly, but the power differential among employees and students and policy-making powers remain with traditional white male establishmentarians. Yet we are witnessing new moments in American history with a first-ever woman of color, Kamala Harris, as Vice President of the United States; the hegemony of white male establishmentarians in the American polity will continue to be challenged as more women and nonheteropatriarchal males are entering positions of power.

Gender Trouble in the Age of Me Too

It seems that some critical theorists and educators have come a long way since Karl Marx first articulated "the woman question" or W. E. B. Du Bois answered the question of what it feels like to be typecast as a problem, as a Black man in a white polity. But one still wonders who continues to be left out in these conversations, which hint at an additive problematic: the awkward and illogical trope of "women and minorities" remains the classic and de jure configuration of affirmative action policies (Nagel, 2014). Yet, it has been superbly troubled in this Black feminist classic primer: *All the Women Are White, All the Blacks Are Men, but Some of Us Are Brave* (Hull et al., 1982). Black feminist scholar, Kimberle Crenshaw (1989) captured this with a brilliant conceptual paradigm shift. She introduced us to the metaphor of intersection, and it has troubled feminist theory and practice in exciting ways. Crenshaw argues that antiracist analysis that does not engage with gender issues reinscribes sexism and heteropatriarchal norms, and feminist analysis that is silent on racial formations also adheres to white supremacist violence (p. 140). The third wave of feminism, including Black feminism and Black womanism, continues to trouble neat divisions and has ushered in a veritable politics of difference. Sexual pluralism in terms of orientation and identities have broken up metaphysical binaries and dichotomies that were unimaginable a century ago when "the homosexual" was invented as a species, in the famous words of white gay philosopher Michel Foucault.

In this book, we tackle race and gender politics utilizing the prism of an intersectional analysis, yet we note that we may not quite succeed with troubling heteronormativity effectively. It is as if Audre Lorde's dictum "The master's tools will never dismantle the master's house" continues to haunt us. There are some small steps that feel hopeful. Generation Z students refer to others with the default pronoun "they/them" and genderqueer and gender nonconforming students challenge the architectural spaces of the twenty-first-century campus—in terms of both traditional classrooms and bathroom allocations and residential life and other student-life centered places. Creating a sense of belonging for increasingly diverse and underrepresented student bodies will be the key challenge for the colleges and universities that fight for survival with the dire demographic projections of a shrinking pool of eligible traditional student cohorts. To give the true meaning of the university as an entity where research, instructions, diversity of disciplines, inclusive student body, and faculty engage in the enterprise of education, diversity, and inclusive leadership will always be indispensable.

Diversity and Inclusive Leadership

There is a plethora of characterizations for diversity and inclusive leadership. The two, diversity and inclusive leadership, go hand in hand. Institutions of higher learning are always in transition because students enroll and graduate constantly. Furthermore, demographic shifts in the student body occur because of birth rates, migrations, and relocations. New faculty and staff join the academy, and committee leaderships, department chairs, deans, and even provosts change position quite often. This transition is not different from what occurs in the nation state as political leadership, international interactions, struggles for equity, and resource distribution, make diversity and inclusive leadership indispensable and irrepressible. Differences in age, race, ethnicity, gender, class, and other diversity categories require leaders to be more inclusive in their leadership style and interaction with students and faculty/employees. A one-size-fits-all leadership style is, therefore, failure-prone in any multicultural and diverse setting. Change-leadership and equity-minded approaches do enhance DEI and inclusive leadership in a culture of cure.

In his seminal essay on diversity and racism in America, Ward (2022) characterizes diversity as "essentially about *quantity*: the range and number of different identities and cultures in any given system. *Inclusion* is essentially about *quality*: the quality of participants across identities and cultures. *Equity* is about *justice*: the policies that ensure equitable outcomes" (p. 9). Educational leaders should be aware that numerical diversity, "quantity," is not a panacea to our racial iniquity issues, and we cannot solve racial inequity problems on our campuses completely with a diversity framework. White institutional presence and policy-making leaders have frequently associated the increases in BIPOC populations on our campuses with improvement in race relations, confusing campus climate with campus culture and at the same time depending on risk management strategies to counteract DEI problems, and this convoluted approaches only creates distraction and frustration for our BIPOC students and faculty.

How Risk Management Affects Diversity Leadership

In these times of global pandemic, most institutional leaders will agree that risk management and safety are more important than anything else is. Nevertheless, college and university leaders have made risk management an indispensable tool for their leadership styles even before COVID-19 turned its ugly head on human existence and caused disproportionately more harm and deaths in BIPOC communities. The irrepressible tension between risk management and diversity leadership cannot be overemphasized. Risk management is how institutional leaders identify, review, evaluate, and control perceived occurrence of risk in an institution. However, as Hubbard argues in his recent work, "Most managers would not know what they need to look for to evaluate a risk management method and, more likely than not, can be fooled by a kind of analysis placebo effect" (2020, pp. 4–5).

Furthermore, the way we analyze risk and our estimation of risk can be tricky, because we have to factor in the frequency of imaginability and relatability that may contribute to the risk. That is, what is the likelihood that something can be dangerous or threatening to the university's image or reputation? There is no way of projecting the future, but we usually count on our best estimations. So, when leaders in the American polity and institutions of higher learning rely on imaginability bias to make diversity and inclusion decisions, we are entrapped in a quagmire of overestimation and underestimation of risk, and misalignment of what is visceral and what is cerebral. As we have mentioned earlier, since diversity and inclusion work is human work and we must be intentional to secure results, risk management does not provide a fertile leadership ground for diversity and inclusion leadership on our college campuses and in the American polity, because the experiences of minorized groups and the best available information is mostly masqueraded in whiteness, lacking DEI perspectives.

Since the tragic shooting incident at Virginia Tech, all public and private colleges and universities have reassessed risk management; many have armed their campus police and even militarized them. Active shooter scenarios are no longer carried out in far-away shooting ranges; rather, they are directly played out in residence halls and classrooms. Fortunately, they are done when no students are present. What does this have to do with our concerns about diversity leadership? When uniformed, gun-carrying campus police had a "coffee with a cop" session at the gym entrance, a Black student shared being triggered by such police presence and wrote his reaction in a poem for a creative writing class. He carries the trauma of "stop-and-frisk" policies in New York city, which was used to racially profile Black and Latino youth for decades.

When Black and Latino students hold social events on campus and they are shepherded by faculty and staff, but campus police still make their overwhelming presence felt, meaningful social gathering becomes infinitesimally diluted. These students' events, designed to define their own social spaces, without having to explain themselves to extra authoritative bodies, defeat the purpose of the students' freedom and ability to define their social spaces in an already highly policed campus. The rationale for police presence needs no explanation for risk managers and those who believe BIPOC students must be "watched" closely all the time (public safety) before they damage the "public good"—whether it is property or service. White campus police who reside in rural white America do not know of such trauma and lived experience. They relish the hard-won access to guns since the Virginia Tech incident seemingly made it a requirement for proper risk management. Prior to Virginia Tech, they were "merely" peace officers and had to rely on city police for any dangerous situation that they could not handle without weapons. Never mind that the city of Cortland has a police station located less than a mile away from campus.

Now, risk management has a new enemy to deal with: a tiny virus that seems virtually invincible. Now, campuses must make new "rational" decisions that pits the health and well-being of the community against sound fiscal policy that demands that classes are held in person regardless of (mental) health status of students or faculty. Such calculus is particularly distressing to BIPOC folx who have lost loved ones to COVID-19. Their concern is not taken into consideration, as no diversity policy has been promulgated to address multilayered issues regarding access, equity, and mental distress. Even uniform policies in an online class are cause for alarm, and, using diversity leadership best practices, it would behoove campus administrators and chief diversity officers to call on faculty to check in with students and prepare flexible guidelines that will serve all students equitably. A case in point: One of our Latino student was immensely relieved and grateful for getting an extension on a term paper from one of us after they contracted COVID-19. They shared that another faculty denied such appeal and it caused obviously great anxiety to the affected student (and, perhaps, to their family members). But we must acknowledge the fact that in such a situation, where risk management supersedes diversity and inclusion considerations, BIPOC students suffer both anxiety and trauma, while most of the student body may only deal with anxiety.

As we have already alluded to above, Trumpism clarified to us an extreme leadership style. Among the various philosophies that we discuss in this book are servant leadership, focusing on equity and inclusion, trust-building, and transformation and transactional leadership, focusing on hierarchy, control, and loyalty. It now seems uncontroversial to suggest that Trumpism endorses a dangerous, reactionary transactional style that borders on a cult of personality—in short, the stuff of dictators (and mafia bosses), who tolerate no opposition to their dictates, as journalist David Cay Johnston (2016) predicted.

Trumpist ideology has taught us, if anything, to review critically the idea of risk management and the problematic silence of college presidents during a long four years of his regime. His policies began with an Islamophobic travel ban, and continued with directives that openly championed racism, xenophobia, transphobia, and anti-LGBT rights, as if those were morally acceptable virtues.

As we completed writing this volume before the summer of 2022, the US Supreme Court decisions confirm that our clarion call to urgent action is well-founded. The high court's decision to overturn the landmark *Roe v. Wade* decision gives a strong signal that reproductive choice is a matter of drawing a geographic lottery card. Seeking abortions in a state that proscribes it in all circumstances, including ten-year-old children, will increase the likelihood of illegal abortions. Seeking legal abortions is impossible for all those on probation who are forbidden from crossing state boundaries, affecting some two hundred thousand persons.

Even before the COVID-19 crisis dismantled international scholarly exchange, academia experienced a real hemorrhaging effect and lost scores of graduate students and scholars to other countries, notably Canada. Indubitably, this will have lasting effects on research and development opportunities in the STEM disciplines, because most of US graduate studies have been populated by international students. We will be forgiven for reminding our readers of the fateful year of 1933 and the beginning of massive expulsion of Jewish professors and students from the German university system, which was at the time one of the best in the world (Ringer, 1969), benefiting students such as a premier sociologist of the twentieth century, W. E. B. Du Bois, who attended the university at Berlin.

Our quest in this project is to join our readers to bear witness to the evolution of DEI and social justice movements that are unstoppable in the academy and society. Nonetheless, without inclusive leadership and a tool kit to tackle the questions and issues of the soul of our democracy, racism, sexism, and the formation of an equity-minded society, it would be difficult to affirm our human realities and mutual potentialities. But to achieve results effectively, we echo what nationally acknowledged expert on preserving inclusive democracy and the recipient of the 2021 Civil Courage Prize, Eric Ward, asserts:

> Each of us has the power to catalyze the change we want to see in the world. That's one of the reasons educators are among my personal heroes and heroines. . . . My own story illustrates that working for racial equity and inclusive multiracial democracy was not inevitable. . . . If we choose equitable options and actions, we will achieve new outcomes: Equity, inclusion, humanity. (Ward, 2022, p. 5)

Conclusion

In conclusion, this introductory chapter attempts to lay out our arguments and the general framework for diversity, inclusion, and leadership, and prospects for our community of learners and the American society, especially in our times of uncertainty and political discontent. The historical contradiction of the processes that resulted in the exclusion of many groups in the American polity, even though the founders envisioned democracy and diversity, had paved the way to the challenges associated with the call for inclusion, equity, and diversity leadership in our organizations and institutions of learning. Traditional white heteropatriarchal leadership is not adequate to serve the needs of all the stakeholders in our institutions. For diversity and inclusive leadership to prevail in the academy, educational leadership should be inextricably linked to our social realities and responsibilities, wakefulness, social justice, and racial equity framework.

The contours of whiteness, white institutional presence, diversity leadership, racism, and sexism are complex in higher education. The evolution of searching for DEI and social justice solutions in our experience started with our own institution, the State University of New York at Cortland and its capacity building efforts, progress, and pitfalls in the multicultural and DEI enterprises. Since story telling is an effective tool for understanding a phenomenon, we believe our readers would be well-grounded and benefit from our story. Consequently, we invite you to come along on the undulating journey of multiculturalism, diversity, equity, and inclusion on a campus of a predominantly white institution (PWI) in chapter 1.

Part 1

How Do Diversity and Inclusion Leadership Matter Today?

Chapter 1

Diversity Studies and Managing Differences

Unpacking SUNY Cortland's Case and National Trends

Diversity, equity, and inclusion (DEI), the politics of difference, and managing differences are important parts of any nation state's agenda. American and European polities are becoming more global and less European in their demographic composition. The 2010 census reports in the United States confirm that workplaces, classrooms, and neighborhoods have already changed their monochromatic makeup and nearly half the population under the age of eighteen are people of color (US Census Bureau, 2010). The 2020 United States census indicates how race and ethnicity have contributed to the change in the population of America, and, while the white population is declining, Latino, Black, Asian American, and people who identify as two or more races are increasing (Frey, 2021a, 2021b). In his collaborative research with the Brookings Institute, William Frey, a consultant to the US Census Bureau makes a projection for the year 2050 that the minority population, mutatis mutandis, will surpass the white non-Hispanic population by over four percent (Frey, 2021). Furthermore, analysis of the 2020 census by census observers indicates that, while whites remain the major race in the United States, the multiracial population of this country made large gains, from 9 million in the 2010 census to 33.8 million in the 2020 census, an increase of 276 percent (Jones et al. 2021). The decline in the white population

---

Another version of this chapter (Nagel & Asumah, 2014) was previously published in the edited volume *Sprache, Macht, Rassismus*.

by 8.6 percent (Jones et al. 2021) and largest increases in the multiracial populations have given, especially white nationalists, a sense of urgent concern. These population explosions, shifts, and the dynamics propel an urgency to transcend the boundaries of multicultural studies because of the fact that all the categories of diversity—race, ethnicity, class, gender, sexual orientation, disability, religion, and their intersections—are highly impacted. In other words, diversity must be carefully and intentionally interrogated, as well as managed to reduce the concomitant tension on our college campuses and in society at large.

As we elaborate in our anthology on diversity, higher education can sustain the forms of learning, pedagogy, and epistemology with integrity only if institutions that profess moral and inclusive excellence are committed to diverse perspectives and people of multicultural orientations (Asumah & Nagel, 2014). Nonetheless, US American-style multicultural studies at this juncture are not the same as observed by many European countries. Even multicultural studies in the United States present their own paradoxical and oxymoronic issues and problems, despite the intensity and scope of their rationale. For instance, general education and academic major requirements put so many constrains on students' academic core requirements that they are left with little room to take courses on multicultural studies that could shape the totality of their lives. Yet, as one multicultural educator mentions, "'Educational Mission' signals the realization that all students benefit from an education that fosters knowledge and competence for a multiracial, multiethnic, multiperspectival and gendered world. 'Transformation' connects all the other dimensions of diversity in fundamental reconsideration of the academy's organizing assumptions—societal, intellectual, educational and institutional" (Smith, 1995, p. 227).

Multiculturalism, as a conceptual framework and a body of knowledge, has slowly merged into diversity. Diversity studies and management of our differences are becoming a sine qua non to the effective administration of our institutions of higher learning. Diversity management is characterized by the recognition of, and provision of, value to differences through effective methodology and implementation of inclusive policies to create a welcoming climate in order to maximize the benefits for institutions and workplaces. Through inclusive diversity, equity, and inclusion management, strategies for recruitment, retention, mentoring, cultural competence, talent development, productivity, assessment, and evaluation can be effectively attained. Diversity management supports an all-inclusive organizational culture of equality, acceptance, respect, and affirmation of our collective humanness.

In this chapter we juxtapose diversity, equity, and inclusion studies and diversity management and examine how State University of New York at Cortland has responded to trends in the United States to mitigate the effects of social alexithymia, whiteness, inequity, and injustice through diversity professional development and institutes. We begin with reviewing the transition from multicultural studies and women's studies at SUNY Cortland to the expanded attention on diversity studies, equity policies, antiracism projects, and the challenges ahead for SUNY Cortland. We highlight some pitfalls and benefits of diversity management, in particular, the concept of "managing diversity," and hope we will contribute to a richer understanding of these concepts, and implementation of policies and procedures at universities elsewhere. Considerable endeavors and actions of civil rights and social justice movements have global implications, as seen with the Occupy Wall Street movement in 2011, which was started by New York City college students. So, our hope is that we may also contribute to a global discourse at the praxicological level—the intertwining of theory and practice. Yet the process of managing differences has a history of its own at SUNY Cortland and the journey to reaching inclusion, cultural competence, and equity has been undulating.

Some Historical Perspectives

In the 1980s, SUNY Cortland was overwhelmed by several self-studies about the campus climate and the monoculturality of the institution. Analyzing the weakness of the institution based on its multicultural and diversity lacuna and offering a number of prescriptions for improving the campus climate became a frequent exercise by progressive faculty members and administrators. Countless studies, meetings, and programs were developed around the campus climate and how to change the chilly campus climate of the 1980s. However, as we have mentioned in the introduction, there are differences among campus climate, campus culture, and campus ecology. Unfortunately, many institutions of higher education spend more time and resources studying campus climate while they totally neglect campus culture and ecology. SUNY Cortland is not an exception to this educational practice of omission and commission in racial and DEI studies. To expatiate, Kuh and Whitt define campus culture as "the collective, mutually shaping patterns of institutional history, mission, physical setting, norms, traditions, values, practices, beliefs, and assumptions that guide behavior of the individuals and groups in an institution of higher education which provide a frame of reference for interpreting the meaning of events and actions on and off campus" (1988, pp. 12–13). In our experience at SUNY Cortland, no one has been interested in the study of campus culture, and we are not aware of any of our SUNY campuses that have done a study of campus culture. Campus culture has influence on the general belief system, behaviors, precepts, and norms for doing business in predominantly white institutions (PWIs) such as SUNY Cortland. Subcultures are parts of the larger campus culture. These subcultures may include the president's cabinet, provost's cabinet, deans' council, labor unions (UUP), student government association (SGA), Greek life, and other student organizations/clubs. Unlike campus climate, campus cultures are difficult to change, because they are deeply embedded in the historical legacy of the institution.

According to Bauer, campus climate includes "the current perceptions, attitudes, and expectations that define the institution and its members" (1998, p. 2). Most universities are fascinated with studying campus climate, because it is a lot easier to tackle current (racial) issues with a bandage or duct tape approach. It is also easier for administrators to play the "waiting out" game with students until they graduate instead of going into the root cause of the problems. In dealing with race and racism on campuses, Hurtado et al. (1998) provide a four-dimensional framework for campus climate. Historical context of inclusion of minoritized groups or the illusion of inclusion and tokenism is the first dimension of campus climate that BIPOC students and faculty face, including SUNY Cortland. For instance, SUNY Cortland is known for being a vanilla campus because of its whiteness of the student population and policy actions. Nevertheless, diversity efforts for the past several years at SUNY Cortland have produced results in attracting more students of color to the campus. Yet numerical diversity becomes meaningless when inclusion and equity are neglected.

Compositional diversity or the aggregate number of BIPOC students and faculty on campus is the second dimension of campus climate (Hurtado et al., 1998). This has been a challenge for SUNY Cortland. The proportionality of the BIPOC students and faculty to that of the dominant culture (whites in this case) is our primary concern. This proportionality must be central in distribution of resources and policy decisions. The third dimension of campus climate is the psychological outlook of how welcoming and friendly or unfriendly a campus is (Hurtado et al., 1998).

This quality is so important because it affects institutional enrollments of BIPOC students, the mental health of minoritized students, and the rate of increases in microaggressions and racial battle fatigue for students of color, resulting to negative campus climate. The fourth and final dimension provided by Hurtado et al. (1998) is the behavioral aspect, which emphasizes how BIPOC students and faculty interact with the major population, which can result in self-separation or self-segregation. At SUNY Cortland most of the organizations of color are relegated to the Student Voice Office (SVO) for their meetings and other interactions. Our white students often ask the question, "Why do all the students of color meet in the Voice Office in the Corey Union?"

While campus ecology defines the environment—setting of the college or university, the inhabitants; students, staff, faculty and administrators, and activities/behaviors; learning, research and development (Banning & Kuk, 2005)—Cabrera et al. (2016) argue that the literature on campus ecology does not factor in whiteness, white privilege, and inequity on the ecology sufficiently. Since critical whiteness studies is nonexistent at SUNY Cortland and the study of the general ecology of the university in relationship to BIPOC students has never been done, we think the university must begin new studies of its campus culture and ecology to strengthen the momentum and retention of BIPOC students and faculty.

The earlier self-studies on campus climate were lean, yet progressive enough to get the ball rolling for change to occur at SUNY Cortland in the 1980s. As a result of these critiques in the campus climatic studies, curricular changes were made and courses on social justice education were added to the general education program as required courses for all undergraduate students. Such courses are concerned with different forms of oppression, namely, racism, classism, sexism; furthermore, they employ other forms of pedagogical approaches to enable students to be exposed to and comprehend the politics of difference, multiculturalism, diversity, and social justice. Nonetheless, several faculty members who taught diversity-related courses treated them as ordinary courses and avoided critical race theory (CRT), critical whiteness studies (CWS), difficult and crucial topics that tend to generate emotional and difficult dialogues (racism, homophobia, white hegemony, white privilege, white fragility). Consequently, the courses that were taught at SUNY Cortland were not making the critical impact needed for a campus that cherishes inclusivity and excellence (in theory and in its pronouncements), but concrete changes were minimal.

Thus, in August 1991, the SUNY Cortland administration decided to take an innovative approach of sending a cadre of faculty members, including one of the coauthors of this volume, Professor Asumah, to the National Coalition Building Institute (NCBI) in Arlington, Massachusetts, for further diversity studies. The institute was based on a prejudice reduction model. The goal of this institute was to provide professional development experience for teams of peer leaders in the most effective way "to empower people to take leadership in reducing racism" (Brown & Mazza, 1991, p. 1). The operating assumptions for this institute included:

- peer leadership training, programs to welcome diversity as an on-going diversity endeavor;
- proactive training programs that focus on intergroup dynamics to respond to specific incidents of racism and other discriminative crisis;
- developing programs that included both visible and invisible differences at the university or workplace;
- prejudice reduction programs not based on guilt or condemnation; and
- anti-racism programs with upbeat and hope-affirming exercises. (pp. 1–16)

The theory and methodology behind the NCBI training are how to tackle institutional racism by working through groups, dismantling stereotypes, dealing with internalized prejudice, recognizing the extent of group oppression, overcoming intergroup conflicts, role-playing, and welcoming diversity. SUNY Cortland's cadre of diversity trainers who were certified by NCBI worked on campus by conducting workshops twice a semester for faculty and staff. Departments and units were mandated to attend the workshop sessions but, after three years, lack of institutional commitment and resistance from seasoned faculty (the old guard) led to the demise of the training sessions. Advocates of the diversity project learned a lesson that even though diversity work should be deliberate and intentional for it to bear fruits, it is still crucial to have backing or support from senior faculty members. A few senior faculty members who were predominantly white males invoked contractual agreements and how the mandate to attend the diversity workshops violated their employment agreements.

Nonetheless, in three years, about 150 faculty and staff participated in the diversity training sessions before the program was discontinued.

SUNY Cortland did not succumb to the monocultural and anti-diversity forces on campus. In the summer 1994, the administration embarked on another major diversity project by sending four faculty members, Drs. Larry Ashley and Kathryn Russell, Professor Deborah Manning, and the coauthor of this chapter, Dr. Seth N. Asumah, to a National Summer Diversity Institute at Williams College, Williamstown, Massachusetts. The title and theme for this summer institute was "Boundaries and Borderland: The Search for Recognition and Community in America." This institute's operating theme was "American Commitments: Diversity, Democracy, and Liberal Learning." The summer institute was a month-long training, which was developed and organized by the American Association of Colleges and Universities (AAC&U). Its goal was using institutions of higher learning to reconcile the presumed difference between diversity and democracy. As the AAC&U training manual states:

> The intellectual heart of the institute—designed to create a learning community most conducive to such interchange—is a series of eight morning seminars, each of which is organized around a different thematic set of readings. . . . Because "Boundaries and Borderlands" pairs diversity and democracy, we are forging intellectual relationships that remain largely separate in the scholarship and educational practices. The scholarship of diversity argues that only through full recognition of diversity are the aspirations of democracy capable of being embodied. (AAC&U, 1994)

The conceptual framework shepherding the genesis of the AAC&U diversity institute is redefining the American individual within the context of diverse communities. What cements Americans of diverse races, classes, genders, socioeconomic status, age, learned ability, and how men and women are socialized is the democratic value of equality and respect. For the purpose of this institute, higher education's goal "should be to deepen public and campus knowledge of the United States diversity histories, to reengage with democratic aspirations as a moral compass for intersecting communities, and to recommit ourselves—as educators and as citizens" (AAC&U, 1995, p. xix). The fundamental difference between the NCBI and the AAC&U diversity training programs for the SUNY Cortland participants is that the NCBI approach was based on a purely normative and behavioral change model to expose participants of the workshops to oppressive behaviors and how to mitigate the forces of oppression on campus and the workplace, an approach some observers labeled as "sensitivity training." On the other hand, the AAC&U models combined normative and transformative approaches, which included intellectual, behavioral, pedagogical, and institutional dynamics for bringing about change.

The faculty who participated in the AAC&U summer institute did not only master the literature on diversity, but they also learned pedagogical techniques for teaching diversity-related courses, how to develop diversity curricula, how to defuse tension based on differences, and how to develop cocurricular programs in order to enrich the campus on diversity issues. The entire SUNY Cortland faculty who received certification from AAC&U created several general education (GE) courses for the university and continued their advocacy in the Center for Multicultural and Gender Studies (CMGS). As a result of the AAC&U program, the 1990s could be credited with high tide for course and curriculum developments and events surrounding diversity. Yet the campus climate on gender, race/ethnicity, and sexual/affectional orientation remained bleak. The efforts of the 1990s were still limited to campus climate, disregarding the critical issues of campus culture and campus ecology discussed earlier. It was not a coincidence that the campus climate at SUNY Cortland was similar to that of the national ethos on diversity at that time.

The United States' historical contradictions on race and racism continue to permeate schools and workplaces. Racial issues are so emotional and contentious that most presidents avoided it in their campaigns or policy programs. The race project in America has a history of its own, and it is so complex that policy-makers and educators would rather avoid it than study it to find meaningful solutions. As some scholars note, "Many practitioners and policymakers face increasing fast-paced conditions for decision making, . . . and white-serving institutions . . . remain resistant to structural and systemic change" (Johnson et al., 2022). The 1960s were pivotal times for confronting racial issues because of the civil rights movement, but since that period laws and actions involving racial discrimination and racism have been implemented on a piecemeal basis. Additionally, as minority groups, who are subordinated in reference to power and privilege, continue to increase in population, the enduring sociopolitical relevance of racial formation and diversity in the American polity could no longer be sidestepped. Realizing the sociopolitical realities and ramifications for ignoring the racial problems in the United States, in June 1997, President Clinton announced his initiative on the Dialogue on Race. The president made references to his childhood experience in the South, bearing witness to the racial divide and the detriment of racial discrimination against people of color. He garnished his inspiration in his second term to take action against racism in America. President Clinton's initiative had five primary goals:

1. to articulate the President's vision of racial reconciliation and a just, unified America;
2. to help educate the nation about the facts surrounding the issue of race;
3. to promote a constructive dialogue, to confront and work through the difficult and controversial issues surrounding race;
4. to recruit and encourage leadership at all levels to help bridge racial divides;
5. to find, develop and implement solutions in critical areas such as education, economic opportunity, housing, health care, crime and the administration of justice—for individuals, communities, corporations, and government at all levels. (Leadership Conference, 1997, pp. 2–3)

University and college campuses were used as platforms for the difficult dialogues on race and discriminatory practices in the United States. President Clinton encouraged university presidents to devote public sessions to the theme of "dialogue on race." SUNY Cortland developed a semester-long program called Let's Talk about Race. SUNY Cortland's president, Judson Taylor, decided to take on the challenge and held a series of public conversations in rooms filled to capacity. President Taylor and the Committee on the Dialogue on Race initiative appointed the coauthor of this book, Professor Asumah of the Political Science Department and the then coordinator of the African American Studies Program (who had, by then, attended three diversity institutes), to serve as the moderator and host for the semester-long program. Asumah and the committee developed critical questions for the forums, introducing several racial and diversity-related issues in the several town hall-styled colloquiums for the entire campus.

The discussions, debates, and conversations were structured to offer avenues for candid and informed, but difficult dialogues. At SUNY Cortland, several faculty members who have taught courses on race and racism for a decade or longer were surprised at the level of commitment that students showed at these forums. After all, many instructional faculty teach courses devoted to anti-discrimination, which, as we mentioned above, all students regardless of their major must take. Inevitably, the instructors of *prejudice and discrimination* courses do face some level of resistance or resentment from students for teaching courses with difficult dialogue and contested subject matter. SUNY Cortland has unique general education requirements and had to seek special permission from the SUNY-wide Board of Trustees to enact the category, titled "Prejudice and Discrimination." It was enacted in the late 1980s after renowned authors such as Chandra Talpade Mohanty gave presentations on how to teach diversity courses. Furthermore, key faculty members, including one of the coauthors of this book, as noted above, were sent to month-long multiculturalism institute at Williams College, Massachusetts. This summer institute was organized by the American Association of Colleges and Universities to expand their knowledge and pedagogical techniques in teaching courses on multiculturalism, anti-oppression, antiracism, and anti-discrimination. These faculty members became the cadre of professors to champion the fight for social justice in the classrooms and to incorporate new materials on diversity and inclusion into their teaching, and they took the lead as trainers for other faculty members.

Engendering the Diversity Institute at SUNY Cortland

Difference and diversity continue to challenge the American society and many university campuses. Democracy and diversity have symbiotic relationships, yet the dilemma in a multicultural democracy is bringing to light often neglected or conveniently avoided difficult dialogues, civic values, and the crucial virtues of a "just society." Our vision for a multicultural democracy in this work, for the nation state, and for colleges and universities includes entities where democracy is relational, and "not only procedural in context. It refers to the ideal that all humans have equal value, deserve equal respect," and must be included in decisions that affect the direction of their society (Asumah & Johnston-Anumonwo, 2002, p. 422). To enable SUNY Cortland to successfully embark on a sustainable multicultural and diversity program, faculty, who were certified at the National Coalition Building Institute (NCBI), AAC&U, and other programs, were active in setting policy and curricular changes through the All-College Curriculum Committee, General Education Committee, and the Center for Multicultural and Gender Studies. The same cadre of diversity faculty were engaged in organizing diversity film series and campus-wide discussions around the film during Black History Month (February) and Women's History Month (March). These faculty also brought intersectional analysis (e.g., of how racism and sexism are interrelated) into the diversity work on campus and into relief.

Yet, when, then-provost Elizabeth Davis-Russell joined SUNY Cortland in 2001, her vision was to bring about social change on campus and improvement of the campus climate at a greater institutional level. She conducted meetings with senior administrative staff and organized programs on diversity and multiculturalism. Some grudgingly attended most of the sessions, but they were present because the chief academic officer, the provost and vice president of academic affairs, believed that, in order for diversity to work, senior administrators must be fully committed to social justice and affirmation of diversity. The university's mission must be congruent with practices—Cortland should "walk the talk" on diversity. McNair et al. are clear and adamant in their work *From Equity Talk to Equity Walk* (2020) about walking the talk: "Unfortunately, some educators only have an equity talk, but not an equity walk. In this category are educators who preach equity [and diversity] but equity values and practices aren't evident in their action" (p. 3). Provost Elizabeth Davis-Russell did not only walk, but she ran with multiculturalism and diversity initiatives and programs at SUNY Cortland during her tenure. The following is her legacy before she was invited in 2008 by the president of Liberia, Ellen Johnson Sirleaf, to become president of Tubman University, Harper, Liberia:

- Provost Davis-Russell accepted and supported the college-wide Committee on Ethnic Studies proposal to create the Department of African American Studies, which used to be a program under the Center for Multicultural and Gender Studies (MGS), and to appoint Professor Seth N. Asumah as chair.
- She affirmed the proposal and request to change the department name and mission from African American Studies to

Africana Studies, thereby increasing the scope and diversity of the discipline and the curriculum at SUNY Cortland.

- Elizabeth Davis-Russell and Seth N. Asumah, based on the models of a number of diversity institutes in the United States, created an institutional model for diversity training—the Summer Diversity Institute for Infusing Diversity and Multiculturalism into the Curriculum and Professional Service. This institute began in 2003 with faculty attending three full days and being paid a stipend. Mechthild Nagel was invited to join Seth N. Asumah as a cofacilitator. She also had the opportunity to attend institutes and conferences such as the National Conference on Race and Ethnicity (NCORE) in her role as MGS director and her decade-long experience with teaching philosophy and women's studies with a focus on postcolonial theory. In 2003, Nagel also founded the online journal *Wagadu: A Journal of Transnational Women's and Gender Studies*, which publishes articles devoted to the intersection of feminist and postcolonial studies.

- Additionally, Elizabeth Davis-Russell and Seth N. Asumah developed the Diversity Film and Dinner Forum, where key administrators and senior faculty were invited to dinners with featured films on diversity. Using films as a point of departure, discussions and workshops led by the Provost and Asumah became regular events on diversity education. Among the films that were discussed are *Race: The Power of An Illusion* (California Newsreel/Ford Foundation); *The Color of Fear* (Lee Mun Wah); *Mirrors of Privilege: Making Whiteness Visible* (Shakti Butler); *What's Race Got to Do with It* (Jean Cheng); and *The Way Home* (Shakti Butler). These films, among others, were purchased and used in other general education courses on campus.

Given Provost Davis-Russell's professional expertise in multicultural psychology, she encouraged faculty to train further in a subject that tended to be marginalized in SUNY Cortland's own faculty advanced educational preparations (e.g., philosophy and political science). Our professional development program could only accommodate twelve faculty members in any given year, with the exception of one year, where Davis-Russell co-led the seminar with Seth N. Asumah, inviting primarily faculty who teach in the general education category on prejudice and discrimination. That summer institute was therefore different in composition. Faculty members who teach courses in prejudice and discrimination (P&D) and those who do not teach P&D but wanted to learn pedagogical techniques in teaching courses with difficult dialogue were invited. Others who participated in the institute were teaching faculty who were interested in expanding their knowledgebase for multicultural and diversity literature in order to infuse diversity into their teaching.

After Elizabeth Davis-Russell retired from SUNY Cortland, the stipends for faculty were discontinued and interest waned a bit. In the meantime, other professional development institutes based on the Asumah model emerged. The Asumah model is premised on the assumption that as a learning community, a proactive and continuing professional development of faculty and students in diversity and affirmation of diversity should become a modus operandi for managing differences and celebrating our similarities. Among the institutes that were developed based on the Asumah model was the Ethics Institute, sponsored by the Philosophy Department, where Nagel also taught at the institute's inception. What is unique about the Diversity Institute is that several faculty members, including part-timers or contingent faculty, have been accepted to *repeat* the seminars. Thus, they are provided the opportunity to deepen their knowledge. Clearly, it is not possible to retrain oneself in three days, especially if one had little or no lived experience/context nor academic preparation in anti-discrimination education. Furthermore, professional staff and administrators have joined the institute to broaden their awareness about managing difference in the areas of international education, residential life, and alumni affairs, to name a few. Nevertheless, one can argue that the narrative for leveling the playing fields for social justice and diversity management in the United States has remained enticing.

The Rise of Diversity Education in the US

At the founding of the United States, constitutional interlocutors at that time engaged in difficult dialogues about the impacts of social diversity on the polity. Interestingly, even at that time, the founders were thinking and talking about managing diversity. Anti-federalist Brutus, who believed in monoculturalism, argued, "In a republic, the manners, sentiments, and interests of the people should be similar. If this is not the case, there will be constant clashing of opinions; and the representatives of one part will continually striving against those of the other" (Brutus, 1787). Yet the federalists won the debate on diversity management even at the inception of the United States. We emphasize that the earlier efforts were about diversity management—how to deal with the differences in Blacks, indigenous people, and the white majority; it was not about inclusion or equity. The three-fifths compromise during the 1787 United States Convention, some may argue, only counted enslaved people as three-fifths of a person. However, other scholars argue that it was not the founders' intention to identify enslaved Blacks as three-fifths of a human and scholars who interpret the Constitution as such have their own political agendas and set out to "defame the Constitution" (Philbrick, 2018). In our reading of the founders' work, we conclude that the three-fifths compromise was designed for taxation, political representation, and identity purposes. Still, no matter how one looks at it, enslaved Blacks were counted as three-fifths of a person for taxation and participatory purposes (Nittle, 2020).

The founders set up a nation state that would take the different categories of diversity, for example, race, class, and gender, into consideration in framing the US Constitution, and again that was about diversity management for convenience, exploitation, and marginalization. The so-called politics of difference in amendments (First, Second, Fourth, Fifth, Fourteenth, and Nineteenth) were designed to solve diversity management problems. For instance, the First Amendment was designed as a diversity management tool to tackle differences in religion, self-expression, different forms of writing, and the freedom to gather together as groups. In a similar vein, the Fourth Amendment shall protect people in the American polity from "unreasonable searches and seizure by government"—a diversity management tool. Statutes, acts, and laws, such as the Civil Rights Act of 1964 and the Voting Rights Act of 1965, perform transformative functions in sustaining diversity, but normative approaches of behavioral changes through information and awareness are also a sine qua non to the legal and institutional approaches. However, what were written in abstraction (laws and statutes) have not easily resolved the issues and problems of social realities in multicultural democracies, and the country had to develop new strategies through diversity education in maintaining a "just society."

Diversity education or diversity studies started for several reasons. The country that professes democracy and equality started its sociopolitical structuring unequally. The historical contradictions in the American experiment with democracy and diversity have to be confronted in order to nurture future possibilities. As the Black poet Langston Hughes invoked in 1935, "Let America be America again . . . where equality is in the air we breathe," so diversity and social justice education are both processes and goals for the country. These goals include reaching equality, full participation of all groups, equitable distribution of resources and power, individuals' ability to shape their own lives, sense of agency, the notion of inclusivity, and mutual respect. Diversity education becomes a challenge, since, practically speaking, it provides a platform for those who have been historically marginalized, oppressed, and voiceless to become the social actors who are appraising society in the process of eradicating the heritage of prejudice and discrimination. Recent studies indicate that after President Obama took office and while some Americans invoked a post-racial America too quickly, it was not a surprise that the electoral colleges that put President Trump in power did so partly as a protest to the Obama presidency. Despite Trump's outrageous campaign based on the "racist idea" (Kendi, 2016) of "Make America Great Again" (MAGA) and his xenophobic approach to the politics of exclusion of dark-skinned immigrants, and regardless of the fact that racism and racial incidents increased during the Trump years, there are still millions of Americans who want Trump back in office. Even though President Obama was the first person of color to occupy the Oval Office, the issues over race and the color line remained virtually the same as in the pre–civil rights era. Many universities and colleges have cited Facebook as a source for confirming issues of covert racism, sexism, homophobia, and Islamophobia as parents review profiles of their children's prospective roommates on Facebook and request changes (Shafer, 2013, p. 3).

So, it is neither epiphenomenal nor anachronistic to discuss and implement policy pertaining to diversity in higher education today. Nonetheless, the multicultural movement that started in the post–civil rights era in the United States in the 1970s was more concerned with multiple racial cultures and ethnicities. Thus far, events that emerged during the civil rights movement prepared the terrain for more demands for social justice, multicultural democracy, and diversity. During the 1960s and 1970s, though, very few people on college campuses talked about "diversity." The political contestations, student-led strikes, and demands in light of the Vietnam War and the civil rights movement brought about the recognition that historically white universities were inaccessible to students and faculty of color. Hundreds of campuses were caught up in a political turmoil, which often was victorious for those agitating on the margins. The first of its kind academic program of Black studies was established at San Francisco State University in 1968.

In 1969 at Cornell, a private Ivy League university with a small land grant public component, armed Black students took over the student union building to demand seismic change in the Eurocentric curriculum and a department was established in a former dormitory in the outskirts of the campus (Penner, 2013). That same year, Cornell University established one of the first Black studies program in the Ivy League (Crawford, 2013). This program would be named Africana Studies and Research Center. One of the student leaders who took over the Willard Straight Hall for the lack of support for Black students, James Turner, eventually returned as faculty to the university and in due course assumed the role of department chair of the Africana Studies and Research Center. SUNY Cortland, not far from Cornell University, developed a Black Studies Department in 1971, only to be dissolved in the mid-1970s because of budget cuts (Ralstone, 1991). The lesson to be learned in this action concerning dissolution of programs and departments is that minority and multicultural programs constantly fight battles to gain acceptance from curriculum establishmentarians, yet these programs are the first to suffer the effects of budget axe during times of austerity measures. Curriculum establishmentarians fight to maintain the traditional status quo in curriculum development and find little reason to accept transdisciplinary courses into the curriculum. However, many SUNY campuses have developed programs in Africana studies, gender studies, social justice education, diversity education, multicultural centers, diversity offices, and affirmative action units to mitigate the problems that emerge due to the politics of difference.

Beyond Affirmative Action and toward an Era of Diversity Management

More often, it is when the incidence of racist microaggressions increase on campus that colleges and universities tend to implement change, for example, hiring a chief diversity officer (CDO) at the executive level. For instance, the State University of New York at Oneonta (SUNY Oneonta) hired a chief diversity officer (at the vice presidential level of authority) after an elderly white woman reported to the police that a Black male had burglarized her during the night. In the investigation of the matter, the local police department contacted the SUNY Oneonta administration and demanded a list of the names of all African American/Black students attending that college. The college administration complied. Many of these students were interrogated and harassed by police officers in the process. Indeed, Professor Asumah, who was not a student at that time, but a faculty member who happened to reside in the city of Oneonta in 1992 was stopped by police officers twice for questioning. So, the incident that started as profiling Black college students mushroomed into general racial profiling of Black people in the city of Oneonta. This incident, labeled the "Black List" saga, attracted national and international media attention. In its aftermath, higher education has become a bit more guarded about handing out student information, lest they be accused of producing a "Black List." After the chief diversity officer left SUNY Oneonta, the position was downgraded to a director/professional level. This diversity professional is now in charge of the Multicultural Center (Richardson, 2012).

But world events also have made an impact on college campuses during the reign (and era) of multicultural studies. In 1992, after the verdict of acquittal for those police officers who beat unarmed motorist Rodney King, a wave of student protests hit campuses and at University of Massachusetts–Amherst, where one of the coauthors of this chapter, Professor Nagel, received her graduate education, undergraduate students of color demanded that a number of faculty of color should be hired across the board. The students also demanded that the student body demographics should start to resemble that of the state, with at least twenty percent being students of color (Couloute, 2011). Nervous administrators whose main building had just been taken over by the students came back in the evening and negotiated with students of color all night about their demands. In the following years, the demographics for students and faculty indeed started to change, and faculty of color's demography mirrored the national average, twelve percent (Couloute, 2011). Such concessions were possible in an era when multicultural discourse was firmly established. Nevertheless, a few years later in 1997, students of color again found themselves occupying a university building because demands of the 1992 accord had not been addressed satisfactorily and the racial climate remained chilly (Couloute, 2011).

A few US Supreme Court decisions later, affirmative action policies that were meant to integrate students, staff, and faculty of color into historically white institutions have practically lost their meaning. In the case of *Grutter v. Bollinger* (2003), the Supreme Court ruled that, based on the principle of *strict scrutiny*, which is the order or pyramid of standards that the court uses to assess governments' interest vis-à-vis the constitutional right to protect individuals, race cannot be used in the admission of undergraduate students. The University of Michigan's diversity-based program for admissions was challenged in the Grutter case. All the same, in the case of *Gratz v. Bollinger* in the same year (2003), the court ruled that race could be used in law school and graduate school admissions. Ostensibly, the University of Michigan proved its case that there is compelling state interest to diversify its law school program, which is predominantly white. With a number of court cases attempting to dismantle affirmation action, which is government policy to "right the wrong" in the American society and college admissions processes because of many past cases of discrimination and "isms." At the same time, there has been no adverse ruling on "legacy admissions," which ensured that a weak student such as former President George W. Bush had a seat at Yale University, where his father also had studied. Universities such as SUNY Cortland still hold on to the administration position of an affirmative action officer, who has an enlarged portfolio including conflict management and running sexual harassment awareness trainings, which are mandatory for new faculty and staff in New York State. However, whether it is in the college admissions process or affirming our humanity, without proper professional development education in handling cases of discrimination, microaggression, difficult dialogues, equity policy, programs, and discourses, issues over diversity and inclusion can be divisive, emotional, and temperamentally tempestuous.

Speaking Truth to Power and Cultivating the Art of Listening: Maintaining Difficult Dialogues

In professional development institutes as well as classroom settings, when it comes to teaching how to unlearn whiteness, racism, sexism, homophobia, and ableism, participants often struggle with using the appropriate language that minimizes offending others. However, this fear of offending others derives from the perception of "safe space" and assumed racial comfort. Spaces are contested in our world all the time and the presumed safety in our classroom and institutes could be misleading—courageous and brave spaces must be encouraged in diversity work. Outside classrooms and professional development spaces, it is not uncommon for students and faculty to frequently engage in microaggressions. Sue characterize microaggression as, "the brief and common place daily verbal, behavioral, and environmental indignities, whether intentional or unintentional, that communicate hostile, derogatory, or negative racial, gender, sexual orientation, and religious slights and insults to the target person or group" (2010, p. 5). The key issue in this context is that the interminable absence of cross-racial, and cross-ethnic engagement, and self-segregation on predominantly white campuses, such as SUNY Cortland, fertilizes the grounds for microaggressions. Furthermore, languages across differences with ground rules on our campuses made by the dominant culture usually offend subordinate groups. When our students of color report to us that they frequently hear the n-word in the residence halls and white students defend it as free speech, there is always a moment of swimming in a pool/ syndrome of "Am I going crazy?"

With reference to a Fanonian framework of analysis, linguistic violence (microaggressions) is rampant in predominantly white institutions and the words of the oppressor (colonizer) can easily become a space for the dehumanization of the oppressed—the colonized (Fanon, 1967). Alas, in the backlash against multiculturalism, such "sensitivity training" (as it used to be called) has been labeled as "political correctness." Such labeling is ridiculed as nonsensical. As critical race theorists, such as W. E. B. Du Bois, Derrick Bell, Patricia Williams, Kimberlé Williams Crenshaw, and Richard Delgado have taught us, using words to name one's own reality, critiquing the social structures of society, and analyzing the intersection of race, law, and power are important for managing diversity. In that respect, critical race theorists have also taught us that words have enormous power and produce much tension and conflict on and off campus. What, therefore, counts as racist expression?

Utilizing Joe Feagin's white racial frame is helpful in questioning the behavior of whites who are not yet allies of people of color. Some white folks often feel licensed to use racist terms as if the past had no bearing on its modern-day usage; or laugh off racist encounters as a simple misunderstanding; or, if none of those strategies of denial work, they target people of color as being overly sensitive. Feagin (2010) notes that racist violence emanates from the elites, who have tremendous power in framing discussions and in gatekeeping (e.g., housing, jobs, law enforcement/criminal justice, club membership, mortgage and other credit attainment). Feagin's white racial frame model explains that the broad framing begins with words:

1. racial stereotypes (a verbal—cognitive aspect),
2. racial narratives and interpretations (integrating cognitive aspects),
3. racial images (a visual aspect) and language accents (an auditory aspect),
4. racialized emotions (a "feeling" aspect), and
5. inclinations to discriminatory action. (2010, p. 25)

Feagin (2010) notes that the frame is very powerful, and it maintains an "overarching and racialized worldview extending across divisions of class, gender, and age." Even though reference is made to a white racial frame, the process of oppression cuts across the diversity categories mentioned above. Race, class, gender, age, religion, disability, and other diversity categories intersect, shape our experience and form the matrices of domination. These matrices of domination are informed by communication and action. Without preparing ourselves cognitively and emotionally, communicative obstacles obstruct our ability to perform properly. Competence in communication includes the ability to navigate controversy with civility and perform productively, hence cultural competence.

If one is culturally incompetent and fails to communicate effectively, underlying this communicative block or incompetence is the tacit acknowledgment that a speaker's *intent* carries more weight than the *impact* on the addressee. If it is not meant in a hurtful way, it clearly could not hurt anybody. Yet the speaker must be ready to mitigate the effects of unintended *impacts*. Much of the Diversity Institute's work lies in practicing rather than avoiding difficult dialogues, which start to recognize the cognitive blind spots or implicit biases we all engage in. Additionally, given the list of topics under scrutiny—that is, history of racism, sexism and heterosexism, dis/ability or learned ability, class oppression and Islamophobia—there could be a topic that one has some discomfort with.

In the US, diversity interlocutors do not label racism as "every-day-racism" unlike in German academic and mainstream discourse. Rather, American educators use the concepts of "covert" and "overt" racism, the latter often associated with hate group organizations such as the Ku Klux Klan (KKK) or neo-Nazi groups, and with racial profiling policies. Furthermore, the dynamics of individual *prejudice* coupled with systemic and institutional forms of *discrimination* are analyzed and much attention is paid to highlighting these important concepts as they emerge in difficult classroom conversations.

Opening the Conversation

Since the participants at the Diversity Institutes at SUNY Cortland are invariably diverse in terms of disciplinary expertise and lived experiences, all of them are usually differently impacted by the program. The cofacilitators define the context of the conversation to include the following:

- initiating candid and informed dialogue
- dealing with difficult dialogue
- emphasizing that diversity work is unfinished with evolving issues
- emphasizing that diversity work is human work and it is complex
- promoting deep learning—metacognition, not bulimic learning
- emphasizing the benefits of intentionality in our policies and outcomes
- building cognitive models for societal realities
- reaching cultural competence and inclusive excellence

In addition to defining the context of the conversation through the techniques above, the facilitators frequently utilize the conceptual framework of diversity education, content integration of historically marginalized groups, knowledge construction for comprehension, investigation, and critical thinking. Prejudice reduction techniques, anti-discriminatory education, and positive attitudes are generated through noncombative or non-guilt-pushing approaches. Inclusivity, pedagogical equity in the methods of talking about race, class, gender, disability, religion, and how men and women are socialized become a centripetal force in the process. The objective here is to take the participants to the sphere of cultural competence by redefining educational culture. We intertwine social justice theories with the best practices to produce praxis. Hitherto, the theories that we depend on are those that provide us with the framework for challenging and questioning oppressive practices to create future possibilities for a "just society."

What has been tremendously helpful is setting up ground rules at the beginning of the institute and making a list of shared values, such as garnering respect and confidentiality—that nothing will be taken outside the safe zone of the institute.

Three additional ground rules are key: the "ouch and educate," "Aha and educate" moments, and using an "I" statement for framing one's position or question. "Ouch and educate" refers to a visceral discomfort with a position held by others and gives one an immediate right to speak up, rather than waiting for one's turn. The Aha moment is about the affirmation of transformative information that could become a game changer in our endeavors in diversity work, and we need to expatiate on it. The "I" statement is significant in so far as claims are couched for one's standpoint only, rather than daring to speak on behalf of a group. However, we note that the pedagogy device of "ouch and educate" has drawn criticism, since it may be perceived as a shaming practice. Here we note that facilitators can draw on diverse rhetorical tools of redirecting the conversation ("calling-in" rather than calling-out) to generate empathic listening among participants. We draw on Loretta Ross (2019), who initiated an important national conversation on the problematic toxic culture of public shaming and offers a pivot: calling-in folks is a "calling-out with love."

Too often, in the classroom of a historically white university, students of color are caught between hypervisibility and invisibility. In the institute, we consider examples of how that occurs and how to take action as a faculty facilitator of discussions. As for hypervisibility, if a student of color enters the classroom late, she is more likely to be noticed than a white student, in particular if it is a habitual practice. And then there is invisibility: Nagel once mentored a Black Caribbean student who told her that she would always make a point of wearing a hat because she was afraid the faculty (of a performing arts department) would mistake her for another Black woman in class. No avail. The student resigned to the fact that she would always be lumped in with the other woman and not graded individually, as the faculty member must have been capable of doing with all the white students.

If the person articulating a racist joke is a person with considerable authority, such as a professor, the negative impact on the audience is magnified, as the recourse is one of powerlessness. In a classic essay,

"Invisibility in Academe," Adrienne Rich proclaims, "When those who have power to name and to socially construct reality choose not to see or hear you, whether you are dark-skinned, old, disabled, female, or speak with a different accent or dialect than theirs, when someone with the authority of a teacher, say, describes the world and you are not in it, there is a moment of psychic disequilibrium, as if you look into a mirror and saw nothing" (Rich, 1986, p. 199).

It is not just feeling invisible in the classroom when one's experiences are neglected, but one faces the lethal effect of failing the course if they challenge the authority in charge of that class. At stake are some of the following: getting a poor grade as retaliation for reporting or confronting the professor personally, getting marginalized among the perpetrator's colleagues, thus losing access to a critical network for recommendations, mentoring, and so on, and a sense of hopelessness in the face of other students' silence or even approval of jokes. The student's negative experience is further magnified, if an institution such as a university has no provisions for an ombudsperson, a chief diversity officer, or somebody who is known to have considerable independent status to provide counseling, support, and other forms of intervention, including notifying the administration of the incident. More recently, administrations have set up advisory boards made up by campus professionals that investigate bias-related reporting. These take the place of student conduct offices and adjudicate in secret. It is unclear how these behavioral incidence teams produce an outcome that is comforting to an aggrieved and traumatized BIPOC student.

In our discussions at the Diversity Institute, we also realize that despite a pretty robust set of institutional support for bringing charges or using dialogue and education, not all students who are impacted would dare to use the infrastructure to demand changed behavior and a welcoming classroom climate. Why call it Diversity Institute? This title was chosen to reflect the national trends that shifted from anti-discrimination and multiculturalism discourses to the broadly conceived terminology of "diversity." Of course, the shift is not without problems. So, we still teach on the first day the appreciation of multiculturalism and contrast it with diversity. What is relevant in these institutes is that "higher education's unique mission as a gathering place for multiple diversities certainly makes us open and vulnerable to the conflicts engendered by our current national dialogue. But our mission to expand human knowledge and capacity also holds us accountable for discovering more productive approaches to the dialogue itself" (AAC&U, 1995, p. 3).

Thus, we have placed the practice of professional development for educators and professional staff members as well as university administrators in a historical context. In the times of the civil rights movement, such an institute would have been labeled in a more oppositional manner (e.g., a teach-in on "anti-racism" or "liberation from oppression") and would probably have moved off campus or precisely in the center of power (e.g., a sit-in at the administration building). However, in the current era of managing differences and accommodating diverse identities, a more politically muted label for the institute had to be chosen. Furthermore, it appeals to an award structure within the academy, rewarding good teaching and service. The peer trainers receive stipends from senior administration along with grants from the state to train faculty at other campuses. This is precisely what occurred from 2008 to 2010 when Asumah and Nagel received several grants to institute a multiyear professional development program so that the SUNY Cortland model could be replicated at its sister institutions, SUNY Oneonta and SUNY New Paltz. Our grant proposals stipulated a certain multiplier effect, and the respective campus trainers were able to reach dozens more faculty with our teaching methods and institute materials. It also motivated us to produce a diversity reader (Asumah & Nagel, 2014), which includes work by a peer faculty from New Paltz, Professor Gowri Parameswaran. Clearly, we are aware that, as faculty and staff peer trainers and facilitators of difficult dialogues, we are doing the university's behest of diversity and inclusion leadership in working effectively with a diverse workforce, with perhaps contradictory effects. At the same time, we find this work immensely rewarding, as it opens up new ways of thinking about diversity education, thinking about our own thinking (metacognition), and the complex ways that identities are discussed and deployed. Finally, given our own identities and those of many institutes' participants as transnational actors, the content necessarily informs global diversity matters, further moving us beyond a narrow United States multicultural context.

Our mission and vision on inclusive education, equity, and global diversity would not be fully realized, as many things around diversity and inclusion are in flux. These events and occurrences include the emergence of the COVID-19 pandemic, the abortive coup d'état by Trump supporters at the US Capitol, SUNY System Administration's new proposals for general education, which includes categories for diversity and inclusion but loaded with language such as "sensitivity training" that needs reconfiguration, the scramble for antiracism programs on college campuses as reaction to the knee-lynching of George Floyd, and recent hate-related shootings in Atlanta and Colorado. The events have ripple effects on diversity leadership. Under these conditions, we attempt to engage in critical consciousness and to project to our students, faculty, and administrators the inescapable interdependence on diversity and inclusion models and narratives as sources of greater comprehension in the human condition in our succeeding chapters.

We continue the next chapter by engaging you, the reader, in a quest for reshaping diversity and inclusive leadership through another narrative approach. This time, we will tell our stories about our lived experiences in different diversity, equity, and inclusion (DEI) spaces that need work. Come with us to Whitehill University, where whiteness is submerged in racial discursive consciousness, epistemologies of ignorance, entity of privilege, and inclusive leadership deficiency.

Chapter 2

The Illusion of Inclusion

Risk Management's Co-optation of Diversity and Inclusion Leadership at Whitehill University

Our nation's campuses have become a highly visible stage on which the most fundamental questions about difference, equality, and community are being enacted.

—AAC&U (1995)

When diversity is characterized by patterned inequity and persistent marginalization of specific groups, it is a symptom of democracy's failure.

—AAC&U (1995)

College leaders are talking more than ever about inclusion. Faculty and students are demanding institutional changes. At some colleges, dozens or even hundreds of faculty members have signed onto open letters that call for anti-racist action and offer criticisms that, depending on one's point of view, will either seem compelling or exaggerated.

—Mull (2020)

Introduction

Educational inclusive excellence in democratic entities is an enterprise that is evolving on undulating terrains and turbulent voyages of the academy because of America's historical contradictions and the fragility of democracy itself. Administrators, faculty, students, and parents have partnerships in maneuvering and renegotiating time, space, place, budgets, curriculums, belongingness, wakefulness, and irrational fear for diversity, equity, and inclusion (DEI) projects. We are inspired by the contumacy of social justice and the persistency of the human spirit to reach a point of equilibrium, equity, and fairness on our campuses, where students and faculty of color would find a welcoming place in the academy. We are hopeful that with resiliency and persistency in DEI work BIPOC students will be treated as active subjects of the learning community and not as objects for someone's research project. It is our position that higher education should champion the modeling of our current and future generations about inclusive excellence, epistemologies of truth, the complexity of curriculum development, and the global human condition beyond whiteness and hegemonic leadership. When the verisimilitude associated with administrative leadership, shepherded by kitsch's fallacious imagery of organized happiness, managed orderliness, and the illusion of inclusion comes in contact with the oppressive and marginalized conditions of people of color on our campuses, there are "moment[s] of psychic disequilibrium" (Rich, 1986) and, consequently, "things fall apart" (Achebe, 1958), and structural racism becomes triumphant. Colleges and universities that engage in miseducation and diseducation of students because of risk management and disregard for cultural pluralism shortchange especially their BIPOC students and faculty. The struggle for social justice on our campuses, creating a playing field that is level for all students and faculty, imparting knowledge for BIPOC students that would make them marketable in future, and not programing them for servitude positions are calls for action. Johnson et al. inform our vision and affirm our mission by giving America this premonition: "As racial tensions mount around the country, especially in our nation's colleges and universities, that aim to undermine progress towards racial equity, access to research-based findings that can be translated into concrete recommendations for practitioners is increasingly important" (2022, p. 13).

We are hopeful that our over fifty years of joint experience in this field, mentioned earlier in this book, would add to the DEI proverbial accoutrements for the fight against injustice and inequity. This chapter would enable interlocutors of the topic of diversity leadership and risk management in higher education to see the similarities and differences associated with traditional leadership, power differentials, systemic oppression, and a call for a change in the American ethos for a more inclusive culture for our colleges and universities. Why are some institutions successful in making BIPOC students and faculty more welcome and productive on their campuses? After visiting many campuses and talking with many faculty of color, we find out that there are too many issues on the campuses we have had access to and too many institutions with similar problems and issues, so we now take an intersectional approach to sharing our narratives. The main thing here is about combining separate stories for the recontextualization of details of real events and processes into a creation that provides readers with a compelling narrative of risk management's co-optation of diversity leaderships.

This methodology works in different contexts; for instance, Collier (2007) develops hypothetical nation states, Prosperia and Catastrophia. The wealthy and prosperous nation state, Prosperia, has a big economy with a growth rate of 10 percent but has a small population. Catastrophia, the neighboring country, has a big population with a declining political economy. When the International Monetary Fund (IMF) and the World Bank analyze the rate of development in the region of Prosperia and Catastrophia, the rule of averages kicks in and the aggregate development and growth picture in that region might be lower than we may think, but Prosperia has skewed the outcomes. The best approach to learn how individuals are doing in the two hypothetical nation states is not by measuring their GDPs and GNPs, but by accounting for the typical person's experiences in the countries of the bottom billion (Collier, 2007, pp. 8–9). By a similar logic, we share our experiences at so many universities and colleges in our quest for social justice in our hypothetical institutions, which serve as an effective laboratory for studying and analyzing the educational ethos of America. Furthermore, the individual narratives of BIPOC faculty and students and how they navigate systemic racism and risk management in the era of diversity and inclusion are related to the reader from the lenses of two institutions, Whitehill University and Whiteview College, where white institutional presence (WIP)—white precepts, norms, ideologies, practices—prevails. As Cabrera et al. remind us, "Whiteness enables the reader to better understand how Whiteness is embedded in the culture of higher education institutions" (2017, p. 9).

Whitehill University (WU) is a microcosm of the United States. This Research 1 (R1) institution is in trouble with diversity and inclusion, just as the US has been in trouble even before the knee-lynching of George Floyd and the global uprising against systemic racism of the 2020s. An

African adage informs us that if we are traveling across troubled waters and making a turbulent voyage to a destination, it is prudent to build bridges and not to destroy bridges. Apparently, Whitehill University's leadership has a different approach to handling risk management vis-à-vis diversity leadership. Whitehill University's leadership capitalizes on risk abatement, neutralizes diversity and inclusion expertise, and engages in diversity and inclusion window-dressing, lip service, and color neutrality (colorblindness) for publicity. Whitehill University is located in the beautiful blue hills of the Wamunda Mountain Region, about seventy-five miles from Charleston, West Virginia. Despite its rural location most of the close to the fifteen thousand student body comes from the Charleston area. As a predominantly white institution (PWI), many of the trials and tribulations of the United States' historical contradictions, diversity and inclusion, and issues in race relations still haunt WU. Just as we see various forms of oppression in the United States, including the symptoms of white supremacy, mobocracy, anocracy, and the insurgency that shocked advocates of American democracy on January 6, 2021, that are difficult to comprehend, we see similar but not identical issues and problems at Whitehill University and the adjoining sister campus, Whiteview College (WC).

Race is a major category in American life and Whitehill University is not different. Many predominantly white campuses have similar issues and problems with race, racism, and risk management. Yet, when students leave their homes to attend college at WU, they anticipate a haven where learning would take place without the ghosts of racism, sexism, homophobia, transphobia, Afrophobia, and all other "isms" and "phobias" haunting them. The irony for students and faculty of color in predominantly white universities is the presumption that academia is sophisticated enough to provide a locus of protection against unreasonable behaviors and racial microaggressions, but that is not the case. Furthermore, students and faculty of color in historically white colleges and universities (HWCUs) presume that before enrolling or securing positions in these HWCUs, their struggles as minoritized groups in a racialized majority world would subside in academia. But do these struggles end because of their presence in these ivory towers? Absolutely not!

In Whitehill University, administrators have made concerted efforts to increase the racial and ethnic diversity rate of the student body and the usual bragging rights about the increases in the student of color population from 2 percent in the 1980s to double digits in 2022 continue to trump the themes of organized events and Whitehill University functions. The administration, in its branding efforts, never misses the opportunity to bombard participants of honors convocation, commencement, chancellor's administrative conferences, chairs council meetings, and other social events on campus with the progress that WU has made in numerical diversity. Many of these administrators and young students see the glory, but they do not know the story of students and faculty of color at Whitehill University. One thing that interlocutors of diversity narratives must not forget is that numerical racial diversity is not the same as authentic racial diversity. Numerical racial diversity deals with pure numerical increases in the people of color in a particular setting. Authentic racial diversity, in addition to the numbers, deals with meeting the needs of BIPOC students and faculty of color, making sure there is a feeling of belongingness to campus, reaching cultural competence, and moving from the state of tolerance to a new position of affirmation. Whitehill University has not reached any level of cultural competence and authentic diversity yet, despite the new numerical preponderance of students of color on campus and, presumably, despite a great effort to hire several administrators within the past decade who focus on diversity and inclusion efforts, such as chief diversity and inclusion officers (CDIOs) and directors of multicultural centers, as well as being in compliance with federal mandates to hire Title IX officers.

As Cross et al. (1989) inform us, there are several elements of cultural competence. Valuing diversity is one of these things and individuals and institutions have to transcend the boundaries of tolerance, acceptance, and respect to reach the levels of affirmation, genuine critique, and solidarity (Nieto, 1992). The capacity of individuals and the institution to engage in self-assessment—examining policy, feelings, attitudes, perceptions of one's own group and for those that are different, including other diversity categories; ethnic, cultural, gender, sexual orientation, religion, disability, and class and affirming that cultural competence is a necessity, not a luxury, should be the university's *modus operandi* (Young & Davis-Russell, 2002).

In this chapter, as we have mentioned above, we utilize a hypothetical case study of Whitehill University to argue that, even though most historically white colleges and universities have taken advantage of the diversity and inclusion movement to increase student of color enrollments, the high rate of risk management vis-à-vis inclusive diversity leadership has become eminent. The new norms of "managing" students and faculty of color on many occasions, have included infantilization of students and faculty of color, backed by a climate of divisiveness, silencing, tone-policing, microaggression, microinvalidation, and new performative antiracist activities, which produce a smokescreen for authentic change for racial justice at Whitehill University. Furthermore, there has been an immense increase in the hegemonic powers of university administrators, especially since the emergence of the COVID-19 pandemic, and, ironically, this priority enables administrators to boost their claim of urgency to protecting the dominant culture and the fiscal strength of the institution while the lived experiences of students of color are mostly ignored. Elise Archias and Blake Stimson (2023) note:

> In other words, the administrative effort to protect students—even for a brief moment, in the name of a Racial Justice Task Force—turned out to be an unwitting institutional endorsement of anti-Black racism. . . . It may simply be bureaucratic arrogance that leads them to think that their managerial titles give them more expertise to address complex and layered social and cultural issues than faculty who are trained in these areas. (p. 9)

The risk management approach to leadership makes events surrounding race, gender, diversity, and inclusion more tricky and complex. Risk management is mostly submerged in identification, prioritization, and evaluation of value that has potential to be lost. Risk perception, the associated judgement or how organizations perceive risk in management, is a major pillar for risk management. Nevertheless, every human activity or endeavor is susceptible to risk. For instance, faculty members avoid pedagogical risk by playing it safe in their lectures. Some faculty even have trigger warnings on their syllabi with lengthy paragraphs about "safe space" without mentioning courageous and brave spaces discussed earlier in this volume. Many faculty members are afraid that in this era of callout cultures (Me Two, Black Lives Matter, and general challenge to hegemonic powers), one has to be careful about what is said in the classroom, so difficult dialogues involving race and gender are usually avoided at the expense of the lived experiences of, especially, people of color, while learned racism and its beneficiaries in a racialized society reign and most often are not challenged. In these days of Black Lives Matter and the divisiveness in the United States, especially after former president Trump lost the elections to Joe Biden, there is a rise of "I-don't-see-color-ism," "I-don't-care-ism," "we-are-all-human-ism," and pretentious safe space vis-à-vis courageous space contests, which invalidate the lived experiences of people of color, and learned racism continues to infiltrate the campus culture. The contemporary nature of whiteness and white administrative powers on our campuses, like Whitehill University, is what scholars such as Feagin and Omi and Winant describe as the structural normativity of whiteness, which expands the privilege of white people in our institutions while at the same time marginalizing BIPOC students and faculty (Feagin, 2010; Omi & Winant, 2015).

Is this a "new" era of in loco parentis—a time where heteropatriarchal hegemons maintain anthropomorphic powers to protect the institutional image and maintain campus culture, rather than defend the rights of all human beings within the institution? What is more convenient for risk management in academia? Is this new approach to reorganizing power differentials in higher education the price we pay for demanding diversity and inclusion on our campuses? Does the fear of making someone "uncomfortable" anywhere—classroom, on campus, study abroad—fundamentally make the intellectual climate in higher education infinitesimally diluted, because of recent callout cultures, diversity "policing," cancel culture, presence of Title IX coordinators, chief diversity and inclusion officers (CDIO), and human resources officers?

At this juncture, we would like to be clear that we are interrogating the risk management model and not supporting interlocutors of the uniculturalist movement, such as Governor Ron DeSantis of Florida, QAnon, and Trumpublicans, who claim diversity disunites America. Who is policing the police (administrators) in the name of inclusion in all these diversity quagmires? Whitehill University is ripe for interrogating diversity management style, equity, and inclusion leadership endeavors. This institution serves as a fertile laboratory for examining risk and diversity management, which are usually masqueraded in the name of diversity and inclusion leadership in higher education.

Whiteness and Whitehill University

Whitehill University, like many institutions in West Virginia and Louisiana, has made concerted efforts to relegate authentic diversity studies and projects to a different lower dimension. Based on national statistical references that have influenced the Whitehill administrators, beautification processes of improving the appearance of the campus's infrastructure, gardens, and the admissions and enrollments are the top priorities. A big budget was allocated to the University Life and Living Center, where students, faculty, and staff can exercise and eat well, instead of developing an intercultural and wellness center, where students can engage in inclusive education, exchange cultural norms, eat cross-cultural meals, engage in cross-cultural activities, and more. The leadership of WU has carefully studied national trends about Generation Z and their desire to attend college. To Generation Z, the educational reputation of an institution is less important than the beautification process of building grand auditoriums, glass-towered buildings, carefully manicured gardens, and ultramodern sidewalks to fight the resistance of not taking selfies in any 100-meter walk on campus. Yes, the sidewalks are Americans with Disability Act (ADA) compliant, yet the pictures and billboards along these sidewalks do not reflect the racial and ethnic composition of the American polity.

Furthermore, while academic indicators for enrollments are relatively higher than most Research 1 institutions, Whitehill University has attracted proportionally more white faculty, administrators, and staff, but it maintains the bragging rights that there has been substantial increments in Black and Latino students—numerical diversity. However, campus climate is so deplorable that there have been organized town hall meetings and petitions by students of color to improve the race and gender relations on campus. Note that campus climate is one thing, but campus culture and ecology, discussed earlier in this volume, like most American institutions of higher learning, are never mentioned at WU. Yes, diversity could be about playing the numbers game, and numerical diversity by itself does not solve the problem of cultural competence and retention. While the Latino student population is increasing at Whitehill, Black (especially males) and indigenous populations are steeply on the decline, the faculty of color population is dismal, and when students of color demand faculty who look like them in their classrooms, they are told it is difficult to find, especially, Black professors who want to come to Whitehill University, in the mountains of West Virginia.

Here, regarding whiteness, as Dyson asserts, "I am not talking about your bodies or your garages or your grocery stores. I am talking about the politics of whiteness. I am talking about an identity that exits apart from the skin you're born in" (2017, p. 44). These forms of social structures and generational inheritances are very illusory, ambiguous, and illusive for white administrators and students to understand. They are so invisible, so white folx cannot get it, but they have societal magic, they are powerful in changing the American narrative on race relations.

Leonardo affirms, " 'Whiteness' is a racial discourse, whereas the category 'white people' represents a socially constructed identity usually based on skin color.... Whiteness is not a culture but a social concept" (2009, p. 169–170). Cabrera et al. (2017) strengthen our comprehension of the concept of whiteness as it relates to the American polity, institutions of higher learning, and (in our case) the saga of education at Whitehall University. These scholars provide us with three "faces" of whiteness and how they define the individual and institutional racial interactions. Whiteness's three faces are (1) refusal and inability to name and identify the shape and form of systemic racism, (2) withdrawal from, nullifying, and avoidance of the lived experiences of BIPOC folx, and (3) deliberate minimization of America's racial history (Cabrera et al., 2017, p. 18). Yet whiteness as discursive consciousness enables some BIPOC folx in WU to engage in the very discourse that is programmed to bring them down and push them to the margins of the American society. How? It is very easy for some BIPOC folx to buy into the narratives of "lift yourself up by your boot straps" and "slavery ended long ago, so it does not bother me anymore."

The history of America is disguised in whiteness and the history of Whitehall University is adorned in whiteness. How can something that is not real—whiteness—maintain so much force of truism and kinetic energy to make things happen personally and politically? So, at Whitehall University, "Whiteness never had to announce its whiteness, never had to promote or celebrate its uniqueness" (Dyson, 2017, p. 64). Whiteness is ubiquitous in America and Whitehall University is not an exception. At WU, many of the white administrators, faculty, and students continue to suffer from the old illness of historical amnesia, cloaked in holy innocence, and intoxicated with racial arrogance. Gore Vidal's (2004) characterization of this historical amnesia as "the United States of Amnesia" is not too far-fetched at WU, as most white faculty tiptoe and dance around difficult dialogues of race, class, and gender in the classroom, and yet students of color are seen as troublemakers when they engage in critical questioning of the course material or find solace in some classrooms through a code of silence, when they refuse to answer belittling questions. Whiteness at WU is a state of mind, a delusion that everything is fine, but "fine," FINE, is just an acronym for "feelings that individuals never express." Administrators deflect questions about inclusion, fail to see color, are shocked to see racist epithets on campus, are quick to dismiss racist and sexist incidents as unconnected events, and scapegoat Black faculty and students who have the audacity to challenge the administrative hegemony.

In his book *Black and White Politics of Race on American Campuses*, Ross (2017) captures the Whitehill campus picture vividly: "And in their most formative years, when their belief in American ideals is the strongest, or being questioned, these African American students will learn that their white university, their white fellow students, their white faculty are not automatic allies in their journey toward educational success" (2017, p. 5). Even more extreme than Whitehill University, is a sister institution in the Appalachian Valley, Whiteview College, that has given up all hopes of diversity, inclusion, and social justice projects. In Whiteview College, many towering statues of white former slave masters and donors overshadow students and faculty of color, reminding them constantly about whiteness and post-traumatic slave syndrome (PTSS)—the residual effects of past carnages (slavery, Jim Crow), current oppression against Blacks due to lack of proper healing from the past, and current dehumanization.

All this whiteness blinds both Black and white students in their educational experience at Whitehill University and Whiteview College. A university or college campus is supposed to be the locus for knowledge development, freedom, diversity of ideas, equity, respect, liberation of the mind and spirit, citizenship, leadership, and liberatory learning. However, are these utopian ideas reserved for white students at Whitehill University only? Whiteness is so ingrained in the educational culture of Whitehill that most white students are submerged in a pool of denial that racism still exists, and white administrators discount racist incidents as isolated events that do not reflect the value of Whitehill University. Most recent cases at Syracuse University (SU) and Ithaca College (IC), for example, are indicative of institutional leaderships that took students of color for granted and minimized the impacts of racist events on campus until the students demanded the resignation of Chancellor Kent Syverud (SU) and President Tom Rochon (IC). Again, the measured statements of many presidents or chancellors when ugly incidents occur at their institutions include labeling occurrences as isolated incidents. There is always minimization or even silence about such events to protect the institution from the media and the world. Ross affirms this bureaucratic tactic and pro forma response in his research on injustice on American college and university campuses: "We're surprised and shocked that this would happen on our campus, and we'd like to say that this racial incident doesn't reflect the value of who we are as a university community . . ." (2017, p. 5).

Taking Diversity and Inclusion Seriously through Faculty Development

Whitehill University's earlier commitment to diversity and multiculturalism was evident, as this predominantly white institution sent six of its cadre of scholars and social justice advocates to several institutes for diversity and inclusion in the 1980s to sharpen their knowledge, skills, and pedagogical techniques in multiculturalism, diversity, and social justice. Some of these faculty and staff participated in faculty development programs from the National Coalition Building Institute (NCBI), American Association for Colleges and Universities (AAC&U) and the National Diversity Institute (NDI) in Washington, DC. These Whitehill University faculty and staff returned to campus to develop courses and projects on diversity and inclusion, including general education courses and a Whitehill Institute for Diversity and Inclusion (WIDI) to provide professional development colloquiums for their faculty and staff. Whitehill engaged the campus with diversity film series, conferences, workshops, colloquiums, student engagements, and mandatory diversity leadership development workshops. Nevertheless, the momentum to make diversity and inclusion a priority subsided as the provost and vice president for academic affairs, Dr. Vindra Azamati, a woman of color, retired from WU. The predominantly white Whitehill Chancellor's Cabinet started stepping on the breaks for diversity and inclusion projects. Some of the cabinet members even accused Dr. Azamati of misappropriation and maldistribution of funding, when she prioritized diversity and inclusion projects. Therefore, misappropriation was used to admonish her for doing too much diversity work. Even so, as the process of budgeting informs us, budgeting experts will assign high price tags to high priority areas in our society to emphasize what is more valuable to the citizenry or the institution. Wildavsky (1988) asserts, "In most general definition, budgeting is concerned with translating financial resources into human purpose" (1988, p. 2). Therefore, due to Provost Azamati's identity as a person of color, her action of prioritizing diversity work was misunderstood by most on the mostly white cabinet.

The departure of the Black provost from Whitehill University created a diversity lacuna in the administrative echelon of the institution. Programs that were organized and implemented did not have the same fervor, as before; even though the student of color population has increased, numerical diversity is not the same as sustainable diversity. Yet Whitehill University hides behind the façade of diversity and inclusion and pretends that all is "fine." Many faculty and students at Whitehill University are dying inside, but they do not know and would not voice out because of power imbalances. Power imbalance asphyxiates ingenuity and diversity creativity in students and faculty who want to see a welcoming campus. Whiteview College, the sister campus to Whitehill University, does not cure much. Even some of its students joined the Unite the Right rally in Charlottesville, Virginia, in August 2017 with neo-Nazi symbols and Confederate flags, causing the death of three people. Yet former President Trump supported these neo-Nazis and called them "very fine people" (Kessler, 2020). At least, Whitehill University is noted for success in struggling to be acknowledged as an inclusive campus by chasing diversity initiatives that encompass delicate and intricate window-dressing of major events to give the appearance of an institution where cultural competence and affirmation of the humanity of people of color reign. But this kind of situation with high performative, feel-good, diversity activities without concrete policy change at PWIs produces racial arrested development, where white students do not face crucial and critical DEI challenges in their "racial selves" and growth in race relations (Cabrera et al., 2017, p. 27).

Students and most faculty members are afraid to complain about macroaggressions, microinsults, microassaults, and microinvalidations or challenge the hegemonic power structures and institutional cultural incompetence. Microaggression, a new form of "ism," is often subtle behavioral, communication, and situational action, whether intentional or unintentional, that communicates discriminatory, prejudicial, or insulting messages toward a minoritized or target group (Sue et al., 2007). Microinvalidation, microinsult, and microassault are subcategories of microaggression. While microinvalidation negates or rejects the experience, presence, and identity of a target group, microassault is a racial verbal or nonverbal attack meant to hurt the intended target, and microinsult conveys a demeaning and insensitive attack on the racial heritage of the targeted group (Sue et al, 2007). Yes, these attacks are rampant at Whitehill University, and they could be characterized as new, invisible, or palpable forms of racism.

Racism is not the only elephant on the campus of Whitehill University. Syracuse University (2019), University of Oklahoma (2019), University of Georgia (2019), University of Mississippi (2019), the University of Arizona (2019), University of Missouri (2019), and Whiteview College (2020) have all had their share of demonstration by students against racism in recent times. There has been gender-related oppression for many years on these campuses, but the federal government has come to the rescue in recent times and has mandated the appointment of Title IX coordinators or directors to organize and tackle gender, transgender, and women-related issues. Title IX is the educational policy amendments that prohibit institutions that receive federal funding from discriminatory practices against female students and employees.

The Irony of Inclusion, Campus Politics, and Microinvalidation: Intellectuals and Impostors

While most colleges and universities are engaged in curriculum development, exercises to improve diversity and inclusion, and professional development to gain proficiency and cultural competence in diversity and inclusion, it is ironic that Whitehall University is more interested in risk management to avoid bad publicity rather than diversity and inclusion leadership. The formation of the Whitehill Inclusion and Equity Council (WIEC), which was charged to lead the campus in diversity and inclusion policy agendas and policymaking, became a popularity contest—the favorites of administrators, political appointees, and sycophants were elevated to committees of power and not necessarily faculty with proven expertise in diversity and inclusion. The politics of omission and commission, politics of anti-politics, political decapitations, exclusions, microinvalidations, and deliberate avoidances of institutional knowledge/history in diversity and inclusion have become the order of the past decade at Whitehill University.

The hegemonic masculinist approach (with the complicity of a couple of white ciswomen) was to reduce the presence of intellectuals in diversity studies/work and silence those who were outspoken, senior faculty, and those who were not afraid to speak truth to power—they have to be politically decapitated. These faculty members have researched, have published extensively, and teach courses in the areas of diversity studies, but that did not matter. The heteropatriarchal hegemons moved to make these scholars impotent in the battle to form the Whitehill Inclusion and Equity Council. Six diversity scholar-activists were invited by the authorities at WU and were asked to "graciously" bow out of most of diversity and inclusion initiatives and membership of WIEC—clear actions of microaggression and microinvalidation. In the place of these scholars, who have led diversity and inclusion efforts for a long time, nonreasoned, inexperienced, and neophytes would join the chief diversity and inclusion officer (CDIO) to do the work of the WIEC. It was not a coincidence that the

CDIO resigned from Whitehill University only after three years of service to WU to join another institution where the leadership is more genuine about diversity and inclusion projects. Apparently, many CDIOs, who join institutions only to be ordained as diversity messiahs by administrators but are desensitized against faculty of color to keep their presumed neutrality, do not outlive institutional memory and those seasoned faculty in diversity and inclusion. These seasoned faculty who have learned how to maintain the craft of maneuverability in troubled waters must be working with the neophytes to serve WU. Diversity of ideas, knowledge production, and microaffirmations are priceless in building a strong and diverse learning community, but WU seriously lacks those qualities.

This process of diversity and inclusion asphyxiation does not only choke the campus out of true diversity oxygen, but it reduces the existential anxiety for intellectual endeavors for diversity and inclusion. It further arms the troops of uniculturalists and white supremacists to attack diversity and inclusion work as "flabby, feel-good exercises." It was not an aberration or epiphenomenal that a former board of trustee of the State University of New York, Candice DeRussy, would characterize women's studies, Black Studies, diversity studies as "feel good" disciplines and a conference on queer studies as "degeneration of an academic forum into a platform for lesbian sex, for public sadomasochism, for anal sex, bestiality and masturbation" (Walker, 1998). It was not a coincidence that after the *New York Times* supported the 1619 Project, a vision of Nikole Hannah-Jones to properly teach the holocaust of enslavement, race, racism, and US history in our educational institutions, former President Trump set up the 1776 Commission to water down the process of teaching and reporting history. It was not unusual for President Biden to dissolve the 1776 Commission on his first day in the White House on January 20, 2021 (Binkley, 2021).

At Whitehill University, there are many wolves in sheepskins, who ride the chariots of diversity and inclusion but whose actions of inclusion are more performative and illusionary. This strategy is what Michael Eric Dyson characterizes as follows: "The ventriloquist effect of whiteness works brilliantly—Black mouths moving, white ideas flowing" throughout the campus (Dyson, 2017, p. 16). So, one of the tools for the illusion of inclusion is to reduce the effects of diversity experts by the process of microinvalidation—making the presence of these experts irrelevant to the diversity and inclusion project on campus. We must ask ourselves, If it makes sense to fight COVID-19 with experts and scientists, why do administrators refrain from working with social scientists and DEI experts in the field of diversity and inclusion leadership? The perception that diversity and inclusion work is everybody's work and nobody's responsibility is destroying the agency of diversity and inclusion leadership not just in Whitehill University, but in most American universities and colleges.

Like the American race projects that define our daily interactions and distribution of resources and power among whites and people of color, diversity and inclusion projects are taking the shape of the race project. Hitherto, in the era of diversity and inclusion, some or most white men of power are maintaining the old power structures, pretending they are all for inclusion. Wolves in sheep skins? Apparently, many historically white college and university campuses have created Black and Latino colonies on white campus (nations) as noted by Chris Hayes (2017). For the state of ethnic politics to thrive, when an American president propounded the concept of "a colony in a nation" Black activists and academics were in the midst of extended debate about the concept of internal colonialism and whether the state of Black people in America was akin to a colonized people (Hayes, 2017, p. 31). The situation at Whitehill University is a microcosm of the American polity, with blackademics, Africologists, Latino, and Africana Studies faculty and students still fighting for decolonization of the curriculum, the mind, and the body, and for the canonization of Africana and Latino knowledge, conditions, and aspirations.

Africology, Africana Studies, Women's Studies, Student of Color Organizations: The Threat to Hegemonic Powers?

The recent emergence of the Black Lives Matter and Me Too movements is an extension of a broader challenge to white heteropatriarchal hegemonic power structures that has helped to shape our lethal experiences and historical contradictions for a nation state that professes democracy, freedom, and inclusion, but, in actuality, has excluded people of color and women in its total experience. The civil rights movement of 1964, multiculturalism, diversity, and inclusion are supposed to provide Esperanto—the international liberating language that failed to save the world from disunity, and a panacea for powerlessness, exclusion, cultural imperialism, and marginalization. However, the legacy of the holocaust of enslavement, colonialism, imperialism, and dehumanization has been complex and more complicated to undo. The lingering effects of these atrocities in terms of implicit biases, microassaults, microinsults, and microinvalidations pose a challenge to our diversity and inclusion projects.

Whitehill University is a laboratory for testing institutional approaches and behaviors in any diversity and inclusion leadership in any historically white college and university (HWCU). Similar to the argument propounded by the Black Power movement leaders (Stokely Carmichael [Kwame Ture] and Charles Hamilton) of the 1960s that America's ghettos suffered from the effects of internalized colonialism and imperialism and it would take Black nationalism to liberate Black folks from the ghettoes, Africana studies and Africology departments are acting as the liberating forces on our campuses in curriculum development, inclusive pedagogy, multicultural programming, and liberatory education. Whitehill University is not an exception to this condition whereby an academic department is in the forefront of the liberation struggle. Unfortunately, in every liberation struggle, the leadership has to pay a price—death, dehumanization, imprisonment, police brutality, assassination, incarceration, and sociopolitical asphyxiation. However, without this struggle, there would be no progress, Frederick Douglass warned us. Nevertheless, 2022 is not 1857, but the struggle continues, and victory is inevitable—*A luta continua, vitória é certa!* This was Samora Machel's (FRELIMO) rallying cry against oppression and the Portuguese colonial presence in Mozambique and Angola. Yes, *a luta continua* (the struggle continues) at Whitehill University.

In addition to the seven disciplinary areas of Africana studies, race defines part of the boundary of Africology as a thrust of the discipline, and Whitehill University as a historically white college and university (HWCU) cannot avoid race as the elephant on campus. Even so, race as a social construct is an ambiguous but major category in American life. Whiteness reigns, but white privilege is a nonissue, an enigma, or a discursive taboo—that is when someone dares to mention it. Blackness has a fictional quality but represents a threat to white hegemony and Africology's taming process involves misdistribution and maldistribution of resources, space, and faculty lines. Furthermore, in Whitehall University, the department chair and senior faculty members who have contributed immensely to the diversity and inclusion projects had to be silenced and directed by the authorities to refrain from or limit their involvement in diversity and inclusion work. This instruction to stop doing diversity work or limit their involvement in diversity activities, even though these faculty members have published more articles and books on the subjects of multiculturalism, diversity, inclusion, and social justice than anyone else on campus, is another of the ventriloquist strategies mentioned earlier in this chapter.

The Africology Department at Whitehill University has organized and led faculty development workshops, conferences, and colloquiums on diversity and inclusion more than any faculty. It is unconscionable that the administration of the Whitehill University would ask them to reduce their endeavors in diversity work—the illusion of inclusion. There is more to this story, but the tyranny of time and space would not allow us to embellish. The rate of microinvalidation increased as interlocutors and experts on diversity and inclusion were instructed to step aside and were disinvited to most diversity and inclusion committees and events. These actions stand diversity, inclusion, and social justice right on their heads at Whitehill University, and they slap the mission statement and institutional priorities right in the face.

Incredibly, for over twenty years, the Africology Department at Whitehill University has graduated students in African studies, African American studies, and Pan African studies without full-time faculty positions. The department chair, faculty affiliates, who work on full-time bases in other departments, and adjunct faculty have been innovative enough to perform their institutional functions—teaching, curriculum development, research, and community service—without proper recognition, the highest stage of microinvalidation and marginalization. Yet, in the face of this exploitation and savage helplessness, students of color, especially, find the Africology Department to be a home away from home and a department that has vested interest in the educational well-being of the student. We cannot discount the facts that many universities and colleges have started responding to calls for social justice, especially since the global response to the knee-lynching of George Floyd, COVID-19 pandemic, and Black Lives Matter protests. The State University of New York system has instituted a program to recruit and retain more BIPOC and women faculty and staff—PRODiG (Promoting, Recruitment, Opportunity, Diversity, Inclusion, and Growth). This is a systemic approach to solving a systemic inequity problem in New York, and Whitehill University must engage in a discussion for such a project with the Virginia legislators and Board of Trustees.

Now, let us share with you the one of the most bizarre findings about hiring practices at WU that defies any regard for diversity, inclusion, respect, and collegiality. After being ignored by the Whitehill administration for over twenty years to hire full-time faculty members for the Africology Department, in 2018 the University Congress of Whitehill University voted overwhelmingly on a resolution that requested the Whitehill administration to act on providing the Africology Department with full-time faculty. To respond to this resolution, the administration disregarded all hiring protocols for the institution—no searches, no consultations with the chair and faculty affiliates, and no interviews were conducted. The academic affairs leadership hired their two best white friends, who share membership with them in a chess club and who have been teaching in the European Axiology Department for a while. Even so, they did not have the academic preparation/qualification to be appointed as assistant professors (but they were nice people), so they became the first full-time lecturers for the Africology Department (with bachelor's degrees in European value systems and gerontology). What a dance with absurdity!

This particular hiring has nothing to do with the needs of the Africology Department and the core curriculum. The faculty associates and external program reviewers were all shocked at this move by the administration, but the Africology Department members cannot afford to be prisoners of this unacceptable practice and condition, so they continued work as usual. The message in this case is that if the University Congress and Africology faculty demanded a faculty line by a resolution, which might be deemed a political move, then the overlords in the administration might succumb to public pressure to do the right thing. Yet the Whitehill University administration had the power to hire anyone they preferred, regardless of the applicant's background and preparation. Could this practice be tantamount to cronyism, nepotism, and prebendalism? Such administrative transgression, violation, and bullying are prevalent at many institutions of higher learning and they perpetuate toxic campus climate and code of silence, because those who speak up could be punished via the tenure/promotion process or charged with insubordination and incivility. It is not a coincidence that the chair of Africology who has championed diversity and inclusion at Whitehill University was turned into an institutional piñata.

The second opportunity to hire a full-time faculty arose in 2022. This time, even though the department chair has been exceptionally productive, creative, dedicated, and one of the most outstanding scholars and leaders at Whitehill University, the institution's all-white hegemons decided to sacrifice him for their bruised egos because of his unswerving support for students of color and leadership in diversity and inclusion. The collective endeavor to dispossess the Africology chair of his legitimacy, intellectual acumen, raison d'être, and humanity marred most democratic principles, diversity and inclusion, critical consciousness, social justice, and the Africana human condition. The leadership (all-white hegemons) wasted no time in summoning the Black chair of the Africology Department to the Chancellor's Office in the middle of 2020 to "congratulate" him for his hard work, long service to the university and outstanding leadership. Thus far, they have decided to hire a new senior faculty and department chair who would perhaps not threaten their power structure. He walked out of the office of the white administrators speechless—another racial battle fatigue consumed the Africology chair in a pool of acquiescence and quiescence.

The chair's Black body was interrogated by all that whiteness in that meeting, but did not show the "angry Black man syndrome" and was detained in utter silence. The chairs of Africology's very presence, filled with institutional memory, who has served for longer tenure than the powers to be, knowledgeable of the politics of anti-politics, who stood tall as a strong Black man, unquestionably revealed that whiteness is just a social construct, just as the foundation of race and gender at that meeting. Yet still, under the mythology of whiteness, power, authority, respect, and hegemonic rule, the Black chair, like many blackademics, succumbed to this abuse of power, because, for that moment, he was not going to become an angry Black man! He was not naive, not a child, not powerless, but he knew that a challenge to the hegemons might shake the whiteness surrounding him and give the authorities ammunition to attack. Acquiescence and quiescence have their moments for the battle to come. He remembered a moment in the civil rights marches, "I am a Man, I am Somebody!" But this sort of behavior is not unusual with risk managers in academia. Dr. Nathan Hare wanted to establish a Black studies department in Howard University in the 1960s and was fired by the administrators—claiming Black studies as a discipline was too radical. San Francisco State University resisted Black studies until students demanded it, and Yale University was no different. It is not just programs for liberatory learning that are not supported, but dynamic activist scholars are also targeted. Dr. Eric Dyson, for instance, was challenged by a white dean to prove himself that he was smart enough to have attended Princeton University (Dyson, 2017, p. 47).

Paradoxically, the preaching of diversity and inclusion by the administration at Whitehill University is put into practice through the exclusion of those who advocate social justice, equity, and inclusion. Furthermore, the tactics of divide and conquer, infantilization of Black folk, and white solipsism are indefatigable at WU. Student and alumni petitions and faculty meetings with the heteropatriarchal hegemons to denounce the administration's plans to decapitate the Black leadership on campus produced some results. The Black community at WU is not naive. The petitions by the students of color amid the Black Lives Matter movement and unrest at many campuses in the nation served as a premonition to those who pursued injustice. By the end of 2022, the leadership's position on hiring another chair was reversed due to outside pressure. Their quest and conquest to apparently dissolve Africology as a department and emasculate the chair subsided but did not end. We learned from the hiring saga that the entire uproar has very little to do with the Africology Department. It is all about the fight to lead the diversity and inclusion project at Whitehill University. Africology was a scapegoat! This was quite a lesson about white power and perhaps white hegemony. If absurdity was not challenged, it could be lethal to the endeavors in diversity and inclusion. Hegemony could be challenged. Hegemony is not finite, as Antonio Gramsci informed us.

The Africology Department has been the safe haven for most students of color and student organizations, such as the Black Student Union (BSU), Africology Student Association (ASA), Whitehill NAACP, Pan African Student Coalition (PASC), and the Whitehill African American Chorale. Members of the Africology Departments are also faculty advisors to these student organizations. The majors, minors, and student organizations become guilty just by their associating with the Africology Department. In addition to their course work, these students and faculty of color continue to do the invisible work of helping to improve the campus climate through workshops, social events, lectures, and civic engagement activities. Yet in doing diversity work, students and faculty of color at Whitehill are perceived as angry Black men and women. Ross reports about a Black student's observation in *Blackballed*:

> We do not get stars or extra credit for forgiving those who hate us. Our worth and humanity shouldn't be inexplicably tied to our capacity to forgive. And our response to prejudice and bigotry should not be a carefully modulated tone. There has to be room for black rage, black frustration and black

discontent if we are going to move forward as a country. If white tears were going to work, this racism thing would have been fixed a long time ago. (2015, pp. 28–29)

The WU Black Student Union (BSU) is a student organization that has championed the issues of social justice, diversity and inclusion at WU. In the era of Black Lives Matter, their strategies for challenging the heteropatriarchal hegemony and helping to create an inclusive campus have included town hall meetings, lectures, sit-ins, petitions, and weekly meetings that are open to the entire campus. In weekly meetings, Black students at WU give meaning to their space by making it a place where they can shape their providence without having to apologize to anyone for being Black. They build connections with other Black and Latino students to redefine their visions and mission and reaffirm their spirits for struggle, resistance, persistence, and inclusive excellence. They are tied together and bonded by what civil rights movement leader Dr. Martin Luther King characterized as a single garment of destiny (King, 1963/2014), though the design of that garment at WU has several pockets of despair, misery, suffering, and sometimes hope for students and faculty of color at Whitehill University.

One may think that we are manufacturing stories to describe the saga of Whitehill University, institutional leadership, and treatment of people of color in the era of diversity and inclusion, but all these issues and problems involving diversity and inclusive leadership are real and truthful. Students and faculty of color are breaking their backs to help improve the campus climate, only to be characterized as troublemakers or people who might engage in lawless behavior in a predominantly white university. The aura of belongingness does not hang around people of color in WU but the phrase of diversity and inclusion is on the lips of everyone. What an illusion! Black and Latino communities have exhausted all avenues in programming about injustice and events of awareness and most of them are suffering from racial battle fatigue (RBF)—the sociopsychological stress of being a person of color (usually male) in a predominantly white institution. In recent times, especially after the defeat of President Trump in the 2020 presidential election, the US has become more polarized. This national divisiveness is affecting many BIPOC students and faculty at Whitehill University. Black men and women are consumed in racial battle fatigue on college and university campuses, which seriously affect their mental health and academic performance.

Students and faculty of color must modify their existence, speech, tone, behavior, culture, precepts, and norms, and, as Dyson mentions, "We are nothing. And the more we remember our nothingness, become experts in the philosophy of nothingness, the better we have a chance to survive" (2017, p. 171). One thing is to accept one's nothingness for survival, but another thing is how to deal with white overlords of the institutions who engage in weaponizing other departments and students against Blackness and engineering divisiveness among Black faculty and students for their benefit—divide and conquer!? After a number of town hall meetings organized by the Whitehill BSU and supported by the Africology Department, the institutional leadership devised a strategy of student leadership lunches for the students of color organizations in order to "listen" to them. Again, these Black students are young but they students are not naive. Yes, we must listen more to our students, but to hold lunch meetings to manipulate and dissuade them from working with the outspoken faculty of color is an abomination.

The Façade of Global Diversity and Inclusion: White Administrators, Model Minorities, and the Saga of Study Abroad in Africa

The illusion of inclusion has also a global dimension. Internationalization of the curriculum, including diversity and inclusion, is a priority for Whitehill University. Whitehill has several study-abroad programs around the world. However, most of the programs are in collaboration with European universities and colleges. There are a few other programs in South America and the Caribbean. The Africology Department spearheaded a push to develop study abroad programs in six African countries. The most popular African study abroad program is the faculty-led semester program with the University of Umzukulu, East Africa. Part of the mission for this semester faculty-led program is to expose whites and students of color to educational experiences other than that of Europe. As we can attest, the true meaning and essence of a university is not just to become a Euroversity! Students must enjoy global diversity and their points of reference must not only be from Euro-American traditions.

The Whitehill-Umzukulu study abroad program is a very successful program as faculty, students and staff seized the opportunity to explore Africa. In 2018, the Africology faculty who developed the semester study-abroad program was on sabbatical and away from Whitehill University and the gods of chance favored him with a prestigious fellowship at the University of Umzukulu. Study abroad students and two faculty members—one Turkish American woman and the other, a white woman, participated in this program. The Africology faculty met the group at the Umzukulu International Airport. Among the students was a mixed-race (Taiwanese and white American) student, who happened to stand out as the class clown. However, her jokes were seriously offensive. "Rise and shine, East Africa, America has arrived!" Shouted this student on her arrival in East Africa. Just as the colonialist chanted with arrogance and ethnocentrism, she hid behind her light olive skin color to demean East Africans as a dormant, lazy people. The Africology faculty called her aside, without public shaming, to point out to her how insulting her joke was. It was utterly painful to witness that a mixed-race woman's triumphant utterance at the airport, perhaps ignorant of the fact that her joke and the implication of it in the minds of the on-looking East Africans, defied all logic. Even though she has mixed-race heritage, she projected the invisibility factor of whiteness and unapologetic attitude after being reminded of her microinsult—nonverbal or verbal, rude, and insensitive attack on the African identity or heritage. She was so invested in her mixed-race identity and privilege that she thought she was infallible. After this episode on the first day, this student almost got the group arrested for taking selfies at the Palace of the King of Umzukulu. In addition, she interrupted a lecture session on international law about consent protocols on voting and refused to collaborate with other students in the study abroad program. When the Africology faculty confronted this student on many of her behavioral issues, she threatened to write up the Black faculty member upon her return to Whitehill University.

The Turkish American faculty (putatively, a model minority), the white staff woman (historically oppressed), the mixed-race student (questioning her identity) decided to collaborate their stories against the Black faculty (powerless, racialized, and culturally imperialized) and group leader because he reminded the group that a study abroad program must not be seen as an academic safari or vacation. At that point, it was evident that oppression Olympics was inevitable—a situation whereby each oppressed group is trying to prove their oppression is more acute. The mixed-race student reported the Africology faculty to the authorities at Whitehill University. Human Resources are usually not advocates for faculty. HR is an office that is designed to support the institution's interest, and it is impossible to fight a system that is designed to make sure that the institution prevails. The hearing of this case did not meet any "due process" provisions or a "fair hearing," as the accused did not have the opportunity to cross-examine witnesses or even be informed of what the charges were. With the assistance of the Whitehill University faculty union, this case would be sent down to the abyss of administrative procedures; however, the Africology faculty had to train another faculty to take over the Whitehill-Umzukulu semester study abroad program and the Whitehill-Umzekulu program has never been the same vibrant overseas program since. Black culture, Black history, Black souls, Black minds, and Black tongues were removed from the educational experiences of especially the Black students of Whitehill University.

The lesson learned in the saga of the global engagement program in the Umzukulu debacle is that Black leadership is very limited in the academy, so far as white hegemony rules—the model of a Black colony in a white nation state remains uninterrupted! A regime that holds sway by the politics of anti-politics and levels of illegitimacy often reacts irrationally against the distributive paradigm of justice when race and gender are concerned. The director of Global Affairs, a white woman; the dean of the Law School, Liberal Arts and Sciences, a white man; the interim provost for Academic Affairs, a white woman; the vice president for Human Resources, a white man; and the provost and vice president of Academic Affairs, a white man, were all involved in this semester study abroad matter. White institutional presence, as we have mentioned earlier, was preeminent in this case and *white sincere fiction* decorated the Umzukulu saga. Feagin and O'Brien (2003) coined the term *sincere fiction* to remind us of how white authorities view modern-day racism as something that they can believe (sincere) and at the same time separate themselves from the empirical reality of racial events (fiction).

The white administrators of Whitehill University infantilized the leadership of the study abroad program faculty and painted his actions as a predatory, insensitive, discriminatory, and sexist (three white women and two Asian American women vis-à-vis a Black man). Here, standing behind the claim of "just doing their jobs," the white administrators did not even have the courtesy to ask the Black faculty what really transpired at Umzukulu. Did they find him guilty because of his Black skin and America's sad history about Black men? Was this another assertion of the never-ending examples of "how [B]lack skin always seems to equal guilty in courtrooms across the country" (Watkins, 2019, p. 5)? Without an office of an ombudsperson in higher education in general, and Whitehill University in particular, quasi-legal proceduralism will fail most Black folx.

We can extrapolate from this experience that whiteness has two major weapons to maintain its hegemony—a weapon to convert and a weapon to destroy. Colonized people in the academy are not different from Black folx colonized in the United States. Frantz Fanon succinctly said this about colonialism: "In the colonies, the official, legitimate agent, the spokesperson for the colonizer and the regime of oppression, is the police officer or the soldier. . . . The government's agent uses language of pure violence. The agent does not alleviate oppression or mask domination. He displays and demonstrates them with the clear conscience of the law enforcer and brings violence into the homes and minds of the colonized subject" (1961/2004, p. 3). We see it happen firsthand at Whitehill University. People of color in the academy are still living in a colony because of heteropatriarchal hegemonic leadership. BIPOC folx deserve the same thing as white folx—a safe and courageous haven to acquire the best and inclusively excellent educational experience.

Conclusion: Reframing Our Beloved Community

Diversity and inclusion leadership at Whitehill University needs overhauling, just as many college and university campuses in the United States. The euphoric prognoses about the hiring of chief diversity and inclusion officers (CDIOs) on college campuses have since subsided, because the rate of oppression against students and faculty of color is on the rise. Many campuses including University of Missouri, Ithaca College, Binghamton University, the University of Colorado, Stanford University, Syracuse University, Oregon State University, Virginia Tech University, and University of Wisconsin–Madison (the list is too long to continue), have had diversity leadership problems and are introducing diversity and inclusion community building programs to mitigate the effects of unwelcoming campus climate. Yet most of these institutions have forgotten about the role of their leadership in stifling faculty and students of color on their campuses. Who is policing the police?

We live by stories and narratives to shape our lives and enterprises in the world. Stories shape our interactions, decisions, and policies. Stories and narratives can help define our visions for tomorrow. This is another story of several injustices submerged in risk management's inertia and co-optation of diversity and inclusion by masquerading excellence in academia. The story or the warrior, who is mightier? It is the story, because the story lives after the warrior is dead. We write this story for the world to be mindful of epidermis-based leadership, which asphyxiates Black ingenuity, creativity, and cognitive advancement. We write this chapter in this book to make it known that even in a place of higher learning, white heteropatriarchal hegemony, whiteness, sincere fiction, and the actions of power holders ironically infantilize our student and faculty of color in their process of education and advancement. We write this piece because top administrative officials and leaders in places of higher learning, who are uniquely qualified and have bona fide occupational qualifications to enhance the spirit of the law and norms of diversity and inclusion on our campuses, have rather chosen whiteness over inclusive excellence for the common good. We write this piece to remind even the most effective leaders that whiteness can be blinding and lethal to the academy. We write this chapter for our white brothers and sisters in leadership positions, who are truthful in their alliances with communities of color to reeducate their brothers and sisters about the mutual benefits of an oppression-free society. We write this story to bring the unspeakable about leadership to light. Robin Sharma or Plato gives us this premonition, "We can easily forgive a child who is afraid of the dark; the real tragedy of life is when men are afraid of the light" (Sharma, 1997). What are these men of power at Whitehill University afraid of?

Beloved students and faculty at Whitehill University, whom we believe, are committed to their institution to become part of the beloved community of learners. We borrow from Martin Luther King, Jr.: "Our goal is to create a beloved community and this will require a qualitative change in our souls, as well as a quantitative change in our lives" (King, 1966). This educational community must be based on social justice, moral leadership, equality before the law, equity in distribution of resources and power, love and respect for all cultures, and the global human condition. For us, our diversity merits the building of bridges, but this endeavor begins with a movement from tolerance to the affirmation of our humanity. White leaders on our campuses must join forces with students and faculty of color to change the heartbeat of our beloved community. It begins with reeducation of the white elites on the Whitehill University campus. Miseducation of white leaders about people of color has contributed to the ineffectiveness of their leadership. Reeducation must involve racial literacy, ethics, and cultural competencies. White leaders must share the responsibility of educating other white folks about what they have learned about themselves and about people of color. Constant contacts by white leaders with people of color could help to improve their inclusive leadership skills. Yet the contact theory informs us that contact could only be effective if Blacks and whites are seen as coequals and have mutual respect, regardless of wealth, leadership, and power differentials.

Finally, redefining alliance formation strategies with people of color could improve white leadership style on a diverse campus. This project should include true and authentic alliance building to eradicate racism, sexism, homophobia, Afrophobia, Islamophobia, xenophobia, and other "isms" and "phobias," not just activities of window dressing. The new alliance building process with people of color must involve ongoing and constant tactics and strategies, which must involve individual and institutional resources and power dispersion, assessment of the environments of diversity, and providing solutions to emerging issues and problems. Effective leadership on any college campus must include but is not limited to the facts that oppression is ubiquitous, that racism and other "isms" cannot be minimized or denied, that whiteness as a social construct has powerful organizational and individual effects and defects, and that concerted efforts are needed to provide resources and support for leaders of color to be effective on our campuses. We must note that winning the battle is not the same as winning the war, and we must be cognizant that, in the saga of the warrior and the story, the story will always be mightier because the warrior will die someday, but the story lives forever. Just as we have learned in American history about the resiliency of Black people from slavery to today, students and faculty of color at Whitehill University are here to stay. There is a troubled Whitehill University in every state of the union. Yet, the question is how to pursue this struggle for dignity, respect, and recognition. Certainly, the grievances mentioned here really outline the need for a dignitarian ethic—one that is vested in Ubuntu ethics, which is truly relational and caring, as explained more fully in chapter 12. With true and genuine diversity and inclusive leadership, Whitehill will rise again.

In the following chapter we showcase best practices of inclusive leadership, which will benefit all stakeholders, building institutions that succeed in ways that are measurable and also contain innumerable other value-added results.

Chapter 3

New Trends in Diversity Leadership and Inclusive Excellence

When those who have the power to name and socially construct reality choose not to see or hear you, whether you are dark-skinned, old, disabled, female, or speak with a different accent or dialect than theirs, when someone with the authority of a teacher, say, describes the world and you are not in it, there is a moment of psychic disequilibrium, as if you looked into a mirror and saw nothing.

—Adrienne Rich (1986)

Conflicts over diversity and multiculturalism in higher education are localized symptoms of a broader renegotiation of full citizenship in the United States.

—Renato Rosaldo (1993)

Introduction

The process of reaching inclusive excellence and cultural competence, and or attaining social justice in the academy has generated new questions for interlocutors of diversity studies and given new meanings for inclusive leadership. In recent years, more attention has been focused on two areas

---

We coauthored a different version of this chapter with Lewis Rosengarten for a SUNY DEI conference, and it was published in *Wagadu* (Asumah, Nagel, & Rosengarten, 2016).

in the academy that implement "diversity management"—admissions offices and recruitment programs for faculty of color, especially after the national protest marches for racial justice in the past couple of years. These units and programs that serve as both diversity agents and gatekeepers for recruitment have come under scrutiny for failing to adopt a culturally competent or even "culturally intelligent" skill set for inclusive excellence. Furthermore, the complex approaches in reaching inclusive excellence in recruitment and retention and hiring faculty of color that involve diversity management, which is ideally ubiquitous in the admissions process and curriculum development, need further reexamination on how diverse cultures have renegotiated change in the academy and the American polity. In this chapter we examine the best practices for inclusive college admissions and recruitment of BIPOC faculty.

In addition, we provide concrete examples of how to infuse diversity and inclusive excellence into the curriculum and professional service. We conclude the chapter by anchoring standards and strategies for dealing with difficult dialogue in the classroom and professional service. We concur with scholars and observers of higher education and the American polity whose research indicate that "higher education leaders rarely acknowledge how higher education's expectations, practices, policies, and unspoken rules further stratify and marginalize students [and faculty of color]" (McNair et al., 2016, p. 13). Our aim is to make sure that higher education is meaningful to all stakeholders in the academy and that it is a value-added enterprise and productive to, especially, students and faculty of color. Inclusive leadership practices and institutional change to make students and faculty who are historically marginalized successful are our focus.

The United States' polity is constantly changing from the original predominantly white, heteropatriarchal, hegemonic, Judeo-Christian, capitalist society to a more global entity with demographic shifts, socioeconomic problems, equity issues, diversity, and multiculturalism presenting new challenges to the emerging societal arrangements. Furthermore, we ask how a diverse populace can negotiate the question of citizenship and the daunting tasks of providing equal opportunity, social justice, and autonomous sociopolitical participation. Global issues and forces of immigration, religious fanaticism, internecine warfare, police brutality, and adverse economic conditions have all contributed to a formidable contestation of the authority of the nation state. Institutions of higher learning are equally bound up in a struggle for recognition, equity, and other social issues. The perceived inadequacy for institutions of higher learning to tackle many of the voices of protest, which are concomitant with the politics of change in the United States, could be related to the ineptitude associated with diversity management and failure to follow best practices of inclusive leadership on our diverse campuses.

Paradoxically, diversity, equity, and inclusion (DEI) are here to stay, but democratic pluralism has not been appropriately designed to deal with the issues of history, geography, space, and the number of people—especially thought leaders—who contribute to the strengthening of the United States' national ethos, identity, and culture. Today's increasing diverse student body, faculty, staff, services, curricula, and infrastructures are among the major challenges facing administrators and faculty of higher education. As we elaborated in our previous anthology on diversity, "higher education can sustain richer forms of learning, dynamic pedagogy, and epistemology with integrity only if institutions of higher learning that profess moral and inclusive excellence are committed to diverse perspectives and people of multicultural orientation" (Asumah & Nagel, 2014). Nevertheless, the sustainability of inclusive excellence in education is dependent upon the diversity of faculty and staff and the quality of inclusive leadership over and above the corporate-style diversity management, which pursues a linear and narrow approach to problem solving.

In this chapter, we intend to interrogate the complexity involved in diversity management, in recruitment, retention, hiring practices, and the process of inclusion. We analyze the agency of difficult dialogue that emerges in diversity management and leadership and associated benefits and pitfalls. We provide examples of some best practices and models for infusing diversity institutions into higher learning.

Diversity Management versus Diversity Leadership

Diversity is concerned with the variety created in society because of the indispensability of sociopolitical categories and constructs of race, ethnicity, class, gender, culture, religion, and differences in the socialization of women and men, including the differences that emerge from sexual orientation, age, disability, and their intersectionalities. Diversity also emphasizes how differences in viewpoints enable society to make meaning for inclusion and social justice (AAC&U, 1998). Diversity is sustainable through individual and institutional efforts, and it has to "be carefully and intentionally interrogated, as well as managed to reduce the concomitant tension on our college campuses and in society at large" (Nagel & Asumah, 2014, p. 349)

Management and leadership have similarities and differences. Both management and leadership utilize influence, collaboration with people, productivity, and attainment of goals. Nevertheless, both Kotter (1990) and Rost (1991) argue that management and leadership are very different constructs. Rost imbues his position in the management/leadership discourse by maintaining that management is unidirectional so far as authority relationships are concerned, whereas leadership is multidimensional (1991, pp. 149–152). Northouse carefully notes that the "overriding function of management is to provide order and consistency to organizations, where the primary function of leadership is to produce change and movement" (2013, pp. 13–14). Hitherto, these authors question the plethora of programs in corporate America and institutions of higher learning that are entrapped in the marketing language of "selling" diversity by thinking that "managing," a mere transactional approach to achieving results, would suffice in any structured diverse entity.

Mor-Barak characterizes diversity management as "the voluntary organizational actions that are designed to create greater inclusion of employees from various backgrounds into the formal and informal organizational structures through deliberate policies and programs" (2014, p. 218). This definition focuses primarily on private corporations and their "voluntary" actions or inactions in managing diversity. Yet we argue that for the workplace and colleges to be inclusive, diversity policies and actions must be intentional and deliberate and must transcend the voluntary boundaries of organizational and institutional structures. Olsen and Martins define diversity management as the "utilization of human resources (HR) management practices to: (i) increase or maintain the variation in human capital . . . (ii) ensure that variation in human capital . . . does not hinder the achievement of organizational objectives . . . and (iii) ensure that variation in human capital . . . facilitates the achievement of organizational objectives" (2012, pp. 1168–1187). This definition is not brief. Neither is it succinct, and, in addition, it relies only on traditional human resources management models for modern issues confronting institutions and organizations so far as diversity is concerned. It also lacks a dignitarian dimension that would center respect and caring ethics for all human beings.

In another chapter in this book, we tackle the issues of leadership vis-à-vis management, and we characterize diversity leadership as the recognition and provision of value to differences through effective methodology and implementation of inclusive policies—solving problems and overcoming difficult dialogues and obstacles (cf. also Nagel & Asumah, 2014, pp. 349–350) Currently, interlocutors of inclusive leadership are advocating models and programs that transcend the limits of diversity management, and we are proponents of diversity leadership as well. Our working definition for diversity leadership is as follows: a leadership style that recognizes diversity categories, inclusivity, equity, cultural difference, values-ladenness, nonhegemonic collaborative agency, and transformative leadership process, not just a position. Our philosophy and perspective on diversity leadership focus on redefining and rethinking problems in creative ways, and they make use of transformational approaches to overcoming difficult dialogues and raising human consciousness to implement goals and policies in order to reach inclusive excellence. For instance, as recruitment and retention of BIPOC students are on the rise in many universities and colleges, there should be corresponding increases in the hiring of BIPOC faculty to mitigate the racial and cultural difference on university campuses. Nonetheless, most faculty recruitment is based on the number of students departments are serving, curriculum relevancy (in the eye of the administration) for the institution, and strategic planning goals for the institution. In institutions where diversity and inclusion goals are not ranked as high as admissions goals for bringing in students (for tuition) and fiscal policy, diversity leadership is displaced by diversity management and transactional leadership.

The call for diversity leadership involves a transformational approach to social change for inclusive excellence. The funnel of diversity leadership in figure 3.1 challenges individuals in higher education to start any diversity enterprise with commitment to diversity and maintaining congruence in one's utterances and deeds. Diversity leaders must walk the talk. If diversity and democracy have a symbiotic relationship, then one should not present diversity projects on our campuses as an option or winner-takes-it-all proposition. Commitment is one of the Seven Cs of leadership that is utilized in the social change model (SCM) of leadership. The other Cs for leadership are citizenship, collaboration, common purpose, controversy with civility, consciousness of self, and congruence (Komives et al., 2009). Komives et al. inform our conceptual framework, thinking and actions that the individual's sense of self is key to commitment (p. 64). Knowing the self and championing the essence of diversity with a common purpose in the academy strengthens the mission of the

84 | Reframing Diversity and Inclusive Leadership

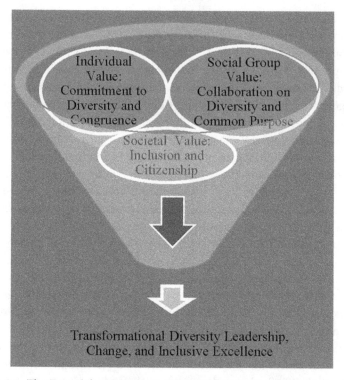

Figure 3.1. The Funnel for Diversity Leadership for Change and Inclusive Excellence. Authors' modified version of Komives et al. (2009, p. 52).

university—a place where a universe of leaners and teachers congregate and people are not excluded because of perceived norms.

Social groups' values become crucial in diversity leadership, when members of the learning community work to transcend the dynamics and effects of prejudice, discrimination, and unearned privilege. Collaboration through collective contributions from faculty, administrators, and students and taking advantage of the power of diversity to reach a common goal of inclusive excellence buttress the campus climate for transformative diversity leadership. When social groups on our campuses effectively collaborate on the leadership's vision on diversity, true citizenship becomes inevitable. "Citizenship occurs when one becomes responsibly connected to the community/society in which one resides by actively working toward change to benefit others through care, service, social responsibility, and community involvement" (Komives et al., 2009, p. 54).

In our case, a university citizen is the one who combines the mission, policy, curriculum, and all student interests to the highest level with responsibility and commitment to diversity, equity, and inclusion. Transformational change in the academy is the ultimate goal for diversity and inclusive leadership. Yet we are aware that social change is not an easy process or without controversy. Difficult dialogues have to be handled effectively for change to occur. The very fact that diversity involves differences and similarities in the process of acquiring social justice means controversies will emerge over limited resources and privileges, and how to negotiate full citizenship for inclusive excellence to transpire. Difficult dialogues are irrefutably embedded in the democratic process. Yet the historical contradiction in a country that cherishes democracy but has the inability to rid itself of the legacy of prejudice and discrimination, which produces the politics of exclusion, is troubling. Developing new ways of dealing with difficult dialogue in the polity beyond Ferguson, Missouri, where diversity mismanagement and lack of leadership caused that city and the United States to reexamine its national ethos and diversity leadership programs, should be placed on the apogee of the nation's agenda. What then is difficult dialogue?

Dealing with Difficult Dialogue

Difficult classroom and workplace dialogues are discussions or policy discourses between individuals or groups involving race, culture, gender, sexual orientation, religion, and any diversity categories. In these dialogues, differences over issues and problems are made public, challenged, or judged to be offensive, often with emotions. Young and Davis-Russell inform diversity interlocutors that, "when in a diverse group, people often avoid discussion of race, class, gender and sexual identity for fear of creating discomfort, embarrassment, or hostility" (2002, p. 41). So, how can we make our campuses inclusive if very few people want to talk about the elephants on college campuses? Why do heteropatriarchal white hegemonic administrators find it discomforting to talk about diversity leadership and the pitfalls of recruitment and retention of groups who have been historically excluded in the admissions process? Administrators and faculty alike are trained in their primary disciplines and are not equipped to confront discomforting and uncomfortable issues in their normal routines. However, the new normal of avoiding difficult dialogue on our campuses for the fear of being characterized as "troublemakers," or making, especially, white heteropatriarchal, agentic, administrators uncomfortable, is unproductive at best and lethal to diversity at worst. We must confront difficult dialogue squarely in the academy.

Dealing with difficult dialogue requires a skill and constant practice in order to be productive in setting university agendas and goals. Young and Davis-Russell propounded four steps in dealing with difficult dialogue: (1) creating a climate of inquiry, (2) focusing on cognitive inquiry, (3) focusing on emotional inquiry, and (4) developing skills of mindful listening (2002, pp. 44–48). Discussions about diversity issues and leadership in higher education have shifted from a focus on academic excellence to inclusive excellence and from cultural sensitivity to cultural competence in our ever-expanding and diverse campuses. In democratic pluralistic societies, difficult dialogue is part of the process of agenda setting and policy formulation and implementation. Nevertheless, difficult dialogues can only be successful when interlocutors or opponents and proponents can effectively combine cognitive knowledge with emotional retorts—what is cerebral must be combined with what is visceral. Creating a climate of inquiry in the classroom, meeting places, and workplaces by generating enthusiasm about asking nonthreatening questions about diversity or university policy, injecting self-reflections in the process, and modeling proper attitude for inquiry, prepares all parties involved to work toward a common purpose.

Academics and administrators can be submerged in intellectual exercises that could derail the underlying context of diversity discussions. Relying too much on research and theories that make up one's discipline could at times render problem-solving on race, class, gender, religion, and disability meaningless. Cognitive inquiry, as Young and Davis-Russell note, is about "going beyond learning about theory and research findings. . . . Sociocultural factors [must be taken] into account" (2002). The actual sociocultural situations of underrepresented groups that are at the point of investigation must become part of the process of cognitive inquiry for it to be successful. Emotional inquiry is essential to the effective interrogation of differences based on culture, race, gender, religion, sexual location, or class. Since emotional inquiry could be different from cognitive inquiry, it is important to acknowledge ahead of time in discussions that feelings are temporal, reactive, and yet diversity issues can ignite deep feelings and emotions and there are times participants in a dialogue could be temperamentally tempestuous.

The process of effective dialogue, discussion, conversation, and collaboration on admissions and retention projects depends on mindful listening. This skill, mindful listening, comprises two channels—listening to the self and listening to the other. Included in this skill is placing one's attention on the other person, being nonjudgmental, paraphrasing statements, engaging in gentle interrogation, and noticing the other person in the conversation. Most often, people who maintain hegemonic power in the academy are too arrogant or unprepared to listen to subordinates on diversity issues; they refrain from mindful listening, which, in turn, produces acrimonious situations and policy myopia in the academy. The road to inclusive excellence and diversity leadership is undulating; however, it is attainable by maintaining stewardship of the intersection of diversity and democracy. Our vision and mission for inclusive excellence must always embrace the active, intentional, and transformational commitment to diversity, specifically in people, the curriculum, the community, and policies striving to use all our resources to provide the best possible learning and working environment. Inclusive excellence, an idea greater than the self, social change, and diversity leadership supported by the best practices in the academy would benefit education for the common good.

Navigating Hidden Double Binds and Double Standards

We now turn to some roadblocks to fulfilling the diversity goals outlined so far, focusing on access to higher education and retention of faculty and students of color. Too often, lofty mission statements about inclusion (of underrepresented groups) and concomitant practices diverge fundamentally. Analyzing this rift, we detect a blame game that adheres to the script of the birdcage scenario, famously penned by feminist philosopher Marilyn Frye:

> Cages. Consider a birdcage. If you look very closely at just one wire in the cage, you cannot see the other wires. If your conception of what is before you is determined by this myopic focus, you could look at that one wire, up and down the length of it, and be unable to see why a bird would not just fly around the wire any time it wanted to go somewhere. Furthermore, even if, one day at a time, you myopically inspected each wire, you still could not see why a bird would have trouble going past the wires to get anywhere. There is no physical property of

any one wire, nothing that the closest scrutiny could discover, that will reveal how a bird could be inhibited or harmed by it except in the most accidental way. It is only when you step back, stop looking at the wires one by one, microscopically, and take a macroscopic view of the whole cage, that you can see why the bird does not go anywhere; and then you will see it in a moment. It will require no great subtlety of mental powers. It is perfectly obvious that the bird is surrounded by a network of systematically related barriers, no one of which would be the least hindrance to its flight, but which, by their relations to each other, are as confining as the solid walls of a dungeon. (1983, p. 4)

Furthermore, Frye explains why a double bind is oppressive: "One of the most characteristic and ubiquitous features of the world as experienced by oppressed people is the double bind situations in which options are reduced to a very few and all of them expose one to penalty, censure or deprivation" (pp. 2).

Frye's model powerfully explains the epistemic gap between ideal and practice. It is easy enough to stay mired within the microscopic lens when fear of the unknown, complacency, or unconscious bias are the fallback positions of admissions officers and tenure-and-promotion committee members. Admissions is particularly risk-averse, despite demographic changes and declining high school graduating classes. None of the actors imagine themselves as "oppressive," but the entanglement of hidden, shared cultural assumptions of a (historically white) institution needs to be named, disentangled and transformed, if the university wishes to promote a deep commitment to diversity and inclusion.

Stephanie A. Fryberg and Ernesto J. Martínez's book *The Truly Diverse Faculty* shines a critical light on the presentation of data with respect to hiring and retention practices of faculty of color. "What does it mean for universities to claim progress with respect to diversifying faculty ranks when 73 percent of faculty of color hold non-tenure-track or adjunct faculty positions that do not provide job security (American Federation of Teachers, 2010)?" (Fryberg and Martinez, 2014, p. 5). We answer that such claims of progress in diversifying the faculty hides in plain sight the fact that a myopic perspective is more comforting to gatekeepers at historically white institutions than an honest look at the macroscopic picture of understanding the diverse pressures faculty of color face vis-à-vis tenure-track level positions, especially at elite colleges or research universities.

In the case of tenure-track faculty of color, Fryberg and Martínez describe the presence of three interrelated narratives:

- "Striving, but Falling Short"
- "Inching toward Progress"
- "Service Is (Not) Necessary"

They caution, "While these narratives . . . are in no way meant to be discrete or comprehensive, they function as part of the uncharted and elusive geography that junior faculty of color must navigate in order to inhabit the university successfully. These narratives exist in tandem, at times overlapping and at times in conflict" (Fryberg and Martinez, 2014, p. 8). In other words, these narratives buttress the birdcage scenario of oppression in so far as navigating within the constraints of the cage is all but a limiting experience that demands superhuman emotional labor to sustain one's well-being for six long years. Having access to union representation and a strong peer-mentoring network, inside and beyond the institution, may assist in strengthening coping practices and overcoming the felt experience of isolation. Yet BIPOC faculty are acutely familiar with the troubling reinforcing mechanism of a double bind: you are damned if you do service, and you are damned if you don't.

Secondly, faculty of color navigate a monochromatic double-standard which is modeled on a narrow model of success; it is used to put a stamp of approval on hegemonic intellectual work and to disqualify the challenging work of "doing diversity." Fryberg and Martínez note that "[e]ither way, junior faculty of color are left with mixed messages and double standards, while the university gets to claim diversity as a core value" (2014, p. 8). A core demand of diversity leadership, as opposed to diversity management, is to evaluate and validate the work of faculty of color as change agents in terms of inclusive academic excellence standards. The caged bird is indeed free to leave the cage and soar in community-engagement praxis, which will "count" toward valuable research, elevating the academy as a place that is accountable to its diverse residents. Historian Darlene Clark Hine exemplifies this "breakout": during the 1970s, she was the only tenured female African American historian professor in the entire state of Indiana. A community member encouraged her to start focusing her research on Black women in Indiana, and Professor Hine agreed. This led to pioneering work unearthing Black women's contributions, and she is a recipient of the 2013 National Humanities Medal (Williams, 2014).

Increasing the number of faculty of color has a direct relation to the level of commitment to admitting, retaining, and graduating students of color. Successful diverse students become professors; without attention to this dynamic, the available pool will remain small. This, added to the systemic difficulties of being hired, conspires to doom diversity in the college setting.

Banning Boxes

At a time when about 700,000 people nationwide are released from prison, and some 2.3 million people are incarcerated on any given day, it is important that colleges and universities as well as unions start paying attention to a population permanently locked out of higher education. The few who try to enter are stymied by threatening forms—the common application. The Center for Community Alternatives (2015) based in New York, documented that over 60 percent of academic institutions screen applicants for prior criminal history. If it is discovered that an applicant failed to disclose, some colleges rescind the admissions offer. Another study also notes that the universities that do not collect criminal history data do not report any compromised safety standard on their campuses (Wong, 2018). In the early periods of the COVID-19 pandemic in 2020, there was a significant drop in the prison and jail populations. However, the drop was a pandemic-related dynamic of slowdown in the criminal legal system and not about concrete policy change. Sawyer and Wagner note, "As the criminal legal system has returned to 'business as usual,' prisons and jail populations have already begun to rebound to prepandemic levels" (2022, p. 2). This means that higher education would have to deal with more prison-based educational programs and education for returning citizens.

Double bind is clearly in effect here: returning citizens are told to engage in higher education only to find locked entrances. One's convict status is (not yet) a protected class. One hundred million Americans have criminal records, which may prevent them from securing easy access to housing, education, and jobs (Vallas & Dietrich, 2014). Thus, the protestant work ethic rings hollow for somebody who experiences legal discrimination.

Prison reform activists have successfully lobbied around the country to "ban the box" for college and employment applications. In those cities and colleges, applicants do not have to check a box on a form, and background checks are done only when an offer is made. Some states have passed "second chance" legislation to permanently seal criminal records. New York finally enacted the Fair Access to Education Act (2016), which calls for removal of the criminal history box from all college applications in New York, so that *all* applicants could be considered on a fair and equal basis. This legislation is "intended to enhance public safety, greater racial fairness, and the economic and social well-being of all New Yorkers by removing needless barriers to higher education faced by people with past criminal justice involvement" (Senate Bill S4068). However, the State University of New York system, possibly the largest system in the world with sixty-four campuses, opted to voluntarily open its doors to the state's diverse population in 2016 (Zimpher, 2016). Upholding the merit and power of "inclusive excellence," we hope to see a shift in admissions strategic targeting of populations and doing their part in disrupting the school-to-prison pipeline. Bold diversity leadership strategies include opening doors to those who have been systematically disenfranchised.

Securing a Place at the Table: Admitting and Supporting Diverse Students

Providing universal access to higher education, and admitting and supporting successful students are essential components of diversity leadership at predominantly white institutions. There are numerous instances of good intentions, but diverse interests remain underserved, often unknowingly. For example, having lowered expectations and standards of students from diverse or challenging economic backgrounds is intended as offering a break or a chance for them to attend college, but unfortunately they may ensure lower achievements (Miller et al., 2005, p. iii).

An institution of higher learning can overcome such obstacles. Many colleges fund offices, departments, and committees dedicated to diversity issues including multicultural councils, gender studies, Africana studies, and educational opportunity programs. Despite their existence, there must be administrative "buy in" to respect, support and listen to these groups' recommendations and to continually accept the possibility that college officials may be unaware of the full dimensional reality of life on campus as experienced by diverse students.

These efforts begin with the admissions process and with the nature of the contact prospective students have with a college. As it is with admitted students, trust and support must also be established early on with the prospective student. Here numerous instances are revealed of a well-intentioned approach, but with unintended consequences. Admission departments may view their main mission as avoiding underenrollment; any consideration they regard as threatening those numbers is discounted. As a result, admissions departments may place no priority on the enrollments and financial aid eligibility process of students who are most at risk and most diverse. Educational opportunity programs' (EOPs) diversity numbers, for instance, can thereby move dramatically in the opposite direction of diversification, as that consideration is trumped by filling a class.

The following case magnifies the birdcage metaphor of oppression. Students and families who are first generation, and may not speak English as their primary language, know little of how to interact with admissions officers and respond to their questions; they are slowed down by, hampered by, and eventually closed out of the process. One student submitted a social services form filled out in Spanish. These forms usually automatically qualify a student financially, but it was rejected for not being in English. When finally translated, it was too late in the process, as white students, some of whom were not first generation, were already admitted, closing out the available spots. These concerns transmit to continuing students who do not have families positioned to offer assistance and advice. Underserved students' family members who are not well versed in producing college papers, conducting research, standardized test taking, and more are left out of the competition for securing a place at the table (entrance), especially at "highly rejective colleges," a fitting term created by Twitter influencer Akil Bello. Standardized test data may tell us more about family income than innate intelligence, Jon Boeckenstedt points out (2020, 2014). These tests are inherently biased in their formulation. Increasingly, admissions offices disregard these high-stakes tests (SAT and ACT), and they were discontinued for the academic year 2020–2021due to a global pandemic.

Consideration must be made for students who demonstrate strong potential through hard work, but who have attended schools that have rendered them radically underprepared for college. It is not simply the case that, if admitting remarkably underprepared students, admissions offices have done their job of providing "opportunity." This perception has the opposite effect. With little potential or ongoing comprehensive support, far too many students of color struggle, incur loans, and ultimately are disqualified, with no expectation of a college degree or a job worthy of assisting in paying off this debt. The recent Biden-Harris administration's student debt relief program for loan forgiveness up to $20,000 is a step in the right direction. Nonetheless, the program must be revisited so that it does not neglect student of color who are talented and have worked hard to acquire graduate degrees but are deeply indebted to the student loan industry, even though they might be making good starting salaries.

Admissions departments must be in partnership with DEI stakeholders in recognizing that the difficult work of diversity leadership begins well before students are admitted and continues long after. They must be compelled to work with the campus professionals who have the expertise and mission in supporting the diversification of the campus and improving the retention and graduation rates for students of color. As Scott (2012) argues, based on her research, diverse students are more likely to succeed if they see themselves represented in the faculty and staff, which alone should provide a compelling reason for the administration's diversification strategic plan. "Studies have shown there is a correlation between African American students and learning at Historically Black Colleges [HBCUs] with African American teachers" (Scott, 2012, p. 126). Howard University is a leader in preparing Black students for professional careers, and it is noteworthy that Kamala Harris, the first woman, the first biracial (Black and Asian) vice president of the US, graduated from Howard. New research shows a new trend in significant enrolment increase of Black students at HBCUs that correlates to an increase in hate crime reports since 2016 (Bauer-Wolf, 2021). Of course, we hasten to note the problem of serious underreporting but as the historical record shows, public leaders' incitement of discrimination clearly leads to normalizing hateful acts.

Academic Advising and Support of Diverse Students: Best Practices

Students of color who demonstrate academic promise, must be motivated and inspired in what for many is a novel and sometimes baffling environment and context. Retention and graduation within six years are important goals and it is also the case that high achievement—not simply "pushing students through"—is a crucial goal. It is contextualized within the demands of DEI that inclusive excellence must serve as a central aspect in student advising. Making excellence inclusive (MEI), as propounded by the American Association for Colleges and Universities (AAC&U), "is designed to help colleges and universities integrate diversity, equity, and educational quality efforts into their missions and institutional operations . . . [for achieving] excellence in learning, teaching, student development, institutional functioning, and engagement in local and global communities" (AAC&U, n.d.). In this case, it is a shared responsibility for the institution and its faculty to ensure that students of color, especially, are college-ready by any means possible and through innovative approaches, not just formal classroom instructions and testing. Specifically, what is regarded as high achievement must be mindful of diversity categories and challenges for BIPOC students. Without a comprehensive focus, diverse students may "confirm" the already lowered expectations and outcomes wrongly associated with them. In the words of Claude M. Steele, these can be considered "identity contingencies" that affect performance (Steele, 2010, p. 3).

Advisors must work closely with students during the admissions decision-making process and summer and fall registration. Advisors thus develop close working relationships with students. Staying in touch with applicants as they complete their files is essential. Working with the guidance counselors throughout the state also raises the probability of good student matches for a particular college and ultimately success. Guidance counselors will already know the emphasis placed on academic achievement and the specific programs offered, and they will be eager to recommend particular students for the opportunity. In her bestselling memoir *Becoming*, Michelle Obama (2018) remembers a painful experience with her guidance counselor, who told her that she was *not* destined for Princeton—despite the fact that Obama was a high achiever and enrolled in the honors program. She was young, gifted—a Black girl without (social) capital. EOP programs that provide intensive summer orientation courses help students to get "comfortable" in a new milieu, especially important for first generation students who are navigating the academy without the academic cultural capital afforded to those whose parents attended college and graduate schools. Note that we use "comfortable" with caution, as we are aware of the fact that whiteness surrounds our BIPOC students in the academy and space everywhere in America is contested and not "comfortable"—sincere fiction! We will say more about "white comfort" in the succeeding chapters. Our students also face additional trials by trying out liberal arts majors, which may have little value at home, such as a philosopher's path.

Thus, our students who do not have academic role models, and will not have had lengthy conversations about college life and its demands, will be challenged each time they return home by friends and even family members who believe they are "abandoning" their roots. This may appear to be at odds with the goal of advisors promoting increasing independence. By acknowledging this push-and-pull dynamic of supporting the drive for autonomy and the need for belonging, potential conflicts and pitfalls are circumnavigated. Indeed, doing right by one's community or origin is a prized good among many immigrants, and deficit-bound logic can be avoided if advisors gain cultural competence vis-à-vis the American fixation on independence and individualism. We will say more about interdependence in our final chapter on Ubuntu ethics.

A focus on peer-mentoring programs to assist with transition to college is key to a successful first-year experience. At SUNY Cortland, career services and alumni affairs are doing more to connect students with alumni to assist them with a tough labor market replete with glass ceilings and sticky floors for BIPOC graduates. The Multicultural Life and Diversity Office offers a Peer2Peer program for underrepresented or marginalized students who are paired with more senior students; they engage in team-building weekend workshops and stay in touch throughout the year with the first-year students. Ideally, the mentee will then transition to a mentorship program with faculty or professional staff members. In the past, the Blake Scott program had a lot of support from faculty and BIPOC students generally succeeded to accomplish their degrees within four years. The program was discontinued for unknown reasons.

Equality and Equity: Moving beyond Diversity Management

BIPOC students are the equals of any student in intellectual capacity and potential, while their needs may be different. Critical race theory helps to explain that educational gaps exist due to schools maintaining "society's current system of socioeconomic stratification," thus encouraging "society's domination of non-white learners" (Scott, 2012, p. 130). Due to the variety of factors outlined above, these students may feel reluctant to compete with students they feel are on a higher intellectual plane or who have been better prepared for college. Students' confidence will soar when they recognize that they have unique and valuable perspectives to offer in class discussion and that they may very well ask the questions no one else will ask. This reverses the effect of "stereotype threat" as identified by Claude M. Steele (Scott, 2012, p. 176). College holds out the promise, sometimes unrealized, that students can challenge assumptions and beliefs, that academic engagement and rigorous debate is part of the learning process for all students. Without their diverse voices, failures, resiliencies, and successes, a campus will suffer in that essential mission.

This chapter has noted some of the Sisyphean struggles people of color face while trying to join the academy or holding on to a good-standing student status or full-time faculty positions. As Alexandra Vollman (2016) informs her readers, faculty at Pomona College and other institutions of higher learning are requiring diversity initiatives and endeavors in their tenure-review processes. Yet, more recently, diversity, equity, and inclusion are under attack in Florida and twenty-three other states and the debates over diversity statements in America are unprecedentedly disruptive to any democratic process and academic freedom (Lu, 2024). Diversity strategic plans tend to get short shrift and are barely implemented in maximizing ways when a university is facing budget cuts. Indeed, diversity efforts tend to be cut first when academic programs are under attack, including Africana studies and educational opportunity programs. Oftentimes, they are "threaded" throughout the strategic plan (such as the power of SUNY), which may obfuscate implimentation of concrete goals and who might be responsible for them. The motto here is "if we are all responsible for diversification of the academy, then, possibly, none of us are responsible." The burden is placed upon faculty of color who lead diversity efforts or Africana or ethnic studies programs to plead in vain for cluster diversity hires or ambitious degree programs. Chief diversity and inclusion officers may feel unable to begin difficult dialogues with managers who are accustomed to managing diversity but not used to a diversity leadership model that presents creative and realistic goals and outcomes for the entire campus community. Are all of us academic stakeholders responsible and ready to hold ourselves accountable to our university leadership lofty diversity mission, vision, and values?

In the next chapter chapter we interrogate hegemony in the academy, multicultural education, and conflict-laden approaches in managing diverse voices that defy the principles of cultural competence and inclusive excellence.

Chapter 4

Risk Management, Hegemony, and the Pitfalls of Diversity within the Academy

Introduction

In North America, the urgency of integration, a key demand of a vibrant civil rights movement of the 1960s, gave rise to corporate concerns on how to manage a *multicultural* workforce. Since the 1980s, the multicultural appeal has lost its luster and corporations have increasingly focused on managing *diversity*. Diversity discourses left an indelible imprint on corporations and academe in the United States and elsewhere. Scholars took note of this political shift. Banks, dubbed "the father of multicultural education," is a case in point. By 1981, he published a primer titled *Cultural Diversity and Education* (1981/2016), to adapt to the conservative turn in public policy. For instance, in the United States, inclusion strategies on the basis of multicultural (i.e., racial/ethnic) and gender identities were considered inadequate. Demands for racial justice and women's rights were followed by a "lavender revolution" (i.e., LGBT human rights) and a struggle for recognition for people with disabilities. Black feminists articulated an intersectionality of social identities approach to protest their endemic exclusion in white feminist and Black political thought. In this chapter, we discuss a brief historical overview of the ideological shift from multicultural education toward diversity and inclusive education, which suggests that the "struggle" paradigm of the civil rights movement has been abandoned in favor of celebrating differences.

A different version of this chapter was previously published in *Wagadu* (Nagel, 2016).

In the chapter, we highlight conflict-laden approaches of managing diverse voices, identities, and discourses within the US academy. Furthermore, we will demonstrate in our discussion that risk management has been rampant in the academy and provide evidence to collaborate with our concerns for the conflict-laden, contentious approaches of managing diverse voices, identities, and discourses within a risk averse, increasingly corporate academy. Calls for a paradigm shift in general education began with the new disciplines of Black studies and ethnic studies, followed by women's studies. Importantly, these demands came from below, engendered by militant student protests, and were not a diversity management decision from above in the 1960s. These interdisciplinary studies programs were granted by besieged administrators (e.g., from San Francisco State, Cornell University, and the City University of New York) as a concession to a revolutionary student body that protested US imperialist wars and racist state repression within its territory, especially on reservations and in cities (cf. Biondi, 2012).

The Black Student Union (BSU), Black Power movement, the anti-war movement and the Free Speech Movement challenged the hegemonic structures in the academy and students and faculty inputs in decision making brought change in the former highly Eurocentric, heteropatriarchal academy. What are the lessons from the movements mentioned above and the civil rights movement for today's DREAMers, Ban-the-Box activists, and the Black Lives Matter social movement within US academia, rallying for citizenship rights, for the rights of persons with conviction records, and for racial equity within historically white institutions? Specifically, what did the struggles and educational practices that aimed at structural reforms look like from the vantage point of administrative report writers, namely, those who are tasked with managing diversity?

To begin with this context, we argue that diversity management pivots around a subtle shift from a demand for *redistribution* to a fairly uncritical corporate frame of *recognition* of diversity (e.g., by addressing bias through sensitization workshops and awareness exercises). Diversifying the academy seems to be an intrinsic good. Here we consider Nancy Fraser's (1998a) famous diremption, recognition versus redistribution, but we do not support her own analysis and critique of recognition struggles from below. Rather, we draw on her critic's objection, that is, that recognition and redistribution (in terms of reform or transformation) are always already intertwined concepts (Young, 1998). Iris Marion Young holds that Fraser and other Left critics of multiculturalism overstate "the degree to which a politics of recognition retreats from economic struggles" (1998, p. 51). To be sure, Young concedes that these "culture wars" have been the domain of university campuses (p. 51). So, we want to ask, Does diversity management always lend itself to an accommodationist strategy, valuing recognition over economics? If so, what are its implications? We offer case studies, from the State University of New York (SUNY) and the City University of New York (CUNY), and we will address what diversity celebration looks like—usually it is about window dressing and what a colleague calls "organized happiness." From the vantage point of those who are minoritized and students who cannot get access to resources and opportunities, and as faculty and chief diversity officers (CDO) who struggle along as they climb the ladder of mis/recognition, these performative exercises in the name of DEI could be disheartening and demoralizing.

The Demand of Access and Equity: The Dream of an Open University (Deferred)

The university has always been a bastion of privilege for the learned (and wealthy, male) elites. The world acquired the term "higher education" based on the social engineering of white elites, which was not intended to be an education for the general populace. This white elitism is reflective of and reinforced by the current socioeconomic inequity in the American educational systems (Geiger, 2005). Cabrera et al., commenting on James Baldwin's analysis of the "Negro problem," insist that "there would be no 'underrepresented minorities' unless White students are currently overrepresented; however, this overrepresentation is not part of the diversity discussion" (Cabrera et al., 2017, p. 29). The *longue durée* approach to fighting inequity in the American educational system is concomitant with deliberate laws, bills, and processes. After 1945, the GI Bill brought a great expansion of the landscape of public colleges and universities, including the establishment of the State University of New York (SUNY) system and the largest urban university system, the City University of New York (CUNY). New York was the last state to establish a public university (Clark et al., 2010; Steck, 2012).

Uniquely, a high school diploma guaranteed many poor Jewish and non-Jewish white residents of New York City access to the Free Academy or City College in Harlem. Putatively, these were the best and brightest high school students; however, dropout rates were very high (Traub, 1994). Residency was a measure of "positive discrimination" as an antidote for *private* colleges and universities that adopted exclusionary practices on the basis of race, creed, color, or national ancestry, targeting Jewish, Blacks, Italians (Berkowitz, 1948). David Berkowitz's revealing report made the case for a public university system on moral and political grounds, prohibiting racist and anti-Semitic admission practices. His is perhaps the first publication that assesses (and validates) Black students' attitudes regarding the importance of addressing a chilly campus climate at historically white institutions of higher learning. The landmark US Supreme Court decision *Brown v. Board of Education* in 1954, which stood *Plessy v. Ferguson* (1896) on its head for de jure discriminatory practices, determined that the chilly educational climate needed to be corrected through systematic integration efforts. That decision created the moral and legal basis for integrating Black and white schools throughout the South (and the rest of the United States).

The lofty goal of integration was accepted by the white male justices with the proviso of "deliberate speed." It meant that the implementation would proceed at a snail's pace and continues to be a dream deferred. Nevertheless, the integration process and forced bussing of especially Black students to white neighborhoods that did not want Black students in their classrooms created traumatic experiences for Black children and anxiety for white parents. We cannot forget the presidential debate between Kamala Harris and Joe Bidden in June 2019 before they became running mates for the office of the presidency. Kamala Harris blamed Joe Bidden for supporting awful legislation for forced busing of students of color after the *Brown v. Board of Education* (1954) ruling that would disrupt the lives of many BIPOC students. "There was a little girl in California who was part of the second class to integrate her public schools, and she was bused to school every day. And that little girl was me" (Honan, 2019). One cannot overemphasize the lingering effects of major legislations in education since the 1960s, which still have traumatic effects on BIPOC students, including the current US vice president Kamala Harris.

As the West Coast of the United States led the country in educational reforms in the 1950s and 1960s, New York state actors also were in no hurry implementing the state university educational system in the 1950s. It was not until Nelson Rockefeller's election as governor that the vision of a massive university system (SUNY) was fully implemented. Governor Rockefeller has also been credited with skillfully maneuvering around the interests of private colleges and universities, upstate constituents, and civil rights activists (Shermer, 2015). The opening of junior colleges, medical and law schools, and Catholic colleges toward the "giddy multitude" (cf. Takaki, 1993) brought along demands for an inclusive curriculum to reflect the lived experience of students and an increasingly diverse professoriate.

Multicultural education, which was an offshoot of the Black studies educational demand/reform, began to shape many general education programs and created further demands for a radical transformation of the university, including diversifying its mostly Eurocentric, monochromatic professoriate. Open and free access for students of color was one such radical goal, won by Black and Puerto Rican students in the famous 1969 Open Admissions Strike at CUNY. They also demanded that education majors take mandatory courses in Black and Puerto Rican history as well as Spanish. In an unprecedented way, the CUNY students not only pushed back the threat of Rockefeller's budget cuts but instead brought about the doubling of the student body of CUNY. Administrators felt under siege and acted fast in order to gain control. Thanks to the continued militancy by the next generation of students, the open admissions policy lasted for three decades, thus transforming an elite white university system into one that welcomed a racially diverse and working-class student body in an unparalleled way. At this point, we bore witness to the emergence of the true meaning of "university," an institution where higher leaning is open to all disciplines, students, and scholars, and not a Euroversity, an institution whose points of reference are European and not multicultural. However, the free tuition policy lasted only some five years ("When Tuition," 2011; CUNY History, n.d.; Traub, 1994).

Rockefeller, the son of the elite, kept pushing for tuition for CUNY schools, but his plans only succeeded after he resigned as governor. While in office, Rockefeller was not only known for his stewardship for a premier public higher education system, but he was also responsible for ordering the mass shooting of prisoners to end the Attica rebellion in 1971. Soon after the above incidents, he established the most repressive drug laws in the nation, which were spearheaded by US president Nixon, who ordered a "war on drugs" to decimate Black Power politics and to repress the Black-led civil rights movement (Hanson, 2016; Perez & Saldaña, 2016). The Rockefeller Drug Laws spurred an unprecedented buildup of prisons in Upstate New York, and it targeted exclusively Downstate Black and Latino nonviolent youth for life-long prison sentences. Dollar for dollar state funding shifted from investment in capital expenditures for SUNY (and CUNY) toward excessive prisons expenditures (Nagel, 2008). Not a single new college campus was built during the last thirty years.

The majority of Black and Latino folks live in segregated neighborhoods with substandard housing, public schools, inadequate access to good jobs, quality health care, supermarkets, recreational resources, and so on. However, the state does not spare taxpayers' money for military hardware for policing, containing, and simply harassing residents of color, such that policy-makers and activists now speak of a cradle-to-prison pipeline. Policy-makers have noticed that when a child fails third grade, a prison cell will have to be budgeted, due to the likelihood of going to jail rather than finishing high school. Race, class, and geography all play a role whether one gets sent to (drug) treatment or to prison (Mauer, 2006). The ascendancy of Barack Obama to the White House did not translate into social or economic uplift for Black working-class America (Alexander, 2010; Drucker, 2010; Porter, 2016; Rothwell, 2016). In *Savage Inequalities*, Jonathan Kozol (1991) already decried the caste system of schooling and found that segregation was worse in 1991 than in 1954, when the Supreme Court desegregated separate and unequal schools.

Alexander's bestseller *The New Jim Crow* (2010) confirms Kozol's bleak assessment and has brought to light the racial caste system vis-à-vis the treatment of Black men in the criminal justice system. The Nixon presidency, and Rockefeller, started the punitive politics of incarceration (mandatory minimum sentences, ending good time, ending furloughs, etc.), which gave rise to the myth of the criminalblackman (Russell-Brown, 2008) and neoliberal policies that dismantled social welfare infrastructure. These, in turn, contributed to massive increases in health-care costs and, of course, in tuition, even for public colleges and universities, where a commitment to grant funding and other subsidies of economically disadvantaged and academically underprepared students has been shrinking. The racist effects present a double containment of Black working-class people with the expansion of the prison system and with the legal and de facto attack on race-based affirmative action programs. The Black Lives Matter movement has demanded a systematic investment in public goods in Black and brown communities, but promises were short-lived with the ascent of the Tea Party, the Trump regime, and a quasi-religious belief in austerity, yet public investments in the penal and military industrial complexes continue unabated.

Let us recall that the Reagan presidency had brought on a systematic attack on affirmative action policies, buttressed by US Supreme Court decisions that ruled against racial "quotas" (*Bakke* decision, 1978). President Kennedy had initiated affirmative action as a political appeasement strategy by offering affirmative action to those who were harmed by Jim Crow (segregationist) practices in the South and by racist discrimination elsewhere. It was meant as an empowerment strategy to give Black citizens opportunities for employment, advancement, and education. However, in practice the pool for eligible affirmative action groups was soon widened and businesses and colleges started to hire white women instead. Today, the biggest group of beneficiaries are veterans of war and white women. Starting with president Reagan's ridicule of disadvantaged groups as "special interests" or racially charged slogans of ending welfare because of (Black) so-called welfare queens abusing the system, we have witnessed an erosion and subsequent co-optation of the civil rights movement's "borning struggle"; this term was coined by Bernice Johnson Reagon (cf. Cluster, 1979) to suggest that Black activists gave birth to a struggle for redistribution and recognition for all other social justice groups (American Indian Movement, second wave feminism, La Raza, the Stonewall uprising by trans, gay, and gender nonconforming Black people, etc.). Even though affirmative action program officers still have a place at the table of human resource offices in the US university, their portfolios focus increasingly on risk management and mandatory sexual harassment trainings, as well as offering resources on how to increase a diverse pool of applicants. There are no sanctions for recalcitrant departments that repeatedly resort to hiring cismen who are straight, white, and able-bodied and have not been trained in decolonizing their disciplines.

The Reagan administration also ushered in a backlash against multicultural education, which conservative think tanks such as the Heritage Foundation furthered with headlines about the dangers of multiculturalism and shored up with Islamophobic sentiments after Samuel Huntington's publication of "The Clash of Civilizations?" (1993). Most recently, conservative journalists use a shrill defense of cultural assimilation (i.e., Euro-American, Christian values) targeting refugees, preferably those who practice Islam, and their left-wing apologists in the academy and encouraging European governments to take note of the peril of non-occidental values and peoples (Gonzalez, 2016). Such a conservative turn is a particularly troubling tendency in primary education, because teachers are often captive to the ideological leanings of school boards and to monocultural standards by federal and state education departments, which schools of education within universities have to adopt in order to get accreditation.

Liberal educators such as Banks also admonish competent multicultural educators not to "make students cynics nor . . . encourage them to desecrate European heroes such as Columbus and Cortés" (1981/2016, p. 11). By contrast, progressive authors such as Howard Zinn, *A People's History of the United States* (1980), Angela Y. Davis, *Women, Race and Class* (1981), Bill Bigelow and Bob Peterson, *Rethinking Columbus* (2003), James Loewen, *Lies My Teacher Told Me* (1995/2007), or Jonathan Kozol, *Savage Inequalities* (1991) go "astray" and offer a cogent ideology critique of triumphalist US history telling. Their counternarratives to crass patriotism provide histories from below that resonate with diverse student populations, whereas standardized, whitewashed victors' histories may hinder quality education and produce oppressive outcomes.

In fact, a Mexican-American studies curriculum in a school district in Arizona was shut down because it defied parroting the patriotic racial frame so prevalent in schools across the United States. Might it be dangerous recognition politics that a Chicana student should find herself reflected in the stories told about conquest, genocide, and persistent struggles against racism? Indeed. A school commission report showed that teaching progressive revisionist history to Chicanos and Chicana children enhances critical thinking skills and increases students' academic performance. White politicians filed a lawsuit and denounced ethnic studies for creating resentment against whites. A judge agreed. Instead of pursuing the commission's recommendation of expanding a Mexican American studies program, it was shut down (Biggers, 2012). Here are the markings of the ultimate co-optation of affirmative action cum multicultural politics of recognition: whites are now the veritable victims of history told from the vantage point of people of color.

The Trump administration, specifically Betsy DeVos's Education Department, instructed institutions to invest in "patriotic education"; of course, this directive was accompanied by threats of defunding academia, which still pursued teaching anti-oppressive, critical perspectives, that is, "anti-patriotic" ideology. At the very end of the rule of Trumpublicans, the administration formed the 1776 Commission to counter the 1619 Project. The 1619 Project, a vision of teaching African American history, systemic racism, the holocaust of enslavement, inclusive pedagogy, Black epistemology, and Black axiology was propounded by *New York Times* journalist Nikole Hannah-Jones (a 2020 Pulitzer Prize winner for her contribution to the 1619 Project), scholars, journalists, and artists for our educational system. The 1776 Commission, formed by an executive order of President Trump, and recently dissolved by the Biden-Harris administration, was designed to project American history from a "patriotic" whitewashed and celebratory approach.

In this politically charged climate and with a veritable corporate intrusion into education and standards, for example, by the British-based Pearson Corporation (Reingold, 2015), the mainstream curriculum that touches on diversity education is filled with feel-good, colorblind rhetoric; the teacher's focus is on prejudice reduction (cf. Banks, 1981/2016) and not raising questions about systemic inequality and divide-and-conquer victor's history (e.g., settler colonialism, capitalism, chattel slavery). Recently, Texas schoolbooks eliminated the word "slave" in favor of "workers" who were transported from Africa, until a Black parent protested and created a social media outburst of resistance (Moser, 2015). More euphemisms endorsed by the Texas Board of Education include the following: "The slave trade would be renamed the 'Atlantic triangular trade,' American 'imperialism' changed to 'expansionism,' and all references to 'capitalism' have been replaced with 'free enterprise'" (Paulson, 2010).

Contradictions prevail in today's diversity landscape. The online newsletter *Insight into Diversity* (May 2016) reports in the same issue divergent trends: an increased focus on diversity and inclusion classroom strategies within Pomona College for tenure review, while in Tennessee, the legislature abolishes the diversity office at the University of Tennessee and redirects its funding to scholarships for minoritized engineering students. The reason: "State lawmakers had been threatening to withhold funding from the office since last year, after staff posted a guide for using gender-neutral pronouns and promoted inclusive ways to celebrate holidays, which angered some Republican lawmakers" (Prinster, 2016). Of course, we are critical of such "limited pie" ideology, which smacks of the British colonial practice of "divide-and-rule." BIPOC students in STEM fields should be supported and diversity offices should be fully funded as well. Trans* struggles have risen in importance and even got unusual support: New York's former governor Cuomo issued a boycott for nonessential state travels to North Carolina. The Southern state did come under fire for its repressive (binary) bathroom politics, nullifying the right of transgender persons to use the bathroom that matches their gender identity (Cuomo, 2016).

"The Fire Next Time"

We will have to keep in mind that representation and redistribution struggles came from the streets and radicalized students took the fight into academia. They included armed takeovers, for example, at Ivy League Cornell University in 1969 (Wilhelm, 2016) by Black undergraduate students who were tired of the hegemonic Eurocentric curriculums. They demanded representation of diverse faculty whom they could confide in as mentors and teachers, who have the (cultural) competence to understand their frustrations and develop cognitive and psychosocial strategies for survival in a historically white institution. (The survival struggles of BIPOC faculty will be discussed below.) Today's Black Lives Matter (BLM) social movement has repeated yesteryear's demands of radicalized students during the civil rights struggle and the anti-Vietnam war activism. BLM started in 2012 with a nation-wide protest about the acquittal of George Zimmermann, a self-appointed vigilante cop who killed an African American teenager, Trayvon Martin, in Florida. The protest action became a national movement in the aftermath of the police killing of another Black teenager, Michael Brown, in Missouri, 2014. In 2015, Black activists around the country took the fight into the academy to protest racism in the classroom, residential life, and sports, and at the level of administrative leadership. In fact, these demands appear to be cyclical, although the methods are vastly dissimilar thanks to the global reach of social media coupled with an intensification of government surveillance.

The government's ability to scrutinize student protesters today is unparalleled with respect to COINTELPRO, the FBI's secret counter intelligence program to spy on a multitude of social/political dissenters and to destroy the Black Panther Party. To date Black Lives Matter has spread to dozens of campuses and its nonviolent actions have led to the resignation of several white senior administrators across the country (Wilson, 2015). During the summer and fall of 2020, BLM 2.0 generated even more support for systematic changes, continuing the pressure for more full-time tenure-track BIPOC faculty and a more diverse general education curriculum. The California State University system is about to institute the first ethnic studies course that is mandatory for all students. Thanks to the vibrant Black Liberation Collective, which encompasses Black Student Unions from over eighty universities, radical terminology and demands for redistribution of resources are back in vogue. They include resisting oppression, disrupting white hegemonic institutional power, and consciously noting the interconnectedness of oppressive systems (racism, heterosexism, transphobia, class oppression, xenophobia, etc.). Their manifesto (BLC, 2015) resonates with that of the Combahee River Collective (CRC, 1977), a Black feminist statement that disrupted the monoculturalism of the second wave of white feminism in the 1970s.

However, the CRC's insurgency demands remain an elusive ideal, and instead their struggle paradigm was co-opted and reframed into a diversity-cum-intersectionality model, which suggests that all social identities have equal value (Wallis, 2015). Will the Black Liberation Collective continue to disrupt the neoliberal ideological hegemony of the academy by demanding no tuition fees for Black and Indigenous peoples and the corporation's divestment from prison shares (Gladney, 2015)? Will the BLC continue to contest administrators who are happy to make concessions to symbolic recognition politics but divert attention away from debt-free demands and monetary reparations to descendants of enslaved persons on university grounds in the North as well as the South? Robin Kelley (2016) is hopeful that the fire this time spread from the town to the campus is consistent with historical patterns. The campus revolts of the 1960s, for example, *followed* the Harlem and Watts rebellions, the freedom movement in the South, and the rise of militant organizations in the cities. But the size, speed, intensity, and character of recent student uprisings caught much of the country off guard. Protests against campus racism and the ethics of universities' financial entanglements erupted on nearly ninety campuses, including Brandeis, Yale, Princeton, Brown, Harvard, Claremont McKenna, Smith, Amherst, UCLA, Oberlin, Tufts, and the University of North Carolina, both Chapel Hill and Greensboro. These demonstrations were led largely by Black students, as well as coalitions made up of students of color, queer folks, undocumented immigrants, and allied whites.

Perhaps CUNY administrators were also caught off guard in 1969, when several African American and Puerto Rican students demanded desegregation. But they had to act quickly, since students occupied buildings and even set one on fire. In the end, they ceded with a compromise to organized labor: open admissions for all city high school graduates. A report's subheading reads "policy by riot" (Renfro & Armour-Garb, 1999, p. 19) and notes with disdain that CUNY sacrificed high standards ("excellence") for mere "access" when dispensing with standardized testing and offering remedial education for all underprepared first-year students: "Access and excellence are CUNY's historic goals. Over the past 30 years, the 'access' portion of the mission has overwhelmed the university at the expense of excellence" (p. 1), a sentiment which James Traub's (1994) book on the City College put in motion with his critique of open admissions, that is, affirmative action. Only recently, "inclusive excellence" has been used to overcome the opposites of "access" and "academic excellence," and politicians from Obama to education department officials affirm the virtues of a diverse classroom as enriching the college experience for all.

Yet, the Renfro report also reluctantly acknowledges that the senior colleges of CUNY have not kept their promise of access to Black and Latino students, thanks, of course, to the prohibition of race-based affirmative action measures. The recent US Supreme Court decision on affirmative action (*Fisher II*, June 2016), reversing over thirty years of outlawing "quotas" and racial diversification of college admissions, breathes new life into "inclusive excellence." Interestingly, because of a shrinking pool of high school graduates, admissions officers of SUNY are now forced to recruit in multicultural schools that they have in the past ignored. For decades, SUNY Cortland mainly recruited students from white dominated areas of Long Island and neglected racially diverse metropolitan areas such as Syracuse or New York City. Today, the incoming first-year cohort is about 27 percent students of color. However, the goal of inclusive excellence rings hollow, when only 25 percent of Black students graduate from the college, while whites graduate at the rate of 72 percent.

The Legal Context: The Meaning of Affirmative Action in an Age of Diversity Management

In 1961, during the militant "borning struggle" of the Black-led Freedom Movement, President Kennedy issued an executive order (10925) to prohibit racist discrimination in the workplace and to encourage business to consider "affirmative action and equal opportunity" and make concerted efforts to diversify their workforce (DiTomaso, 2013, p. 257). In his famous "I have a dream . . ." speech, Martin Luther King (1963) powerfully noted that Black people are still not free and, furthermore, they have been given a bad check, which reads "insufficient funds." Kennedy had made a timid reparative gesture to Black America: apply to jobs and colleges and enter historically white (and some elite) academic institutions, which were denied to generations of Black Americans due to Jim Crow practices of exclusion. It was a promising proposition: to attain placements despite cumulative disadvantages in education and second-class citizenship status.

The dream was deferred: in the end, the executive order concerning "affirmative action" was amended to address sex discrimination in the Johnson administration (DiTomaso, 2013, p. 257). As such, it turned out to be a corrective measure benefiting white middle-class women to break glass ceilings and invisible elevators in many professions. Thus, an elastic interpretation of "affirmative action" opened doors to white women, who were thought to "fit" into a white male boardroom with much greater ease than Black people and other folks of color. To date, what is left of Kennedy's lofty ideal is a mere nod to "equal opportunity." Or, everybody is affirmed, because we are all diverse.

Favoring a focus on "diverse voices" is akin to moving chairs around so that some workers of color will have front row seats (and being given prizes for their diversity work), but few, if any, new chairs will be added to the white dominated workplace, offering a cohort of people of color a seat at the table. Such liberal focus on awareness raising about inequalities has also left its imprint in the academy. Diversity trainers inform us about a plethora of social identities, which all (ought to) take up equal space: racism should be dealt with on a continuum of challenges such as classism, ableism, and sizeism/weightism/lookism (Wallis, 2015). And Audre Lorde (1983) is (mistakenly) quoted for her bon mot: "There is no hierarchy of oppressions."

So, it is interesting to see that, today, military veterans are the single largest beneficiary group of scholastic opportunities and government employment, and many of them are white men. At all colleges and universities, another trend is noticeable: many of the Black students enrolled (and a number of faculty/staff) are first (or second) generation immigrants, outnumbering Indigenous Black students (Massey et al., 2007; Tauriac & Liem, 2012). It is easy to blame the victim, as politicians are quick to do. However, the deeper root of the problem, namely, a prison epidemic that has ensnared practically every US Black family: one in three Black men will face incarceration in his lifetime. In an era of mass incarceration, there are more Black males in prison than enrolled in colleges and universities. This has a lasting psychic impact. Testing has shown that Black male applicants *without* criminal records have a higher chance of being denied a job than *convicted* white males (with parole status, etc.). As Devah Pager writes, "The effect of race was very large, equal to or greater than the effect of a criminal record. Only 14 percent of black men without criminal records were called back, a proportion equal to or less than even the number of whites *with* a criminal background" (2004, p. 46).

President Kennedy did not sign a true reparative measure that included "guarantees" of jobs and education (never mind housing or excellent k–12 schooling). It was simply "an opportunity." So, in the new "colorblind" era, people of color may be handed a job application, but it is not assured that they will get a call back, even when they are more qualified than white counterparts. Academia also had its own policing mechanism, because criminal records have to be disclosed on the admissions' application form. There used to be one notable exception. A major public university system in New York state, namely, CUNY, had a long tradition of welcoming court-involved people; they do not have to check a box disclosing a felony conviction when they apply to CUNY schools.

Thanks to the social activism by multiracial coalitions and celebrity authors such as Michelle Alexander, whose book *The New Jim Crow* (2010) critiques a decades-old racist drug policy, the Obama administration rallied some two dozen universities and colleges together, including SUNY, to take a pledge to ban the box for student applicants with prior convictions (White House, 2016). The SUNY system finally agreed to the demand, partially, that campuses ban the box. The neoliberal, risk-averse academy may admit a person with misdemeanor or felony records to attain a "second chance," but there are many secondary-checks that follow the student, including petitioning for living on campus, studying abroad, taking overnight fieldtrips, or attaining an internship, thus ensuring that a "record" still will follow the person for the rest of his or her life, hampering significant educational opportunities and gainful employment (CCA, 2015). Furthermore, high school disciplinary records follow a student and may derail their college admissions. Critics of "zero tolerance" policies enforced in K–12 schools have noted the disparate impact on Black and brown students who experience the brunt of the pushed-out effect and the proverbial school-to-prison pipeline (cf. Morris, 2018). However, this criminalization "pipeline" needs to be investigated at the college level. Few have focused on this troubling phenomenon, in part, because it is difficult to compile data. "Studying-while-Black" at white colleges and universities is perilous, as campus police ticket and arrest students who drive "suspicious" cars; Black students, faculty, and staff have to show identification in office buildings, on campus walking paths, and thus these stakeholders learn that they are not welcome on a campus that authorities have deemed exclusively white spaces.

Why is all this relevant for an analysis of diversity management? Who deserves inclusion in the academy? While all white institutions clamor for gifted US born Black applicants, they also quietly pursue an internationalizing strategy, as their data of Black students (or faculty/ staff) tend not to separate out national origin status, and the presence of African or Caribbean faculty and students will be all that matters to make the university look diverse. It is a matter of presenting a score sheet that receives a "diversity" stamp of approval by national organizations such as the National Association of Diversity Officers in Higher Education, DiversityInc, and regional educational accrediting agencies.

Diversity Tactics: Roles of Chief Diversity Officers in the Neoliberal University

Diversity management is a *corporate* approach that, for the most part, ignores the complexities of lived experiences, of intersectional oppression, and lacks praxeological clarity. It is a failure of understanding the interaction of critical discourses and practices. As mentioned above with respect to the exclusion of applicants with convict status, it is a *risk-averse* approach, and it is peculiar how effortlessly diversity management has been introduced into the academic institutional framework. Students of color, still labeled by administrators as "minorities," disappear into aggregate statistics about recruitment, retention, and graduation rates. The term "diversity" lends itself to much confusion, being a hot topic among academics who engage with the term in a critical way, while administrators use it normatively or instrumentally (Vertovec, 2014, p. 1).

In the SUNY system, which encompasses sixty-four campuses, various chancellors have pursued ambitious diversity strategic plans promising to become "the most inclusive university system in the United States" (Zimpher, 2015, p. 3). Under the previous chancellor, Nancy Zimpher, every campus had to appoint a chief diversity officer to coordinate diversity management of all units and departments (Zimpher, 2015). So far, so good. In reality, these officers have this (impossible) mandate:

1. to conduct trainings of search committees in order to diversify the workforce while being one of a few diverse persons among the senior administration (reality of tokenism);

2. to assuage any conflicts rising from the student body (the most likely body that speaks up or, worse, occupies the presidential suite) by inviting select students to join a diversity council;

3. to issue reports on diversity scores (aligning with national standards and practices);

4. to be the "fall person" in case something goes awry (the next racist incident, sexual assaults against women in fraternity housing, etc.)—it will be the diversity officer who will take the blame, thus preventing a holistic review of systemic failures of providing a welcoming and safe environment for all;

5. to lead positive directives (award ceremonies given to those who have an equally positive outlook on diversity management); and

6. to partner with faculty on curriculum initiatives. (cf. Worthington et al., 2014)

For any person considering advancing to the level of chief diversity officer (CDO), it will be prudent to study some historical cases. For those of us who are employed by the State University of New York (SUNY) system, it is paramount watching Gallagher's documentary film *Brothers of the Black List* (2013), which chronicles the aftermath of the SUNY Oneonta administration's fateful decision of turning over a list of 125 Black male students to the city of Oneonta's police department in search of a suspect. This blatant incident of egregious racial profiling occurred a mere twenty years ago and the litigation was one of the longest civil rights suits in US history. The film shows that the multicultural resource director failed to be a resource for traumatized students; instead, they turned to a Black college counselor for crisis intervention and advocacy.

Despite best intentions, the diversity officer's key role, in this hyper-real world of diversity management, is to shield the president and other power brokers from liability and to provide maximum damage control. Because they are "management confidential" or otherwise worry about job retention, these diversity officers are unlikely to go to bat for a Black student applicant with a criminal record and draw the ire of a powerful admissions director. If they are savvy, they call on allied faculty (with tenure) diversity workers to do the job they (as diversity officers) were hired for: assist in diversifying the student body, participate in "difficult dialogues" with an admission officer, and so on.

In fact, the diversity management blueprint for universities authorized by the National Association of Diversity Officers in Higher Education outlines the following social identity categories: race/ethnicity, gender, age, sexual orientation, disability, religion, national and geographic origin, language use, socioeconomic status, first generation, veteran/military, political ideology (Worthington et al., 2014). So, in addition to protected classes of groups, one's worldview (including pagan or atheist) is also a notable diversity dimension. This blueprint is mentioned in SUNY chancellor Zimpher's policy memorandum (2015).

After Chancellor Zimpher's departure from the SUNY system, George Floyd's knee lynching, and the global resistance against racial injustice, SUNY in general has increased its efforts in recruitment of faculty of color through PRODiG—Promoting, Recruitment, Opportunity, Diversity, Inclusion and Growth program. PRODiG aims at increasing diversity in SUNY's students and faculty populations. SUNY has suffered in the areas of, especially, recruiting faculty of color, whose population in the system is now only 8.6 percent compared to the BIPOC student population of 28.0 percent (*SUNY PRODiG 2019-2020 Cohort Data*, 2021). This disproportionality of students of color to BIPOC faculty in the SUNY system has debilitating effects on the workload, teaching, and research of faculty of color. It also affects students of color in that many of them complete their educational experience without interaction with diverse faculty. Furthermore, the PRODiG program, which was very well-intentioned, continues to experience the local politics of anti-politics, where campus leaders' (usually white males) perceptions of "diversity and inclusion" are most of the time interpreted to suit their own risk management needs. Departments in the natural sciences that need women faculty have attracted more white women. Moreover, administrators have determined who is financed in the PRODiG program on the local campuses and smaller departments like Africana Studies or Philosophy have not benefited from the program. With the emergence of COVID-19 and concomitant budgetary and austerity measures, diversity and inclusion projects in the SUNY system are in a state of inertia.

Diversity Discourses—Civility Discourses
("We All Need to Get Along")

So far, we have argued that the gains of the civil rights movement have been slowly eroded. Discursively speaking, this means the virtual disappearance of critiques of power, hegemony, oppression, and ideology, and, of course, resistance to systemic injustice (cf. Bart, 2016). Cultural critic Robin Kelley (2016) implores student activists to keep pushing the institutions into a life-affirming direction. He notes, "Resistance is our healing. Through collective struggle, we alter our circumstances; contain, escape, or possibly eviscerate the source of trauma; recover our bodies; reclaim and redeem our dead; and make ourselves whole. It is difficult to see this in a world where words such as *trauma, PTSD, micro-aggression,* and *triggers* have virtually replaced *oppression, repression,* and *subjugation*" (his emphasis). What was formerly discussed as problems of structural or systemic injustice is now being reduced to personal slights or personal responsibility, replete with counseling sessions and risk-management assessment reports.

In what follows, we present a case of managing diversity: The Black Student Union held town hall meetings on behalf of the chief diversity officer and the campus administration. The president of BSU read out managerial language ostensibly to make such meetings safe for senior administrators and white students. Ground rules for engagement even suggested refraining from labeling one's traumatic experience as "racist." Instead, the speaker was encouraged to speak of it as "racialized experience" and do so within one minute of allowed airtime. Audience responses were collected and perhaps discussed at a president's cabinet meeting. A faculty/staff committee on campus climate never received the responses and failed to make recommendations for a campus that values inclusive excellence. Perhaps these campus conversations offer up the hope that discussions about racism can be carried out in a "safe space" and welcome interracial dialogue. Yet social media with anonymously posted hate mail or classroom discussions that pit students of color against the white teacher, who educates the class about race as a biological fact, speak volumes of the presence of a racist climate, not a "racialized" one. Social media may be new; however, what is not new are the complaints of students of color.

At SUNY Cortland, a report, *Toward a More Equitable, Inclusive, and Diverse Academic Community* (Steck et al., 1992), makes clear that students of color should not be unfairly tasked with "instant expertise" on matters of urban affairs in a classroom, something that continues to haunt well-meaning white teachers' pedagogy today, as students' feedback makes clear. The Steck report also emphasizes the role of meaningful mentoring and recommends the expansion of a mentoring program for students of color. Twenty years later, this program that helped to retain students on campus was disbanded by an administrator, because it did not include white students. However, all strategic proposals regarding overcoming achievement gaps between white and student of color cohorts emphasize the role of advising and mentoring as a key to retention and graduating students of color within six years. Diversity management "levels the playing field" in a way that this tactic again disadvantages ethnically and racially diverse students on a white dominated campus. A subsequent report, *Recruitment and Retention of Ethnic Minority Report* (Peagler, 2000), focuses on key offices, including admissions and recommends: "The College should establish an on-going assessment of what is being accomplished related to campus climate and issues pertinent to diversity" (p. 14). However, such committee has never put together an annual progress report (card), nor has it been tasked to report to the president of the college, as the Peagler report had advised.

Part and parcel of a risk-adverse strategy is to champion a "crucial conversations" re-education campaign. The ideological framework is focused on the *individual* (disgruntled) employee, who will need a "stern, but kind talk" with her supervisor. "Crucial conversations" packaged workshops were first tried out in the corporate world and then imported via human resources and affirmative action officers to the academic context. This "effective communication" program whisks away any need for "diversity dialogues," for example, regarding intent and impact of speech; it steers clear from any critical discussion of systemic powerlessness, whiteness, and a cycle of oppression. We are all supposed to belong (and behave civilly). And (ideally) employees would be "allowed" to talk back at their unkind boss, as long as they follow the civilly outlined rules of conduct. Supposedly, the workers do not have to fear retaliation. But noting a pattern of sexism or racism in the manager's actions would be anathema to the corporatist agenda of "crucial conversations" conduct: those are construed as fighting words and the complainant might face reprimand.

Diversity management often devolves into "managing" diversity: a homogenous, white (male) management presides over a workforce that may have a few white gays or lesbians or straight-identified persons of color in decision-making roles, but otherwise it relegates gender queer or gender fluid persons as well as ethnically and culturally diverse cisgender workers to the backroom, low-paying, and invisible, glass-ceiling and sticky-floors jobs such as janitorial staff (cf. Cox, 1991).

Hence, despite the ideal-case scenarios played in workshops and attention to socioeconomic class (in theory), few workers, especially secretaries, administrative assistants, or professional salaried staff members dare to challenge a supervisor by challenging her to a "crucial conversation." Working-class college professors with working-class roots and first-generation identity, because their parents never attended college, are also unlikely to speak up, even in contentious department meetings, lacking the required cultural capital and self-esteem (Kadi, 1996).

Within the US, this management model thrives on a post–civil rights business ideology of nominal inclusion of diverse populations and interest groups in the workforce and academic institutions. The model's focus is squarely on diversity trainings that minimize conflicts. For instance, Brennan Nevada Johnson (2023) in his advice on bad company culture, itemizes ten things never to say to a Black coworker in the office; even though they might be well-intentioned, they can nonetheless be received as microassaults, microinsults, or just plain offensive. In the academic context, the awareness-raising approach is adopted by professionals who manage student affairs. Studies of private business companies show that training programs that simply target managerial bias are fairly ineffective, whereas "affirmative action plans, diversity committees, and diversity staff positions are more effective in increasing [workforce] diversity" (Wrench, 2014, p. 259). The business case for outcomes, that is, diversifying the workforce, is indeed helpful and addresses the findings of perception research, identified by Sara Ahmed (2012): "One project finds that external communities perceive the university as being white. Rather than responding by accepting this perception (and thus assuming the task of modifying the thing perceived as white) the perception becomes the problem. The task becomes changing the perception of whiteness rather than changing the whiteness of the organization" (p. 184). This means that diversity managers draw the wrong conclusion by including more students of color in glossy welcoming brochures and promotion pictures in the admissions office. But the pictures of white professors adorning the hallways or offices of most departments cannot be changed, can they? However, one change might be, following Ahmed's analysis, that the smiling photographs of the white professoriate disappear from the walls. By contrast, effecting transformative change and making a "business" case for diversification, cluster hires of faculty of color have been quite effective in increasing their retention rates. Yet businesses also report a rise of conflicts in a diverse workforce and question the efficacy of conflict management. Do they simply reinforce double standards and double binds, or do they dismantle structural, cultural, psychological barriers, and systemic exclusion?

Facing the Double Bind and Professional Double Standards

The shared realities faced by BIPOC faculty in historically white institutions, can be summarized as "Sisyphean." Stephanie A. Fryberg and Ernesto J. Martínez's book shines a critical light on the presentation of data with respect to hiring and retention practices of faculty of color: "What does it mean for universities to claim progress with respect to diversifying faculty ranks when 73 percent of faculty of color hold non-tenure-track or adjunct faculty positions that do not provide job security?" (2014, p. 5). Such claims of progress in diversifying the faculty hides the fact that a myopic perspective is more comforting to gatekeepers at historically white institutions than an honest look at the macroscopic picture of understanding the diverse pressures faculty of color face vis-à-vis tenure-track level positions, especially at elite colleges or research universities.

In the case of tenure-track faculty of color, Fryberg and Martínez describe the presence of interrelated narratives that have all the trappings of a double-bind oppression, outlined in Marilyn Frye's (1983) classic article on oppression. What is considered meritorious research tends to be contested ("Striving, but Falling Short"), even as some scholars are applauded for tackling diversity or ethnography ("Inching toward Progress"), and their clincher: "Service Is (Not) Necessary." Several Ivy League institutions have been under scrutiny for failing to tenure their faculty of color and Black Lives Matter gives new attention to these interrelated oppressive narratives. Take the case of Professor Aimee Bahng who was denied tenure at Dartmouth College. An angry student post reads: "Professors who engage with activism & advocate for students are disproportionately denied tenure #Fight4FacultyOfColor #DontDoDartmouth" (May 13, 2016). Her colleagues say Bahng stands out for her innovative work in Asian-American studies, for gaining national attention for leading a faculty collective on Black Lives Matter, and participating in a collaborative book project. Yet it seems that she ran up against Dartmouth's "culture of politeness" for confusing service with activism (Flaherty, 2016; Silverstein, 2016). Echoing Fryberg and Martínez's shrewd analysis of faculty of color as the university's convenient diversity jugglers, Professor Ellison voices her disillusionment with Dartmouth concerning the exploitation and marginalization of faculty of color. Fryberg and Martinez rightly note:

> Beyond tenure denials, some faculty members of color have left Dartmouth on their own. In a Facebook post about the

> departures, Treva C. Ellison, a lecturer in geography and women, gender, and sexuality studies, wrote that the "lack of critical faculty here always means that any new person hired who can feel what direction gravity pulls in is going to be inundated with more work than their white cisgendered male counterparts and other zero-G hires." Dartmouth doesn't have a "diversity problem," she added, "rather, the temporary, precarious, and disavowed labor of people of color at Dartmouth is their purposeful and intentional diversity solution." (cited in Flaherty, 2016)

The neocolonial university relegates faculty of color to the ranks of precariat labor while showing off in glossy magazines that they are "doing diversity." This leaves junior faculty of color "with mixed messages and double standards, while the university gets to claim diversity as a core value" (Fryberg & Martínez, 2014, p. 8).

Inclusive excellence goals are still tenuous, especially in research universities, which prize publication with certain publishing houses and journals; and they devalue faculty committed to action research and publish those in "low impact" journals. Faculty who pursue such work and still hope for tenure and promotion need to be mindful that service to the community and the profession does not really count toward enhancing their reputation. For some junior faculty of color, it is simply impossible to pursue a false choice, that is, of either being part of the struggle or being an acceptable public intellectual who will keep politics out of the classroom (June, 2015). With increasing attention to assessment, what can be said about something as simple as disaggregated recruitment and retention data of US and international faculty of color? A data-driven university will cloak itself in silence over such simple analysis. Fryberg and Martínez (2014, p. 3) clarify: "With rare exceptions, universities frequently invoke narratives of progress in lieu of providing measurable outcomes (Moreno, Smith, Clayton-Pedersen, Parker, & Teraguchi, 2006). This often comes in the form of over idealizing administrative 'goodwill' and generalizing campus-wide 'efforts.'" Universities such as Yale are under increasing scrutiny on why faculty of color are not receiving tenure. Often, Black Student Unions are driving this social justice call for action, unwilling to settle for empty gestures by administrators who favor discourses of equity and inclusion and cultural competence.

Fryberg and Martínez perceptively note another constraint imposed at research universities, which cannot break free from narrowly conceived academic standards:

> Women of color feminism as a field of study would not have existed without the 1980s and 1990s institution-building labor of creating publishing houses like Third Woman Press and Kitchen Table Press. Groundbreaking volumes of interdisciplinary inquiry like *This Bridge Called My Back* (Moraga & Anzaldúa, 1981), *Making Face/Making Soul* (Moraga & Anzaldúa, 1990), and *All the Women Are White, All the Blacks Are Men, but Some of Us Are Brave* (Hull, Scott, & Smith, 1982) might not have been published without these alternative publishing venues. More important, the methodologies that arose from these volumes—methodologies that now form the foundation of established schools of thought in the humanities and social sciences—would never have reached their paradigm-shifting potential, if these writers had waited to be published separately in journals or individual single-authored books. (2014, p. 7)

Part of the paradigm shift is a nod toward the intersectionality of "unruly categories" (cf. Young, 1998) in contemporary North American feminist and critical race theoretical discourses, which are clearly indebted to the transformative texts by women of color. For several decades, the progressive women of color INCITE! collective has organized inspiring grassroots conferences and published activist-oriented books, for example, *The Color of Violence* (INCITE!, 2006). Their intersectional work helped make connections between the mutually reinforcing oppressive matrices of oppression, settler colonialism, racism, and heterosexism, and the connection that feminist work entails being vigilant about one's complicity with agents of the criminal justice complex. White feminist activists and scholars often failed to critique the role of police and social workers vis-à-vis stigmatized work, sexual violence, and relationship violence. Black Lives Matter's feminist founders Alicia Garza, Patrisse Cullors, and Opal Tometi (Garza, 2014) brought international attention to what is at stake and with this new social movement were able to influence discussions in all sectors of society, including, of course, the university curriculum and social climate. BLM signifies the power of coupling the politics of recognition with the demands of structural change.

In these volatile times, college presidents and their diversity actors are advised to create real accountability measures on structural diversity questions, which clearly go beyond perfunctory celebrations of diversity or unity. In an environment of diversity management, they may ask themselves whether they can rely on the support of the institution's diversity officer, who has been trained to diffuse resistant practices. Sara Ahmed suggests a different approach: "We might need to be the cause of obstruction. We might need to get in the way if we are to get anywhere. We might need to become the blockage points by pointing out the blockage points" (Ahmed, 2012, p. 187). Yet, so often, the academy leaves no room other than leaving one's post, as Sara Ahmed did in May 2016. In her resignation letter she writes, "Sometimes we have to leave a situation because we are feminists. Wherever I am, I will be a feminist. I will be doing feminism. I will be living a feminist life. I will be chipping away at the walls." Clearly, world-renowned Professor Sara Ahmed, Professor of Media and Communications and Director of the Centre for Feminist Research, did not feel included at Goldsmiths and as "feminist killjoy" scholar-activist certainly could not be "managed" within a risk-averse institution.

Arguably, "diverse" members of any campus community who face some or all aspects of the "five faces of oppression," outlined by Iris Marion Young (1990)—namely, powerlessness, exploitation, marginalization, cultural imperialism, violence—have little if anything to "gain" in a corporate model of "diversity management." The effective exclusion of their affective physical and emotional labor can be quite carefully managed under the elusive goal of diversity, inclusion, access, and equity.

In the following part 2 of this book, several chapters focus on specific, historical faces of oppression and movement politics, foregrounding dimensions of Afrophobia and Black feminist critiques of white feminist blind spots. We conclude with an analysis of leadership models that are particularly inclusive and redirect the reader's attention on why we must reframe diversity by focusing on the intersections of race and gender.

Part 2

Anti-oppression Traditions and Oppressive Practices

Searching for Interlocking Systems

Chapter 5

Race, Questioning Immigrant Bodies, and Heteropatriarchal Masculinity

Rethinking the Obama Presidency

The concept of race, developing unevenly in the Americas from the arrival of Europeans in the Western Hemisphere down to the present, has served as a fundamental organizing principle of the social system. Practices of distinguishing among human beings according to their corporeal characteristics became linked to systems of control, exploitation, and resistance.

—Michael Omi and Howard Winant (2015)

"Respect" was what I heard over and over when talking with men . . . , especially black men. I interpret this type of respect to be a crystallization of the masculine quests for recognition through public achievement, unfolding within a system of structured constraints due to class and race inequities.

—Michael Messner (1997)

I argue that identities are grounded in social locations, and I make use of resources from hermeneutics and phenomenology to explicate the epistemic, the metaphysical and politically relevant features of identities . . . in social theory and practice.

—Linda Alcoff (2006)

A different version of this chapter was published in *Wagadu* (Asumah, 2015).

> Immigration policy has long been controversial in the United States and has at times been used in openly racist ways. It has become even more controversial in the new century, as a plan proposed in Congress to both tighten border security and provide a path to citizenship for estimated 11–12 million undocumented aliens already present in the United States failed in 2007 amid opposition from both sides. . . . Afterwards, for the first time, the United States began to construct a fence along its border with Mexico to keep people out.
>
> —John E. Farley (2012)

Introduction

Race, ethnicity, and social identity are complex phenomena in the United States and the rest of the world. The discourse over race, heteropatriarchal masculinity, and immigration policy, like other critical political issues, makes racial analysis for the American presidency novel in the minds of many scholars. Yet, even though race matters and race is a major category in American society, the lack of agency for race, especially in Barack Hussein Obama's presidency (2009–2017), his deliberations on racial issues, and immigration policy, tend to puzzle many sociopolitical observers. Under Obama, the antagonisms against undocumented immigrants of color, especially Chicanos and Latino folx, pushed the conversation over race and immigration beyond the Blacks/whites paradigm. The euphoric prognosis about the Obama presidency, the first president of color, post-racialism, and the politics of change will make America less divisive and more racial-friendly subsided in Obama's second year in office.

Even though many Americans were and are still in denial about the agency of race, even when racial spaces and critical race theory (CRT) today are under attack. Race was (under the Obama presidency) and still is (during the Biden-Harris administration) a major conversation piece and the elephant in the room, when any American president interacts with the United States Congress or engages in any public space. The issues of Obama's electability, reelection, respectability, masculinity, leadership style, policy-making and implementation, and approval rating were and are all submerged in a convoluted discursive consciousness of the American people. The interlocutors of race, immigration narratives, and racial matrix of domination have reached a new level of contumacy, perhaps because of the recent movement Black Lives Matter, the murder of George Floyd, the first woman of color as vice president of the United States and President Obama's racial identity and background. On January 27, 2010, after President Obama's State of the Union Address, Chris Matthews, MSNBC host, had this characterization of President Obama: "He is post-racial, by all appearances. I forgot he was black tonight for an hour" (Matthews, 2010). Did this statement then or does this statement by interlocutors of race and racial issues in the United States, such as Matthews's, mean anything to the racial narrative of the country? What has happened to racial categorization and group political consciousness of racial issues since Obama became president? Has white privilege, an unearned advantage for whites because of their skin color and status, changed or have Blacks gained any privilege in recent times because of race? In order to answer these questions, one has to interrogate racial history, racial group dynamics, identity politics, and group prejudice plus institutional power with reference to policy-making and implementation. Even though President Obama intentionally avoided the race question for the first six years of his presidency and had episodically made statements involving race, in his interview with the *New Yorker* magazine, he impugned, "There's no doubt that there's some folks who just really dislike me because they don't like the idea of a black president. . . . Now, the flip side of it is there are some black folks and maybe some white folks who really like me and give me the benefit of the doubt precisely because I'm a black president" (Remnick, 2014, p. 7).

Hitherto, did President Obama's race combined with his limited dependence on the agency of race and the presumed challenge to his masculinity in the policy sphere, call to question his position on racial issues and immigration issues? Did the African American and Latino unemployment rates during his presidency, the Louis Gates debacle, the Trayvon Martin case, Michael Brown's killing by police officer Darren Wilson, Ferguson, Missouri, questions about the president's "My Brother's Keeper" initiative to save boys and young men of color, the police chokehold killing of Eric Garner, and nonindictment decision by the grand jury, and presidential immigration action through an executive instrument tickle America's consciousness about Obama's approach to dealing with race? In disrespect to the president and direct confrontation to his policy agenda, in the advent of the immigration policy reform myopia, the states of Arizona and Alabama created their own "show me your papers" laws that tended to target people of color and challenged the president's executive authority in immigration policy-making and implementation. The agency of race permeated all the issues and topics above. Race was and still is the elephant in the American polity that most people like to avoid because of the country's historical contradictions surrounding race and immigration.

Furthermore, the Obama presidency and his policy initiatives were stifled because of the hegemony of heteropatriarchal masculinists in the American polity. What then is the heteropatriarchal masculinity that haunted the Obama presidency? Heteropatriarchal masculinity is a polity that is sustained and protected by the elite ruling class and predominantly middle- and upper-class males who define personal, professional, socioeconomic, and political issues based on the normalization and superordination of whiteness and patriarchy, and the subordination of others by perpetuating the matrix of domination and interlocking systems of oppression (see Harris, 2011; Hoagland 2007; Smith, 2008). Both critical race theory and feminist theory inform our analysis that heteropatriarchal hegemons depend on paternalism, devaluing of women's skills and role in the polity, and using legal and moral theory to exclude lesbians, gay, bisexual, transgender, two-spirit, queer, questioning, intersex, asexual, and pansexual persons (LGBTQIAP), and, especially, Black males. The reawakening of heteropatriarchal masculinity under the Obama administration and the intersectionality of heteropatriarchy, racism, classism, and sexism produced a toxic condition for the politics of difference, thus affecting the Obama presidency and his legacy as the first and only president of color in the oldest democracy in the world. Moreover, heteropatriarchy stifled the endeavors of many Black heroes, like Dr. Martin Luther King, Jr., who is the most cited Black person in the world, especially in times of struggle for racial justice, but was reduced by a bullet to an ordinary Black man in black suit and a mortal being in Memphis in 1968. Such intersectionality of oppression (race, class, gender) is glaringly in the forefront of anyone concerned with the legacy of the civil rights movement, as major milestones are being dismantled under the guise of "states' rights," "originalism," as the US Supreme Court has begun to weigh in on matters of reproductive rights, dignity for LGBTQIAP folks, immigration policies, recent deceptive flights and busing of migrants and asylees from their ports of entry to Martha's Vineyard, Massachusetts, and other places in the "new" politics of attention-grabbing, and so on, during another "hot" political summer (of 2022).

In the balance of this essay, we argue that the macroscopic nature and complexity of the concept of race, heteropatriarchal masculinity, microaggression, and immigration issues put President Obama in a double-bind situation during his presidency, which affected his style of inclusive leadership and any attempt for productive decision/policy-making involving especially race and immigration. Double-bind situations produce limited options and exposure to penalties no matter what approaches President Obama took in confronting racial issues, immigration reform, and a challenge to heteropatriarchal masculinity in the United States. Furthermore, racial and heteropatriarchal hegemonic masculinity, which shape the policy-making process asphyxiated most of Obama's attempts for effective decision-making and policy reforms. This asphyxiation emasculated President Obama in his policy confrontations with lawmakers who are/were predominantly white heteropatriarchal hegemonic establishmentarians, such as the current Republican Senate Minority Leader, Mitch McConnell, whose interest in producing gridlocks and policy myopia is paramount to his ego and whiteness, instead of the country's well-being. As a heteropatriarchal hegemon, McConnell's legislative obstructive/destructive behavior has continued even under President Biden. In Obama's case, the position of discontent for a Black president was so obvious that the election of one of America's worst and most racist and sexist residents, Donald Trump, was a direct reaction and response to the apparent disapproval and backlash associated with putting a Blackman in the White House. President Obama himself noted in his memoir, *A Promised Land*: "It was as if my very presence in the White House had triggered a deep-seated panic, a sense that the natural order had been disrupted. . . . Which is exactly what Donald Trump understood when he started peddling assertions that I had not been born in the United States and was thus an illegitimate president. For millions of Americans spooked by a Black man in the White House, he promised an elixir for their racial anxiety" (2020, pp. 671–672).

President Obama's racialized body, his father's African ancestry and immigrant body, his audacity to venture into whites space as the first president of color in the White House, and his own confidence (or political naiveté) in America where "sincere fiction" obstructs race relation, combined with white heteropatriarchal hegemony, contributed to his asphyxiation in leadership and the policy arena.

To place this discussion in context, our usage of the term asphyxiation is symbolic of Black struggles for liberation in sociopolitical contumacy in a suffocated polity for the oppressed. Asphyxiation also invokes a state of urgency in the United States, where especially Black males, such as George Floyd, in Minnesota, could easily be murdered by knee-lynching. Floyd called his dead mother to save him from the white police officer, Derek Chauvin's knee on his neck for 9 minutes and 29 seconds before he died. And Eric Garner in Staten Island, New York, was put in a chokehold by white police officers until he died without much legal repercussion (except for the civilian person who happened to videotape the killing). The last call for help Mr. Garner made was "I can't breathe." Nevertheless, it is not only ordinary Black males that are suffocated to death, but a commander-in-chief of the United States who happened to be a Black man could easily suffer from political asphyxiation because of the systemic heteropatriarchal hegemonic political manipulation of predominantly white policy-makers, who thwarted President Obama's policy initiatives. Asphyxiation is therefore an evocative and symbolic concept of the totality of the recent Black condition in the American polity.

This chapter is intended to make some theoretical contributions to the study of the presidency and heteropatriarchy in America by interrogating the Obama presidency and how it could serve as a microcosm for examining identity politics, institutional policy-making, and the intersectionality of race, gender, masculinity, class, and their impact on racial and immigration issues. Yet, still, President Obama is viewed by many observers as someone who occupied a failed heteropatriarchal masculinist position during his presidency because of his personal experience, which embodies the Black experience and immigrant characteristics. If a picture could speak a thousand words, Arend Van Dam's cartoon below (see fig. 5.1), depicting President Obama's inability to breathe politically, sums up our perception of asphyxiation and Obama's own take on political suffocation in his memoir, *A Promised Land* (2020), in this chapter (see van Dam, 2014).

Race and Racism Revisited

The literature on race and racism is impressive. Many Americans could write books about race and racism with little trouble because of the United States' history with these concepts. The concept and texts of race and racism are already grounded in the cognitive structures of most Americans,

Figure 5.1. "I Can't Breathe! A Better America," by Cartoonist Arend van Dam. Used with permission.

and they elicit racial groups' moral character. Americans have been put into racial categories for convenience since recorded history. The first census in 1790 developed a racial classification scheme and the following twenty-three federal censuses have not been any different. The statistical races and the social construct of race continue to dominate American lives. These categories of race have taken on forms of their own, shaping our precepts, norms, cultures, policy, and patterns of political interactions. So, in the American polity, race matters. Race plays a critical role in individual endeavors and political ones. If the implications for race on the presidency and immigration policy remain unquestioned, the results could be overpowering and debilitating racial problems for the totality of the American populace.

To negate the adverse effects of race, one must understand the meaning of it as a social construct. Omi and Winant define race as a "concept which signifies and symbolizes social conflicts and interests by referring to different types of human bodies" (2015, p. 110). Though the human bodies referred to in this definition employ characteristics of humans associated with biological phenotypes, these organisms maintain sociohistorical and political properties because of their selection and operation in any society. For instance, in American history, under the

Supreme Court ruling of *Dred Scott v. Sanford* (1857), Blacks were only considered as pieces of property, not quite human. The status of Blacks in the American polity has been defined by the society, and now Blacks are accepted de jure as "somewhat coequal" of whites. If the definition and selection of race depend on a political process, then race itself is an "unstable" concept, constantly changing with the political process, and it is concomitant with groups' competition to sustain their interests or resolve conflicts. Issues concerning racial categories, for the above-mentioned reason, will continue to be sociopolitical. The racial categories and hierarchy propounded by the power holder at the inception of this country (United States) created a white ruling class that benefited from the structures of race and racial interactions. As Feagin alludes, "People do not experience 'race' in the abstract but in concrete reoccurring relationships with one another" (2014, p. 13). Superordinate races therefore benefit from racial arrangements that place them on the apogee of the racial hierarchy, while subordinate groups and races are reduced to the status of the oppressed and the disenfranchised.

The origins of America's rejection of other peoples (races) could be traced from European racial reasoning, what Cornell West describes as "a division of deceptive consensual racial position based on the history of domination and subjugation of one race over another" (1994, p. 8). When Carolus Linnaeus, the Swedish botanist and European father of taxonomy, wrote his essay titled *Systema naturae*, he created a racial position for whites in his hierarchy of human classification with the white race at the apogee of that pyramid and Blacks at the bottom (1735, pp. 5–60). Count Arthur de Gobineau (1854), the French diplomat and scholar, maintained a similar sociopolitical position on the concept of race when he published his work, *Essay on the Inequality of Race*. He was providing a synopsis and amplifying the white supremacist ideas of the then Euro-American perception on race (1854/1915, pp. 2–15).

Reginald Horsman correctly recapitulates: "In the first half of the nineteenth century many in the United States were anxious to justify the enslavement of the blacks and the expulsion and possible extermination of the Indian. The American intellectual community did not merely absorb European ideas; it also fed European racial appetites with scientific theories stemming from the supposed knowledge and observation of blacks and Indians" (1995, p. 3).

Yet, the science Horsman talks about was nothing more than pseudoscience to justify white hegemonic thinking and attitude. Kendi asserts,

"Already, the American mind was accomplishing that indispensable intellectual activity of someone consumed with racist ideas: *individualizing* White negativity and *generalizing* Black negativity. Negative behavior by any Black person became proof of what was wrong with Black people" (2016, pp. 43). To maintain a lasting racial hierarchy, white racist behavior was seen and assessed through a white racial frame as individualized deviation from any general white behavior. So, from such early development of negative perceptions by whites about the Black race, the people and decedents of Ham (Blacks) were condemned in the American polity, doomed, and relegated to the position of the wretched and deplorable—even in the minds of many white Americans today.

John Dewey cites Thomas Jefferson, one of the authors of the declaration of American independence from Great Britain who asserted, "In memory they are equal to whites, in reason much inferior. . . . I advance therefore . . . that the blacks, whether originally a different race, or made distinct by time and circumstances, are inferior to the whites" (Jefferson cited in Dewey, 1940, p. 52). Such pseudoscientific characterization of race even by an American president was easily transformed into socioeconomic and political privilege for whites. Racial formations are therefore not natural. They are constructed by societies to affirm racial positions for public policy agendas. Race is currently understood as a sociohistorical and political concept. Schaefer notes, "Race is a social construction that benefits the oppressor, who defines which groups of people are privileged and which are not. The acceptance of race in a society as a legitimate category allows racial hierarchies to emerge to the benefit of the dominant 'race'" (2019, p. 12). Nevertheless, this universal racial hierarchy was historically constructed by Europeans and supported by American Founding Fathers to benefit Anglo American socioeconomic and political systems of oppression, and because of generations of fortification of its foundation, it may take generations to deconstruct the negative agency of race. Yet, while whites have used race a tool for racial domination, Schaefer correctly affirms that, "in general, White people do not think of themselves as a race or have a conscious racial identity. A White racial identity emerges only when filling out a form asking for self-designation of race or when Whites are . . . surrounded by people who are not White" (p. 130).

Many students of race tend to confuse the concept of race with that of ethnicity. The English word "ethnic" is derived from the Greek *ethnikos*, the adjectival form of *ethnos*, meaning "a nation." Later, the meaning of *ethnos* evolved to become paradigmatic for conceptualizing groups of different humans in the 1920s and 1930s (Asumah & Johnston-Anumonwo, 2002). Ethnicity emerged as a conceptual challenge to the prevailing biological approach to race, which made people of the Black race inferior. Ethnicity has been used as a tool for ethno-nationalism and ethnic cleansing in recent times. Ironically, in America, many whites refuse to associate themselves with the term "ethnicity." For some obscure reason, whites on most college campuses do not associate with the term "ethnic group." Whenever one hears the term "ethnic students," it is easy to associate it with Blacks, Latino, Native Americans, or some groups other than white. The statistical races constructed conveniently by the United States government are white, Black, American Indians, Asians, and Native Hawaiian/Pacific Islanders, all based on the color scheme of eighteenth-century thinking of natural scientists and the color choices of white, black, brown, yellow, and red (Prewitt, 2013, p. 6).

What then is ethnicity? Ethnicity is an affiliation or classification of a self-conscious group of people who share similar racial, kinship, cultural, and linguistic values (Barndt, 1991, p. 5). Ethnicity is a sociocultural phenomenon. Ethnic stratifications occur in multiethnic societies where a hierarchical arrangement of ethnic groups could emerge as one group establishes itself as a superordinate group, with power to shape the nature of ethnic relations. Within both Black and white races there are different ethnic groups. The politics of difference and racial categorization present their own ambiguities in defining what is race and what is not. Latino people, for instance, are not considered a race in this connection. Latinos are ethnic groups within the Black and white races. All the same, one must not consider Latino folx as exclusively mixed-race people.

Racism and all other "isms" operate on a common premise. Most "isms," including racism, have a control group that exercises power and privilege and a target group that is dominated, subjugated, and marginalized in resource and power distributions. Racism does not only rest on individual action and ignorance. Institutional powers make racism viable. From Main Street to Wall Street, whites control the institutional structures of power. From the village council to the national government, the same group has the marginal propensity to make most policies in America. In 2014, grand juries in Ferguson, Missouri, and Staten Island, New York, that made the decisions not to indict white police officers who killed Black men in both cases were predominantly white. It was only in the case of George Floyd and Derek Chauvin, where the world observed the brutality associated with the knee-lynching on video (live) and the global response via protests, the grand jury had no option but to indict. Given these premises, and by making reference to racism as group prejudice plus institutional power, whites in America control and maintain the dominant structures of power to impose their will upon other groups and therefore benefit from racism. Certainly, not all whites are racists, but every white person implicitly or explicitly participates and benefits from the system that racism fosters. Furthermore, white supremacy harbors the most toxic forms of racism such as the George Floyd knee-lynching in Minnesota, the Rodney King beating in Los Angeles in 1991, the Jasper, Texas, killing of James Byrd, the killing of Michael Brown, Ferguson, Missouri, and the chokehold killing of Eric Garner in 2014 in New York, to name a few.

Peggy McIntosh informs her readers about the historical "white privilege" that white America has over the rest of the general populace. McIntosh is particularly clear about this "unearned" privilege for whites in America (1988a, p. 2). With this privilege and power, whites are in a better position to solve America's racial problems by developing a positive white identity. This is not a crusade to push undue responsibility on white Americans and their image development. However, it is a truism that white Americans constantly fail to acknowledge their race as a group phenomenon, and that whites, as a group, maintain an "unearned privilege" to tackle America's racial problems. Noel Ignatiev, in his attempt to distinguish between being white and whiteness makes this assertion: "Whiteness is nothing but an expression of race privilege" (1994, p. 84). If in this perspective race privilege is written over everything we can possibly think about in our sociopolitical interactions, why is it so difficult for white folx to accept their racial identity and race privilege to help mitigate the issues and problems associated with America's race project? Once whites, including the heteropatriarchal hegemons, have developed a unified, positive group identity, they can effectively shape public policy regarding racial issues.

American presidents who have confronted issues and problems concerning race and racism intentionally, as a policy agenda, have usually transcended the universality of whiteness and spearheaded civil rights and human rights initiatives. However, the American presidency is an institution that has historically been submerged in racism. Most of the Founders were racist, and political scientists have developed models for categorizing the intensity, scope, and a president's racial reasoning, actions, and policy goals to determine whether a president is a racist or not. Content analysis of what presidents have said in private about race and their policy agendas on race could help one determine whether the president was/is a white supremacist, racist, racially neutral, racially ambivalent, and antiracist (Smith, 2010).

Presidents who fit the white supremacist model believed or believe that Black people are innately inferior to whites. American presidents from 1789 to 1869 (Washington, Jefferson, Madison, including Abraham Lincoln (1861–1865), who appeared as both a white supremacist and antiracist after his policy on slavery, had maintained a racist, heteropatriarchal polity. President Woodrow Wilson (1913–1921) and Richard Nixon (1969–1974) were both white supremacist and racists according to this model. President Trump has maintained a racist posture and policy perspectives (2016–2020). When observers characterize former President Donald Trump as one of the racist American presidents in modern history, they examine his verbalizations, behavior, and policy. Among the many are his embracement of birtherism, calling African nation states as "shithole countries," attacking Congress women of color and asking them to go back to where they come from, insulting Chicanos as "rapists," and affirming white supremacists as being on the good side, just to mention a few.

Racially neutral presidents had/have no concrete position on race and racism. President William McKinley (1897–1901) and William Taft (1909–1913) could be categorized as racially neutral. Interestingly, President Obama (2008–2016) at the inception of his presidency could be considered a racially neutral president. Racially ambivalent presidents vary from racially neutral to antiracist. President Ford (1974–1977), Reagan (1981–1989), George H. W. Bush (1993–2000), George W. Bush (2000–2008), and Obama (2008–2016) are examples of presidents who did/could not take a clear position on race and racism. Antiracist presidents exhibit behavior and actions that are aimed at dismantling racism and racial subordination. Included in this category are President Lincoln (who appears twice in the chart because of changes in his utterance and actions), Grant, Truman, Kennedy, Nixon, and Clinton. The Obama presidency somewhat changed by the end of his term in office (2016). Former President Obama is still fighting to keep his legacy on the American race project clean, but the time is not right to perform a premature autopsy on his racial program endeavors after his presidency (see table 5.1).

Table 5.1. A Typology of the American President—Samples of Presidents and Categories for Racial Attitude/Behavior and Policy Action

White supremacist	Racist	Racially neutral	Racially ambivalent	Antiracist
George Washington (1789–1797)	George Washington (1789–1797)			
Thomas Jefferson (1801–1809)	Thomas Jefferson (1801–1809)			Abraham Lincoln (1861–1865)
Abraham Lincoln (1861–1865)		William Taft (1909–1913)	Ronald Reagan (1981–1989)	
			George W. Bush (2001–2009)	William Jefferson Clinton (1993–2001)
		Barack Hussein Obama (2009–2017)	Barack Hussein Obama (2009–2017)	Barack Hussein Obama (2009–2017)
Donald Trump (2017–2021)	Donald Trump (2017–2021)			
				Joseph R. Biden (2021–)

Source: Modified Version of Smith's (2010) typology.

Identity Politics, President Obama, and Heteropatriarchy

The 1790 first United States census developed a racial classification scheme that differentiated race and ethnicity and promoted the idea of colorism. Racial groups were color-coded as white and Black, and yet brown, yellow, and red are colors that have been associated with Latino, Asians, and Native Americans in American history. In the 2010 United States census, Barack Obama's racial identity and racial reasoning were tested. President Obama, even though a mixed-race person, identified with Black because he contended that he was socialized as Black, even when he resided with his white mother and grandparents when his Black father left the United States for Kenya. To the over ten million mixed-race families in the United States at that time, President Obama's failure to acknowledge his mixed-race identity was a blow to their own group political consciousness. The 2020 census indicates that mixed-race Americans are the fasted growing group in the country with over thirty-three million people (Foster-Frau et al., 2021). Did Obama neglect this fastest growing group of Americans as "a big, powerful phenomenon" (Foster-Frau et al., 2021)? Perhaps the important question here is whether Obama's particular attachment to his Black identity inhibited his leadership capabilities and coalition politics. Do issues concerning individual identity captured in terms of identity-based movements and identity politics change in presidential politics? The answers to these questions are indubitably affirmative in most racialized societies. Capitalism by its composition, nature, and dynamics at its inception sustained social ordering based on racial and gender categories and identity markers, supported by resource and role distributions. Capitalism therefore strengthens identity politics and heteropatriarchy.

Nathan Glazer and Patrick Moynihan (1963) argue that strong ethnic identities and identity politics emerge because of the politics of exclusion. When groups are excluded and remain invisible to the superordinate culture, they come together to strengthen their affinity. Feminist theory informs our knowledge on gender identity formation, which is usually a byproduct and condition of oppression (Alcoff, 2006). Nevertheless, Schlesinger (1991), Hollinger (1997), and Fraser (1998b) argue against social identity and how these social identities may create political liability, cause separatism, reification, and contribute to group think, which limits the individual's ability to be creative. However, in a racialized society where whiteness possesses the privilege of defining others, should identity politics matter to those who think particularism subverts the universal?

Some interlocutors of identity politics, such as Schlesinger (1991) and Fraser (1998b) maintain that identity group formation disunites a nation state and that the politics of identity are a plot by intellectuals to mystify the dynamics of race relations and dislodge the uniculturalists agenda of patriotism. Both of these scholars believe that a strong social identity may have political liability. Yet Ashely Jardina argues that "an identity—a psychological, internalized sense of attachment to a group—can provide an important cognitive structure through which individuals navigate and participate in the political and social world" (2019, p. 4). To Jardina, identity politics was an asset to Donald Trump after Obama's racial identity in the presidency rubbed many whites wrongly (p. 4). Could that have been a reason for President Obama to distance himself from identity politics earlier in his presidency? Based on Schlesinger's (1991) and Fraser's (1998b) argument, could there be a reverse social liability if one avoids identity politics, but nevertheless becomes identified with it; they could be identified by groups and institutions with a particular identity that that person attempts to avoid? This discussion is somewhat submerged in binary analysis—Black and white America—even though other minority groups such as Latino are the majority of the minoritized groups. What does that do to the traditional Black/white model for racial analysis?

The Black/White Paradigm and Race Relations under Obama

The discourse over social justice and race has been dominated by the Black/white binary model. Some interlocutors of race and racism advocate examining racism beyond the Black-white paradigm. One can easily say that the Black-white model contains what Elizabeth Martinez calls "the devils of dualism"—the irreducible oppositional elements of good and evil, mind and body, civilized and savage (2010, p. 98). However, the model accurately describes the American psyche in race relations. Scholars, including Elizabeth Martinez (2010), Linda Alcoff (2006), Frank Wu (2002), Richard Delgado (1996), Elaine Kim (1993), maintain the position that race and ethnic issues must stand scrutiny beyond the historical Black-white model, because the United States is much more diverse and discourses over race become color-restrictive if we continue to utilize the Black-white model.

Countering the camp that would like to move away from the Black-white binary model are Mary Frances Berry (1980) and John Hope Franklin (1993), who contend that the Black-white paradigm is meaningful, pragmatic, and historical. African American exceptionalism, crossover experiences, unfinished civil rights issues, and the recent Black Lives Matter movement are testimonies to the indispensability of the Black-white model. Furthermore, the fact remains that the Black-white paradigm cannot be blamed for Asian and Latino immigrant problems and lack of political efficacy despite their numerical preponderance is paramount to using the model for analysis. It is important to note the fight over this paradigm is championed by that Latino and Asian American scholars on

138 | Reframing Diversity and Inclusive Leadership

one side and Black/African Americans on the other. One may think these scholars are competing in an oppression Olympics to determine who is more oppressed. Yet we find a new twist to the Black-white model. More recently, the model has shifted from Black-white to Black, white, and blue, as police (blue) brutality has taken on its own institutional framework in dealing with Blacks and especially Black men—for example, Amadou Diallo, Patrick Dorismond, Ousmane Zongo, Timothy Stansbury, Jr., Sean Bell, Michael Brown, Eric Garner, Freddie Gray, George Floyd, and Ahmaud Arbery, have all suffered from the lethal force of police brutality. However, as the movement for #SayHerName points out, Black cis and trans women such as Sandra Bland, Breonna Taylor, India Kager, Korryn Gaines, Atatiana Jefferson, and Kayla Moore, are also brutalized and murdered by police. Moore's last words were "I can't breathe" (African American Policy Forum, 2020).

As cartoonist Matt Wuerker reminds us, the color of justice in America could only be seen in Black, white, and blue (see fig. 5.2). President Obama has responded differently to each of these racially tragic issues in the United States. When Harvard University professor Henry Louis Gates, Jr., was arrested for disorderly conduct by a white police officer, James Crowley, for attempting to break into his own home, President Obama mentioned on national television that the white police officer has "acted stupidly" and racism is "deeply rooted" in the American society ("Police

Figure 5.2. "The Color of Justice," by Cartoonist Mark Wuerker. Used with permission.

Who Arrested Professor," 2009). A "Beer Summit" brought President Obama, Professor Gates, and Sargent Crowley together to discuss one of the major problems in the United States—racism. Most interlocutors of race were not appreciative about a "Beer Summit" and the photo opportunity (see figure 5.3). The president himself tried to dispel the characterization of the meeting over racial issues as a "Beer Summit." Unfortunately, the imagery was worse—the president toasted the two adversaries, Professor Gates and Sergeant Crowley, with a chilled mug and Bud Light, Professor Gates enjoyed the occasion with Sam Adams Light, and Officer Crowley had his day on the White House lawn with Blue Moon beer (Feller, 2009). Many observers believed that President Obama made light of a serious issue such as racism by conducting a "Beer Summit" with a "light" beer. The imagery and symbolism read into the "summit" were somewhat disturbing for race scholars and those who have suffered racial prejudice and discrimination in the United States. Furthermore, Obama had the opportunity to address the logarithm of race and the algorithm of racism in America, but instead he downplayed the issue of policing Black bodies and systemic racism during his presidency.

In the cases of the killing of Trayvon Martin, Lennon Lacy, Michael Brown, Eric Garner, and George Floyd (killed during the Trump era), the

Figure 5.3. The Beer Summit. Photo by chief official White House photographer Pete Souza, 2009. Used with permission.

analytical framework has moved beyond the Black-white model, and it has developed a newer dimension of "blue" for the police, so far as justice is concerned. As commander in chief of the United States and the chief executive officer of the country, who happened to be a Black man, should Obama have stood aside and watched while many Black men were being killed under his watch for things that are not worth dying for? What happens to law-governed multicultural nations and the oppressed, when white police officers are not charged with a crime by a grand jury for killing a Black man and the two top government officials in the country to deal with the brutality against Black men were also Black men—President Obama and Attorney General Eric Holder (before he resigned from the position)? Even though some observers think race should not become a factor in the cases above and it should be all about justice, it is indubitable that race motivated the white police officers to profile and kill Black men. Race motivated the grand jury not to indict and race demotivated both President Obama and ex-attorney general Eric Holder to be somewhat silent over the critical issues of the killing of Black folx by white police officers and predominantly white grand jurors voting not to indict the officers. In a more recent case, not under the Obama administration, and perhaps because of the reinvigorated Black Lives Matter movement, the white police officer, Derek Chauvin, who knee-lynched George Floyd while the world watched, was convicted and sentenced to 22.5 years in prison. Justice at last?

In all the brutal killings mentioned above by police, President Obama's position and his race tend to asphyxiate him from acting. In commenting about the brutal killing of Michael Brown in Ferguson, Missouri, President Obama's and Eric Holder's inaction, Luke Visconti of DiversityInc asserts, "In essence, you're asking two Black men to urge calm amongst the mainly Black constituency, after that constituency was subjected to extreme, persistent, and racially biased law enforcement. . . . I don't think it's fair to ask President Obama or Attorney General Holder to cover for all the nonsense in Missouri" (2014, p. 1). Yet, in the Eric Garner police choking-death case of another Black man by white police officers in Staten Island, New York, which was recorded by a number of bystanders, President Obama said, "My tradition is not to remark on cases where there may still be an investigation" ("Obama on Garner Decision," 2014). Nevertheless, what is confusing is that the president had been commenting on cases without concrete administrative action. He commented on the Skip Gates issue, Trayvon Martin, Michael Brown, and even on the Eric Garner case. But were these comments just performative rhetoric or window dressing?

In order to continue his carefully calculated politics of race, Obama maintained that he was not the president of Black America, even though deep down, he would like to do something about race and politics. He elected to do what was prudent for a Black president of majority white America. For some Black communities, President Obama was a disappointment to the Black community as far as race, class, and justice are concerned. Michael Eric Dyson, MSNBC network contributor and a professor at Georgetown University, asserts, "President Obama's refusal to wade into the Ferguson situation is a 'low point' for his presidency. . . . Obama 'failed' black people and the nation for trying to come up with an excuse to 'not speak about race'" (2014, p. 1). Furthermore, given President Obama's rhetoric about Black life after devoting $200 million public-private partnership project, My Brother's Keeper to short-circuit the school-to-prison industrial complex pipeline, the Black community did not favor his lecture about the fact that "there are young black men that commit crime. And we want to argue about why that happens because of the poverty they were born into or the lack of opportunity or the school systems that failed them or what have you, but if they commit a crime, then they need to be prosecuted because every community has an interest in public safety" (Henderson, 2014).

After the Ferguson, Missouri, uprising against the jury's verdict of not to indict the white police officer, Obama's racial rhetoric changed to good community policing. However, a reductionist approach of confronting racial problems as just one of the many of America's problems without a concrete position or solution kept President Obama in a racial quagmire.

Obama himself has suffered from white racial imagery and many contemporary racist actions. It is evident from the above discussions that there has been more racial tension since Obama started his presidency for obvious reasons. There had been several racialized attacks on the president and some of these attacks come from elected officials such as Tom Coburn of Oklahoma, who stated that President Obama's legislative "intent is to create dependency because it works for him . . . as an African American Male [who received] tremendous advantage from a lot of these programs" (Krehbiel, 2011). Racist images of the president as a chimpanzee were/ are widespread on the internet and many of these racist slurs have been extended in poor taste against First Lady Michelle Obama. For instance, in Nashville, Tennessee, a hospitality organization depicted the First Lady as someone being married to Cheetah, the chimpanzee, from the racist Tarzan movie (Garrigan, 2011). Heteropatriarchy coupled with misogynoir does not spare even the First Lady of the United States, since the dynamics of heteropatriarchy includes the institution of marriage. Senator David Vitter of Louisiana, appearing on a show on Glenn Beck Radio, disrespectfully admonished President Obama for doing worse for Black people than his slave-owner ancestors. Obama has played into the hands of the white heteropatriarchal hegemons by siding with capital and removing himself from the horrible conditions Blacks faced under his command.

Racial Formation, Obama, and Questioning Immigrant Bodies

In the American polity, race has an agency in almost every sector, including presidential politics and immigration policy-making. Race matters in a heterogeneous, patriarchal society such as the United States. Race has been used as an instrument for acquiring different forms of results, whether positive or negative. Race will continue to secure a permanent domain in both our individual and institutional patterns of interaction. Consequently, denial of racial elements and race as an irrepressible agency in immigration policy-making process could only lead to grave public policy paralysis or policy myopia, with implications not only for recent immigrants, but also for native-born Americans. President Obama campaigned to gain the Latino vote in his run for the presidency and reelection by challenging restrictionist sentiments to propound a fair immigration policy. Yet, under his administration, more undocumented immigrants were deported than his predecessors. Furthermore, in his second term, there was nothing concrete about immigrant bodies and immigration reform.

However, the discourse over the US immigration policy under the Obama presidency, like other "wedge" issues such as unemployment, racism, sexism, classism, and crime, evoked cultural, racial, and socioeconomic disquietudes. Immigration issues of late have been made even more contentious with quasi-political parties and social movements like the Tea Party, and by state legislatures such as Alabama, Arizona, California, and New Mexico. Moreover, after the election of President Obama, the stakes rose even higher, with his calls for "level-headedness" and "fairness" in any discussions regarding immigration. However, the 2012 Republican Party presidential primaries debates were submerged in name-calling over US immigration policy as Mitt Romney accused Newt Gingrich of labeling him as anti-immigrant and Gingrich, former Speaker of the House, lashed back at Romney, former Massachusetts governor, about running an advertisement in which Gingrich called Spanish "the language of the ghetto" ("Latino Leaders Throw Support," 2012). Issues involving undocumented Latino topped the chart in these debates, yet a number of the Republican presidential candidates, including Newt Gingrich, were too busy talking about voluntary deportation or what to do with eleven million undocumented grandmothers who may have lived in the United States all their lives. This may have been an important, but not the most serious issue, and perhaps politicking with the topic by circumventing the most critical issues about US immigration policy was a contributing factor to why America lacks a concrete direction in dealing with immigration crises. Thus, immigration issues have gained a centripetal position in policy debates, because the number of foreign-born, non-European persons has reached the highest level in the United States' history. Furthermore, the characterization of Black and brown people from Latin America, Africa, and Asia as depriving United States citizens of jobs and tainting the American national ethos, culture, and norms is at best unfounded and at worst restrictionists' agenda against new sojourners and racial categories in the United States. The discourse over race, racial identities, and immigrant bodies implicitly or explicitly, runs through every public policy agenda, whether it is on the national or local levels.

Blacks and Brown Bodies, "Deporter-in-Chief" and the American Dream

Early in the history of the United States, Thomas Jefferson and other political leaders of the country recognized the benefit of large-scale immigration. This form of immigration provided cheap labor to build the nation, technology for reconstruction, and trade that provided fuel for the economy at that time. US immigration policy followed an open-door approach, where immigrants were not restricted from entering into this country. "From 1875, the United States Congress instituted measures for excluding certain categories of people. Among these people were prostitutes, criminals, the handicapped [people with disabilities], and people who had the chance of becoming a public charge" (Mitchell, 1992, p. 11).

Many of these immigrant categories still remain on the books today as part of US immigration law.

Many attempts at rethinking immigrant bodies and creating a comprehensive immigration reform before the Obama presidency had failed, and the 2007 major attempt was not an exception. The 2007 immigration reform endeavor included five major essential areas: (1) developing a strategy to increase security increase through the funding and hiring of twenty thousand border patrol officers, new fences, and vehicle barriers at high crossing areas of US borders; (2) creating procedures to expedite the process of permanent residency and citizenship for undocumented aliens through a new "Z-visa" system with a waiting period of eight years before obtaining a "green card"—yet these undocumented people must return to their countries of origin and pay a fine of between $2,000–$5,000 for beating the system and remaining in the United States illegally; (3) a guest-worker program under a new "Y-visa" would have been created to enable immigrants who would like to work and stay in the country for two years to do so legally; (4) the law would have eliminated dependent family members of US citizens, except for spouses and children; (5) the policy would have integrated the DREAM Act, which would have allowed undocumented immigrant children to complete college or render their services to the United States Department of Defense (Farley, 2012, p. 500).

The conservatives were the majority of lawmakers and heteropatriarchs who killed the bill because they argued that the new policy would have granted amnesty to too many illegal immigrants and that would have been a bad signal for those who are attempting to enter the country illegally. Nevertheless, those who favored the bill argued that it was designed to temporarily repatriate undocumented immigrants and pay a fine before their readmission to the United States. All in all, most US citizens did not support the bill, because they did not believe it would curb immigration and improve the state of US economy. Furthermore, the new waves of xenophobia and Islamophobia in the country did not serve the bill favorably. Immigrants, both documented and undocumented, continue to make their way to the United States, nevertheless. Yet, as Belson and Capuzzo (2007) correctly note, the failure of the United States Congress to reach an agreement on a new immigration reform act has given incentives to especially anti-immigrant border states within the Union to generate their own policies which are generally xenophobic in nature.

The Politics of Racial Exclusion, Building Fences and Obama's Executive Instrument

The Obama administration supported the US immigration policy (that started before President Obama took office) to create a physical barrier between the United States and Mexico with a 670-mile concrete wall has generated another philosophical and diversity debate. The Secure Fence Act of 2006, which has been revised a couple of times, does a few things: it separates the two nation states, divides United States public opinion about illegal immigration, and creates a philosophical debate about US perception of our neighbors to the south. As interlocutors of the border policy continue their debate, proponents of the policy have called the project a "fence," while opponents have labeled it a "wall." Whether it is a fence or a wall, the facts remain that the United States has built a structure that divides the US and Mexico. The Associated Press opinion poll conducted in March 2008 indicated that Americans are split right in the middle about the 14-foot-high border fence; 49 percent of those who were polled were in favor and 48 percent were against it. Nevertheless, 55 percent of respondents maintain that the wall will not make a difference in deterring illegal immigrants.

The states of Texas, New Mexico, Arizona, and California are sharing the 670-mile fence with nearly half of it in the state of Arizona. About 370 miles of the immigration wall was aimed at stopping Mexicans who attempt to walk or sneak through the border and other 300 miles was to deter unauthorized vehicles from crossing the US-Mexican border at the fence-states mentioned above (Chertoff, 2008). Proponents of the fence maintain that it is not only deterrence to illegal immigrants, but it will also prevent terrorist from entering the United States through Mexico. Yet James Carafano, a senior defense and counterterrorism analyst, points out that the augment about the wall/fence stopping terrorist from entering the United States through Mexico is far-fetched and unfounded. Carafano asserts, "Fixating myopically on the wall is just bad public policy. . . . Looking for terrorists by standing watch on the border is stupid. It's looking for a needle in a haystack" (Karaim, 2008, p. 750). It is indubitable that the wall's primary goal was to deter undocumented Mexicans in particular and illegal immigrants in general from entering the United States. Opponents continue to argue that the terrorism argument is just a smoke screen in the politics of exclusion. Nevertheless, wall or no wall, the magnetic attraction of the United States to Mexicans will not stop until the quality of life in Mexico and especially the border towns has improved substantially. When people are desperate to improve their quality of life, they will do anything to make it happen. As most Mexican dwellers of the border towns will say, "Show me a 12-foot wall and I will show you a 16-foot ladder." Nonetheless, after Obama's presidency, "build the wall" would become the slogan that energized Donald Trump's campaign for the presidency and his tenure in office.

An interesting but troubling observation is that national statistics reveal that the difference in the pre-fence and post-fence apprehensions at border remained roughly the same, 1.2 million people in both 1992 and 2004 (Kariam, 2011, p. 185). This means we have to do more about dealing with immigrant bodies and immigration policy that would encourage our neighbors across the border to stay home instead of risking their bodies and lives and coming to the United States to be excluded and exploited. Furthermore, with the cost estimate of $47 billion to maintain the fence for the next twenty-five years (Kariam, 2011 p. 200), it makes sense to jointly develop a program for guest-workers and attractive job avenues with the billions mentioned above, which could yield revenue from investment in jobs instead of being mean neighbors with a fence that psychologically screams at the rest of the world, "Keep Out!"

US states, such as Texas, Arizona, New Mexico, challenged President Obama's executive authority and his masculinity by writing their own immigration laws, which created a conflict in the principles of federalism. The state governments were challenging the federal government in its own legislative and executive spheres. The immigration system was broken, and President Obama had to take action with or without the Republicans (the opposition party). Therefore, in 2014, Obama circumvented the US Congress and created an immigration reform via an executive instrument to allow people without documentation who have been in this country for more than five years to file the right immigration papers. President Obama also included streamlining legal immigration to promote a stronger US economy through work authorization for those who have already applied for a green card. Yet most Latino people, especially those whose reside in the border states, believed President Obama to be the "Deporter–in–Chief" instead of maintaining the role of the president as a commander-in-chief. The Congressional Black Caucus and the Progressive Caucus introduced immigration bills in previous years, but the white supremacist hegemons killed these bills. However, President Obama did not demonstrate leadership in immigration policy-making to counteract the maneuvers of the opposition. Was Obama's lack of leadership in immigration a function of his relationship to capital and heteropatriarchy in the business sector? Congressional/executive relations became more acrimonious since the Republican Party gained majority of the seats in the midterm elections of 2014.

Moreover, heteropatriarchal, masculinist, congressional hegemons threatened lawsuits against President Obama for taking immigration reform action via executive order, even though many presidents since George Washington have issued executive orders on different policies. As Spitzer (2014) notes, "This raises the political context of Obama actions on immigration. . . . Obama's action: a) alters policy without going to Congress; b) telegraphs to the Latino community his support, and that of his party; c) spurs Congress to act." Nonetheless, it is not just a political question Obama's action raised; in addition, it raised a racial question, since the majority of those affected by the executive orders would be Latino and Black folx.

Heteropatriarchal Masculinity and the Obama Presidency

Obama's presidency was confronted by actions from heteropatriarchal toxic masculinists, who think that President Obama was soft on many issues ranging from leaving Afghanistan, ending the war in Iraq, failing to lead his party to capture seats in the US Senate and the House of Representative in the 2014 midterm elections, failing to be a unifier for the country as he promised during his campaign, failing the Black community, as Black unemployment was twice that of white unemployment (11.4 percent versus 5.3 percent), and the list continues (Chapman, 2014). How does one associate the emasculation of a president to weak inclusive leadership style, failed policy, or policy myopia? Heteropatriarchal masculinity invokes a system where the rule of male, heterosexual, and elitist biases are prevalent in the nation state. One can easily recognize a system where masculinities are essential components of the prevailing male projects in democratic capitalism (Collinson & Hearn, 1996). In this perspective, whiteness prevails and white men are usually the power holder and the primary actors in the political economy of the state. Furthermore, the political hegemons are not just any white men, but business tycoons, financiers, and political movers and shakers. These are men whose locations in the racialized and gendered sociopolitical institutions are often reconfigured by their ability to utilize their masculinity. Heteropatriarchal masculinity remains a disputed phenomenon in that some scholars think it should be pluralized because they are several ways of being a man and it is beyond the implication of a binary analysis of contrasting masculinity with femininity (Acker, 2006). Furthermore, as we have argued earlier, the institution of marriage supports the hegemony of heteropatriarchy. The institution of marriage is a normative structure for the American presidency and heteropatriarchy. Out of the forty-five individual presidents of the United States and forty-six presidencies, only one was not married—James Buchanan (1857–1861). Of course, he was engaged to be married but his fiancée died before Buchanan became president.

President Obama does not fit the description or characterization of the typical heteropatriarchal masculinist president as did his predecessors and that made it difficult for him to navigate his way through the turbulent policy-making waters in American politics. Race and gender are attributes to the sustenance of a system dominated by heteropatriarchal masculinists. The politics of social programing are devalued in a system that favors the main game of strongmen in racial capitalist empire. Obama's policy of creating a national health-care system, immigration, and race issues became a contest for those who have the traditional socialization to become heteropatriarchal masculinist in the policy arena. He became an outsider to many Republicans who fit the norms and descriptors for heteropatriarchal masculinist. In the 2015 State of the Union Address, President Obama became the first president to ever use the terms lesbians, gays, and bisexuals in such an address. This was historically an unprecedented and unheteropatriarchal statement. The absence of such conversation in the American presidency is supported by institutions of socialization such as churches, workplaces, legislatures, and executive branches spearheaded by heteropatriarchal hegemons, and President Obama broke with tradition to make reference to LGBTQ plus persons in the State of the Union Address. His comments about helping the middle class, minimum wage, paid sick leave, free community college attendance, and equal wages were seen as programs that were not attractive to Republican heteropatriarchal hegemons and are signs of weakness for President Obama. While some chanted after the speech that "Obama was back," some still believed race, immigration, and soft social programs tainted Obama's legacy.

Conclusion

Barack Hussein Obama's presumed failed heteropatriarchal masculinity as president of the United States (POTUS) faces several analytical trajectories. These vectors and indicators include the function of his Blackness, immigrant bodies and characteristics, friend of capitalism, deviation from the normative structural arrangements of the American presidency, the paradigm of justice based on a new model of Black, white, and blue, and whether Obama had the qualities to become the first Black heteropatriarchal president. Nonetheless, during and after his presidency, the racial microaggressions against him have continued among lawmakers and segments of the American general populace because of his race. We are not ready to perform an autopsy on the leadership and legacy of President Obama, because it would be premature to do so. However, in presidential politics, we are made aware that the racialization of Spanish as a language of the ghetto could be different and at the same time similar to the racialization of the former president of the United States's family as chimpanzees or Michelle Obama as a naked slave woman, supporting the heteronormative arrangement of the institution of marriage and invoking a new slavocracy. The level of disrespect for the first president of color in America has been unprecedented. Sue et al. assert, "brief and commonplace daily verbal, behavioral and environmental indignities, whether intentional or unintentional, that communicate hostile, derogatory, or negative racial slights and insults to the target person or group" can be characterized as microaggression (2008, p. 273). The level of disrespect and hatred still prevails even after his presidency (Bailey, 2017). President Obama has suffered microaggression throughout his presidency because of his race and the policy goals he has selected for his legacy. In a system where whiteness and hegemonic masculinity are prevailing projects in a racial capitalism system, Obama lacks the essential quality to maintain the historical connection to heteropatriarchal hegemony and the traditional office of POTUS. Even though he held presidential power, his race tends to devalue that power and the heteropatriarchal establishmentarians continue to maintain their position in a structure in which gender and race are built into the hegemony of "democratic" capitalism and the class process through the long historical socialization process that makes the job of a Black president unattractive and toxic in the United States. Using the American presidency as a microcosm for evaluating race, gender, heteropatriarchy, and the dynamics of immigration policy, the following questions may open avenues for further research: Is the microaggression suffered by President Obama concomitant with the inability of Black people to breathe anywhere on the planet, and has that ever moved any presidential or executive authority who is part of the heteropatriarchal hegemony or not? Would it change the racial narrative if President Obama has the qualities to be characterized as a Black heteropatriarchal masculinist, or would it change the equation if President Obama has been successful in dealing with racial and immigration policy reform?

Immigration crises continue to haunt the American presidency, diversity, and inclusive leadership. In the next chapter, we examine the elements that contributed to this and how his successor, an obsessive, narcissistical, heteropatriarch, former President Trump, whose ascendancy to the presidency was a direct result of what some may say is Obama's failure in leadership and as a traditional POTUS. Trump, challenged by immigration reform also, engaged in a politics of difference, and exclusion in the era of DEI.

Chapter 6

The Politics of Racial Exclusion in the Era of Inclusion

Seeing More Than an African Immigrant in US Immigration Policy

The bosom of America is open to receive not only the Opulent and respectable Stranger, but the oppressed and persecuted of all Nations and Religions; whom we shall welcome to a participation of all our rights and privileges.

—George Washington

Lots of the news from sub-Saharan Africa is about war, famine, poverty or political upheaval. So it's understandable if many Americans think most Africans who immigrate to the United States are poorly educated and desperate. That's the impression that President Trump left with his comments to members of Congress opposing admission of immigrants from "shithole countries" in Africa and elsewhere.

—Ann M. Simmons (2018)

Introduction

Since the inception of the United States from a complex arrangement of different racial and ethnic groups; white Europeans, Africans, indigenous people, Asians, and others sharing a space in this country, US immigration policy has been submerged in a pool of implicit bias and microinvalidation at best, and has been totally racist at worst. In its current form, the United States' immigration policy remains controversial and exclusionary, as the debate over immigrants of color, caravans of Central Americans seeking asylum at the US-Mexican border continues. Furthermore, thousands of unaccompanied children from Central America awaiting immigration hearings, and migrants being flown from some of the southern states of the union to Martha's Vineyard by Florida's Governor DeSantis under President Biden's watch, increase the nature of political circus, without clowns, around US immigration policy. Accessing the viability of the uncompleted wall/fence between the US and Mexico under the Trump administration and the status of African immigrants in general have reached the apogee. Immigration policy discourses are always entrapped in "wedged" politics that educe a historical, racial, ethnic, cultural, socioeconomic, and religio-political sense of disquietude.

The Trump administration, Make America Great Again (MAGA) "patriots," conservative policy-makers, and former President Trump, in particular, did not help the current discourse about US immigration policy. His rhetoric about immigrants of color—including his characterization of Mexicans, Haitians, and Africans as "criminals," "all Haitians have AIDS," Nigerian immigrants should "go back to their huts," and Africans are from "shithole countries"—has left a lasting impression on most immigrants from these countries and immigrants of color (Watkins & Phillip, 2018; Silva, 2018; Dawsey, 2018). What was obvious about the President Trump's statements (which were sometimes denied by the White House) was the fact that the attacks were usually about immigrants of color and his intentions of excluding them from the American polity. Yet the politics of exclusion in US immigration policy is not exceptional with President Trump. This politics of exclusion is contradictory to what the Founding Fathers envisioned, yet it has become part of the American racialized national ethos. Furthermore, in contemporary terms, when racialized reasoning for immigration policy is engulfed in opportunism for political gains and targets minoritized immigrant groups in the United States, linguistic violence, xenophobia, Afrophobia, and Islamophobia become the new order of the day for race relations and the "new" race project.

In the backdrop of the patterns of immigration in the US, we recognize the fluctuation of the numbers of immigrants from different regions of the world, because America's immigration policy is mostly based on the politics of the party in power—Democrats or Republicans. Our observations are also shaped by the regions and cities, where neo-sojourners settle, and the countries of origin immigrants come from for whatever the reason. The recent fluctuations indicate there have been more immigrants and migrants from Latin America and Asia to the United States (from the 1980s to the 2000s) than from Africa (Schaefer, 2019). In the 2000s, the rates of European immigrants legally entering the US has dropped drastically from 8 million immigrants in the 1900s to 2 million in the 2010s, while at the same time the rate of immigrants from Asia and Latin America has jumped from 2.5 million to 10.4 million from the 1950s to the 2010s (p. 99). Furthermore, Asians have topped all immigrants coming to America since 2010. Despite these immigration patterns, the rate of xenophobia and Afrophobia was higher than that of Sinophobia until the recent attacks on Asian Americans since the global pandemic, COVID-19. If Black Africans are not in the equation of this recent immigration fluctuation, why then are they targeted and scapegoated in the discourse over immigration?

In this chapter, we argue that, despite the claim by the United States as the "land of the free," US immigration policy has always included the politics of exclusion in the era of inclusion, and the macroscopic nature and complexity of immigration issues, concomitant with recent increases in African immigrants in the US with degrees in higher education, and their rate of employability have contributed to the labeling and scapegoating of Black Africans in the immigration debate. Furthermore, the neo-racial structural model, neonationalism, patriotism, and heteropatriarchal hegemony, which tend to shape the contemporary policy-making apparatus, have asphyxiated immigration policy initiatives but have increased the conservatives and former President Trump's policy myopia, fueling the attacks on African immigrants. In the balance of this chapter, we will provide some historical trajectories of African migration and immigration to the US, the politics of exclusion in US immigration policy, characteristics and qualities of African immigrants in recent times, failures of US immigration policy goals, reasons for scapegoating Black Africans, agency of the racial despotic state in immigration policy, and the urgency for the demystification of the Black African "self" in the American psyche. Angela Helm (2018) correctly notes, "In light of President Donald Trump's recent 'shithole' remarks, followed by exceptional-immigrant stories on social media to refute them . . . , it should be noted that the facts actually bear out that this nation would be much better off with more black Africans." It on this premise that we interrogate the politics of Black exclusion in the era of inclusion.

Some Historical Trajectories of the African Presence in the United States

Early American history informs readers about the need for large-scale labor to build the US nation state. Political leaders such as Thomas Jefferson recognized the benefits of large-scale migration and this form of immigration and migration provided the basis for cheap labor, technology, and trade that provided the engine bloc for an emerging nation state at that time. African people were one of the first to be brought to the United States by force or threat of force to provide free labor to build the country. America therefore has a long history of Black immigration fueled by the holocaust of enslavement and Maafa (the Transatlantic holocaust), even though free Black immigration from Africa may be seen by some uninformed observers, including former President Trump, as a relatively recent phenomenon.

Historian Charles Joyner (n.d.) carefully describes how Africans were violently brought by force and the threat of force to build America with their blood, sweat, and tears: "Slaves who were herded into the slave ships, into the dark, landed on unsanded plank floors, chained to their neighbors, their right foot shackled to the left foot of the person to their right. Their left foot shackled to the right foot of the person to their left. . . . The slaves had no way of knowing where they were going [or] when, if ever, they would get there. And indeed it was a long trip [to America]."

This ugly historical reality of how Africans were brought to the United States must be understood carefully in order for interlocutors of the immigration debate to comprehend the contemporary dynamics, perceptions, and misperceptions of the African immigrant. We will continue to suffer historical amnesia and myopia if we forget how America "enslaved Africans to work these appropriated lands [from the indigenous people]. . . . The color and cultural differences of Africans typically made them easier for Whites to identify for the purpose of profitable enslavement and sustained control" (Feagin, 2014, pp. 35–38).

The first recorded information about Africans reaching the region of the Americas was in 1519 and the destination was Puerto Rico, which is now a commonwealth and territory of the United States (Eltis, 2001, p. 17). So, even though 1619 has been noted for the African presence in the United States, Africans have been forced to this region from 1519 to 1865, when slavery ended (p. 17). As Nikole Hannah-Jones (2019) mentions in the 1619 Project, "In August 1619, just 12 years after the

English settled Jamestown, Virginia, one year before the Puritans landed at Plymouth Rock . . . the Jamestown colonists bought 20 to 30 enslaved Africans from English pirates." Point Comfort was the first place of contact for Africans in America, and many Africans would follow during the holocaust of enslavement to build the new world. Out of the ten million enslaved Africans that were brought to build the western hemisphere, an estimated 360,000 ended up in the United States (Eltis, 2001, p. 17). So, for observers of African migration and immigration history and the United States' policy toward Africa, the analysis must begin from the inception of the United States, those whose sweat and blood helped to build this country, and the descendants of enslaved people who continue to fight against the injustices associated with the distributive paradigms of justice, the interlocking systems of oppression, and the politics of exclusion.

The Politics of Racial Exclusion: Africans and Immigrants of Color

In American immigration history, the politics of exclusion started around 1875 with prostitutes, criminals, and people with disability who were seen as a potential liability to the nation state (Mitchell, 1992, p. 11). Interestingly, many of these groups of people are still excluded from entering the United States and that part of immigration law currently remains firm. As the quest for diversity and inclusion continues, it is hopeful that people with disability would not be put in the same category as criminals. Racial and ethnic groups gradually became victims of the same law that prevented criminals, prostitutes, and the disabled to enter the United States. The Chinese Exclusion Act of 1882 and the Japanese Exclusion Act of 1907 are notable racially based laws that United States had propounded against people of color (AAC&U, 1994). In 1910, for instance, as Japanese population in the United States reached 72,000, with more than 40,000 residing in California, exclusion of Japanese reached the apogee (Daniels, 1993). While Asians were the main targets during these times for exclusion, Africans in America were treated as nonentities, properties, influenced by the Supreme Court cases of *Dred Scott v. Sanford* (1857) and *Plessy v. Ferguson* (1896), where segregation and exclusion were affirmed in almost every human activity and interaction.

To support the United States' discriminatory actions in immigration issues, the National Origin Act of 1924 was propounded for Eurocentric biases and to discriminate against immigrants of color (AAC&U, 1994).

Eugenics, the Ku Klux Klan, and the Progressive Party at times joined forces to fabricate racial, ethnic, and religious reasoning for targeting minoritized groups. It is interesting to note that during the same time period, while people of European pedigree were highly welcome to the United States, over 400,000 people of color, mostly Mexican Americans were being deported. Eighty-five thousand European refugees (the preferred people) were admitted to the United States (AAC&U, 1994). Again, when immigration policy is based on white supremacy, Afrophobia, and xenophobia, the American Dream becomes meaningless to those who do not have white privilege and preference.

In the 1950s, McCarthyism and the "Red Scare" about communism and communist sympathizers within the United States gave the US fertile ground to germinate lethal and mean-spirited policies such as the 1950 Internal Security Act, that targeted people based on their organizational affiliations for deportation and imprisonment. The United States immigration policy of exclusion and cultural imperialism remained on the books until 1965 when the Immigration and Naturalization Act became effective. This act stood the past discriminatory immigration policy on its head. The Civil Rights Act of 1964, a forerunner for challenging the state of metastability in United States discriminatory practices facilitated the 1965 Immigration and Naturalization Act, which was signed at the base of the Statue of Liberty, with Emma Lazarus's inscription of "Give me your tired, your poor, your huddled masses yearning to breathe free." America, at this time, was ready for introspection, self-examination, and critical consciousness for all the past deplorable actions against people of color in the "land of the free." Yet Langston Hughes, the American poet, playwright, and novelist, in his poem, "Let America Be America Again," would give us the premonition, "There's never been equality for me, Nor freedom in this 'homeland of the free'" (Hughes, 1935). Africans and BIPOC folx are still fighting for freedom that is concomitant with immigration and migration to the "land of the free."

Immigrants in recent times come from countries of color, the developing world, with Mexico, not Africa, sending most people to the United States. The two-thousand-mile border that Mexico shares with the United States makes border patrol difficult and, regardless of a wall, as the Trump administration advocated, Mexicans, people of the Northern Triangle of Central America—Guatemala, El Salvador, and Honduras—and South American countries will continue their influx into the United States. The fiasco in the zero tolerance immigration policy of the Trump administration that separated children of asylum seekers from their parents and detained the children in cages was another of the anti-immigrant and anti-people-of-color stunts pulled by the United States government. It was absurd that former US attorney general, Jeff Sessions, used biblical quotes to support this cruel and unusual punishment against children. Sessions asserts, "I would cite you to the Apostle Paul and his clear and wise command in Romans 13, to obey the laws of the government because God has ordained them for the purpose of order" (Long, 2018).

Whether it is about asylum seekers from Central America or Africa, the United States has a history of separating children of immigrants of color from their parents. Such horrible behavior occurred during the Chinese and Japanese internments in 1882 and 1907; so this policy approach of separating immigrant children from the parents in 2018 and 2019 was not a new thing. As Viet Thanh Nguyen, Pulitzer Prize winner, puts it, the "idea of good and bad immigrant is convenient amnesia. . . . Even at this moment in history, where the xenophobic attitudes that have always been present are reaching another peak, even those who don't like immigrants nevertheless believe in the immigrant idea" (Nguyen, 2018). At the point of writing this chapter in March 2021, over 9,200 unaccompanied children were in custody of the US Department of Health and Human Services (HHS) refugee office per new Biden administration policy (Hesson & Rosenberg, 2021). This number is higher than the US has experienced in many decades. Whether President Biden is a nicer person than President Trump, studies indicate spikes at the US-Mexican border occur after the change in administrations. Nonetheless, African migration patterns have different push-pull factors. So, Central Americans and Africans could be bad immigrants today, and tomorrow other groups can be characterized as immigrants from "shithole countries" in Africa.

Afrophobia and Black African Migration Scare in the United States?

Historical records and interlocutors of world immigration and migration trends would easily inform readers that an estimated ten million African slaves were forced to come to the western hemisphere to build what is now most of the developed world at the expense of the African continent. Capps et al. (2011) maintain that, out of the ten million enslaved Africans, about 360,000 landed in the United States to develop the New

World. It could be argued that even before America's independence from British colonial rule, African slaves were working this "land of the free." Yet, even before Africans reached Puerto Rico in 1519, Ivan Van Sertima (1976) has argued, the Indigenous people of the United States had informed Christopher Columbus of the presence of Black Africans and their secret trade routes to ancient America. Sertima asserts, "On this third voyage he [Columbus] came upon more evidence of the contact between Guinea and the New World. . . . These were the earliest documented traces of the African presence" (1976, p. 14). As one remembers, the superordinate culture in the United States fears to accept the fact that Africans have been in the US even before Columbus, and Sertima was ostracized from the learned society of anthropology for a long time for speaking truth to power about the African presence in the United States before the Founding Fathers settled on this land. Aside from the ancient contact of Africans with the Americas and the holocaust of slavery, one could argue that voluntary large-scale movement of Africans to the United States is a relatively new phenomenon.

The over one million Black African immigrants recently residing in the United States tend to make white America particularly nervous. What is this nervousness all about? Is the fear of blackness the problem or the fear of Black Africans? Very little is said or heard about white Africans or Africans of Arab descent migrating to the United States. Yet the 1.7 million Black Africans who live in the United State make up only 4% of the 43 million immigrant population (Zong & Batalova, 2017). Eighty-three percent of 2.1 million immigrants from Africa are Black Africans, but most of these immigrants are not what President Trump characterized as nincompoops or at worst from "shithole countries." The quality of Black Africans in the United States will be discussed later on in this chapter, but the fact still remains that as Black Africans are becoming one of the fastest growing immigrants in the US, it is easy for them to become scapegoats of a nation-state that is facing tumultuous times in race relations, Afrophobia, xenophobia, Islamophobia, transphobia, racialized sexism, sexualized racism, and misogynoir.

The percentage increase of Black Africans among immigrant populations in America in the 1980s through the 1990s was about 100 percent. In the 2000s this increase has jumped to 200 percent (Capps et al., 2011, p. 1). As the Pew Research Center Fact Tank indicates, the Black African population in the US continues to climb steadily (Anderson, 2017a). Nothing scares white supremacists more than this rapid increase of the

Black population in the United States. The same way the early English American colonists in the seventeenth century paid attention to skin color and biologized-racism of "Christians" for themselves and "Negroes" for Africans and people of African descent, white supremacists are nervous about the Black African immigrant population today.

As Feagin carefully notes, "Powerful Whites have periodically dressed it [population increases and racism] up differently for changing circumstances, although much of its racist reality has remained the same" (2014, p. 81). So, the attack on Black African immigrants is not a new thing. It is in the American psyche, spearheaded by powerful whites and masqueraded by ordinary Americans who are usually the oppressed and disenfranchised. Ordinary white Americans become scapegoats to the politics of exclusion. Many whites who follow the power elite to denounce Black African presence in America are suffering from the politics of convenient amnesia—forgetting American history of enslavement and demographic facts of the nature and statuses of recent Black Africans in the United States. Yet, hypocrisy reaches a high level when some of these critics of Black Africans are the first to talk about the United States as a post-racial and anti-racist society, even as the same people and the birther movement attacked former President Obama as a Kenyan, a Black African, and an African American, who does not have what heteropatriarchal presidents had—whiteness and white privilege.

Black African migration scare and Afrophobia have been on the rise in recent times because of the political ineptitude of elected officials to tackle immigration policy issues and immigration reform. Additionally, the caravan of over 7,000 migrants and asylum seekers from Honduras who attempted to cross the borders of Mexico in order to enter the United States under the Trump administration's watch brought a heightened awareness of waves of undocumented immigrants flooding the borders of the United States, which in turn caused a scare for some of the anti-immigrant public. These asylum-seeking folks pushed the Trump administration to politicize the immigration issue further. Unfortunately, Africans become the soft targets for this anti-immigration rhetoric. When the rhetoric is turned into a high level of threat perception for American citizens who are xenophobic, bigotry and racialized policy agendas ensue.

There is an African proverb that when the rot is at the top, it can affect those at the bottom. President Trump's derogatory characterization of African immigrants and immigrants of color does not remain in the White House. It transcended the inner circles of the president's cabinet and even immigration officers and some agents at the US Homeland Security Office have called Black and Latino workers and immigrants "monkeys." As reported by DiversityInc, "Racist behavior is commonplace and encouraged by management at a Department of Homeland Security investigative office in Virginia. . . . For example, a supervisor called Black and Latino employees "monkeys," and an agent had a racist photo on his cellphone—a Black child in a fried-chicken bucket. Numerous racial incidents are said to have occurred" (DiversityInc., 2018, p. 2.). If white Norwegians were the immigrants of the Trump administration's choice, then it was not surprising for the president of the United States to characterize African countries, Haiti and El Salvador as "shithole countries" and people from those countries must "be taken out" of the United States (p. 2).

Interlocutors of the US immigration debate and policy against influx of Africans and other people of color are entrapped in issues from the Secure Fence Act of 2006 or a physical wall, which will supposedly stop undocumented immigrants from coming across the 670-mile border in the states of Texas, New Mexico, Arizona, and California. However, the 370 miles of the immigration wall was aimed at preventing illegal immigrants from Mexico from entering the United States. Still, as James Carafano, a senior counterterrorism analyst once said, "Fixating, myopically on the wall is just bad policy. . . . Looking for terrorists by standing watch on the border is stupid. It's looking for a needle in a haystack" (Karaim, 2008, p. 750). Fencing the border should not be the concern of most African immigrants. Nonetheless, Africans are still targeted in the United States by Afro-xenophobes and those suffering from Afrophobia.

Characteristics of Black African Immigrants in the United States

The saga of the African immigrant in the United States cannot be based on innuendos and political rhetoric until the recent African presence in America is fully examined. The prevailing narrative about Black Africans in the United States, without knowing the facts and statistical analyses, is that they do not have the same "quality" of characteristics as Norwegians or other Europeans, as President Trump would like to put it (Fox, 2018). Utilizing conventional criteria such as age, levels of education, employability, occupation, and poverty rate, one can determine whether the alarming concerns about African immigrants by sufferers of Afrophobia have any legitimacy.

From 1980 to 2010, the population of Black African immigrants in the United States doubled every year. In 1980 only 130,000 Black African immigrants lived in the United States. By 1990, the number of Black African immigrants has jumped to 364,000—more than a 100 percent increase. The year 2000 saw 881,000, followed by 1.32 million in 2010 and 2.1 million in 2015 (Anderson, 2017a, pp. 1–4). The substantial increases from 1970 (only 80,000 people) to 881,000 in 2000 is triggering the population explosion alarm to conservative white America. This overall increase in the Black African population is what has become a critical concern for many anti-immigrant Americans and especially the interlocutors in the Trump administration; Trump supporters would say, "You seem eager to know what it would be like to be in the driver's seat. You need [to] look no further than Zimbabwe and South Africa. When people like you started driving the bus, the wheels came off. That's what terrifies people like me" (Pitts, 2021). Furthermore, compared to other recent immigrants, especially, Europeans, in the past ten years, Africans register the fastest growing group and growth rate in America. In addition, out of a 4.2 million Black immigrant population in 2016 in the United States, Black Africans made up more than 50 percent of this group (Anderson, 2018, p. 1). The chart below presents a visual nightmare for white supremacists and the anti-Black immigrant movement in recent times.

Where Do Black Africans in the United States Come From?

According to the Pew Research Center, the Black immigrant population has increased five times since 1980. In 2016, there were 4.2 million Black immigrants living in the United States, and this number shows an increase from 816,000 (1980) to the 2016 number (see figure 6.1). The number of Black immigrants residing in the US has increased by 71 percent since 2000 alone (Anderson, 2017a), and this increase is what is scaring Afrophobic native-born Americans. Out of the 4.2 million Black immigrant population in the United States, Black Africans make up more than half of this number (see fig. 6.2). Nigerians make up the majority of Black African

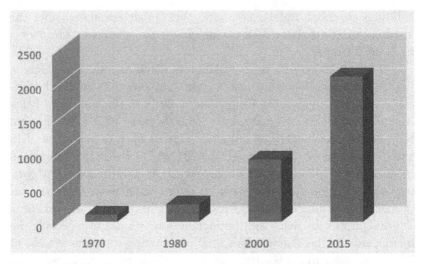

Figure 6.1. Black African Immigrant Population in the United States, 1970–2015. Author provided.

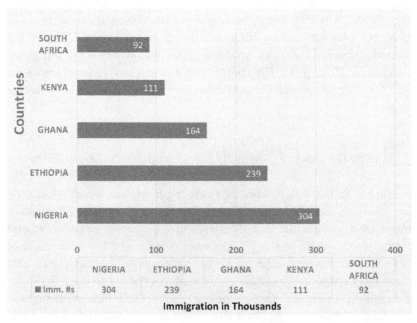

Figure 6.2. Where Do African Immigrants Come From? Author provided.

immigrants, with about 304,000, followed by Ethiopians (239,000), then Ghanaians (164,000), Kenyans, South Africans, and Somalis are included in the top five countries in Black Africa that send immigrants to the United States (Anderson & Lopez, 2018). From 2000 to 2013, Africans from the five top sending-countries (to the United States) increased their efforts in the process by 41 percent, which provided Africa the fastest growth rate in sending immigrants to the US, a whopping 137 percent (Anderson, 2018).

Age, Youthification, and a Threat to American Society?

It is not only the numerical preponderance of Black African immigrant population that is alarming for white supremacists and anti-Black African immigrant advocates, but age and youthification of recent Black Africans have become a rising concern for even native-born Americans, who are experiencing the power of urban redevelopment, increasing young Black African presence in their neighborhoods, the "Forever 21s" or "forever young" and their lifestyles that are somewhat different from native-born youth. This life-style includes the modernization of African cultures with touches of American/Western ones. Black African youth projects, Afrocentric fashion, "going natural" hair style, consumers' of Afro Beat, Hi-Life and Hip-Life music. These youthful Black Africans have the ability to balance leisure with education and work, and at times become agents of the youthification forces that enhance gentrification of high-density urban redevelopment, which is concomitant with youthful population—cycling, small household sizes, residential rental price increases, police racial profiling, and ageism.

Black African immigrant youth population is slightly higher than most immigrant groups in America. These are children under eighteen years old. The general immigrant population stands at 6 percent, according to the US Census Bureau (2015) information. Nonetheless, the ages range between eighteen and sixty-four is the area of concern for many anti-Black immigrant groups. Black African immigrants top the chart with 83 percent. All immigrants of this category (18–64 years) make up 80 percent and native-born United States citizens in this category make up only 60 percent of the population (see fig. 6.3).

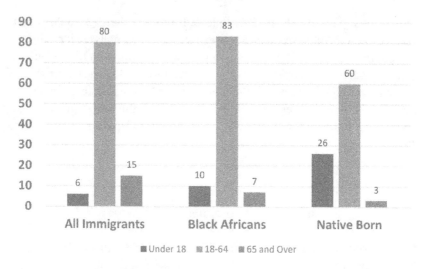

Figure 6.3. Age Distribution: Youth, 2015. Author provided.

Educational Levels and the Apparent Threat to the Beloved Country

An educated populace is one that most nation states would work hard to acquire. The level of the educated populace tends to correspond with productivity, scientific ingenuity, creativity, and artistic endeavors. Furthermore, the type of education one receives is very important to the contribution one makes to the polity. Africans have suffered from miseducation during the colonial and immediate postcolonial eras. Previous educational standards were designed either to fail Africans or to serve the needs of colonial powers. Missionary educational systems provided some basic literacy standard, but it was meant to serve Christian interests and to spread the gospel according to Europeans (Khapoya, 2013). These missionaries brought the Bible and stole the gold and other natural resources from Africans. Religious education facilitated the process of Westernization for the benefit of the colonizer. Western communication patterns and behaviors made it easier for the acculturation process and cultural imperialism of the colonizers to occur through education. Lastly, missionary education attempted to elevate the productivity of the African laborer in order to adequately serve the colonizer—miseducation, diseducation, and dysfunctional semi-educated people roamed the continent for a long time in the postindependence era.

Paradoxically, many Black Africans and their children who left the continent to improve their education returned to the places where they were undereducated or miseducated—Europe, United States, and Canada. In the United States, the diversity visa program or visa lottery, as it is called, requires immigrants to demonstrate that they, at least, have earned a high school diploma or two years of training in an occupation that requires two years or more preparation in that field. Most African immigrants who have taken advantage of the lottery system are well-educated. Nevertheless, the Trump administration questioned the credibility of the visa lottery system by asking whether the diversity visa program was really sending the "worst of the worst" to America.

This is a sociopolitical question concerning Black Africans coming to America. It is a question of whether these immigrants would add to the forces of resistance of Black Americans in a racialized despotic state. The diversity visa program enables 25,000 Africans annually to make the United States their homes (Asante-Muhammad & Gerber, 2018). Even though the Trump administration threatened to end the diversity visa program, the US State Department announced that the program would continue until fiscal year 2021 and 2022. However, countries that have exceeded the quota of 50,000 immigrants in the US in the past five years will not be allowed to participate in the diversity program (Capps et al., 2012, p. 12). This policy therefore affects Nigeria, one of the leading countries in sending immigrants to the US.

In 2012, the United State passed a milestone when more than 30 percent of its adult population held a bachelor's degree or higher (Perez-Pena, 2012). Yet African immigrants in the US maintained a higher educational level than the US native-born citizens. A study of four countries with high immigration levels by the US Census Bureau at this same time period indicated that Nigeria, one of the leading countries of immigrants that President Trump characterized as "40,000 Nigerian visitors would never go back to their huts" in Africa after they see what the US looks like, leads the US in educational attainments (Mark, 2017).

As the bar chart below indicates, while US total population educational attainment levels for bachelor's degrees and above are only 28.5 for adults twenty-five years and older, Nigerian immigrants of the same category are 61.4 (see fig. 6.4). So, the American president might be suffering from

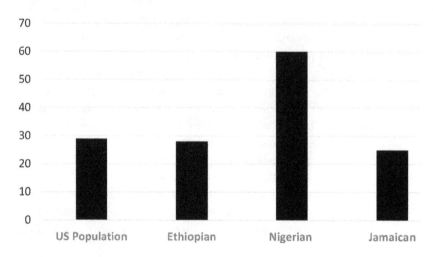

Figure 6.4. Education Levels. Author provided.

a high dosage of convenient amnesia or strategic misinformation. Labor force participation in the same survey indicates that Nigerians, Ethiopians, and Jamaicans engage in the labor market more than United States citizens. In 2015, as the US Census Bureau indicated, more sub-Saharan African immigrants (80 percent) engaged in the job market than the US-born population (60 percent), even though most African immigrants were generally more underpaid than their US counterparts and that picture has not changed much in 2022 (Tamir & Anderson, 2022), as Tamir and Anderson report for the Pew Research Center's analysis on Black immigrants from Africa (2022).

Interrogating the Racial Despotic State and the Politics of Exclusion

Considering the nature of United States' hegemonic politics and the process of democracy, heteropatriarchal hegemons continue to make public policy and immigration policy. Heteropatriarchal hegemony is a polity that is sustained and protected by the elite ruling class and predominantly middle- and upper-class males who define personal, professional, socioeconomic, and political issues based on the normalization of superordination of (white) men and subordination of others by perpetuating the matrix of domination and interlocking systems of oppression (see Harris, 2011; Hoagland and Penelope, 1980; Smith, 2008; Asumah and Nagel, 2014). In entities like the United States, where heteropatriarchy combines forces with the despotic state, immigration policy will continue to exclude immigrants who do not look like the power holders. Omi and Winant note that, in racial state despotism, "first, they define 'American' identity as white: as the negation of racialized 'otherness'—initially African and indigenous, later Latin American and Asian as well. . . . Second, racial despotism organized—albeit sometimes in an incoherent and contradictory fashion—the 'color line' . . . Third, racial despotism consolidated oppositional racial consciousness and organization" (2015, p. 131). It is in this perspective that the US immigration policy is organized and it is in the same context that we write to raise consciousness, resist oppressive immigration policy and the politics of Black Africa's exclusion.

Furthermore, former President Trump's unfortunate and myopic "shithole countries" characterization of Black African countries and an attempt by Trump's former campaign manager, Corey Lewandowski, to defend the president's position of excluding Black Africans from coming to the United States but, then, invite white Norwegians to come to America is presumably based on "the high per capita income of Norway compared to African nations" (Aurdal, 2018). However, ceteris paribus, this argument stands the reasoning behind that statement on its head. Without getting into an oppression Olympics—who has suffered the most because of US immigration policy—it is important to stress the point that Black Africans who take advantage of the diversity visa program to immigrate to the US tend to be better educated and more productive than Norwegians. The *Los Angeles Times* reported, "Research found that of the 1.4 million [sub-Saharan African immigrants] who are 25 and older, 41% have a bachelor's degree, compared with 30% of all immigrants and 32% of U.S.-born population. Of the 19,000 U.S. immigrants from Norway—a country Trump reportedly told lawmakers is a good source of immigrants—38% have college educations" (Simmons, 2018).

Besides, one cannot dispute that fact that overwhelming evidence indicates that Black African immigrants make a substantial, positive contribution to the United States economy by sustaining more than $40.3 billion in purchasing power, contributing more than $10.1 billion in federal taxes and more than $4.7 billion in local and state taxes (Simmons,

2018). Black African immigrants pay their fair share in taxes, they are as productive as any other American citizen, commit less crimes, take their civic duties seriously, and deserve better than the mischaracterization, dehumanization, and microinvalidation that are designed to perpetuate the evils of the racial despotic state and unfortunate rhetoric of the heteropatriarchal hegemons of the United States.

Conclusion

How did the United States reach an anti-Black and anti-brown immigrant nation state status without immigrants? How can the former president of the United States, the frontrunner for a leading party of a country of immigrants and former leader of the free world, claim, without real and concrete evidence, that the country is full and America cannot accept any more Black and brown immigrants, but that statement does not apply to white immigrants? The answers to these questions of the politics of exclusion can be found in the American psyche, the racial despotic state, whiteness as property, social alexithymia, and the white racial frame. Needless to mention, after the 2020 elections, it has become even more frightening to ponder about a divided nation and the rise of hatred. Racial despotism assigns America's identity as white and people of color as "others" who are not welcome to the country. Social alexithymia numbs and separates white hegemonic masculinists' emotions from their demeaning actions, including anti-Black immigration policy. "White racial frame" (Feagin, 2010, p. 25), provides the racial infrastructure for the race project that depends on racial stereotypes (Africa has "shithole countries"), racial narratives (universalized cognition), racialized images (Nigerians live in "huts"), and inclination to discriminatory immigration policy against Black Africans (Feagin, 2010). Without any concrete, recent, well-thought-out immigration policy consensus between US lawmakers and former President Trump, Black African immigrants, even though they are well educated and make great contributions to American society, will continues to suffer the politics of exclusion, omission, and commission. The Trump-style travel ban on Africans to come to the US continues to affect many Africans. A pastor of the Agape House of Worship, in New Jersey, Jide Lawore, sums it up this way: "We feel we don't belong in this list. . . . We have made a lot of positive contributions to the United States. We are educated, a lot of us are professional people in the United States, we are shocked by it"

(Alvarado & Gomez, 2020). African immigrants are also not monolithic. Immigrants come from fifty-four countries (excluding Western Sahara and Somaliland) of the African continent, and there are significant differences in education, for instance, between Nigerian (60.5 percent with bachelor or higher) and Somalis (with only 15 percent) (Chikanda & Morris, 2021). Many African leaders are relieved that the Biden administration will take another and better look at African immigrants in the US. However, the current situation at the Mexican border has preoccupied the Biden-Harris leadership and immigration policy agenda. It will take a cultural and racial paradigm shift, reeducation of our current leaders and the less-informed populace on the African immigration narrative to begin unlearning and relearning the nature and locus of the Black African immigrant's position in the American polity.

In the next chapter, we move from the politics of exclusion, immigrant wars, and leadership failures of the Trump administration to mass racial participation, agitation, the struggle against anti-Black racism, and why Black lives must matter to the American polity and the world.

Chapter 7

Black Lives Matter, All Lives Matter?

Black folx live in a three-dimensional world—one with the Black self, then with the Black "other" (from other spaces, places, and regions), and ultimately with the life that has to be maneuvered around the irrepressible forces of whiteness (not just in the US but all over the world). The life that is concomitant with Blackness can always be misunderstood by those who do not share the lived experiences of Black folx, those who continuously disregard the irrefutable history of the holocaust of enslavement, colonialism, capitalism, Jim Crow, the interlocking systems of oppression, matrices of domination, the current forms of institutional and systemic racism, and those who assign universality to all things intangible, such as life, but control the pure existence of Blackness. When universality (all lives) is staged to deprive the particularity (Black lives) of its true value to privilege whiteness, we miss the opportunity to solve critical racial and ethnic problems because of the easy and convenient generalization that all lives are the same and all lives matter. Nevertheless, it does not take quantum physics to explain to interlocutors of the US race project that living while Black is an extreme sport. "To be black in America is to exist in a ceaseless state of absurdity; a perpetual surreality that twists and contorts and transmutes equilibrium and homeostasis the way an extended stay in space alters human DNA" (Young, 2019, p. 9). That is Black life, and one cannot put it any better than how Young describes it in his book *What Doesn't Kill You Makes You Blacker*. The superordination of the white racial frame tames Black lives and reconditions the generation of wealth and power that strengthen whiteness vis-à-vis Black lives.

In this chapter, we discuss antiracist activism in the streets and on college campuses during the times of the Black Lives Matter movement. We also show how pedagogical and epistemological efforts fall short when faculty use a white racial frame even when they teach about social justice and diversity. In this context, we mention Todd Pittinsky's positive psychology neologism of "allophilia," that is, developing a friendship, liking, or love with those who are different from us. We note that this kind of love is not agape love, but it includes the sense of white goodness, niceness, and the friendship that constantly echoes, "I am too nice to be a racist." Yet allophilia for many reasons sustains systemic racism. Are college intergroup dialogues the answer to raise awareness about anti-Black racism? We cannot dismiss how critical whiteness studies (CWS) and Fanonian theory of safety caution us about college intergroup dialogue. Although intergroup dialogues can be valuable in many cases if conducted by experienced and well-trained professionals, they can nonetheless become an avenue for linguistic violence against people of color (Leonardo & Porter, 2010). We contrast Pittinsky's approach with Frantz Fanon, who focuses on "disalienation of the Black man." Fanon gives a foundational account of white reasoning for anti-Black racism. He analyses how Black bodies are organized to survive a social world that is designed for white enterprises. Black feminist Monique Morris investigates school policies (e.g., zero tolerance) for creating very different and inequitable pathways to success for racialized children. In the US context, an abridged version of diversity and equity still leaves Black and brown children behind, as many studies of the nefarious processes of criminalization through heightened surveillance and disparate punishment have showcased. Importantly, we highlight the impetus for change emanating from Black Student Unions who want more than symbolic and representational diversity in the new era of Black Lives Matter.

Which Is It? Black Lives or All Lives?

The police murder of Michael Brown, an unarmed Black teenager, ushered in a sustained movement around a single dignitarian rallying cry of *Black Lives Matter!* in 2014. Even President Obama responded approvingly, and the Justice Department engaged in consent decrees with several cities' police departments (which were rescinded under the Trump administration). In Ferguson, Missouri, and elsewhere, the police response to protests was fierce, as they acquired and used the federal government's military surplus and other martial equipment (tanks, riot gear, etc.). The police created a new mythological narrative: "The Ferguson effect." This narrative suggests that violent assaults, presumably by a Black militant populace, would dramatically increase, especially against (nonviolent) police. Their counter rallying cry was predictable: "Blue Lives Matter"—a war cry for proponents of predatory policing and police brutality. In New York City, police engaged in a massive work slowdown (calling in sick, working to rule, and using police discretion on nuisance "crimes"), in order to show the mayor and the public that without them, violent crime would dramatically increase. In fact, their protest action actually decreased the violent crime rate (Khan, 2017).

In 2020, during the Trump presidency, the major backlash motto became "All Lives Matter," which, for all intents and purposes, is nothing other than creating a reductionist approach and a racist response to the Movement for Black Lives. Not only do such white people display their outrage by defacing street murals, but also maiming and even killing protesters, using cars and trucks as new weapons to assault their nonviolent opponents. In fact, diversity educators and those steeped in critical appreciation of a revisionist American history already know that *White Lives Matter Most and Other "Little" White Lies* (Meyer, 2019). Matt Meyer connects the two "movements" in the following way: "From the days of Jim Crow lynching to the police-Klan realities of 'blue cap by day, white hood by night,' America has always meant White Lives Matter Most" (2019, p. 10). The benefit of disguising white supremacy in colorblindness is that such an "all lives" movement will not see the wrath of the Justice Department as being labeled a "terrorist organization," which certainly has, by contrast, befallen the proponents and activists of Black liberation. These freedom fighters would subsequently face the new repressive versions of FBI's COINTEL (counterintelligence) surveillance program that was once used to destroy the Black Panther Party.

At the time of George Floyd's murder by Minneapolis police in May 2020, another video went viral, with over forty million views by July 2020. In Central Park, New York City, Christian Cooper, a life-long bird-watcher, recorded his encounter with a stranger, an irate white woman, Amy Cooper. His sister posted it on Twitter. What the video displayed was the raw power of weaponizing white female fragility: she intentionally used her status and identity—her whiteness coupled with femininity—while placing a 911 distress call, telling them that she is threatened by a Black man in the park. The dispute was about leashing her dog, which she refused to do, thus violating park policy. The frontal anger that she articulated to Mr. Cooper, nothing other than assaultive speech, was enacted with coy anguish when she addressed the operator who received the 911 call. Ms. Cooper (no relations to Christian Cooper) performed the call with such precision that it looked and felt like she had rehearsed such shrewd demonization and character assassination of other Black folks before this recorded event. Does Ms. Cooper's behavior fit the profile of a Central Park Karen, a psychological personality profile with low-level self-esteem and high-level narcissism? Alternatively, we surmise that she grew up with mediated images of Black men and boys cast as "superpredators," especially always already being a threat to white femininity.

These historical trends are repetitious, and they serve as reminders to what a Central Park Karen could do to a Black man: Emmett Till's gruesome murder for whistling at a white woman in Mississippi and the destruction of Rosewood, Florida, by a lynch mob who "revenged" the lies of another white woman—a Central Park Karen—by burning down an entire Black city. From the birth of blackface minstrel shows in the 1820s to *Birth of a Nation*, a film celebrating the KKK and the most watched film of its time, the threat emanating from Black promiscuous masculinity crossing racial borders, endangering the life of white ladies, is securely emblazed in the American public's collective unconsciousness or consciousness. It just felt *natural* to Amy Cooper (Central Park Karen), an upper-class white woman, to use threatening speech, decorated with linguistic violence. If the lynch mobs of the past are any indication, the specter of the myth of the dangerous Black male rapist is replicated in the police, who perform as guarantors of security of white female, fragile bodies.

Amy Cooper's entitlement was on full display in performing tearful vulnerability to the 911 operator while using threatening, authoritative speech toward her target, Mr. Cooper. Such duplicitous performance seemed to be drawn from the playbook of "Ms. Ann," the white imperial lady of the plantation. Today's "Ms. Ann" has been dubbed "Karen," generally, referring to white women who use whiteness as property and their white status to put people of color out of contested spaces and "in their place." Liberal feminists have called out this meme/name for being sexist and ageist, because it typically refers to women over 40 years old (such as Amy Cooper). The call-out culture of social media is certainly distressing and often destroys a person's reputation, which is also the case for Amy Cooper. However, the response of tit-for-tat, "I call you out for your racism, which now makes me a sexist" is highly problematic. Such knee-jerk reaction smothers the epistemological testimonial of Christian Cooper altogether, effectively silencing his claim that Amy Cooper's escalating aggression needed to be videotaped (cf. Dotson, 2011). Such critique of the meme "Karen" forgets conveniently that enslaved people created their own defiant language and secret codes, to ridicule the behavior of the oppressor and to warn each other about "Ms. Ann's" life-threatening actions.

Astonishingly, Mr. Cooper continued to videotape her antics, remaining calm, poised, and collected, even encouraging her repeatedly to call the police. Such stoicism is all the more remarkable because, as a Black man, he can never forget Black American history and that police contact might present a clear and present danger to him. He used his polite authoritative speech to remind her of her own transgression, since park signs clearly state that her pet has to be leashed at all times.

Amy Cooper worked (she was fired after this encounter went viral) in an investment firm in a superdiverse metropolitan city where somebody in her position of leadership clearly must see Black men freeze-framed to subservient roles, as transit workers, janitors in her corporate office—folks who are invisible to her and are supposed to follow her orders. If they do not perform to her expectations, she knows to turn this information to the (white) authorities who execute swift justice. Thus, her entitlement to anonymous white public space, including the bird sanctuary of Central Park, is not only white supremacist, but also smacks of colonialism, because she gets to rearrange the "law" and "orders" it as she sees fit. She is not particularly concerned that Mr. Cooper starts recording her racist antics after denying his request. Dog owners similar to Amy Cooper seem to have had a reputation to *unleash* their dog and confront strangers who rebuke them. Such is the enormity of entitlement weighing down the soul of Black folks, *pace* Du Bois. In her own mind, she expresses justifiable rage, because she is humiliated through a verbal leashing by a queer Black man. She knows to stand her ground and reminded by American history that whiteness is property (cf. Harris, 1993) by fighting back, using the ghosted script of Jim Crow and chattel slavery: a Black man has to be put back in his place in contested spaces, when he threatens to challenge the white supremacist order of things. She lets him know that she will tell the cops that a Black man is threatening her and her dog—a videotaped statement, no less. In her world, Black men have no position of authority, do not use command language (even if that means gently pointing out the law). He has no reason to share her space as Harris expatiates, "The law has accorded 'holders' of whiteness the same privileges and benefits accorded holders of other types of property" (1993, p. 1731). In addition, in her perceived arrogance, he cannot challenge her power of interpreting the law as she sees fit. Living in the Trump era where "law and order" has renewed cache, the regime quells white anxiety and reassures the Amy Coopers: America can be *made white again*. Public space is clearly white space (again) and Black men always already have criminal intent.

Having the naturalized right (or entitlement) to make fraudulent distress calls by using her white femininity as a weapon is certainly part of that upper-class, colonial, white supremacist playbook. Chris Cooper, to date, refuses to make counter charges. He could sue her for causing him emotional distress through her threatening speech and invading his personal space. He is heard to plead "Step away from me!" when she charges towards him impersonating the white shining knight of public order, not looking particularly afraid. Her call is part of that aggressive demeanor, because she tells the cops that a Black man is a clear and present danger to her own life. By contrast, Mr. Cooper maintains his stoic, peaceful demeanor and notes that she has been punished enough. He even approves of her apology. He is not interested in revenge. In her apology, she justifies her behavior noting that she "misread" his verbal promise that she would not like what he would do next (Cooper, 2020). Mr. Cooper stated that it referred to his act of offering treats to the dog to entice the dog away from the vegetation that serves ground-nesting birds. What gets lost in her apology is that he asks her to maintain a social distance and that he encouraged her to call the cops. And, in the end, Mr. Cooper even thanked her for finally leashing the dog and went on his way. This is not what threatening demeanor looks like, subjectively or objectively. At this point, surely, it would have been her civic duty to call 911 again and tell them not to send police.

When his video of the traumatic encounter went viral, we also note the intersection of animal rights activism with antiracist protest. First, the animal shelter, which gave Ms. Cooper the dog, demanded the return of the dog, since she was seen yanking on the collar, when she finally leashed the animal. (However, they returned the dog to her after seeing no visible animal abuse.) Secondly, she lost her corporate job. Viewers may watch different truths and narratives being played out, depending on one's implicit bias, ideological framework, and propensity for empathy. Some may only have an eye for the dog in distress and voice outrage about Amy Cooper's leashing behavior. Others may focus on white female victimhood. If historical traumatic events are any indication, it is the favorite rallying ground for terrorist behavior of the white nationalist brotherhood, acting in civilian clothes, or, as Matt Meyer argues, in code blue, because it gives them a raison d'être under the mantle of protector. They will also rebuke Christian Cooper for threatening the dog with treats; after all, kindly strangers could poison animals. This time, now, filmed by the victimized person himself, many saw an assault on Black male dignity. Unleashed dogs or leashed dogs held by white slave patrols or modern-day cops also have been used to catch runaway folks and to terrorize and bite protesters on the Edmund Pettus Bridge, during the Selma-Montgomery marches in 1965 or elsewhere during the civil rights movement. Given that this incident played out in Central Park, Amy Cooper also drew on the weaponized narrative that Donald Trump used effectively, when he called for the death penalty of five framed Black teenagers for the crime of raping and almost killing a white female upper class jogger.

Thirty years ago, Trump instigated this witch-hunt, taking out advertisements in all New York newspapers calling for the death penalty. Even today, some of the white public is unconvinced that they are innocent. Never mind that a serial rapist confessed to committing the crime. In the celebrated film series *When They See Us*, renowned director Ava DuVernay (2019) portrays the racist witch-hunt, the trial, and the men who grew into adulthood spending over a decade behind bars, showcasing the humanity of each of the five men. After the traumatic encounter with Amy Cooper, ABC News filmed bird-watcher Christian Cooper at his favorite spots in Central Park and gave a sympathetic portrayal of his passion for birds, his great skill of identifying different calls, and being a professional comic writer, who is concerned about the lack of LGBTQ themes in the genre and invents queer characters ("After Racist Encounter," 2020).

The Scottsboro case, Emmett Till, the Central Park Five, and so many lynching victims of white supremacist triumphalism still ghost the American imagination—the familiar master narrative of Black aggressor(s) and white female victims. Marlon Riggs's documentary *Ethnic Notions: Black People in White Minds* (1985) powerfully narrated the way art imitates life, which in turn imitates art. The criminalization of Black bodies *and* white impunity is at the heart of such a traumatic/traumatizing script. Furthermore, Joe Feagin's white racial frame model in *Racist America* (2018) indubitably exposes Americans to the dangers of white manipulation and superordination through stereotypes that become the national narrative, and fabricated stories that are turned into public policy agendas. Is it not epiphenomenal that a whitewashed narrative could become a public policy that condemns a total race into the dungeons of disenfranchisement and inhumanity?

For the sake of justice, New York's district attorney Cyrus Vance stepped in and charged Amy Cooper with placing a false report, the first ever of its kind to be made against a white person in the US (Ransom, 2020). How does Black Lives Matter play out in historically white academic spaces? While the last wave of BLM, beginning in 2015, brought about the institutionalization of chief diversity and inclusion officers (CDIO) and revisiting the weight of history upon those institutions who benefited directly from enslavement of people of African descent, what might be the meaning of this new intensified wave of multiracial protests of racist police brutality, immigration policies, and of racist ramifications of a pandemic for academic leadership? When do truly *all* lives matter in the ivory tower? The following section highlights a narrative, perhaps the master narrative of white academe, that does not discuss racial identity and racism at all. We suggest it performs the illusion of inclusion.

Single Stories and Individualized Lenses

In the spring of 2019, a keynote speaker of a literacy conference shares messianic messages of hope and endless opportunities for students' own self-improvement, always under the guidance of a supportive teacher. For a moment, Hesiod's image of Pandora's jar (mistranslated as a box) comes to mind; when its lid was opened, misery, diseases, and other ills spread onto humans—only hope (*elpis*) remained in the jar. It is the only positive good remaining to humans, making sense of their dreadful condition. The cisgender white speaker and seasoned English teacher even shares her own resources for generating hopeful moments in her life—the PowerPoint presentation is filled with photos of her supportive nuclear family and their joining the speaker at her own graduation ceremonies.

As our friend, a faculty of color who teaches US history as multicultural history, points out, not once did the speaker mention her and her family's whiteness, economic privileges, or social and cultural capital, which surely delineate the straight pathway of merit and success. However, the speaker is fond of positive psychology and mentions allophilia (https://www.allophilia.org), which, as we have mentioned in the preface of this book and preview of this chapter, is a term coined by Todd Pittinsky, signifying the "Other" of prejudice, that is, developing a friendship, liking, or love with those who are different from us. It is meaningful in intergroup dialogues, and websites show the ubiquitous depiction of a Muslim boy embracing a Jewish boy or a white girl holding hands with a black girl on a playground. The speaker dwelled more on allophilia than on empathy, which she downgraded to a *negative* effect, because we feel bad when sorrowful feelings inflict others we care about. Does this mean that empathy creates a distancing effect that is overcome by allophilia? Yet a white person might have complex reasons for developing a liking for somebody who is a person of color; one such problematic reason might be using the person as a "trophy." This purpose cannot be considered as allophilia, because the white person seeking the "trophy" has an ulterior motive and an exploitative intention.

The lecture is surely useful for students aspiring to be well-meaning teachers and current teachers. It packages a good deal of positive reinforcement for those who have endured adverse childhood experiences and portray a "can do" attitude and optimistic/heroic attitude that Americans are famous for. This optimism and yearning for upward mobility as exemplified in the script of the American Dream draws self-chosen immigrants to join US academia. In our case, it inspired us, as immigrants, to attain terminal degrees and to join the American "teaching machine," to borrow from literary critic Gayatri Spivak, who is an immigrant woman of color outsider teaching in the ivory tower (Spivak, 1993).

However, this white solipsistic ideology conveys a portrait of American apartheid in so far as it *disappears* effortlessly structural and systemic barriers such as residential and educational segregation, natal alienation, or a foster-care-to-schooling-to-prison pipeline through positive psychology memes. Faculty who are analytically invested in critical and liberatory education find themselves despairing at white student teacher candidates who offer lesson plans about slavery simulation. These are well-meaning students, who have been taught by their (white) kindergarten to twelfth-grade teachers that the past is dead and chattel slavery, its legacy, and imprint on daily life does not haunt the US republic anymore. How is anti-oppression being taught? When do we frankly talk about racist oppression and other interlocking systems of oppression and matrices of domination, including the violence of poverty, ableism, ageism, lookism, colorism, and so on? How do we diversify the curriculum without retraumatizing students at all levels with recurring misrepresentations and oppressive classroom exercises? Do schools of education curricula invest in a candid self-reflection? At what point does one address issues pertaining to oppression in the classroom, power relations, and systemic domination-subordination? At what point do safe spaces in the classroom become courageous and brave spaces? These far-reaching questions do not suggest that we can afford to dispense with tackling psychological issues in an individualized way. Frantz Fanon, famously, wrote a book about the disalienation of the man of color (*Black Skin, White Masks*), and, recently, Black psychologist Joy DeGruy Leary (2017) has focused her attention on the *Post Traumatic Slave Syndrome* disorder and has developed community-oriented guides to assists young Black men in promoting wellness and respect.

Furthermore, it became clear that the keynote lecturer used social justice in a shorthand form for individualized attention to a particular student's needs. This can be validated as an equity approach to pedagogy and certainly we have learned about respectful evaluation of students' writing and focusing on a strength-based way. Nevertheless, the abridged social justice–individualized method provided by the lecturer does not and cannot stand in for liberatory education, as illustrated in bell hook's *Teaching to Transgress: Education as the Practice of Freedom* (1994). In these turbulent times of searching for righteousness, arguably, social justice and inclusive education have become empty phrases for a color-blind approach to pedagogy that does not take into account the deep-seated systemic and historical inequities of our educational system. Black children are disciplined more harshly than other children of color and whites from pre-K through high school, making the schooling experience a preparatory ground for "reform schools" and ultimately adult prisons. Black girls and gender nonconforming Black children, as well as Black children with disabilities, do not earn empathy "points" and face higher levels of sanctions, including suspensions under "zero tolerance" rules, as Monique Morris shows in her timely book *Pushout: The Criminalization of Black Girls* (2016). Morris's study shows that Black girls get school suspensions for trivial matters, including forgetting to wear a belt (thus, not adhering to the strict dress code), for asking too many questions, for questioning the teacher's standard of fairness, for protesting racist double standards (e.g., witnessing leniency regarding white girls' behavior). Morris concludes with the following warning: "The hyperpunitive climate of many educational environments, particularly those that have adopted zero tolerance policies, is antithetical to the cultural norms associated with Black feminine expression (e.g., the use of verbal and nonverbal cues to process information, or the practice of speaking up in the face of adversity)" (p. 188). Black girls want educational environments that do not look like prisons (pp. 192–193).

How then do we keep hope alive given this caldron of systemic, intertwined oppressions, which at its core feeds anti-Black racism? How then can we keep hope alive if hope keeps dying in every major indicator for Black America; poverty, unemployment, incarceration, housing, health, education, income, policing, and quality of life? What instead is called for is a culturally competent approach that is infused with a healing-informed caring perspective and sound restorative justice practices. In that way, cultural competency is mobilized for cultural efficacy. In cultural competency, we are more interested in one's ability to perform properly in a diverse space or entity. This is a space that is somewhat different from the one of the performer. Performance in this aspect must be inclusive of attitudes, behaviors, and institutional policies. So, cultural competence encompasses both individual and institutional consciousness, as Nieto (1992) avows. The individual and institution have to transcend their original circles of tolerance, acceptance, and respect, and reach new interlocking circles of self-assessment, affirmation, solidarity, and productive critique. Valuing diversity and inclusion, adaptation, institutional knowledge base, and a movement from diversity window-dressing to action, equity, and inclusion are what strengthen the individuals and the institutions. Cultural competence is indispensable to inclusive excellence, and it is not a luxury.

The Power and Efficacy of Student-Led Protests

Since the advent of the national Movement for Black Lives, Black student leaders have been adamant about bringing lasting changes to historically white institutions: diversify the student and faculty body, invest in a broad, interdisciplinary antiracist curriculum, and create mandatory trainings for all faculty/staff/administration, to name a few. Black Student Union leaders on college campuses have donated an enormous amount of time to meetings with administrators and with the campus community on their demands. In fact, as Abyssinia Lissanu, alumna of Princeton University, complains, students have been "committeed to death" without seeing tangible commitments to structural change (Mull, 2020). The new student-led movements are increasingly tired of symbolic or, as Lissanu notes, "cosmetic" change. Only one of the five demands of a coalition of student of color organizations was finally acknowledged by the Princeton leadership: dropping Woodrow Wilson's name from the renowned policy school in July 2020. We note that this concession is actually very significant, since the previous student generation did not succeed in taking down the name of a president who is the epitome of anti-Black racism in public administration and public policy. Wilsonian policy from 1913 to 1921 was the most effective tool for removing Blacks and other people of color, especially, from top-level government positions.

Even though he is remembered for winning the Nobel Prize for Peace, strengthening the League of Nations, and supporting women's right to vote, there was more evidence that he was a racist and a white supremacist. Should his name continue to haunt students of color at Princeton? This time in the wake of national and global Black Lives Matter protests, there was no need for a university committee to study the name change. It was done in the urgency of the moment—to placate a student movement that wanted much more: reparations for descendants of enslaved people who worked for Princeton's presidents and board of trustee members, divesting from funds that support the prison-industrial complex, adopting antiracist mandatory courses in the policy school, and more (Black Justice League, 2020). In addition, the Princeton students have learned to adapt in the times of the American chief diversity and inclusion officer: they will no longer be satisfied with symbolism, representational diversity, or cultural competence trainings. The new student movement excels in reviewing the archives and keeping institutional memory alive; in making big connections to other social movements such as prisoners' justice causes and comparing notes with students at Ivy League schools, such as Harvard University and other Hidden Ivy League schools, such as Georgetown, where descendants of enslaved people who were sold off by Jesuit presidents will have a right to free education (Swarns, 2019).

With the renewed vibrancy of a Black liberation movement, which is dispersed and does not have hierarchical structures or figureheads, change is coming with incredible speed. Washington and Lee University is contemplating a name change, again, a very significant (and costly) act, given that the confederate legacy is being subjected to scrutiny like never before. General Lee, the hero for the Confederate cause, even though he lost the war against the Union forces, is subjected to cancel culture, statutes, named streets, universities, and all. However, there may come a time when President Washington will also be scrutinized more, for his nickname among American Indians is "town destroyer," referring to his use of biological weapons and wholesale destruction of Indian life in the territories of the Iroquois Confederacy. We note heightened interest in rethinking monochromatic literature for all ages and genres, beginning with antiracism guidebooks—*How to Be an Antiracist* (Kendi, 2019) and *White Fragility: Why It's So Hard for White People to Talk about Racism* (DiAngelo, 2018)—and history books—*Lies My Teacher Told Me: Everything Your American History Textbook Got Wrong* (Loewen, 2007) and *A People's History of the United States* (Zinn, 1980).

Chicanos and Asian Americans are demanding inclusion in the school curriculum. These protest movements will eventually shake up the textbook industry, which has whitewashed American history for all too long. Most recently, history textbooks distributed in Texas gave the master narrative that "workers" were brought from Africa. A Black mother who publicly protested first noted this disappearing act of the brutality of the transatlantic slave trade and the meaning of chattel slavery for people of African descent. When she reached a national audience, the textbooks were recalled (Fernandez & Hauser, 2015). However, we must be prepared for backlash culture to reimpose the hegemonic ideology. It has already happened in Arizona, when a thriving Chicano studies curriculum was recalled from schools, even though it was linked to better outcomes and graduation rates for Chicano students. It was just not patriotic enough. Perhaps parents who are now experts in homeschooling thanks to the COVID-19 pandemic might just stay engaged enough to demand the diversity of the home experience be included in the school curriculum. When anti-imperialist narratives such as Roxanne Dunbar-Ortiz's *An Indigenous People's History of the United States* (2014) will be included, there will truly be progress and divergence from the normative triumphalist and exceptional history-telling that (white) Americans are so used to hearing.

Prosecuting Hate Speech?
The Use of Slavery Terms in the Academy

It is probably fair to say that college administrators, especially deans of students and residential life directors, fear the fall semester the most, since it brings first-year students to campus and residence halls and all their deep-seated prejudices and phobias. Due to residential segregation, dubbed "American apartheid" (Massey & Denton, 1993), many white students have never shared public spaces with people of color, especially in classrooms. Black students and their parents will be treated to Afrophobia, because some white students may request another roommate who looks just like them.

At our institution, issues of alienation and rage came to a head through a particularly heinous incident of racist hate speech. In spring 2019, the Black Student Union (BSU) at SUNY Cortland organized several town hall meetings protesting the "plantation" conditions faced by food service *student* workers of color and systemic racism in classrooms. They invited the campus to attend a meeting on the food service provider Auxiliary Service Corporation (ASC). The Student Government Association refused to send the email invitation on campus, so the Black Student Union sought the assistance of the Africana Studies Department to disseminate the invitation all over campus to improve attendance. The email invitation designed by the students but sent on campus by the department was provocative: "ASC: Auxiliary Slave Corporation?" Black studies/Africana studies departments in the United States have always provided agency for Black students to educational and political movements on campuses of American colleges and universities and this case was not different from those of University of California at Los Angeles (UCLA), Yale University, San Francisco State University, or Cornell University. On the day of the meeting, senior food service administrators were summarily fired. One of the BSU demands concerned organizing a student workers union, since student workers were the only nonunionized group on campus.

It was a politically charged period, as it occurred in the wake of several incidents of racist graffiti found in classrooms. At a previous town hall meeting during Black History Month, 2019, the BSU had offered a list of ten demands that included mandatory diversity trainings at all levels of employment and for the entire student body; hiring more faculty and staff of color; and demanding diversity statements from all faculty search candidates. Black students have raised several of these demands over a thirty-year period, resulting in several faculty-led taskforce reports, which reiterated the students' demands. However, little progress was made on key structural and curricular challenges. In the recent decade, substantial efforts were made to attract Black and Latino students to campus; however, retaining Black men has been a particularly difficult challenge, leading to a Black-men initiative and a peer-to-peer mentoring program, which have been quite meaningful to our students of color.

The packed BSU town hall meeting was followed by a dynamic presentation of Lawrence Ross, author of *Blackballed: The Black and White Politics of Race on America's Campuses* (2015). His talk was an unapologetic interrogation of whiteness, and white, make-nice politics after racist incidents, which, he says, always follow the script of "minimize, trivialize, individualize" (Ross 2019). This white supremacist script was in place when a student reported that a cafeteria worker bossed her around saying: "I am a slave master, and you are the slave!" The remedy given to the traumatized student was moving her to another campus cafeteria. When the student shared the experience at a public meeting, there was backlash and racist escalation. A supervisor put together a memo to full-time workers (but *not* student workers), telling them that they should use the word "taskmaster" instead of "slave master," adding insult to injury with minimizing the effects of the traumatic experience and trivializing it profoundly. That supervisor was fired just hours before the next BSU meeting. However, the student needed police protection to walk to her dorm after a late-night shift, because somebody in a pickup truck was following her. Her grades suffered due to severe PTSD, and she ended up transferring to a historically Black college. The offending cafeteria worker still has her job to date. Was this a matter of protected speech? Workplace harassment definitions focus more often on reoccurring offensive speech rather than on one instance of an egregious utterance that has lasting traumatic impact on the person and all those affected around her.

Hate speech is very difficult to prosecute, linguistic violence is rampant, and the white-dominated courts have tended to deny that it is actionable. The US Supreme Court has constantly acknowledged the offensive nature of hate speech, as in *Virginia v. Black*, 2003 (cross-burning case as free speech), and *Matel v. Tam*, 2017 (racially disparaging trademark case), yet the justices have strictly scrutinized hate speech as free speech, ruled on the side of it as free speech, and have been reluctant to impose restrictions on hate speech. Using hate crime legislation may even have unintended consequences, for example, by targeting Black people rather than remedying effects of white supremacist actionable conduct through tort law. It is often said that it is best to counter hate speech with "more speech," an echo of J. S. Mill's treatise *On Liberty*. We are not so sure that this is the case. Racialized groups (e.g., students or Black and Latino faculty and staff) are retraumatized and triggered by telling their stories, mostly in public forums, always carrying the burden of making themselves vulnerable to majority white audiences, who "consume" the information without necessarily acting on it in active-bystander intervention/disruption. Folx of color also have to endure listening to "white fragility" stories, which, in turn, gives legitimacy to whites feeling victimized and not confronting their own accountability work. Would some of this work be best shared in focused group dialogues? Intergroup dialoguing has shown promise in bringing together cohorts of folks with two differing social identities and have them discuss systemic oppression and privilege regarding race, religion, citizenship, gender, or sexual orientation. This relation-building discussion model has been touted as helping to raise whites' awareness about racism and greater empathy (Schmidt et al.,2020). However, research shows that whites actually learn more from other whites, because, in that setting, they do not put up defensive strategies such as retreating to guilt or shame mechanisms. Michael Eric Dyson directs white folx in this way: "You must *school* your white brothers and sisters, your cousins and uncles, your loved ones and friends and all who will listen to you about the white elephant in the room. . . . They may not be defensive about you, so you must be an ambassador of truth to your own tribes, just like the writers Peggy McIntosh, Tim Wise, David Roediger, Mab Segrest, Theodore Allen, and Joe Feagin" (2017, pp. 203–204).

Intergroup dialoguing (IGD) between social groups who do not share class identity seems to be a more challenging one. It will be too easy for somebody with class privilege to play a victim-blaming game: Why is it that you and your family cannot lift yourself out of a cycle of generational poverty? The individualized American Dream ideology plays a powerful role, which working-class people also succumb to. It shows that the IGD model has a limited vision when uplift liberal ideology clashes with a class-conscious, revolutionary model of struggle politics for transformative justice and an anti-capitalist demand for reclaiming the commons. With reference to the scenario above, a student worker's traumatic experience with a white, unionized supervisor with no college education, how would such dialogue look?

Here we wish to draw on the lessons of the transformative justice movement that imagines different ways of taking responsibility (cf. Dixon & Piepzna-Samarasinha, 2020). What if a community accountability process had been proposed to the worker? It would include others who are standing in for the victim because she would have been too traumatized to participate. Such process would allow for grievances to be addressed and may continue till certain goals are achieved: raising awareness of what hate speech is and its impact on the victimized and the Black community, including future students and alumni; a sincere apology, accompanied by meaningful redress and repair of the relationship (monetary or community service); and addressing other structural issues such as changing policies within the foodservice industry (which has monopoly on most college and university campuses) proposed by participants.

Teaching to Transgress? The Pitfalls of Teaching about Racism

What seems to be at stake is how effortlessly concepts like social justice and diversity are co-opted and whitewashed, and it takes visionary student activists and theorists like Lawrence Ross, Beverly Tatum, bell hooks, Angela Y. Davis, Monique Morris, Michael Eric Dyson, and Cheryl L. Harris to show that Black lives truly matter and that deep-seated anti-Black racism is still part and parcel of the American landscape. What our students of color demand is that, at the very least, they should not be dehumanized, they should be treated fairly and equally, and white faculty should stop treating racism as a taboo topic in classrooms of historically white institutions. Moreover, when racism as discussion topic comes up, it may be introduced in a clumsy or toxic way. Power differentials between faculty and students have enabled professors, and especially white instructors, to use students of color as teaching props and aids—this is particularly distressing in situations of hypervisibility. For instance, a sole Black student feels as if they are in the hot seat when discussion of chattel slavery comes up—all eyes turn to them, and the white teacher might even do a cold call—asking the student to explain what slavery means to them. The effects of such relentless microaggressive targeting accumulate week after week and affect the mental health of Black students. Additionally, white faculty should also stop using students of color as stand-in teachers, hiding these teachers own content-specific deficiencies based on training from graduate schools that continue to teach a white-solipsistic curriculum. As we have noted, the response to white solipsistic education (thesis) are Afrocentric resistance (antithesis) and multicultural/inclusive education (synthesis). Yet the synthesis is still looking for cultural competence and efficacy. Reid and Curry, frustrated about the political science white curriculum template in the United States, assert, "All of us have inherited a white, heteronormative, male, template, and our institutions perpetuate it" (2019). While there is nothing wrong with offering inclusive pedagogy and positive psychology ideals accessible to all in our classrooms, we cannot reduce social justice to a symbolic gesture of individualized good will.

Early on in his campus lecture, Lawrence Ross treated us to a quiz: "Who are you?" He freely offered that he is a Black man and clearly requested that we also be honest about our social/racial identity. It would have been positively helpful if the literacy speaker referenced above had dwelled for a bit on her own social identities and showcased that achievements are hope-inspired for some on a fairly stable, linear ladder of progression. For others, the ladders have missing steps or topple over altogether, as scholar and policy analyst Estela Mara Bensemon (2016) so powerfully demonstrates in her equity score charts when she discusses differential access to college education due to class and racial apartheid structures in US schooling.

Whitewashing the Ultimate Taboo Subject: Racism in Academic Spaces

Race remains a major category in our lives. Race has agency and it is irrepressible. So, whitewashing social justice and diversity issues in a racialized institution of higher learning only provides us with a "duct tape" approach to confronting the real issues on our campuses and the racial projects cannot be relegated to amateurs to handle. Nor can the bourgeois ivory towers pretend race will dissipate into thin air because of the elitist and exclusive nature of higher education. We constructed race and we can deconstruct it. It is on us!

We argue that whiteness profits from its normative and descriptive frame of invisibility. Such an invisibility frame is convenient and, in fact, hegemonic in so far it never dawns on its adherents and beneficiaries that they have to apologize for never making their frame apparent, that is, visible. There have been notable attempts in critical whiteness studies to unearth the secret machination of white supremacy. Joe Feagin (2018) produced a useful term with the "white racial frame," as did George Lipsitz (1998) with his book *The Possessive Investment in Whiteness: How White People Profit from Identity Politics*. Lipsitz's later study *How Racism Takes Place* (2011) starts appropriately with a chapter titled "The White Spatial Imaginary," which traces the politics of redlining. Lipsitz shows persuasively how the logic of hostile privatism and defensive localism shapes public policy and private investment in the US. He follows up with a chapter on "The Black Spatial Imaginary" and continues with a critique of the systematic oppression faced by Black Americans today.

Peg McIntosh's (1988b) classic essay on white privilege does *not* tell a story of white racial frame, except for tarrying with the negative. Her perspective actually focuses on how Black people lack the kind of invisible cards of access and vast opportunity that whites enjoy. Of course, McIntosh provides a helpful list of "items" of relative privilege to those who have never thought of themselves as "white" in a settler colonial white supremacist nation state. However, there is a risk of smugness, after the first "aha" moment wears off, and the analysis does not necessarily embed a call for action to undo racism. Some recent work on critical whiteness studies has focused on the concerted resistance to change. One may accept, after all, that one is a beneficiary of privilege and oppressive policies, but it seems easier to accept it with a sigh of relief—"at least, I am not a person of color!" It seems impossible to do antiracist work, even for the most well-meaning white people, when everybody in the (class) room is actually white. The fish does not see the water, just as whites are not taught to see white supremacy, and cisgender men take patriarchy for granted (cf. Mills, 1997).

Undoing racism means to refuse to take a racist system of domination for granted, and there are rare individuals who make that their calling card at great personal cost or even pay dearly with their lives such as Lydia Maria Child or John Brown. If we continue to limit antiracist workshops to discussions of "privilege reduction," we will never get to the critique of the oppressive nature of white supremacy. Undoing privilege minimizes and individualizes. It served its purpose in the beginnings of critical whiteness studies by white scholars, but it very much serves to maintain the status quo: managing diversity in the age when it is Black lives that should matter. At the bare minimum, the *individual* white person's acknowledgment of being privileged is a necessary, but not sufficient condition to raising awareness about *systematic* racist oppression. It is also noteworthy that McIntosh's (1998) companion piece on criminalization of Black bodies rarely gets a mention. But still, even in this sequel, McIntosh insists on talking about a system of "over-advantage," which does not get to the root of the problem, namely, that folx who experience oppression deal with double-bind scenarios, where there is no good, easy solution to problems. If we remain at the "privilege" and "advantage" analysis, it seems that we simply have to remove the obstacles one-by-one, and we do not get a hold of the deeply enmeshed, entangled, intersectional level of the inner workings of oppression.

As we mentioned earlier in this chapter, Lawrence Ross (2000), who visited with us during our town hall meeting organized by the Black Student Union, has penned a comprehensive study on fraternities or Greek lettered organizations in the academy focusing on Black sororities and fraternities. He shares an incisive analysis on institutional white amnesia in his more recent work *Blackballed: The Black and White Politics of Race on America's Campuses* (2015). He illustrates the logic of minimization and denial by white administrators when an "individual" racist incident occurs on a historically white campus. Whether it is about the inconvenience and embarrassment of racist chants, a staple of white segregated fraternities, or blackfacing, the system quickly insulates itself from blameworthiness and controls the messaging through quick condemnation, coupled with assurances that these are isolated incidents. Overt Jim Crow signage might be a thing of the past, but systemic and institutional racism, even in its overt demonstrations, continue to exist. However, whites on a college campus are afforded with a tunnel vision and can easily ignore all the red flags and signposts of the persistence of white supremacy. The privilege of "not seeing" continues unabated on the backs of students, faculty, and staff of color:

> Even when forced to confront overt racism, white America has been slow, reluctant, and dishonest in recounting that memory, a memory that is deep in their guts, a memory that they know is true. As individuals, white Americans have learned that they can deflect, defuse, and delude as a way to maintain the charade: "This is not a race issue. The people who did this are jerks, but this is not about race"; "This may have been insensitive, but can we move on from this and get back to normal?"; "Because you're talking about racism, you're being racist, and that's the reason why we can't get beyond race in this country"; "This is not who I am. This is an isolated incident." (Ross, 2015, p. 2)

McIntosh's list gives us a good inventory of the handy tools of white supremacy, but it does not hold whites accountable, misusing the list to their own advantage: "This is what white privilege looks like, but I am a good person, and I don't define my actions by such tools of convenience." Deflect, defuse, resist, and, in turn, demand that people of color reorient their lives around the needs of whites. Ross recounts the persistent efforts of colleges across the nation to deny Black students entry into the bastion of white, male privilege. But when they opened the doors a crack, it came with the exhortation that Black students better conform to the ethos of the campus and adapt and assimilate to the norms of whiteness; that imposition meant that there was no grievance procedure for Black students who were confronted with racist violence or microaggressions (Ross, 2015, p. 39).

When we finally turn our gaze toward white allies, can we expect a different attitude from them? In *Teaching to Transgress: Education as the Practice of Freedom*, bell hooks (1994) accuses white feminists of appropriating the work of Black women, which they had earlier dismissed—in fact, hooks could not find a publisher for her bestseller debut book *Ain't I a Woman?* (1981) till white women turned toward studies of gender *and* race (hooks, 1994, p. 121). By engaging with Black women's literature and theory, white women scholars now "reproduce the servant-served paradigms in their scholarship" (1994, p. 104). It means that Black women serve the needs, desires, interests of white scholars, who in turn never blink and review what race, that is, whiteness, has to do with them and whether they commit their analysis to critical antiracist introspection. Why actually bother and name one's social identity by outing one's writerly voice in an introductory chapter or as principal investigator who interviews Black women, when it does not serve to hold the author and authority of the subject matter accountable? bell hooks notes that whites desire studying the "black experience" and do not pay any attention to "the meaning of 'whiteness' in their lives, the representation of whiteness in their literature, or the white supremacy that shapes their social status" (1994, pp. 103–104). Resorting to allophilia will continue to placate and comfort white minds to look at racism at a distance, and they will continue to be challenged (and made upset) by students, community activists, and radical faculty who dislodge the status quo of white (supremacist) complacency and acquiescence.

Conclusion

Will Black Lives Matter have outlived its rallying cry for freedom, equality, and justice some day? Whites quickly tire of its impetus and administrators dream of more subdued times. In the meantime, Black and Latino students are restless and will not be mollified with toppling of names from named schools, buildings, and other symbolic acts of acquiescence by nervous (white) administrators and boards of trustees. Too much is at stake for history not to repeat itself, which would signal an end of the illusion of inclusion. A truly multicultural, inclusive, equity-minded, campus must confront its past on a daily basis and will be a place where all stakeholders feel the urgency of racial justice.

As we continue to struggle to give meaning to the lives of our students and faculty on our campuses and in society, new challenges make the struggle for justice, fairness, DEI, and inclusive leadership even more complex. The knee-lynching of George Floyd and the color of COVID have magnified the levels of inequity, injustice, leadership ineptitude, and cultural incompetence in our society. What lessons can we learn for American society and on our campuses in the succeeding chapter?

Chapter 8

The Color of COVID-19 and the Knee-Lynching of George Floyd

Interrogating Systemic Racism and Inclusive Leadership

> Black workers at universities are among the most vulnerable people on campuses. But they often are left out of conversations about racial justice.
>
> —Lilah Burke (2020)

> Eventually doctors will find a coronavirus vaccine, but black people will continue to wait, despite the futility of hope, for a cure for racism. We will live with the knowledge that a hashtag is not a cure for white supremacy. . . . The rest of the world yearns to get back to normal. For black people, normal is the very thing from which we yearn to be free.
>
> —Roxane Gay (2020)

Introduction

The years 2020–2021 confirm for many observers and interlocutors of social justice what Black folx in the United States and the rest of the African diaspora already knew—a country whose founders advocated freedom, justice, and the pursuit of happiness but treats some of its own citizens as inanimate objects, who are disposable. In the midst of the global pandemic of the early 2020s, white supremacy reigns high and Black men, especially, continue to succumb to a sociopolitical system that was not built to work for Blacks, Indigenous, and people of color (BIPOC). The sobering realities of recent events and the tasteless public exhibition of a racist burlesque of a white police officer knee-lynching, taunting, and humiliating George Floyd ignited global demonstrations to remind the world that Black lives matter. George Floyd's murder by state agents—the police—was an indictment of American democracy and our gargantuan appetite for injustice in the global court of public opinion. Furthermore, interlocutors of global affairs, including Fareed Zakaria of CNN's *GPS* news magazine, who noted correctly in the *Washington Post* that the irrepressible force of COVID-19 is dragging everything in the world with it and global inequity is expanding more than ever in world history: "The pandemic has intensified other trends, too. For demographic and other reasons, countries will likely see more sluggish economic growth. Inequality will get worse, as the big get bigger in every sphere. Machine learning is moving so fast that, for the first time in history, human beings might lose control over their own creations" (Zakaria, 2020, p. 2).

Yet Zakaria is somewhat hopeful that human ingenuity and the global human condition could be sustained through human agency. We are already interrogating the present in order to see the future that human agency and the ingenuity of our scientists and leaders may develop. This respected CNN journalist maintains that "people can choose which direction they want to push themselves, their societies and their world. In fact, we have more leeway now. In most eras, history proceeds along a set path and change is difficult. But the novel coronavirus has upended society. People are disoriented. Things are already changing and, in that atmosphere, further change becomes easier than ever" (Zakaria, 2020, p. 2). While the impact of COVID-19 picture painted by Zakaria was bleak, the future for post-pandemic world is still hopeful for most societies, as vaccinations for the virus and bivalent boosters have been developed by Moderna and Pfizer companies. Nevertheless, Black, Indigenous people, and people of color (BIPOC) who live in a racialized world continue to suffer the effects of Maafa, that is, the holocaust of slavery, post-Maafa citizenship questions, antebellum America, Jim Crow, and post–civil rights inequities in the United States. The damage caused by the coronavirus pandemic could take another sixty years (a time span equal to that from the civil rights era to Black Lives Matter era) to mitigate and reconcile, let alone the high mortality rate of BIPOC folx in this pandemic. It is actually a syndemic—systemic racism and the killing power of COVID-19. We use the acronym BIPOC for Black, Indigenous, and people of color for its symbolic and linguistic significance in this work. Since the knee-lynching of George Floyd in the era of COVID-19, the protest movements have gained new group-political consciousness to emphasize the intensity and scope of historic and systemic oppression of Blacks and Indigenous people—a reminder for not engaging in reductionism—grouping people of color into one sociopolitical entity.

We are hopeful, but we are not as optimistic as some observers, because, when global catastrophes happen, Blacks and Indigenous people suffer three to four times more than whites. If historical amnesia continues to prevail in our society, then we can write off the effects of the *longue durée* of global disasters and catastrophic events that have shaped the lives of BIPOC folx. The 2020s will always top whatever BIPOC have witnessed since colonial times for taking account of their struggles in different dimensions and endeavors for making progress on race relations. The 2020s would also serve as an instrument for gauging leadership ability and inability, malfeasance, nonfeasance, and ineptitude in dealing with crises—testing ground for DEI and inclusive leadership.

In this chapter, we argue that even during crises and catastrophes, when most people and institutions must demonstrate compassion, systemic racism exacerbates the levels of prejudice, discrimination, white hegemonic power, and white supremacy, resulting in disregard for Black lives and the rise of policy myopia, which present new challenges to inclusive leadership and moral consciousness. Furthermore, we offer this chapter as testimony to America and the world that even though many white Americans are becoming more racially conscious and reawakening (woke), our work in justice and racial equity has many miles and years to travel. Contrariwise, despite a plethora of multiracial demonstrations and denunciation against police brutality after the killing of George Floyd in Minneapolis by a white police officer, Derek Chauvin, most non-BIPOC folx in "comfortable" spaces/positions in the United States are still in denial about systemic racism. The omnipresence of systemic racism has obscured and obliterated our objective racial lenses so much that this country's educational and political leaders have settled for the status quo since the civil rights movement (1960s), until the global pandemic and the murder of George Floyd on May 25, 2020, provided yet another wakeup call to America for racial justice.

The racial status quo continues to reward white America at the expense of BIPOC folx because of the structures and systems that support the nation state, namely, the philosophy and ideology of whiteness and plantation capitalism. *Rhizomatous racism* infiltrates every system like dangerous roots of a powerful tree that penetrates and destroys the foundation of the house that we have built—America. Power holders of the racial hegemony and the American caste system, beneficiaries of the caste system, and those who profit directly or indirectly from all sorts of systems—social system, economic system, political system, and the interlocking system of oppression—cannot feel the lethal effect of these systems. As Michael Eric Dyson, one of the deepest critical thinkers of our times on race and University Distinguished Professor of African American and Diaspora Studies at Vanderbilt University, notes, "Every entity whose name ends in the word 'system' has been used to methodically exclude Black bodies and prevent Black well-being—while providing comfort to the white masses" (2020, p. 215).

These hegemonic systemic beneficiaries find system-supported comfort that fortifies their spaces from any intrusion. Most white masses are also clueless about the intensity and scope of rhizomatous racism and if they learn about it, they are numb to the pain that racism inflicts on BIPOC folx. The people who destroy Black bodies and Black lives enjoy sustenance in the structure of comfort and privilege that barely holds them responsible for the destructions they cause. Ta Nehisi Coates in his book *Between the World and Me* describes the racial status quo and what that does to Black bodies: "But all our phrasing—race relations, racial chasm, racial justice, racial profiling, white privilege, even white supremacy—serves to obscure that racism is a visceral experience, that it dislodges brains, blocks airways, rips muscles, extracts organs, cracks bones, breaks teeth. . . . You must always remember that the sociology, the history, the economics, the graphs, the charts, the regressions all land, with great violence, upon the body" (2015, p. 10).

Continued violence against Black bodies in America has been magnified by the agencies of COVID-19 and the demonstrations that emerged after the knee-lynching of George Floyd. Black bodies have endured individual and state violence based on the matrices of domination—the intersectionality of race, class, ethnicity, sex, gender, geography, culture, age, disability, religion, and more. These diversity categories will not cease to interact with race and the body politics in any locations regardless of crises. As coauthors of many books and articles, who have done research and worked together for over twenty years on diversity and inclusion projects, we are cognizant of how these diversity categories shape our own racialized bodies and thinking. We know the effects of racialized policies and microaggression on Black bodies and spaces.

Both of us, the coauthors of this work, have multiple diversity identities that provide us with different lenses for viewing COVID-19 and George Floyd's murder, perhaps differently from other observers and interlocutors. One of us is a Black scholar and the other, white. One of us has both Ghanaian and American nationalities, the other, German and American nationalities. Both of us have recent immigrant roots, and, yes, we claim United States' citizenship with all the honors, privileges, and responsibilities that come with it. In terms of ethnicity, one of us is African American, the other, European American. Both of us share a wide experience of three continents—Africa, Europe, and the Americas. One of us is female, and the other, male.

Yet, in addition to our educational preparations, disciplines, shared interest in philosophy, political science, Africology, and research experiences, the racialization of our bodies, connection to the American body politic, and social justice serve as a major mandate to how we place value on elements in our environments and in our worldviews. After all, all scientists are products of their environments. The recent health crises produced by COVID-19 and a racialized American polity made more evident by the murder of George Floyd provide us with a new stethoscope in examining the American body politic and the politics of difference in the United States.

Making Sense of Race Neutrality, Crisis Leadership, and COVID-19

When the COVID-19 pandemic attacked the United States and institutions of higher learning to an unusual dimension in March 2020, many observers accessed the early conditions from a global humanist disaster appreciation perspective—we are all in this together. Yet many experts in epidemiology, immunology, pandemics, and disaster analysis were too busy reviewing the disaster in general terms and they forgot about the infection and mortality rate among different diversity categories and COVID-19. Race, class, gender, age, and disability as diversity categories, did not draw the attention of most experts for a long time. Americans engaged in a global oppression Olympic—how many people have suffered/died in China, Italy, Germany, United Kingdom, Canada, Brazil, and Mexico?

At our own university, when we received instructions to move all our classes virtually, synchronous and asynchronous, and use MS Teams or WebEx as our instructional platforms (Zoom is not supported by the institution), diversity and inclusion were not on the lips of anyone, just as diversity and inclusion were not on the lips of leaders during most crises in the United States. Reductionism—reducing all political subjects into one entity prevailed. Yes, "we are all in this pandemic together," has been the gallant slogan to conquer COVID-19, even though nobody seemed to know the nature of the pandemic earlier on in 2020. At the writing of this chapter, we are still looking out for each other as a global big family. Nevertheless, the shift from face-to-face instruction to an online (virtual) platform for many teaching faculty and especially faculty of color was like building an airplane and flying it at the same time.

Administrators seem to be more interested in the economic calculus to keep institutions open and continue with face-to-face instructions. To enable most schools to pretend to be as normal as possible or return to normalcy, formulas, including at least 40 percent face-to-face instructions per department were devised. Classroom occupancy capacity was reduced. Faculty with pre-existing conditions and those who were qualified for exemptions went completely remote. BIPOC faculty in general had very little to say in this situation. BIPOC students were caught in a double-bind situation—a situation that does not produce positive results, no matter what one's options are—if you do, you are dammed; if you don't, you are damned. Minoritized students who are underserved and economically deprived prefer face-to-face learning because most of them do not have the best computers and Wi-Fi systems at home. Nonetheless, these same groups of students are the ones with family members who work on the front lines or who have lost their jobs because of COVID-19 and have disproportionately faced more fatalities. We do not know how many condolences we have to extend to our minoritized students during and after most class sessions. Yet very little of their conditions and situations were ever addressed in the numerous COVID-19 related faculty meetings we attended.

Faculty pushback was high in most institutions, but in numerous virtual meetings that were held on many campuses about the state of instructions and COVID-19, administrators in most institutions made up their minds before meeting with faculty. The decision to handle COVID-19 related classroom design was left to individual faculty members, which was chaotic for our students—when to attend in-person vis-à-vis virtual classes. Concerned faculty continued to hold their own meetings to counter some of the decisions of predominantly white hegemonic masculinist institutions. The following assessment is not an aberration or epiphenomenal: "We are putting economic concerns above health concerns, said Robert Cassanello, associate professor of history at Central Florida and president of its American Federation of Teachers—and National Education Association-affiliated faculty union. Rumors are swirling that universities are facing political pressure to go in-person before they're ready or face deeper state budget cuts. Healthwise, Cassanello was 'concerned there may be vulnerable faculty who do not fit nicely' into the university's current set of exemption criteria" (Flaherty, 2020).

The position of most administrators was and is still clear. Anything that could be done to maintain the economic viability of the university is what must happen and perhaps balance that with the safety-first argument. University presidents demonstrated their kind consideration by assuring faculty that they would do what it takes to avoid layoffs, by dissolving departments, and by cancelling programs, yet many adjunct/contingent faculty lost their jobs or teaching loads in the saga of COVID-19. In-person instruction, campus interaction, and return to normalcy appeared to champion the thoughts of the powers that be. A Florida University president, Kent Fuchs, mentioned in his memorandum to the university community that, "although we are justifiably proud of the effectiveness of UF's online instruction" over last spring and this fall, "the full experience of a residential university includes in-person instruction" (Flaherty, 2020). Ignoring the Centers for Decease Control and Prevention (CDC) guidelines, the University of Florida even instituted a surveillance app so that students could report anonymously faculty who decide to take their classes online without administrative approval (Ivanov, 2021). It is clear to us that BIPOC faculty will be impacted differently than their white colleagues in at least two ways: students will feel more emboldened reporting defiant BIPOC faculty and the facts of racism will not be counted as a "pre-existing condition."

As social justice advocates, we even joined in the global empathic approach by modifying our syllabus. We modified universal humanist statements from the *Chronicle of Higher Education* and other publications like the one below that was shared by most concerned faculty who added a version of this statement in their revised syllabi:

> Nobody signed up for this and nobody asked for this. Not for the sickness, not for the social distancing, not for the sudden end of our collective lives together on campus. Not for an online class, not for teaching remotely, not for learning from home, not for mastering new technologies, not for varied access to learning materials. The humane option based on the human condition is the best option. We are going to prioritize supporting each other as humans. We are going to prioritize simple solutions that make sense for the most. We are going to prioritize sharing resources and communicating clearly. We cannot just do the same thing online. Some assignments are no longer possible. Some expectations are no longer reasonable. Some objectives are no longer valuable. We will foster intellectual nourishment, social connection, and personal accommodation. . . . Nobody knows where this is going and what we will need to adapt. (Supiano, 2020)

It was not only college and university administrators who demonstrated the lack of leadership and guidance for their faculty and students on what to do during crisis; leadership position and debates on COVID-19 at the national level were convoluted by science/politics and politics/administration dichotomies. This time, it was not the type of politics/administration dichotomy argument carefully propounded in the Wilsonian era (1914–1920) about the role of public administrators and that of elected officials in government—administrative professionals vis-à-vis elected politicians. This time the politics/science dichotomy was a typical former President Trump approach to discrediting reputable scientists about the nature and dangerous effect of the coronavirus. He even labeled COVID-19 the "China virus" to distract his critics from commenting about his inaction and encouraging white nationalists to engage in ethnophaulisms—pandemic-specific ethnic and racial slurs against Asians and specifically, Chinese. Unfortunately, our colleagues and students who are Koreans, Vietnamese, and Filipinos all suffered from abuses from former President Trumps' ethnophaulisms and the color of COVID! To white nationalists, these Asian Americans all look like Chinese.

The former president of the United States, Donald Trump, was too busy rallying his base and stirring up insurgency among his followers for his failed attempt of securing a second term in office that he hardly listened to his own advisors and the scientific community about safety during COVID-19. He refused to wear any facial covering even after he contracted COVID-19. The American polity, for this politics of anti-politics from the top, suffered the most casualties from the battlefield of COVID-19.

There is an African adage that when the rot is at the top, it affects innocent ones below. Another African adage is that when you think you are cheating uncle spider, you might be cheating yourself (*Wu sisi Kweku Anansi, wu sisi wara wu hu* [Twi language]). Yes, the rot in leadership during this pandemic did not only remain in Washington, DC; it affected every state of the union. Trump's cheating of the COVID-19 precautionary measures affected him, his family, and many coronavirus victims who are Trump followers. In January 2021, over 21.8 million cases of COVID-19 have been reported and 367,046 fatalities, the highest in the world, have been reported by the Center for Disease Control ("Coronavirus in the U.S.: Latest Map and Case Count," 2021) and CNN. By the October of 2022, there were 98.66 million cases and 1,084, 893 million people dead in the United States (Worldometer, 2022). The death toll by the summer of 2023, after the emergency COVID-19 period ended, was 1,130,662 (Elflein, 2023). The politicization of the pandemic at the national level affected state and local governments too. Disagreements between Republican governors (e.g., Brian Kemp, Georgia) who were towing the president's line vis-à-vis Democratic mayors (Keisha Lance Bottoms, Atlanta) who were more concerned about health and safety and Democratic governors (e.g., former governor Andrew Cuomo, New York), who were requesting federal assistance but were against Trump's politics on COVID-19 ensued while Americans perished.

As academics, we have struggled with how and when to tackle the larger intellectual question of analyzing general problems or crises through cross-cultural lenses and appreciating the politics of difference; the COVID-19 pandemic was not different. How does one bring up the questions and concerns of those who have been historically excluded and marginalized at a time when the majority culture is relentlessly singing the songs of "we are all in this together"? How do we navigate the sociopolitical and universal humanist life and our intellectual and cognitive structures in the politics of difference in order to ascertain that our students and faculty of color have been given proper attention even in these times of crises?

Hurricane Katrina was a rude reminder that when the levees break, the poor and BIPOC folx suffer the most. Other disasters like Hurricane Fiona and Hurricane Ian in Puerto Rico recently are reminders of how Black and brown people suffer more than other racial groups in most disasters. Yet, in time of crises, difference is not quite valued over homogeneity. Lucius Outlaw reminds us that, most of the time, "where difference is prized over forced homogenization—or the hegemony of one group and its values and practices over all while masking this dominance in liberal, democratic dress" (2016, p. 414), minoritized groups become victims of this democratic masquerading. In the COVID-19 pandemic debacle in the United States and on many college campuses, it is the universality of perception and approach by the dominant culture to tackling the crises that give rise to the disproportionality of fatalities of Black and Latino folx. Yet for Black and Latino students—the particular vis-à-vis the universal—creates a suffering because of the "accidental differences" of race and ethnicity, which exposes them to the lethal force of the color of COVID-19. Study over study indicates that the health inequity in the United States is reflected in COVID-19 cases. The Centers of Disease Control and Prevention Health Equity Tracker statistics reveal that while Black/African Americans have 17,822 COVID cases per 100,000, Latino folx have 22,600 per 100,000, our Indigenous people have 23,513 per 100,000 people, and whites have 15,494 cases per 100,000 people. Based on the percentage of the American population, minoritized folx have disproportionate cases of COVID-19. For instance, Blacks are 12.2 percent of the population with 12.3 percent of all COVID cases and Latinos 18.8 percent of the population with 24.8 percent of all COVID cases (CDC, 2022).

Aside from the infection rate, what our minoritized students had to go through during the pandemic for the virtual-learning aspect (2020–2021) was unprecedented; BIPOC students have to face a serious double bind. Our students and their parents have shared that certain material conditions prevent access to excellent learning environments at home: they may not have their own spaces at their homes (share rooms), they have very unreliable Wi-Fi systems, and they have to choose between the public library and sharing resources with their family members who are also utilizing what they have at home. At the same time, they dreaded coming to campus, being exposed to other carefree students in classrooms and residence halls. Furthermore, COVID-19 decision processes and discussions (in most institutions) have been predominantly monocultural and lack inclusive lenses. Administrators can be proactive and intentional: instead of denying BIPOC students the right to remote learning, deans and chairs should wave rigid procedures and allow for students to be on campus *and* engage in remote learning. Such flexibility would signal students and their mentors that the institution is responsive to the dual pandemic: racism and COVID-19.

Short of such an action plan, those who are becoming extinct are not at the table. They do not have a place at the table. We, as educators and student advocates, have to speak for the voiceless. When administrators suggest to all faculty to cut workload, faculty of color also are in a bind—it feels irresponsible to say "no" to marginalized, minoritized students. In other words, Black faculty, specifically, do not have the luxury of "saying no" to Black students. "National survey bears out discontent according to the 'color line.' 51 percent of students agreed with this statement: 'the way my institution handled the pandemic this past semester made me trust its leadership less.' By contrast, 63 percent of Black students agreed with the statement according to a survey conducted by Third Way, a policy organization" (Hiler et al., 2021).

Colorblindness and *Kumbaya* (God Come by Here) Does Not Work for COVID-19

The fall semester of 2020 will remain infamous for what the ugly head of COVID-19 did and continues to do to the American national ethos. However, it was a semester of compassion and *kumbaya* sessions among students and faculty, asking "God to come by here" and save us all. "We are all in this together," is a favorite slogan from the human resources and the public relations offices at our own institution. We learn how to say to students and colleagues that, "it is okay not to be okay," to console our students and colleagues, and yet coronavirus continued to do damage. At the writing of this chapter, over one million Americans have succumbed to the mortal blow of COVID-19 and millions who may have survived are suffering from chronic illnesses because of this pandemic. Many more people died by the end of 2022 based on the report on the daily dashboard of the Center for Diseases Control (CDC) and Johns Hopkins University.

Even though the Pfizer-BioNTech, Moderna, and AstraZeneca COVID-19 vaccines, among others, have been in supply since early 2021, the planning and fiasco surrounding distribution networks of the vaccines were/are compounded by the continual politics of anti-politics because of lack of leadership from Washington, DC, and the fact that the United States does not have a centralized national health program. For some states, such as New York, hospitals and clinics through state mandates are/were serving as distribution centers for the vaccine and pharmacies, and labor unions and other distribution networks are participating in the process, but the range of efficiency/inefficiency continuum is so broad that it is difficult to say anything with certainty at this point. Furthermore, the federal government that oversees the supply chain did not have adequate supplies to provide the states in demand for vaccines at the beginning of the distribution cycle. It was shameful that the federal government under the Trump administration that promised before the presidential election that it had reserves of vaccines backtracked (or reversed course): there was no such thing as "reserve vaccines" (Holmes & Murray, 2021).

The years of the COVID-19 pandemic have been those that have elevated race consciousness and a universal appeal to end the denial that America is a racist country, and not even COVID-19 is neutral to systemic racism. These years (2020–2022) in review will become years of undulating terrain for health, racial, economic, and sociopolitical human challenges and endeavors. We write this chapter in these years (2020–2022), but it is our hope that God will reprogram these awful years, by many accounts, to go away. Therefore, we have elected to write in both present and past tenses, hoping that things will be normal before this book is available to our readers. We are hopeful, but not optimistic, as over a million Americans and disproportionate minoritized folx have already lost their lives to the pandemic by the summer of 2022. Hitherto, these are years that could serve as a measuring rod for the American psyche, even though we dwell in moments of psychic disequilibrium, for we are uncertain about the power of COVID-19. The racial dynamics within the American polity are fluid, because COVID-19, a pandemic that has killed more Americans than any other nationalities, and what some call an equal opportunity killer, has killed Black folx more than four times per capita than whites. Dyson makes this assertion: "The cities of our country are burning once again because of Black death. A vicious virus is stalking the globe, a disease that—sadly, predictably—has attacked Black flesh with tragic specificity. The pandemic has thrust us into the vortex of Black vulnerability. In America, coronavirus has exposed ugly truths that are far from novel. They are in fact part of the barely acknowledged preexisting condition of racial oppression" (2020, p. 15).

The atrocious denial of Black folx and lack of access to good and affordable health insurance and health-care systems and the concomitant high rate of heart diseases, high blood pressure, colon cancer, diabetes, obesity, asthma, and other diseases mean BIPOC folx are more vulnerable to the coronavirus. It was against this backdrop of the color of COVID-19 that the brutal knee-lynching of George Floyd occurred. It is evident that rope-lynching of Black folx may be outdated, but knee-lynching is in vogue. At the same time, we must note that it is significant that a noose hung from the press scaffold during the January 6, 2021, white supremacist insurrection. While COVID-19 has disproportionately consumed the lives of Black and Latino folx, the brutal killing of George Floyd signifies and symbolizes the extent and scope of white supremacy and the use of force by elements of the state against Black bodies. For Black folx, there is a continuum—dual pandemics: COVID-19 and systemic racism.

The COVID-19 pandemic has affected the global human condition in north, south, east, and west. Nonetheless, in this pandemic, China, the United States, and the Global North is suffering more than the Global South that has historically been the victim of recent pandemics—Ebola, AIDS, and the Zika virus. These sufferings are encapsulated in terms of lives lost, health and immunological nightmare, leadership deficiencies, economic deprivations, racial inequities, systemic and structural paralysis, and global immobilization. Ironically, Black America has suffered everything that has occurred in the Global South that has been notorious for pandemics, even though Black America is in the Global North.

The fall 2020 semester started discouragingly with many universities and colleges gambling on whether to keep students on the college premises or send them home in the first couple of weeks and hold classes virtually after the infection rate of COVID-19 multiplied. A number of institutions cut their originally scheduled face-to-face instructional year short in response to concerning positive test numbers. These institutions included our own university, SUNY Cortland. Some colleges and universities quarantined whole residence halls, sent students with COVID to nearby hotels to be quarantined because there were less spaces available to house those who had tested positive but were asymptomatic. Institutions engaged in several emergency meetings between administrators, department chairs, and human resources folks about what to do for the rest of the fall 2020 semester. Meanwhile, in the State University of New York (SUNY) system, the Oneonta campus became a victim of bad planning, malfeasance, and a leadership lacuna. SUNY Oneonta was shut down about three weeks into the semester and their new president, Barbara Jean Morris, ended up resigning. In the midst of that leadership chaos, SUNY's former chancellor Jim Malatras announced that SUNY Oneonta's president was not fired because of her mishandling of the COVID-19 situation on that campus but the "decision to resign was of her own volition" ("After COVID-19 Outbreak," 2020, p. 2). In the end, the Cortland campus had the sad distinction of having the highest number of COVID cases of the entire SUNY system.

SUNY Cortland suspended in-person classes before the planned Thanksgiving break and issued study-in-place directives for students for one to two week periods to allow for contact tracing and to get the case numbers under control. Meanwhile, some universities with some of the highest reported case numbers in the country pressed ahead with in-person semesters with no plans or transparent threshold for shutting down. During these times of crisis, planning and discussions took the "we are the world" approach without regard to diversity, inclusion, and the politics of difference. While the authorities consoled the institutions with *kumbaya* and "we are all in this together," most of our students and faculty of color fell through cracks of the system during these times of crisis. In fact, even as we began the spring 2021 semester, there continued to be no strategy, no plan of action, to address the unique challenges faced by the BIPOC community.

Across the US, academic institutions continue to approach plans to curtail the COVID-19 pandemic differently. The SUNY system created a centralized dashboard for all its sixty-four campuses, the largest higher education system in the world, which were updated daily. In addition, SUNY's individual campuses were allowed to separately develop their own dashboards. As one investigative journalist noted, "The centralized approach means the same basic level of information about case numbers, total tests administered by the campus and the percentage of positive tests, quarantine capacity and hospitalizations and fatalities is available whether you attend or work at a major research university or at a smaller four-year institution or community college" (Redden, 2020). These numbers were only good for general record keeping, but very little was done on campuses about the infection rates of BIPOC folx.

Related to COVID dashboards for releasing the infection rate of many campuses, testing, including pool testing, remains disorganized and sometimes chaotic. We frequently received information about pool testing that cuts into our classes and appointments. Students are pulled out of classes randomly for testing. While we mostly agree that the pandemic is no child's play and must take precedence over our daily lives, better planning could have alleviated much of the chaos. Yes, the pandemic is first of its kind to all of us, but the politics of anti-politics all the way from Washington, DC, made matters worse. It was not uncommon to learn that, with reference to testing strategies, "more than 1,400 colleges by researchers affiliated with the College Crisis Initiative at Davidson College in North Carolina found that two-thirds of colleges and universities have no clear testing plan or are only testing 'at-risk' students, those who are symptomatic or who have had contact with an infected individual" (Redden, 2020). The risk factor for institutions of higher learning and especially residential universities extend beyond the confines of the university campuses; they affect the health and safety of the larger communities. Nevertheless, for the minoritized students who reside in urban areas such as Brooklyn, the Bronx, Philadelphia, and Newark, New Jersey, for examples, it becomes a double-bind affair—a situation that no matter where they go, the odds against them are three times more than our white students.

Just as the national trends indicate, it is not only students of color and faculty who are impacted disproportionately by COVID-19; BIPOC frontline workers on university campuses are/were also affected. Workers of color who clean the classrooms, cook in the dining halls, and clean the offices and residence halls have disproportionate risk of contracting COVID-19 and being hospitalized, if they are lucky. Minoritized faculty in predominantly white institutions are fewer in number than the majority, and when a formula for in-person instructions was developed, no consideration was given to racial and ethnic diversity categories in most institutions, including our own. To keep their positions and fulfil departmental quota of at least 40 percent face-to-face instructions, BIPOC faculty become sacrificial lambs and victims of the system.

We are not the only people writing about COVID-19's effects on BIPOC folx. To affirm our observation above, five legal experts, three of whom are distinguished law school professors from the University at Albany Law, Yale Law School, and Rutgers Law School, a distinguished professor of sociology at Duke University, and an assistant professor of African American studies, ague in *Bloomberg Law* that "people of color are . . . more likely to be the essential workers in the university setting who are exposed to more risk—those who clean university spaces, who interact with students as support staff, the facilities managers, adjuncts and food service employees" are chief targets of COVID-19 (Roithmayr et al., 2020, p. 2). It is clear from observations of social justice experts that COVID-19 has reinforced and mimicked America's system of injustice and racial inequities. BIPOC folx on and off many college campuses shoulder uneven burden of risk, quarantine, hospitalization, and even death. Because of systemic oppression against BIPOC folx, the level of preexisting health conditions is higher than the white population. Moreover, BIPOC are less likely to gain and maintain access to effective medical insurance and health care and the COVID-19 situation exacerbates their already vulnerable conditions for any pandemics, including COVID-19.

There are several studies that indicate that Blacks, especially, are killed by COVID-19 more than other groups. A recent MIT Sloan School of Management study found evidence that race may be as vital as preexisting health conditions in determining a person's marginal propensity of dying from COVID-19. The researchers Christopher R. Knittel, the George P. Shultz professor of applied economics at MIT Sloan, and Bora Ozaltuna, a graduate research assistant in the Center for Energy and Environmental Policy Research (CEEPR) lab, examined a number of factors that lead to death from COVID-19, including patients' race, age, health, and socioeconomic status, and other environmental factors. The researchers found that, among these factors, race, on its own, contributes more highly to one's chances of dying from COVID-19 (Moller, 2020).

The researchers posed the following questions to tickle our racial consciousness and racial literacy. "Why, for instance, are African Americans more likely to die from the virus than other races? Our study controls for patients' income, weight, diabetic status, and whether or not they're smokers," Knittel affirmed. "So, whatever is causing this correlation, it's none of those things" (Moller, 2020). All along, most Black people did take COVID-19 very seriously because of the historical contradictions in American life. The color of COVID-19 only makes manifest what Black America has been saying for many years about systemic racism—this is just another wake up call for America.

The Syndemic: Mixing COVID-19 with Systemic Racism and Reframing George Floyd's Murder

It is not a coincidence or an aberration that the events mentioned above were also shaped by the emergence of the American racial narrative, racial formation, the continuing challenge to the American polity, and the racial landscape that provided the space for the knee-lynching of George Floyd, a Black man, by a white police officer in Minneapolis. This inhumane killing of another unarmed Black man was the last straw that broke the camel's back. A Black teenager, Darnella Frazier, filmed the prolonged, horrendous murder and received the 2020 Courage Award from PEN America in December 2020. Hitherto, the killing of George Floyd only tops a historical trend of police brutality, Afrophobia, Afrocide, and anti-Black racism that has characterized American life for over 400 years—the holocaust of enslavement, Jim Crow, plantation slavery, lynch-laws, black codes, convict labor, mass incarceration, the death penalty, racial injustice, socioeconomic injustice, and systemic racism.

The murder of George Floyd is symbolic for America's knees that have been embedded in the necks of Black Americans from the holocaust of enslavement, that is, Maafa, to antebellum America, to Radical Reconstruction, to the Great Migration, Jim Crow, the civil rights movement, the Black Power movement, and the Black Lives Matter movement. The major turning points in Black lives in the United States redefine Black spaces and Black bodies. Yet Blacks continue to redefine their spaces based on white comfortability, white disbelief, white racial frame, white sincere fiction, and white rejection of Black reality. COVID-19 just provided another lens in viewing Black reality and how George Floyd's death, with a twist of martyrdom, awakened America—a true lesson in *wokeness*—a state of being aware of social problems from a state of previous and perceived dormancy.

The fatalities of COVID-19, killing of George Floyd, global support for Black Lives Matter, an organization started by three strong Black women to save Black lives, the passing of perhaps the last icon of the civil rights movement, Congressman John Robert Lewis, the flipping of the United States Senate to Democratic Party control in 2021, the elections of Joseph Biden as president and Kamala Harris as first Black/Asian American woman vice president, have penetrating forces in race relations. Furthermore, the insurgency of *Trumpublicans* to disrupt the sacred ritual of certifying the electoral votes in the US Congress on January 6, 2021 (only the third time this insurgency has happened since the War of 1812) and the second impeachment of President Trump on January 13, 2021, for inciting the insurgency against America, all made 2020–2022 unusual years. All the same, the events of 2020–2022 cannot be limited to a particular playbook in American life and world affairs. These are/were years that cannot be duplicated by many accounts.

In the United States, the Black Lives Matter movement demonstrations, especially in 2020, were sometimes performative and symbolic of the social asphyxiation of Black folx in this country because of systemic racism. Conditions surrounding the COVID-19 pandemic, such as general frustration among races, unemployment, disproportionate deaths of Blacks and Latino folx, behavioral issues during quarantine, and despair may have contributed unusual violence in the general populace. However, Gorge Floyd's murder was an account of the saga of Black killings, which include but are not limited to the white police officers' chokehold death of Eric Garner for selling cigarettes outside a bodega in Staten Island, the massacre of Alton Sterling for selling CDs outside a supermarket was another one. The list continues with the murder of Mario Woods, for walking away from a white police officer; the murder of Laquan McDonald for walking towards a police officer; and the killing of Freddie Gray, for making eye contact with a white police officer. The murder of Trayvon Martin by a white community security officer, for wearing a hoodie, is one that questions Black mobility in America. Taking the young life of Tamir Rice, a Black child playing with a toy gun, troubles our consciousness that even Black boys cannot play peacefully in the park without getting killed.

The butchering of Amadou Diallo for offering his wallet to police who requested identification card should outrage any rational human being who likes to follow orders from authorities. The killing of Stephon Clark by a white police officer for relaxing in his grandmother's garden and talking on his phone informs Black folx they have nowhere to run to, not even their own homes. Murdering Philando Castilo for driving his girlfriend's car with a child in the back seat sends a message that these state-supported killers have no respect for infants or the elderly. The brutal murdering of Armaud Arbery by a white former police officer and his son for jogging in a white neighborhood is another statement to Black America that they are unwelcome to this country even though America was built with the blood, sweat, and labor of Black folx. This is a clear example of whiteness as property in critical whiteness studies (CWS) and America's infatuation with property rights instead of civil rights. And the needless wrongful killing of Breonna Taylor after a no-knock search warrant entry into her apartment, again, tells Black America that they may not rest in their own homes. These killings are systemic and highly institutionalized for structures that were not designed for the safety and protection of Black bodies and people of color.

In a white supremacist polity, George Floyd's videotaped murder sends a message to the world that can never be erased from the global psyche and American sociopolitical conscience. Afrophobia and the hate of Black bodies in America from the holocaust of Maafa, through the massacre of Emmett Till, to the knee-lynching of George Floyd are all chapters in the playbook of white supremacy and barbarism. The slave police, which may now be the state police, remains the greater part of the tools for Black random motility. Black bodies are easy targets for enraged white cops because of the white racial frame that controls especially Black and white racial interactions. We Americans have to come to terms with the encounter between George Floyd and Derek Chauvin before his death.

Eight minutes and forty-six seconds is too long to asphyxiate any human-being. During the jury trail, the world bore witness to the monstrosity of the knee lynching on videotapes that were not released to the public until April 2021. We learned that the actual time officer Chauvin kept his knee on the handcuffed George Floyd's neck was nine minutes and twenty-nine seconds. How long is too long? We have said this in the civil rights movement. How long is too long to choke Black bodies. How long is too long for white knees to be placed on Black necks? The figure 9:29 will remain on our global consciousness forever. To officer Chauvin, the emasculation of the big Black body of Floyd was very important for sustaining white masculinity and heteropatriarchy. Floyd who had already lost his job to COVID-19 had suffered a double agony with his masculinity—no job and police dehumanization. The Cup Foods employees who called the cops on George Floyd and his friends are/were doing what white America does best in any altercation—whether they are right or wrong—call the police on Black folx. In the exchange that transpired a frightened unarmed civilian appealed to the police not to shoot him because he had been shot before and he knew what it was like to be shot. After the police dragged Floyd's helpless Black body to their car and he fell near the police car, two officers, Lane and Kueng, put the handcuffs on Floyd with his hands behind his back (*Grio*, 2020). George Floyd was restrained by the police officers by their knees on his legs and on his neck, even with the handcuffs on him with his hands on his back. What threat does he pose with his hands cuffed behind his back? George Floyd pleaded for mercy, he called his mama on the verge of dying, he informed the officer that he could not breathe, but all went on deaf hears (Adams, 2020).

To the white police officers, the call and response communication style, as it is done in Black culture and Black gospel music, is offensive to them. These Black calls and responses tend to trigger blue fragility. As Robin DiAngelo apprises us, "Though white fragility is triggered by discomfort and anxiety, it is born of superiority and entitlement. White fragility is not a weakness per se. In fact it is a powerful means of white racial control" (2018, p. 2). Blue fragility has four times the power of white fragility, because it has to be multiplied with a badge, lethal weapon, state support, and heteropatriarchy. Hitherto, when most white police officers are queried about their anti-Black behaviors, blue fragility always kicks in with overexerted occupational hazards and suffering, demanding the highest form of qualified immunity from their atrocious and deadly actions. Blue fragility is weaponized to kill Black bodies. The men and women in blue now stand in for the trope of the white innocent woman during lynch terror a century ago. We ask why is it so difficult for grand juries to indict police officers and for juries to convict police of murder or manslaughter of unarmed Black folx?

Both George Floyd and Eric Garner informed their arresting officers during the chokehold and knee-lynching episodes that they could not breathe. "I can't breathe" has become a phrase for caution about police interaction with the general populace and signpost for rallies for racial justice since the deaths of Garner and Floyd. Black America continues to suffer from physical asphyxiation, social, economic, and political asphyxiations—yes, we cannot breathe. One of the saddest moments of the killing of George Floyd was when he calls onto the spiritual world to bring back his mother who had passed away. The symbolism of this message is overwhelming in Black culture. Dyson affirms, "Floyd's calling out for his recently deceased mother is especially hard to hear. Mothers are broadly cherished in this country, but Black mothers have a special magical place in Black culture. When he cries 'Mama,' he is crying out for his maternal root, his most loving supporter, his first and foremost advocate and protector" (2020, p. 76). Law professor Paul Butler's book *The Chokehold: Policing Black Men* (2017) serves as a grim reminder that this outlawed police practice is not just a metaphor for the terror wielded by police across America but part of the arsenal of deadly police encounters that replicate and continue lynch-law of yesteryears by men donning white sheets.

At the end, we can analyze the Floyd murder case further with Joe Feagin's (2010) white racial conceptual frame model that captures the essence of what has shaped white America's thinking process when it comes to racial encounters. Racial stereotypes, both verbal and cognitive aspects would quickly push any white authority figure—with a badge and a gun—to look for racial narratives that would fit a big Black man like Floyd's perceived demeanor. The interpretation of the racial narrative by the white police officer, Chauvin, is that Floyd is a dangerous "beast" and he has to be restrained by any means. The racial imagery that is received from this thinking is the visual and auditory signals that come from Floyd. His Black body, his language, perhaps using Ebonics, are different from Chauvin's. Officers Chauvin would quickly equate differences with deficiencies or danger. He spits out venomous racialized emotions—the feelings of killing a big Black man, based on the American socialization process that elevates the falsity that the Black man must always already be criminalized and pathologized; he cannot be trusted. Pervasive cultural bias, implicit bias—what more? Chauvin, the white police officer strictly, scrutinizes the white racial frame, and he is inclined to knee-lynch George Floyd to death. Even postmortem police reports render Floyd's body pathologically dangerous because the state's autopsy report reveals the existence of illicit drug consumption. Floyd, in death, will be remembered as a drug user, or, worse, fitting the stereotype of racialized images of drug pushing. Whether it is the state-backed force of police power that brutalizes Black bodies or state mismanagement of COVID-19 endeavors, Black bodies are condemned by the system of oppression and matrices of domination.

Conclusion

As we write this work, we are still dealing with different variants of the COVID-19 pandemic and the aftereffects of the George Floyd's murder without a closure for the deplorable state of physical and mental health of BIPOC folx, reform of the criminal justice system, reparation, restitution, and envisioning America's divisiveness and leadership. Over one million Americans have perished and the economy has shattered. President Biden's stimulus checks of $1,400 that went into the bank account of most Americans in need in March 2021 cannot bring relief to most financially stressed and marginalized BIPOC folx. The student loan forgiveness program would not do much for BIPOC folx. Two years after we started this project and as we have cited Roxane Gay (2020) at the beginning of this chapter, it is again important to bring her into our conclusion by repeating her unforgettable statement that, "eventually doctors will find a coronavirus vaccine, but black people will continue to wait, despite the futility of hope, for a cure for racism." She is right, we have many coronavirus vaccines and boosters now, but no cure for systemic racism. Yes, most Americans, who have transcended the boundaries of vaccine confidence and trust thresholds, have already been vaccinated against the coronavirus. Others, including many BIPOC folx, who do not trust the government and health systems, are still waiting for more information. Yet still, many Americans of color will not expose themselves to historical amnesia, such as the Tuskegee study of untreated syphilis in Black men, which tricked and duped them into becoming victims of sterilization, prolonged torture, and death.

America's race project is not principally about empirical data and evidence about a given research thesis statement and a statement of purpose. It is the lived experiences of BIPOC folx that we interrogate and the perceptions that the general white populace have developed and turned into policy that we must deconstruct. We seek revival of the principles that shape the global human condition and appeal to our leaders who are in places of power to be transparent in their processes of decision making. Mindful listening to those who are disenfranchised and do not have a place at the table when decisions are being made, because of the irony of democracy, especially in times of crisis, should enable decision makers to save lives—and Black lives. Inclusive leadership—which involves attitudes, behaviors, antiracist policies, accountability, special responsibilities in terms of dealing with racialized communities, and a racial equity framework—must shape our vision, mission, and actions.

The Color of COVID-19 and the knee-lynching of George Floyd only provide America with the unfortunate opportunity to reexamine its moral compass on systemic racism and to rethink its leadership sensibilities, especially in the time of crises, including COVID-19. The gallant and reactionary calls for antiracist nation states, inclusive college campuses, and equitable sociopolitical institutions only give way to the illusion of inclusion and performative responses that masquerade as fairness during the times of hideous murders and oppressions that leave the structures of injustice intact. Americans must move beyond reactionary and performative leadership responses and be proactive in recognizing and accepting responsibilities, which are concomitant with generations of denial and injustice for reconciliation to occur. Without healing our fragile and broken democracy, a pandemic such as COVID-19 and an unforgivable act like the knee-lynching of George Floyd will continue to engulf the flame of injustice. On April 20, 2021, the jury on the George Floyd's murder case completed its deliberations. When the judge announced the guilty verdict on all three counts—manslaughter, second degree unintentional murder, and third-degree murder. The world jubilated with chants of "All three counts" and "Say his name, George Floyd." Some say justice was finally served, but systemic racism and vampire policing are still with us. Yes, a step in the direction of justice, and America has to seriously work on justice for all.

Our hope in writing this chapter is not premised on the general race to eliminate COVID-19 and new reforms in police departments after the murder of George Floyd. We attempt to use this chapter and our other essays in this book to shape and strengthen the cognitive structures of students, faculty, administrators, policy-makers, and caring readers about the continuing struggle to reinterpret the American psyche and this country's violent past and present and to lay a stronger foundation for a better America guided by inclusive leadership.

The succeeding chapter will enable readers to understand the dynamics of how being shut down by whiteness, historically white male hegemony, and institutional structures for a long time, because of power and gender differences, could produce counter dynamics, for those who have been neglected and silenced, to the gathering of strength to form social movements and organizations in order to challenge the power structures, because hegemony is not permanent. Yet these movements are not monolithic. Just like the women's right moments, and feminist movements, the Me Too movement has its idiosyncrasies, instrumentalized agencies, and racialized elements in dealing with male hegemony. Read on!

Chapter 9

Me Too, Me Two, and Misogynoir

From Margin to Center: Black Women's Testimony in the Age of Me Too

The #MeToo meme was created by Black activist Tarana Burke in her work supporting women of color, who disclosed having experienced sexual assault, beginning in 2006. When white Hollywood celebrity women used the meme, their rallying call for action went viral in 2017. Burke immediately became worried about its misappropriation (Brockes, 2018). This is a reasonable concern considering the history of a concerted "reasoning from race" by white women. The monochromatic feminist movement is mired in a well-documented history of appropriation, misappropriation, and concomitant silencing of the struggles of resistance by Black women in the last two centuries, beginning with the struggle for the abolition of enslavement through to the struggle of ending Jim Crow.

Clearly, the hashtag was meant as a feminist gesture of solidarity for *all* victims who accused Hollywood film producer Harvey Weinstein of sexual assault and rape. However, who is a victim whose life truly matters? At first, Weinstein's public relations handlers and lawyers retreated to the standard denial of allegations and, at the same time, announced that the accused checked into a therapy center for persons accused of sex offenses. Once Black women shared their testimonials, such as Oscar winner Lupita Nyong'o, Weinstein and his handlers, denying culpability, mounted a vociferous attack on the victim's character. Some interlocutors of victimology who would question the premise upon which the victim, Nyong'o, provided a massage to Weinstein in his bedroom, while the family was not far away was bizarre. Yet the meaning and benefit of massages to actors that the victim learned at Yale School of Drama in connecting body, soul, and mind and redefining space, body, and power relations should dispel any confusion about Nyong'o visit to Weinstein's bedroom. Those who have doubted the victim's visit continue to dwell on the old tactics and legal maneuver of assassinating the character of the witness and victim. Furthermore, it follows the racist heteropatriarchal logic that women of color ought never to be believed. This logic emanates from an empathy deficit, delegitimizing Black suffering and tort claims.

This chapter engages in a comparative analysis of recent social movements, inspired by specific hashtags on twitter and social media in general. We analyze the logic of misogynoir and cultural appropriations and instrumentalization of race, looking at current and historical examples. In a way, "Me Too" was the rallying cry of white upper class US women who participated in abolitionist circles, condemning the practice of chattel slavery. By instrumentalizing race, too often Black women disappear from view. Kristie Dotson's (2011) analysis of epistemic oppression will be useful in reviewing what exactly is detrimental to Black women's agency and how Black women and organizations are resisting testimonial quieting. In the balance of this chapter, we draw on contemporary examples that are indicative of the assaultive microaggression of "misogynoir," a term coined by Moya Bailey in 2008, which then went viral, again without proper attribution to its originator, a Black feminist queer scholar. Bailey uses the term misogynoir specifically in highlighting misogynist and racist media representations of Black women (Bailey & Trudy, 2018). We conclude the chapter with an analysis of the Black Lives Matter movement outside the United States to strengthen our case for global applicability of movements: Black Panther, Black Lives, women's rights. In Europe, specifically Germany, the Me Too movement was dubbed Me Two by antiracist activists.

Examples of Misogynoir Practices

We start with an example in sports. Selecting professional athletics helps at one level to shine a light on practices and narratives that may perpetuate microaggressions. On another level, they also magnify such biased behaviors, especially where celebrity professionals are targeted. Let us begin with the white supremacist, sexist world of professional tennis. (It is noteworthy that so many *individual* sports are still the bastion of white privilege and depend on the material infrastructure readily available in the white wealthy suburbs: tennis, golf, lacrosse, hockey, badminton, soccer, track and field, swimming/diving.) We have not intentionally neglected America's favorite sports, American football and basketball, in our examples above. Yet we leave the analysis of how whiteness, white privilege, and the plantation hypothesis in sport, where owners and coaches are predominantly white in those sports, for another project.

The Williams sisters have changed the playing courts of tennis in the world. Tennis fans and all those who believe in challenging hegemony, as Serena announced her retirement from tennis during the US Open in 2022, will miss them. In 2018 during the US Open final match, Serena Williams stood up to umpire Carlos Ramos and contested his unfair penalties, which ultimately cost her the championship game against newcomer Naomi Ōsaka, a Haitian-Japanese tennis star. This controversy is no trifling matter. Given Williams's reaction (and hefty fine, after the fact, compounding insult and injury, of $17,000), the umpire association threatened a boycott of any further games that involved the tennis superstar. In the press conference following the championship game, Williams calmly shared that she stands up for gender equality in tennis and noted that there is a serious double standard in the sport. In her tweet some weeks before this championship game (in August 2018), Serena Williams complained about being unfairly singled out for drug testing, being tested with more frequency than any other top woman tennis player for performance enhancing drugs, even though she has never tested positive.

As Frederick Douglass put it so poignantly a century earlier, there is an assumption of imputing crime to color. In all US institutions, we see a misogynoir logic that inevitably draws attention on Black girls and women, who are unduly singled out, pushed aside, and punished. Serena Williams and her sister have been subjected to scrutiny their entire lives in a sport that is dominated by white players, coaches, and so on. It is very clear, then, that a Black woman might raise the flag for gender equality (even for strategic reasons) before she will highlight the intersections of racism and sexism that she confronts and resists on a daily basis. This strategic defense is different from the common, problematic defense of white women, who just tend to "add up" the oppressions (considered the additive approach): "As a woman, I can relate to what you are going through when you deal with racist bias." This "sympathetic" nod amounts to micro-invalidation, as such a comment never makes sense for anybody who has experienced oppression in an intersectional way; women of color, specifically Black women, have extraordinary difficulties making their grievances intelligible. Drawing on sociologist Patricia Hill Collins's Black epistemology, philosopher Kristie Dotson (2011) notes that Black women's narratives may not find credibility in white public spaces—painfully, their testimonials continue to be invalidated, which is one of the forms of microaggressions.

Many white feminists continue to struggle with an intersectional analysis, preferring the additive approach instead, which isolates one form of oppression (e.g., sexism) and makes problematic comparisons with another one (e.g., racism) (cf. Nagel, 2014). In a classic victim-blaming and -shaming narrative, they revert to the tired stereotype of the angry Black woman. Germaine Greer, a first-wave white feminist, calls Williams a sore, patronizing loser, and Greer could not see any racism by the umpire's actions, either. Greer conceded that the Australian blackface cartoon, universally critiqued for its blackface misogynoir tenor, may be construed as sexist. Regarding Williams's performance, Greer opines: "The game was gone already because she dropped the first set and she was looking for a way out. . . . I found the way she behaved really repellent, especially when she put her arm around the poor young woman who actually won the bloody thing to say, 'I am the grand dame and you have done quite well, deary.' When what she had really done is thrown the match" (Honeysett, 2018). Appallingly, even Williams's graceful, comforting gesture towards Ōsaka, who clearly idolizes Williams and thanked her during the ceremony, is profoundly misread by a cynical white privileged woman, Greer, who chooses to overlook the institutional mistreatment of Williams at previous US Open matches spanning over more than a decade. Greer's white solipsism calls into relief the urgency of understanding the politics of misogynoir. It is not for white women to evaluate whether Black women experience racism, because whites' social ontological position disallows them from seeing racism in the first place. As Charles Mills so provocatively writes, as the fish has no practice seeing water, similarly, whites cannot understand their own entitlement in a white polity—it is natural to them (1997, p. 76). Privilege produces implicit bias and is at the center of profound misunderstanding, what Mills calls epistemological ignorance (p. 18). Dotson's (2011) analysis helps us to understand that Greer also displays *pernicious* ignorance—white speakers who use the microaggression of invalidation regarding BIPOC speakers' testimonies. And Applebaum strengthens our case about Greer's utterance and behavior through white epistemologies of ignorance: "One of the significant features of White ignorance is that it involves not just 'not knowing' but also 'not knowing' what one does not know and believing that one knows'" (2010, p. 39). Furthermore, white epistemologies of ignorance insists that one knows (because of whiteness and white privilege) even if they have no clue what they are talking about.

Such misinterpretation of the world is the foundation of Greer's cavalier dismissal of an Australian cartoon's vitriolic hatred of Serena Williams. The cartoonist uses distorted images from the enduring blackface tradition: Williams is depicted as an enormous Black raging toddler with unkempt hair in a masculinized aggressive pose. While her opponent Ōsaka, who identifies as a Black woman, is depicted as a petite woman with blond hair and demure demeanor, deploying the racist stereotype of Asian women's docile character and model minoritized person imagery to appease the predominantly white tennis audience. The umpire, cast as white master and overseer, counsels Ōsaka, "Just let her win!" After international protests, the cartoon was later pulled from the website. However, racist microaggressions, specifically the patterns of invalidation and assaultive speech, remain unaddressed.

The racist, misogynoir cartoon also played up the anti-Black trope of "pickanninny," depicting a Black child, who is not gendered—a staple of Hollywood cartoons. In these devastating images, Black children's lives are constantly threatened by wild omnivore animals such as lions and crocodiles (Riggs, 1987). The white gaze pathologizes Black children's lives who are not worthy of protection. Thus, a white audience seeks pleasure in a necrophilic, cannibalistic way, whereby young Black children are sacrificed on celluloid. At that the same time, lynching of Black women, men, and children occurred in broad daylight and hundreds and sometimes thousands of white terrorists participated.

This 2018 cartoon follows a familiar script: in the past, other white Australian men had mocked the Williams sisters in blackface misogynoir (Brennan, 2018). Such vitriolic contempt shows how the commercialization of Afrophobia and misogynoir, the fear and hatred of Black women's embodiment, travels globally to another white colonial settler nation, Australia, which still has to own up to its ghostly atrocities against Indigenous Black people. Here, we draw on criminologist Viviane Saleh-Hannah's (2015) theory of Black feminist hauntology, which complements Bailey's theory of misogynoir; both name and excavate the legacy of injustices that speak to Black cis and trans women's experiences. These theorists refract the rich Black feminist tradition, including the Combahee River Collective's

(1977) manifesto and legal scholar Kimberlé Crenshaw's theory of intersectionality (1989), which highlights the concerns of legal activist turned Episcopalian priest Pauli Murray that sexist and racist discrimination does not get instrumentalized in a parallel fashion, but in an interconnected manner. Crenshaw's groundbreaking article ends in this prophetic manner:

> It is not necessary to believe that a political consensus to focus on the lives of the most disadvantaged will happen tomorrow in order to recenter discrimination discourse at the intersection. It is enough, for now, that such an effort would encourage us to look beneath the prevailing conceptions of discrimination and to challenge the complacency that accompanies belief in the effectiveness of this framework. By so doing, we may develop language which is critical of the dominant view and which provides some basis for unifying activity. The goal of this activity should be to facilitate the inclusion of marginalized groups for whom it can be said: "When they enter, we all enter." (1989, pp. 166–167)

When Black women's voices (their intersectional experiences) are being heard in the white mainstream, when Black cis women and trans women's lives start to matter, all of our lives will matter.

However, we should note that, of course, not all Australians delight in misogynoir. Another Australian newspaper highlights the cruel double standard that Williams is subjected to and draws sensibly on Claudia Rankine's (2015) feature article in the *New York Times Magazine*. According to Rankine, Serena Williams does not hold back when she is on the tennis court. Despite the decade-old misogynoir body policing, Williams continues to demonstrate defiance instead of despondence:

> For black people, there is an unspoken script that demands the humble absorption of racist assaults, no matter the scale, because whites need to believe that it's no big deal . . . But Serena refuses to keep to that script. Somehow, along the way she made a decision to be excellent while still being Serena. She would feel what she feels in front of everyone, in response to anyone. And in doing so, we actually see her. She shows us her joy, her humor and, yes, her rage. She gives us the whole range of what it is to be human, and there are those who

can't bear it, who can't tolerate the humanity of an ordinary extraordinary person. (Rankine, cited in Holmes, 2018)

In her award-winning book *Citizen*, Rankine (2014) also reminds us of the white Danish tennis player Caroline Wozniacki who mocks Serena Williams' physique by stuffing towels in her top and shorts at an exhibition game. This obscene gesture occurred on December 12, 2012, just two weeks after Williams is named WTA Player of the Year. Such a misogynoir blackface routine serves as a harsh reminder that a most valuable player is blatantly humiliated in an elite white supremacist tennis court. Even the greatest player of all time is not welcome in this white public space. We know of no warnings or penalties that Wozniacki may have incurred for humiliating Williams.

Over and over, Black women are told to abide by the politics of respectability and civility, to smile stoically, while facing all kinds of misogynoir insults. Williams' accusation ("You are a thief!") hurled at the umpire in the 2018 US Open deserves merit. He piled up penalties, disregarding her complaints, and reinforced the perception that tennis is rife with double standards: men do not get punished for being perceived as insulting the umpire on the court. John McEnroe, for instance, was nicknamed "Superbrat" for yelling and insulting umpires, but tennis audiences just loved it. Moreover, Williams's monetary punishment of $17,000 was also extremely severe. Afterwards, the Umpire Association even threatened to boycott Williams's next games. Nevertheless, Williams was voted 2018 WTA Comeback Player of the Year. In 2017, she had given birth and almost died having to endure a surgery following the birth of her daughter. So, given this feat, being back on the tennis court in high stakes tournaments, it is even more astounding that the referee Carlos punished Williams severely for a transgression of her coach (giving hand signals during the match) that is actually common practice in tennis (and never incurs loss of points). Her anger found its expressive release in smashing the racket on the floor, breaking it, which incurred another penalty. We would like to point out that such outburst was a safe release of the humiliation she felt, which she so well articulated: "I have never cheated in my life" (with respect to the hand signal penalty). The embodied experience of shame is not well understood in the fields of psychology or psychiatry. And it is time that justified angry expressions be evaluated as a shame response to rejection (Thomas, 1995). In Williams's case, it was the exacerbated articulation of referees' invalidation-microaggressions over decades.

Implicit bias, harsh one-sided punishment follows Black players in all sports. Andrew Dix's (2018) study reveals that women's basketball teams from HBCUs are particularly discriminated against. He analyses the referees' practice of calling fouls given to individual players, noting that Black women drew the most number of fouls. This has repeatedly been the case for both Williams sisters, Serena and Venus, throughout their tennis careers. Being habitually invalidated by referees and audience members led these superstars to boycott the US Open Tennis Championships for over a decade. Serena Williams suffered through five bad fault calls in one game in 2004. In the end, the referee's faulty misogynoir judgment was supplanted through the installation of a "neutral observer": Hawk-Eye technology (Rankine, 2014, p. 27).

Dix's study is hugely important to give readers and observers independent evidence of implicit bias and the microaggression of invalidation, specifically where Black women are targeted. At the very least, it validates elite players' complaints of being unfairly singled out. In another context, studies have been used to investigate racist and sexist patterns in housing, jobs, and so on. Since, the 1990s, white mainstream media got involved in testing implicit bias with hidden cameras, as exemplified by *True Colors* (Sawyer, 1991) and *The Fairer Sex* (Sawyer, 1993). *True Colors*, a CBS investigatory documentary project, follows the lives of a Black man and a white man, who test housing, shopping, employment opportunities, and simply strolling in St. Louis, Missouri: walking-while-Black clearly is a perilous activity where he gets threatened by uniformed officers and white truck drivers for being in the "in the wrong neighborhood." In *The Fairer Sex*, it is a white woman and a white man who test for sexist discrimination in employment, shopping for cars, and leisure activities (e.g., golf). In this documentary, they do not expose the white woman to the perils of testing her personal sense of safety walking alone or entering bars at night. Such methodology still sidelined unique concerns of Black women; presumably, this is the case, because testing for intersectional claims of discrimination is simply too messy.

Finally, misogynoir microaggressions also target somatopolitics (a fear and hatred of the body). US athletes Serena Williams, her sister Venus, and Olympic gymnasts such as Gabby Douglas and Simone Biles have all endured humiliating body shaming. Not fitting the white, fragile mold of femininity, white trolls shame these women for "being too strong." It is noteworthy how these all-star Black women fought back misogynoir and somatophobia on their social media accounts and in public interviews, refusing to be silently facing the racist, sexual evisceration of their personhood and accomplishments, and taking a political stance—taking pride in their embodiment and superlative athletic prowess, the work of thousands of hours in the gym and on the tennis court. They are acutely aware of their pioneer and role-model status, especially for all Black girls and for the next generation of Black girls in the US and around the world aspiring to be superstar athletes.

In the case of the South African Olympic star athlete Caster Semenya, the epidermal, visceral hatred and jealousy was accompanied by an all-out invasive and public demand of gender testing—led by white women athletes who felt robbed of their entitlement when Semenya, a newcomer, stole the show and the medals in 800-meter races. Are Black cis women actually women—or aliens of a different kind? This is, of course, a provocation, but it echoes Katheryn Russell-Brown's (1998) critical trope of the criminalblackman, rendering Black men into a third species. It was not lost on South African feminists that Semenya's humiliation was a painful reminder of the colonial exploitative exhibit of an ancestor, Sara Baartman, dubbed across Europe as Hottentot Venus (Orgeret, 2016). Necropolitics, settler colonial Afrophobic aesthetics continue to haunt sports and every other aspect of life.

It is ironic that *corporate* social media platforms now are being used to magnify the voices of Black women whose athletic merits have been devalued and they strategically speak back and control the narrative with an ever-increasing youthful fan base globally. These women refuse stoic silence, and they critique both the racist trope of being marked as superwoman *and* vilified as subhuman. Williams, Douglas, and Biles refuse to accept their status as *anthropos*—that species studied and dehumanized by the white colonial gaze—but rather they express powerfully their *humanitas*, claiming their humanity in a white supremacist polity (cf. Osamu, 2006).

White Feminism and Anti-Black Racism: Reasoning from Race

What happens to the meaning of the rallying cry #MeToo by the oppressed when persons of immense status and prestige invoke it for their peculiar power struggles? We look at its performance in two ways: (1) when it is directed against third parties, and (2) when it is redirected against the party who first decried the injury. Broadly conceived, these are concerned with epistemological privilege and resistance, and epistemic injustice (Fricker,

2007; Medina, 2012; Dotson, 2014). Whose voice and truth are being heard and understood by the hegemonic historiography? Whose testimonial is instrumentalized or smothered? Is it ever alright to reason from race, that is, to use African-descending peoples' freedom-cries for one's own harm experienced, when this harm has nothing to do with enslavement, Jim Crow, convict leasing, criminalization, and pathologization? We submit that such reasoning from race amounts to a false, disingenuous, and dangerous analogy. It leads to a trivializing and disappearing of the testimonial outrage and pain expressed in authentic diasporic enslavement narratives (and neo-slave narratives after 1865).

Exhibit 1: The American Revolution and False Analogies

We begin with freedom fighter *and* slaver Thomas Jefferson. In the Declaration of Independence, he complains that King George treats the white male American fraternity of rebels like slaves. And, worse, the king has the audacity to turn the enslaved against him and his fellow slavers—a criminal act, no less. The original text also included a long passage about Britain's hypocrisy for installing the "peculiar institution" in North America, which Southern slavers disliked and struck from the document. How can it be possible to defend the position of anti-abolitionism and antislavery? This is a contradiction that Ibram Kendi calls "classic Jefferson" (2016, pp. 108), a Janus figure. On the one hand, Jefferson professed egalitarianism invoking a guiding principle for humanity that "all men are created equal"; on the other hand, Jefferson struggled with a belief that some men must be kept in the holocaust of enslavement to provide free labor needed to build the foundation for the new and violent "democracy" project.

Jefferson's contemporary critics who were abolitionists did not buy his convoluted logic. A Rhode Island preacher, Samuel Hopkins, rebuked Jefferson's false comparison with enslavement, calling his grievance "as lighter than a feather" in contrast to the lived experiences of enslaved Africans (Kendi, 2016, p. 107). Ben Franklin also used this infamous comparison, complaining that England turned "American whites black." White British public intellectual Samuel Johnson quickly demolished this complaint by noting ironically, "How is it that we hear the loudest yelps for liberty among the drivers of negroes?" (Kendi, 2016, p. 103). It should also be noted that Johnson adopted his manumitted Jamaican servant Francis Barber and his family who lived with him for thirty years and inherited Johnson's estate ("Samuel Johnson [1709–1784]," 2014). As we show below, the analogy of oppressive conditions, especially of this kind—"My misery is a kind of slavery!"—is repeatedly invoked in protest movements throughout US history.

Exhibit 2: Abolitionist Betrayals: Origins of
White Women's Suffrage Movement

Two hundred years after the beginnings of a white abolitionism, it is worth taking stock again of the racist roots of white feminism. On the one hand, white Quaker women abolitionists Sarah and Angelina Grimke clearly saw the brutal reality of enslavement and acted in solidarity with Black women (and Black men), as Angela Y. Davis notes in *Women, Race, and Class* (1981). However, many other women of status did not share these insights. Instead, elite white women who participated in the abolition movement, misidentified their lot as housewives with perpetual servitude und racial capitalism and borrowed Jefferson's false analogy for their own purposes. This misanalogy is birthed from an epistemology of ignorance. Seeing the world in such a racist way, white educated women believe their victimization under patriarchy to be just as terrible as those human beings who were considered chattel. We note that such casual reference to a system of white terrorism serves to *erase* the lived experiences of Black women and men, marooned or enslaved in the African diaspora. It is no coincidence that the inception of the white women's suffrage movement took a turn toward vicious expressions of racism decades later. Northern white elite women such as Elizabeth Cady Stanton, who had penned the Seneca Falls Declaration of Sentiments in 1848, felt enraged about enfranchisement of Black men with the passage of the Fifteenth Amendment (the last Reconstruction Amendment) to the US Constitution. By 1869, she had "forgotten" that it was pro-feminist Frederick Douglass who came to her rescue when Stanton introduced the controversial suffrage demand in her manifesto for women's rights in 1848—Seneca Falls! After all, many white women abandoned the convention at that point, because they felt that voting rights for women were too revolutionary. Douglass spoke up in favor of suffrage, and it was thanks to his persuasive power that many women stayed and signed the declaration. It still took seventy-two years to garner white men's support for the nineteenth constitutional amendment, and another additional fifty years to enfranchise Black men and women, who survived the nefarious Jim Crow era of convict leasing, lynch terror, and other forms of state-sponsored violence.

After the Civil War, Black women felt the brunt of white women's abandonment of civil and human rights struggles and learned to distrust whites' intention of "helping" and being "allies." After 1865, white suffragists made common cause with white Southern politicians to further their cause at the expense of Black women's enfranchisement. Such unprincipled alliance put a massive rift into the alliance that had carried white and Black abolitionists toward the victory over the Southern chattel slavery cause (of course, the passage of the Thirteenth Amendment brought no relief from state-sponsored enslavement in the form of the prison system). In the 1920s, after white women had received the right to vote, fractured relations were manifested in the struggle for the Equal Rights Amendment (ERA). Alice Paul's National Woman's Party again cultivated alliances with Southern white supremacist politicians for decades to come; it bore fruit in the heat of the civil rights movement, when a white Southern senator wanted to derail the Civil Rights Act by adding the word "sex" to the antidiscrimination clause that focused on race. It seemed to be a revisit of the fight over the Fifteenth Amendment that enfranchised Black men but not Black women or white women.

However, this time Black feminist Pauli Murray was prepared and counseled the antiracist coalition to accept "sex," because, after all, Black women were not able to untangle sex from race and would benefit from the antidiscrimination act. Murray's brilliant strategy helped to keep a fragile coalition together and to articulate the need of an intersectional analysis, instead of thinking of "race" and "sex" in parallel terms (Mayeri, 2011). Black feminist legal scholar Kimberlé Crenshaw (2018) credits Murray's "unsung legal genius" with preparing the ground for such intersectional feminism (cf. Crenshaw, 1989), which finally gives us a conceptual framework for critiquing problematic analogies and comparisons.

EXHIBIT 3: ASSESSING MISOGYNY AND OPPRESSION OLYMPICS

However, the logic of gendered racism continues to be profoundly misunderstood. Specifically, how do we challenge misogynoir occurrences using a truly intersectional feminist methodology? A headline titled "Christine Blasey Ford's Experience Was Just as Bad as Anita Hill's—Maybe Worse" by white *New Yorker* writer Margaret Talbot (2018), showcases an impossible comparison, and a common strategy of "reasoning from race," which, in the end, quietens Black women's testimony. The journalist stages a version of "oppression Olympics," a term that was coined by Elizabeth Martinez in the 1990s and Audre Lorde had warned us against. Talbot plays into a misogynoir script by erasing Hill's struggle in front of white male politicians who would and could not listen to a Black woman's allegation against her former boss, Clarence Thomas. His defense strategy ended up being effective when Thomas rebuked Hill for engaging in modern day hanging of a man for a crime he did not commit—"high tech lynching." This is, of course, a perverse logic, as if Hill somehow reinscribes Klan terror. This attack worked, and Hill's own history was interrogated by white male senators in lurid sexualized manner. In the end, Hill's testimony of enduring sexual harassment had no standing, even though some 1,600 Black women came to her defense in a very public way—listing their support on a full-page *New York Times* ad (Crenshaw, 2018). Would another (white) woman's victimization in an intraracial incident be heard? Blasey Ford testified to the Senate Judiciary Committee in September 2018, revealing a violent side of Brett Kavanaugh, who was nominated for Justice Kennedy's seat on the Supreme Court. Interestingly enough, the white male guard of Republicans learned an important lesson. They did not want to repeat the embarrassment of the past, when they vilified Anita Hill in the Thomas hearings. Therefore, they hired a female sex crimes *prosecutor* to question Blasey Ford. Few observers wondered why a prosecutor would question the veracity of a victim, rather than a seasoned defense attorney. What was also different is that this time, on the Democratic side, a Black male senator, Corey Booker, served on the committee, in addition with several women, lending their support buttressing Blasey Ford's credibility. She did not suffer from the phalanx of inappropriate or obscene questioning Hill endured.

So, how does Talbot conclude that Blasey Ford's experience was worse? Surely, receiving death threats is a terrible reminder to sexual assault victims in the US that coming forward comes at a steep price. However, Hill faced a divided Black community, where many Black women supported Thomas's nomination—using identity politics to find another Black justice to replace the honorable Thurgood Marshall, but Thomas is no Marshall. Scholar Orlando Patterson, using his own girls' narrative, chastised her for being less than playful at the office. In addition, Black women are not supposed to air sexual assault complaints to a hostile white public (Crenshaw, 2018). Here again, Kristie Dotson's (2011) analysis of epistemic violence is helpful. By going public with her testimony, Anita Hill crossed the proverbial line of the politics of respectability. By speaking up, she was quietened (a form of epistemic violence) by powerful white senators as well as by Black men such as Thomas and Patterson. And Hill also endured hostile opprobrium by other Black women who supported Thomas's nomination. Kristie Dotson explains, testimonial smothering occurs "when a speaker smothers her/his own testimony when an audience demonstrates testimonial incompetence for unsafe, risky testimony owing to pernicious ignorance" (2011, p. 250). Clearly, a public display of vulnerability, doing what is right, came at a high personal cost. In hindsight, Hill should have smothered her account, and, because she committed a public break with the tradition (to keep silent in the face of intraracial violence), the backlash was as raw and violent as it was predictable.

By contrast, feminist support for Blasey Ford was quite unified, where white and Black women demonstrated at the Supreme Court, and even shut down Washington, DC, during the hearings. Using social media and other outlets, a fierce Me Too movement, flourishing into #WeBelieveHer, fought back against toxic masculinity. Nevertheless, Kavanaugh prevailed, although it was the lowest confirmation vote for a Supreme Court seat at that time. None of that unified feminist protest was present when Anita Hill was barraged by misogynoir vilification. She felt literally quite alone on the Senate floor and in the streets, yet she still worried more about her parents' well-being than her own. The most visible support came from prominent Black feminist women such as Crenshaw, Angela Y. Davis, and hundreds of others who took out a full-page advertisement supporting Professor Hill (Crenshaw, 2018).

By going public with her story (and not bowing to the pressure of testimonial smothering), law professor Anita Hill made history in more than one way. Her testimony was heard by thousands of working women who started filing sexual harassment claims—a Me Too moment avant la lettre. The concept of such harassment had just been coined by feminist legal scholars such as Lin Farley and Catharine MacKinnon, and this language of empowerment that put a concept to a pervasive behavior was a watershed moment in redefining workplace spaces (Siegel, 2003). Yet it took the testimony of a Black conservative woman to create a sea change in the prevailing patriarchal, misogynoir narrative of public opinion. Today, it is commonplace in the US academy that sexual harassment training is mandatory for professors and staff. Still, we ask for more, since diversity training and antiracism training is still optional. Additionally, we need to be vigilant about not repeating mistakes from the past, assuming a stance of "reasoning from race," instead of mobilizing resources for a complex intersectional understanding of how different systems of oppression are operationalized and how we might build strategies of resistance that address them in a kaleidoscopic way.

Christine Blasey Ford's testimony found tremendous support from women of the Me Too movement, and yet it was also haunted by a new misogynist backlash in the form of "himpathy"—elite heteronormative men being portrayed as the new and latest victims of feminists. (Never mind that it was Ford who received death threats and had to move her family.) In the bestseller *Down Girl: The Logic of Misogyny*, white feminist philosopher Kate Manne (2017), also called the "philosopher of #MeToo" (Doherty, 2019), differentiates misogyny from sexism. While both are aspects of the patriarchy, she considers misogyny to be the law enforcement apparatus of patriarchy, articulated in policies, and sexism expressed in ideological terms (Doherty, 2019, p. 20). Himpathy refers to "the disproportionate or inappropriate sympathy extended to a male perpetrator over his similarly or less privileged female targets or victims, in cases of sexual assault, harassment, and other misogynistic behavior" (Manne, 2017, p. 197). In *Entitled: How Male Privilege Hurts Women*, Manne (2020) opens with a reading of the Kavanaugh hearing as an exemplar of "himpathy," namely, Kavanaugh is quite naturally owed a position. Senator Graham presented a furious defense for the white male contender for the Supreme Court, declaring the hearing nothing short of "hell" instead of a proper job interview (Manne, 2020, pp. 5–6). Kavanaugh's own prepared speech and his overall conduct was laced with an emotional appeal to entitlement, quite the opposite of somebody who has a sober, dispassionate character, the kind of temperament necessary to serve the high court. We are reminded of the entitlement embodied by Thomas, who had complained of "high-tech lynching." Himpathy meets misogynoir, as his attack was directed at Anita Hill.

We end this exhibit with Eric Schneiderman, the disgraced attorney general of New York. He had championed women's rights, became a self-styled leading supporter of the Me Too movement, had sued Harvey Weinstein, and had even written a law against strangulation. *The New Yorker* broke a story with four women corroborating lengthy histories of abuse (Mayer & Farrow, 2018). A former girlfriend calls Schneiderman a misogynist and sexual sadist. He defended his physical attacks including chocking as "consensual play." The article ends with one of the women victimized, Tanya Selvaratnam, expressing defeat: "What do you do if your abuser is the top law-enforcement official in the state?" Three hours after the publication, this law-enforcement official resigned. He was never prosecuted for any of these allegations. It is significant that these courageous women decided to come forward during the height of the Me Too movement instead of continuing to smother their testimonials; it was also strategic to do so collectively, so that they would be able to withstand potential cyberbullying and worse. Like Weinstein, Schneiderman taunted the women that "he was the law" and that nobody would believe them, and he also threatened to kill them. From their perspective, clearly, he was *not* play-acting and neither did any of them consent to his emotional and physical violence.

From Black Lives Matter, Me Too, to a Global Me Two Resistance Movement

The genesis of one of the most powerful movements in the United States since the civil rights movement happened during the Obama presidency when three Black women community organizers—Alicia Garza, Tometi Opal, and Patrisse Cullors, two of whom identify as queer—rewarded the US and the world with the Black Lives Matter movement (https://blacklivesmatter.com). In 2012, they mobilized national protests in the aftermath of the acquittal of vigilante self-appointed neighborhood watchman George Zimmermann who shot and killed an unarmed Black teenager, Trayvon Martin. Their call to action gained global support, after another Black teenager, Michael Brown, lay lifeless for four and a half hours on the street in Ferguson, Missouri, in 2014. That Black lives indeed matter is a radical call to love that has reverberated through the ages since 1619 (cf. Green, 2019). BLM's call to action has only intensified with calls for defunding the police since the brutal police murder of George Floyd in May 2020. The summer and fall of 2020 saw national protests at a massive scale not seen since the civil rights movement of the 1960s. This popular resistance movement has generated new protest touching the ideological and institutional fabric of society, including "monument-history"—some icons of white supremacy are starting to tumble. Abroad, it has created vigorous discussions about the legacy of colonialism and more tumbling of statutes followed, including a British slave trader's statute being tossed into the river ("Edward Coston statue," 2020).

The Me Too (https://metoomvmt.org) and Time's Up (https://www.timesupnow.com) movements focus on giving support to survivors of sexual assault and sexual harassment in the workplace. By 2018, new mass protests by women for women sprang up around dozens of countries. It was an exciting time to see women refusing to smother testimonials and engaging in risky practices outing powerful men in the academy, in theater, and in politics, to name a few, some of whom lost their jobs, their position of influence. In Weinstein's case, he is serving prison time while awaiting more trials at the time of this writing. However, we also caution against a defense of carceral feminism. Abolitionist journalist Victoria Law describes the term as "an approach that sees increased policing, prosecution, and imprisonment as the primary solution to violence against women" (Law, 2014). In the aftermath of successful hate crime legislation, we have learned that the law has not benefited BIPOC. Queer and gender nonconforming BIPOC groups across the US and Canada have opposed enhanced criminalization. Even though these laws were meant to serve as deterrent to white supremacist terrorizing behavior such as burning crosses, bodily harm and murder have morphed into tools benefiting police departments who have a record of targeting poor, queer BIPOC. Thus, queer communities of color complain that police officers have been implicated in hate crimes, perpetuating homophobic and transphobic acts, but they are hardly ever prosecuted (Swiffen, 2018, p. 131).

Me Too, just like BLM, found a global echo in protests and demonstrations occurring worldwide. We are here interested in another "Me Too"—of European dimensions, specifically reviewing the German context. The Me Two movement originated in the world of European soccer in 2018 (see *causa* Mesut Özil and Trevor Noah on French Soccer in another chapter of this book). It started with international soccer star Özil, who quit the German national team by decrying racist treatment in several tweets. Born in Germany to Kurdish parents who fled Turkey due to discrimination, Özil said that he has a Turkish heart and a German heart. On the soccer field, he is praised when he scores goals "as a German" and he faces racist Islamophobic vitriol when his team loses (becoming Turkish Muslim Other). Hate messages intensified after the German team lost early in the qualification matches and when Özil met with Turkey's President Erdogan ("Germany Gripped," 2018). In solidarity with Özil, journalist Ali Can created #MeTwo—in defense of binational people, and he encouraged other people of color to share their experience of "everyday racism" (*Alltagsrassismus*) in Germany (Darwish, 2018). Can, who is also an intercultural peace activist and educator, mobilized over 200,000 Afro-Germans, Afropeans, and other binationals who tweeted their outrage of dealing with the effects of white supremacy in every aspect of their lives, specifically in education, housing, and employment. The Me Two movement challenges white Germans to look at their own racism and Can noted that the tweets show that white Germans should stop denying that racism is rampant—this is an allusion to the denial committed by Germans who denied knowing about concentration camps after the liberation by the allies. Specifically, he calls on German school teachers to get a robust antiracist training ("Germany Gripped," 2018).

The *New York Times* followed up with a survey and heard from five hundred readers in 2018 and published a few of their stories in 2019, marking three decades of unification and increased xenophobia and right-wing parties who have won seats in the German parliament. SchwarzRund, a queer feminist Afro-German writer who lives in Berlin, responds to the *Times* survey: "The more you research, the clearer it becomes: Germanness is about whiteness, as it's the racist assumption of a shared white experience and supremacy. It's not about episodes of violence here, but rather daily violence. In 1990 my black father was almost killed by fascists. My school years in the 2000s were marked by the N-word, racism and black friends who were suicidal because of the German school system" (Takenaga, 2019).

SchwarzRund now "writes back" from a capital in the Global North. Berlin, the site of the 1884 conference that led to the carving up of African territory by European colonial empires, has come under renewed scrutiny in 2020: Afropeans demand the renaming of streets that celebrate white German men associated with genocidal murder of the Nama and Herero of Namibia in 1904. And the Namibian government still awaits the declaration of these murderous acts as "genocide," repatriations of the bodies of the ancestors, and reparations from the German government (US Holocaust Memorial Museum, n.d.).

In no uncertain terms, the police murders of George Floyd and Breonna Taylor have led to a renewed reckoning with anti-Black racism and Islamophobia in Germany. As elsewhere in Europe, it includes renewed protests against the glorification of the colonial period whose memory is marred by unacknowledged genocide. And Afro-German activists are still seeking answers about a case of possible police murder of Oury Jalloh, an asylum seeker from Sierra Leone who was burned to death in police cell in Dessau in 2005. It was declared a suicide by the state prosecutor. Racial profiling and criminalizing immigrants of color are part and parcel of legitimate police violence work (Chimbelu, 2020; Thompson, 2022). Specifically, the Working Group for the UN Decade of People of African

Descent accuses the German government of anti-Black racism in the judicial system, regarding Jalloh's death under suspicious circumstances and police killings of African women N'deye Mareame Sarr and Christy Schwundeck, among others (Bruce-Jones, 2017). The German public also seems to know more about Trayvon Martin, Michael Brown, or George Floyd than about police murders on German soil, since the German media and public seem partial to the police narrative of self-defense. Thanks to Black activists on the ground, the families of murder victims receive support and media coverage and, increasingly, there is a critical discourse about precarious Black life in Germany and the need for civil society to address racist policing, widespread bias-related harms and right-wing demagoguery of politicians and party members.

Conclusion

Black women have always been in the forefront of nonviolent resistance against state violence. The Combahee River Collective's manifesto makes it clear that lesbian separatism is not a feminist practice that Black lesbians endorse. Garza, Cullors, and Tometi, the spiritual daughters of the Collective, Audre Lorde, Angela Davis, and Assata Shakur, made it their mission to bring attention to young Black men's murder by the state. And yet their contributions of uplifting Black cis and trans women often disappear even in the age of social media. By 2016, mothers who lost their daughters to violent police encounters created the #SayHerName Mothers Network in the US. These mothers sent a supportive video message to the mother of Breonna Taylor in 2020 (African American Policy Forum, 2020).

At a time when border policing along with a relentless war on drugs continue to target minoritized groups across the US and Europe, it is noteworthy that those who are the most vulnerable, namely, refugees, DREAMers, people without documentation, still show up and protest. They have good reasons to stay invisible, to smother their testimony of suffering injustice on the streets.

Some Europeans and white Germans, especially, often decide to measure racism on their own terms: "It is quite bad in the US and its racist police and judicial system," and they reassure themselves that people of color are governed by the rule of law in Germany and Europe, and white supremacist behavior is an aberration of neo-Nazis. Many Black women authors have put this myth to rest in the past three decades. Thanks to

Audre Lorde's visit to Berlin in the 1984 Black Germans self-organized into the Initiative of Black people in Germany (ISD) and its sister organization ADEFRA (Afro-German Women), founded by Black feminists and lesbians. Lorde coined the identity "Afro-German" in 1984 (Florvil, 2017). A first Black German collective work was born with *Farbe bekennen: Afrodeutsche Frauen auf den Spuren ihrer Geschichte* (Oguntoye, Ayim, and Schultz, 1986), later translated as *Showing Our Colors: Afro-German Women Speak Out* (1992). Reckoning with misogynoir, these writers and activists set the stage for addressing racism and the colonial past, as it is reinvigorated with a global Movement for Black Lives. And, importantly, they are inspired by the possibilities for resistance and renewal as shown in the struggles and perspectives of US Black feminist scholars and activists of the past and today.

This chapter along with the previous ones makes a case for a reframing of historical narratives under a Black feminist, critical whiteness studies (CWS), and critical race theory (CRT) lens. These also illustrate a commitment to diversity leadership that takes a bold stance at a time when CRT has come under political scrutiny in many states of the US. In the following chapter, we outline what kind of diversity leadership we favor.

Chapter 10

An American Kaleidoscope

Rethinking Diversity and Inclusion Leadership through the Prism of Gender and Race

> The mind thinks all the time, but most often it does not think about its own thinking and the activities of the brain.
>
> —Seth N. Asumah (2022)

Introduction: First Thoughts, the Great Man Theory, and Leadership Demographics Today

In this chapter, we offer a pathway out of the traditional and heteropatriarchal hegemonic deficit model of leadership prevalent in corporate America and institutions of higher learning by interrogating some of the traditional leadership models through the prism of gender and race. We analyze two different leadership paradigms and insist on the urgency of inclusive leadership. One is concerned with the gendered and racialized pattern of leadership styles and the other deals with the broader diversity and inclusion process of leadership, as the process of leadership is more important in a relational democracy than a position, per se. We argue that these different approaches and processes ought to be subjected to an intersectional analysis, which foregrounds gender and racial equity,

---

Another version of this chapter (Asumah & Nagel, 2020) was previously published in *The Routledge Companion to Inclusive Leadership*, edited by Joan Marques (2020).

inclusive excellence, and social justice considerations. Furthermore, it is our contention that in the American polity gender and race continue to structure our lives with deeper implications and impacts on women and people of color because of the historical contradictions of American life and the enduring agency of heteropatriarchal leadership in these changing times. Gender and racial stratifications, formations, and oppression continue to shape our leadership approaches and models, and how that affects diversity, equity, and inclusion (DEI) and social justice is important to our work.

The recent emergence of global Me Too and Black Lives Matter movements have given rise to a critique of racialized institutions and toxic masculinity and their articulations in organizational mismanagement, insensitivity to oppressed groups, and missed opportunities in responding to sporadic crisis and patterns of abuse of power. Our focus will be on effective diversity and inclusion leadership and dealing with gender and racial crises in academic institutions in the United States. To that end, we interrogate the transactional approach frequently associated with business models of leadership and suggest a social change model that rests on the pillars of transformation, supported by the combined metaphoric forces of the leadership qualities of the eagle and the crow—powerful vision, fearlessness, nurturing, strength, adaptability, intelligence, and inclusion.

The euphoric prognosis about the state of diversity and inclusive leadership by the appointments of chief diversity and inclusion officers (CDIOs) on all of the sixty-four campuses of the State University of New York in the past four years seems to have subsided, as a plethora of issues involving diversity mismanagement affecting several college and university presidents and others in leadership roles have resulted in many resignations and expulsions. Among the college presidents, provosts, and deans whose leaderships and authorities were challenged recently were the president of Ithaca College, Tom Rochon; Tim Wolfe of the University of Missouri; and Jack Thomas of Western Illinois University. Yet colleges and universities, including Duke University, South Carolina State University, Syracuse University, SUNY Cortland, Binghamton University (SUNY), the University at Albany (SUNY), University of California, Los Angeles (UCLA), University of Nebraska–Lincoln, Arizona State University, University of Florida, San Jose State University, University of California–Irvine, University of Connecticut, and The University of Alabama, have problems associated with diversity mismanagement on their campuses (Cole & Harper, 2017).

What is interesting about the majority of these leadership positions in higher education is that most of the presidents and their cabinets are mostly white, traditional, heteropatriarchal leaders, who have accumulated and consolidated power in the academy for years, despite this era of diversity and inclusion. Many of these leaders are mostly removed from their students and faculty, depending strictly on transactional leadership style, which, like the traditional Great Man model, is linear, hegemonic, risk-averse, masculinist, rational, practical, and unidirectional. Furthermore, a basic course on Diversity Leadership 101 could have informed these college and university leaders about three important elements/tests for leadership success: (1) diversity leadership work must be intentional; (2) diversity leadership work should be about human relations and not about "things"; and (3), during crisis management, one's rhetoric must contain an alignment between intent and impact. The college and university leaders in most of the aforementioned institutions failed these tests (Cole & Harper, 2017). The leadership qualities mentioned above, which do not seem to work in institutions filled with students of Generation Alpha, Generation Z, and Millennials, have been ingrained in our minds since the body of knowledge in leadership studies was propounded in the 1800s. Nonetheless, many institutions still operate on the Great Man leadership model in the twenty-first century. Is this leadership model and its concomitant application a product of unconscious bias, and the irrepressible reliance on old business models of transactional leadership?

We teach courses on diversity, equity, inclusion (DEI) and leadership. We also direct and cofacilitate diversity and inclusion professional development institutes in the United States and around the world. In our workshops and classes, when we ask participants and students to engage in an exercise called "first thoughts," what one thinks of first when, for instance, manager or leader is mentioned, we receive a long list of stereotypes and archetypes: men, white males, competitive, strict, businesslike, boss, WASPs, head, chairman, administrator, master, taskmaster, in charge, head honcho, and boss man, to name a few. Our students and participants represent a cross section of Americans in higher education or in the general populace. Some of these stereotypes and archetypes may not have validity, but most of them are products and images of the old records that constantly play in our minds. Yet we know that not all leaders and managers in the United States are white males or boss men, but these images become the narratives, the narratives become our realities, and the perceived realities are turned into policies, hiring practices, and programs—in short, we are dealing with a WRF—white racial frame (Feagin, 2014).

Mapping Out Gender, Race, and Leadership

Before we map out the traditional transactional management and leadership styles, let us look at the state of senior leadership demographics in US-based Fortune 500 companies and the academy. We might also ask what changes, if any, have occurred since the civil rights revolution of the 1950s and 1960s? What are the prevailing changes in leadership in the post–civil rights era and the recent period of the politics of inclusion or the illusion of inclusion?

While women from all ethnic/racial backgrounds and people of color have entered the workforce in record numbers, they have not really broken the glass ceiling and the glass escalators, which enable white men to be promoted and retained in leadership positions, fortifying the leadership color line. Why do men who enter "pink-collar" careers still get a male privilege of riding the glass escalator? People of color who, per chance, enter leadership positions are mostly in auxiliary capacity such as chief diversity and inclusion officers (CDIOs) with little or no power for policy-making, if they do not serve on the president's cabinet, and most CDIOs do not. Furthermore, with reference to leadership positions in our world today, we cannot ignore the forces of intersectionality of gender and race. Omi and Winant assert, "The intersectionality of race and gender gains particular importance because sex/gender also is a corporal phenomenon. The chattelization of the body has been a common experience for both people of color and women. In many ways racial differences and sex/gender-based differences resemble each other because they are both grounded in the body. Millions of people, after all, are both people of color and women. Gender differentiation resembles racial differentiation in numerous discomfiting ways" (2015, p. 258). Our observations and informed opinions in leadership discourses is that what affects most people of color has similar trajectory for all women, and an approach to mitigating the inequities in leadership both in higher education and diversity categories all over the world is long overdue.

A decisive change in leadership demographics is only apparent in countries where decisive affirmative action, mentoring, and quota systems are in place to diversify company boards and executive chambers as well as members of parliament and ministers (Iceland, Norway, Sweden, Rwanda). Of course, structural equity measures to enhance leadership advancement for people who have been historically disadvantaged such as legal instruments regulating pay equity, work-family balance, and parental/family leave benefits accompany such quota policies. Even so, in the United States diversity hiring is based on the pool of applicants that apply and not quotas, since the case of *Bakke v. Regents of the University of California* (1978) made quotas illegal but affirmative diversity based on percentages is acceptable.

The measure of all (heterosexist) things still seems to be Aristotle's natural complement theory. The philosopher and scientist seems to defend all that is noble and good for mostly white men and relegates women to undesirable aspects of the masculinist self-expression and social identity. It reinforces a reasoning/body dichotomy, whereby "reasoning" is reserved for white males and "body" for Black men and all women. The woman's body is objectified and Black bodies are sanctioned for physical labor and athleticism, in this perspective. Aristotle's misogynist ideology has had lasting effects through the millennia. Table 10.1 gives us a clarification of masculine and feminine ideal attributes that differentiate personality dispositions, skills, and interests within the heteronormative, *white* American nuclear family.

It is a binary table of ideal dispositions, that is, they are mutually exclusive and thus reinforcing differences. The ideological claims of such biologically based, essentialist complement theory are expressed in a rigid

Table 10.1. Gender Stereotypes

Masculine	**Feminine**
Active	Passive
Independent	Dependent
Assertive	Receptive
Self-interested	Altruistic, caring
Physically competent	Physically weak
Rational	Intuitive
Emotionally controlled	Emotionally open
Self-discipline	Impulsive

Source: Author provided.

gender (and sexual) division of labor: cisgender men and women have biologically different capacities and interests; the social cohesion will be guaranteed when each gender accomplishes tasks that they are best suited for. Finally, women and men are "separate but equal." That means that men have power in the public sphere, pertaining to the economic and political order, while women have power in the private sphere (domestic life, family). In the end, such biologically determinist theory suggests that gender roles and the division of labor are not sexist (that is, they are not unequal, unfair, discriminatory toward women).

Of course, such claims are easily debunked. The cultural traits defined as masculine are seen as positive in a dominant heteropatriarchal society, while the traits defined as feminine are negative, specifically, inappropriate for the public domain. These same cultural traits that refer to heteropatriarchal masculinity apply specifically to white males in powerful positions. Second, biology does not determine social destiny: male aggression and female submission and maternal "instincts" are products of society, not biology. Therefore, gender expression is on a continuum, where masculinity does not necessarily exclude femininity. Racial categories are also socially constructed and are not biologically structured and race projects intersect with all the diversity categories of gender, class, religion, disability, and sexual orientation. Race projects are sociopolitical identities based on phenotypes, combined with social agendas and structures to enhance racial groups' representation and struggle for rights and resources within a polity. Omi and Winant maintain that a "racial project is simultaneously an interpretation, representation, or explanation of racial identities and meanings, and an effort to organize and distribute resources" (2015, p. 125). Finally, in reality, women and men actually do not play in a "separate but equal" realm. Separate but equal did not start with *Plessy v. Ferguson* (1896)—affirming segregation—nor did it end with *Brown v. Board of Education of Topeka* (1954)—undoing de jure segregation. We continue to struggle with both equality and equity even today.

Despite equal protection and antidiscrimination gains in the workforce, women still have less economic and political power than men; there still is a glaring pay equity gap; in a heterosexual relationship, a woman still does much more unpaid care labor than her partner, which increases with parental responsibilities. Arlie Hochschild's (1989) extensive studies on the second, unpaid shift describes it as the upstairs-downstairs division of labor: the male partner is responsible for basement activities (e.g., light household repair, but the laundry machine, which may also be deposited in the basement, still is her responsibility. He gets to do glorified public chores such as taking out the garbage and mow the lawn, and she gets to do everything else [behind the scenes]). Another analysis gives us an even clearer picture of the *structural* inequity of unpaid domestic labor: "Feminine chores are mainly indoor and done frequently: cooking, cleaning, laundry and child care. Masculine chores are mostly outdoor and less frequent: taking out the trash, mowing the lawn or washing the car" (Miller, 2018). What are the psychological effects of such unequal task-sharing in this cisgendered heterosexual matrix? Women get anxious and resentful and men do *not* see themselves as over empowered, enjoying the benefits of male unearned privilege. As Aristotle would remark on this distribution of goods: "It is the natural order of the *oikos*."

Such reified binary disposition of "public man, private woman," in the famous words of Jean Bethke Elshtain, is so powerful that it seems even today that working men or women have difficulty accepting the fact of competent leadership from a woman CEO, college president, or head of state, let alone general secretary of the United Nations. In the workforce, gender essentialism means that women are pegged into secretarial, supportive social roles even where it is incongruent with their professional disposition. A natural science researcher boasts having achieved gender parity in his lab; the advantages being that women do the meticulous, detailed-oriented experimental work, whereas men are the decision makers and grant-writers who have the birds-eye view and put teams together; however, men are incapable of doing "more routine work for a longer period" and it's best to delegate such work to women (Linkova, 2017, p. 58). Marcela Linkova notes that this male team-leader displays benevolent sexism of typecasting women into performing analytic support work and leaving the big picture, synthetic cognition to male researchers. The latter style is more valuable because it leads to successful grant writing. We note that his unconscious bias is also a case of microaggression, namely, one of microinvalidation with clearly punitive consequences for women researchers, condemned to a life of data entry. It is clear that the prized good is grant writing, and women would lose out on bonuses and other types of compensation and leadership recognition.

Black and Latino women and men are entrapped in a similar quagmire. Whether it is acquiring a PhD or becoming a corporate executive, dean, provost, or president of a college, the achievement gap is real. Miseducation of the Black elites, diseducation of the Black masses (to serve capitalistic needs), white syllogism that casts Black and brown folx out as failed races in leadership, white solipsism, which sustains white privilege, cultural imperialism and the mindset that whiteness is both discursive and normative agentic entity, and stereotype threat, which sets Black and brown people up for failure, are all programmatic agencies sustained through social engineering. We can add to the awful list above: Black immiseration, the part of the undergirding of the capitalism that detains Black people in the bottom billion and helps to promote material fetishism of Black folks for the marketplace; Black and Latino infantilization, a childlike position placed on Black and Latino folx by the dominant culture, which reduces their anthropomorphic status; and post-traumatic slave syndrome, the lack of clinical healing for the Black race since enslavement and Jim Crow. These are some of the reasons for lack of Black leadership in corporate America and academia. Of course, race is a major category in America and racism is the elephant in the room.

As might be expected and without getting into an oppression Olympics (oppressed groups competing for medals for who has suffered the most in the system of oppression), it is evident that white women are the prime beneficiaries of affirmative action and white male veterans are the fastest growing group for affirmative action benefits, not Blacks. So, the lights and reflections on the leadership kaleidoscope are not only gendered but highly racialized. Racial categories and racialized bodies are contained in workplaces and spaces, where Black bodies run an unequal opportunity race to the top without much success. When spaces are given authoritative meaning in terms of leadership and management, they become mostly white heteropatriarchal places and spaces. Black bodies were "questioned" in our history for personhood and leadership. "Questioned personhood" did not start with disability studies, because we can travel as far back as the Supreme Court decision of *Dred Scott v. Sanford* (1857), where Black bodies were not regarded as fully human properties. Founding Fathers like Thomas Jefferson believed Blacks were "dumb," "have very strong and disagreeable odor," and are "unable to utter their thoughts in plain narration" (D. Smith, 1998). Yet Jefferson cherished an under-age teenager Sarah Hemings in order to have a relationship with her for over thirty years (D. Smith, 1998). Paternalism and heteropatriarchy shaped Jefferson's mindset to group women and Black folk in a category that would always be subjugated and yet protected for economic benefits of the system.

Joe Feagin's (2014) white racial frame (WRF) encapsulates the saga of America's racial formation, racial project, and race relations that reduce Black Americans to servitude and minoritized positions. In this white racial frame, which supports and sustains white privilege, the unearned advantage of whites because of history and skin color, white racial stereotypes of Black people (lazy, childlike, predator), are turned into racial narratives and interpretations loaded with negative images of Black folk. Racial images are transformed into racialized emotions. Racialized feelings are transformed into racist perceptions, and these perceptions are turned into public policy and discriminatory actions combined with lethal social trust that prevent Black folx from securing leadership positions (Feagin, 2014).

However, interlocutors of the racial project and leadership may question the election of the first African American president of the United State, even with an Islamic name—Barak Hussein Obama as primus inter pares of world leaders. Racial projects shape American lives through the connections of structural entities, systems, and racial representations. These racial projects facilitate the nature of racial formations and racial group's ability to lead or rule (Omi and Winant, 2015). Obama's election was a test case for the American presidency and the United States' racial projects. This test case included Obama's mixed-race identity; a challenge to white heteropatriarchal hegemony of the US political establishment and the presidency, and the extent to which "no drama Obama" could remain racially neutral in a racialized society. In the assessment of white supremacists and heteropatriarchal masculinists, Obama failed all three measures above (cf. Asumah, 2015).

Dealing with the dynamics of the white racial frame for Black and brown folx and women leadership is one thing; the other thing that has threatened Black and brown leadership efforts is the concept and effects of social trust. Social trust is the precepts, norms, and beliefs associated with integrity, honesty, and reliability of a group of people or a nation state (Putnam, 1993). Social trust sounds simple but the impact of it on Black and brown leadership and African nation states is devastating. When a group of people is perceived to be deviant and deficient in social trust, they are not given the opportunity to aspire to be leaders, managers, or administrators of programs, institutions, or nation states. The PEW Social Trends Survey indicates that in the United States, whites are more trusting than Blacks and Latino (PEW Research Center, 2007). This distrust is also translated in leadership roles and responsibilities. Who would entrust a leadership position in the hands of a distrustful person? This might be a rhetorical question, but the answer is an important one when studies about distrustful groups and nations point to the Black community in the United States and Africa (PEW Research Center, 2007).

On the global scene, studies conducted in the West indicate Black/African countries and their leaders are more distrusting than Scandinavians, Americans (PEW Research Center, 2007). Does white solipsism, the epistemological and cognitive position that since Black knowledge base is outside white spheres of reasoning and behavior means that Black folx cannot be successful leaders? Does it tickle our moral consciousness that in American football—National Football League (NFL), a sport populated by Black men (65 percent)—the most important positions that involve leadership, quarterbacks (23 out of 32 are white) and center positions together are 82 percent white in the 2013 season (Mudede, 2017; Ralston, 2019)? The narrative is not different in corporate America. According to *Fortune* magazine (McGirt, 2018), there were only three Black CEOs in the Fortune 500 companies in 2018. This number was down from six CEOs in 2012 (McGirt, 2018). It is not a coincidence that in the wake of the murder of George Floyd and Black Lives Matter protests around the world, *Fortune* recently reports of the number of Black CEOs jumping back to the 2012 levels of (miserable) six in 2022 (McGlauflin, 2022). In academia, the American Council on Education (ACE) 2017 annual report indicates that African Americans make up 8 percent of all college presidents and women of color make up only 5 percent of this leadership position (ACE, 2017). Women of color are the most underrepresented group in university and college leadership. Again, after George Floyd's murder case and Black Lives Matter protests in 2020–2021, the *Chronicle of Higher Education* reports that while white women make up 45 percent of provosts, 45 percent of deans, and 57 percent of vice provosts, only 13 percent of minoritized folx are provosts, 14 percent vice provosts, and 16 percent are deans in American higher education (Kafka, 2022).

Social trust and implicit bias are powerful motivators to maintain the status quo. The Harvard-based Project Implicit self-testing exercise serves the purpose of unearthing our deep-seated unconscious fears about women and Blacks in the workforce, in white male-dominated careers, it also offers testing about disability, racism, and many other diversity indicators. As we will demonstrate in the section below on transformative ethical leadership, only through conscious effort and repetition, old habits can be broken and an equity mindset and habitus can start to germinate in each of us and our lifeworld. Furthermore, it is our conviction and our enduring sense that it is in the institutions where diversity educators and thought leaders are able to report directly to the top leadership that inclusion and equity flourish. We have heard many times in our diversity and inclusion institute that we codirect at SUNY Cortland the frustration of white colleagues about their inability to deal with their biases if these prejudices are "unconscious" in the first place. Our answer to such a perspective is that we must work smarter and inclusively to make the unconscious conscious, so that the personal and institutional cycles of oppression can be broken.

Furthermore, breaking discrimination patterns at the individual (conscious) level is necessary but not sufficient. If it were sufficient, antidiscrimination policies and procedures (de jure legislation) would have immediate deterrent effects and persuasive power. As we have seen, the legacies of white supremacy, including chattel slavery, the convict lease system, Jim Crow, and the perpetuation of a racial caste system in the carceral system are lingering on. Astoundingly, Black Americans have one tenth of the average wealth accumulated by whites in 2019. In response to federal pressure, southern states enacted their own anti-lynching laws during the height of lynch terrorism of African Americans. However, state actors (sheriffs, etc.) never bothered to enforce the laws, and the white lynch mob was never indicted, prosecuted, or convicted of the thousands of deaths they committed during the Jim Crow era. The enduring effects of the Jim Crow era was a mass exodus, dubbed the Great Migration, of hundreds of thousands of Black Americans to northern states. But accumulation of networks did not ensure generational wealth there either, thanks to redlining enshrined in the "whites only" New Deal legislation of the 1930s. In this perspective, race, a master category in the American polity, strengthened systemic oppression and made ample space also for resistance. Racialization facilitated superordination and subordination with leaders and the led. Yet the led were not passive. Resistance, marches, rallies, protests, and insurgencies were all part of the struggle for democracy and inclusive leadership.

Finally, the civil rights moral revolution and legal changes were supposed to present a break from a white supremacist past: the universal right to suffrage, integration of schools, and even affirmative action federal policies went beyond formal antiracist measures to endorse substantive educational and economic opportunities for Black people.

Or so it seemed. As we mentioned earlier in this chapter, with the US Supreme Court decision of *Bakke v. Regents of the University of California* (1978), it was made clear that any race-based policies that favored Black applicants for universities or employment, that is, that had the tinge of a "quota" system, would be abolished. In the end, the Kennedy initiative of equal opportunity and affirmative action to undo the racist legacies of the past benefited another group of people: white women. Decades later, they found themselves displaced by veterans of war. And today, redlining continues to be the status quo—residential segregation is as prominent as it had been in the 1950s and many African American children now (again) are educated in schools that have fewer than 10 percent white children. The difference is that today most of them are educated by whites and no longer have Black role models as teachers, guidance counselors, or principals (hooks, 1994). White teachers teach most Black students and those who control institutions and processes of education can easily use them to maintain their leadership roles and superordination, while subordinate cultures are enmeshed into subservient and not leadership roles. Many African American males are sadly placed in special education programs, and these boys by the fourth grade are set up for failure. Kunjufu (1995) calls this process that kills the educational enthusiasm of Black boys the "fourth-grade syndrome," a stage where Black boys begin to lose enthusiasm in education and leadership. White teachers are unprepared to assist them, and, at the age of nine, these boys are seen as a burden to society (Kunjufu, 1995, p. 33; Asumah & Perkins, 2001). We are hopeful that recent inclusive educational practices would counter the process of miseducation, diseducation, fourth-grade syndrome, inadequate educational financing in public schools, and mitigate the forces of the stereotype threat to enable Black students to be fully prepared to enter college and be ready to take up leadership roles.

The topic of women of color, specifically of Black girls and women, continues to be systematically excluded from gender equity discussions in educational institutions. Over and over, Black feminist testimonies deride the fraudulent claims of the Moynihan Report, which was supposed to present a status report on the Black American Family. What Senator Moynihan's study effectively does is resort to a "blame the victim" gendered-racist framework (Davis, 1981; Hill Collins, 1993; Harris-Perry, 2013). Moynihan resorts to the tired mammy stereotype and opines that Black women as mothers and wives are simply out of step with the normative (i.e., white, patriarchal) ideology of the cult of domesticity and therefore ill-equipped to deal with rearing their sons and providing proper (domestic) moral support for Black men. However, the Black man is characterized as a caricature, predator, and destroyer of the Black family. The Black man was emasculated through reduced alpha image, vacant esteem, and nihilism—the feeling of hopelessness and nothingness because he cannot fully provide for the Black family. The Moynihan Report emasculates the Black male by citing matriarchal family structures of the Black community and their demerits vis-à-vis heteropatriarchal white family structures as the normative measure of the American family.

Astoundingly, Moynihan concludes that Black women are to blame for the lack of educational and employment opportunities of Black boys and men. Thus, in one magic trick relying on historical amnesia, all racist, sexist systemic, oppressive inequities are disappeared from the political landscape and (white, male supremacist) policy-makers are offered assurances to treat the ailments of the Black family with "benign neglect." The Black family's enduring struggle is as much about coping with the post-traumatic slavery syndrome, as Joy DeGruy Leary notes, which continues to be an irrepressible racial and gendered apparitional structure that haunts Blacks in the American society. So, "what originally began as an appropriate adaptation to an oppressive and danger-filled environment has been subsequently transmitted down through generations" (Leary, 2005, p. 15). Angela Y. Davis (1981) notes, what also disappears from such racist framing is the fact that through the centuries, the Black family has enjoyed a much more egalitarian und supportive gendered relationship than what was offered to white middle-class women with the allure of the cult of domesticity. To patriarchs (such as Moynihan), such egalitarianism is deliberately misread as a threat to the power structure and Black women are deemed to diminish the ideal of (toxic) masculinity prescribed by Aristotle some 2,500 years ago.

A common complaint of scholars of color who work in the white ivory tower is that their service expectations are monumental, creating a racial-gendered fatigue syndrome for cis and trans women and men of color. Such unfair service burden is coupled with a perennial suspicion that their scholarship is just not good enough—again, a serious case of microinvalidation. This cultural taxation, the invisible labor of faculty of color (unpaid service), which is concomitant with the exacerbation of enrollment of students of color without adequate support systems and limited hiring of faculty of color. As Audrey Williams June (2015) in the *Chronicle of Higher Education* notes, "Professors who carry heavy service loads do it at the risk to their careers." In academe, being perceived as a productive scholar is often an entrance ticket to respectable leadership positions such as dean or provost.

Rethinking Leadership Models for the Disadvantaged

Like any valuable commodity, leadership is highly sought after in both corporate America and academia. While good leadership is a sine qua non in any successful business, institutions of higher learning have recognized that fact and have developed many leadership courses and programs. Research in the area of leadership continues to grow, examining the theoretical frameworks and processes of leadership. Even the basic definition of leadership runs the gamut from "the ability to impress the will of a leader on those led and induce obedience, respect, loyalty, and cooperation" (Moore, 1927, p. 124) to "leadership is a process whereby an individual influences a group of individuals to achieve a common goal" (Northouse, 2018, p. 7) and to "leadership is concerned with effecting change on behalf of others and society" (Komives et al., 2009, p. xii). Nevertheless, very little research and few books address the emerging field of diversity and inclusive leadership. As far back as the Great Man theory of leadership in the nineteenth century was propounded by white historians such as Thomas Carlyle (1888), who in 1847, had the idea that leaders were born and not made, white women and people of color were absent in that school of thought. Great men—heroes were prophets like Jesus, poets such as Shakespeare, kings as Napoleon, and philosophers such as Rousseau were the leaders of the time. We wonder where Yaa Asantewaa, the most eminent African queen mother, leader, and warrior of the Ashanti Empire, who fought against British colonialism, and Frederick Douglass, the African American scholar and philosopher, would place in Carlyle's mind.

The evolution of leadership theories has circled around mostly white male traits, those who are born to lead and those who are "natural" leaders. Process-orientated leadership places emphasis on the interaction between the leader and the led. Here, leadership is seen as something that could be learned and it is behavioral. In recent times few Black, brown, and women leaders have risen to the occasion. Martin Luther King, Jr., a civil rights leader, Nelson Mandela, former president of South Africa, who brought apartheid to its knees, and Oprah Winfrey, a television talk show host who rose from rags to riches, are some of the leaders who combined traits and behavior in their leadership style.

While traits and behavior seem to dominate the theoretical framework of leadership, one should not be surprised to learn from many corporate and higher education leaders that they admire Greenleaf's work on servant leadership. "A servant-leader is servant first. . . . It begins with the natural feeling that one wants to serve, to serve first," Greenleaf notes (1977, p. 27). We have had the opportunity to review and submit an evaluation of two college presidents and two candidates for the position of president and it is not a coincidence that all of them mentioned stewardship, service first, and the servant-leadership model.

Transactional and Transformational Paradigms in Leadership Development

As we have mentioned earlier in this chapter, there are many theories about leadership; the dominant ones have crystallized as theories on transactional versus transformational leadership. A growing body of literature tackles the thorny issue of leadership styles with respect to racial and gendered stereotypes and stereotype threat (Rudman & Glick, 2001; Eddy & VanDerLinden, 2006; Madden, 2011; Ellemers et al., 2012). With reference to gender stereotypes, they argue that the agentic style is congruent with expectations of male leadership, while women are expected to lead using a collaborative style. Building on Eagly and Karau's (2002) role congruity theory of prejudice, Margaret Madden, former provost at SUNY Potsdam, notices that when a woman leader adopts an agentic style, direct reports (i.e., subordinates) have more difficulty accepting her leadership, because she does not fit into the expected supportive, caring, collaborative mold of femininity. Whenever women are in senior leadership positions, their work tends to be devalued. As soon as she retires and a (white) man, *usually*, is hired, power and legitimacy again are vested with that office.

For a Johns Hopkins study done in 2002, senior women faculty/administrators were asked the following: "Are women faculty attracted to leadership positions as currently designed?" Francesca Dominici and her team found that women are systematically devalued in the academy; they lack informal networks and mentoring that prepare them for the traditional advancement (from department chair to dean, etc.). Furthermore, the Hopkins study notes that "success in such positions often seems to depend on having a spouse who can shoulder domestic responsibilities"—often on a full-time basis (Dominici et al., 2009).

Surprisingly, the Hopkins study also notes that where women have focused a lot of energy on is in building interdisciplinary centers that "address important unmet needs." They labor to find office space and scarce internal resources and build these centers with external grants because they often have national/international reputation; yet these center directors find only tacit approval by department chairs and deans, even though the university's reputation is greatly enhanced due to an increase in research productivity (Dominici et al., 2009). Here then is a paradoxical situation: women find traditional leadership workload onerous but do not mind spending equally endless hours building centers, organizing conferences without any compensation or administrative office support. Again, aspiring women leaders are supposed to enjoy service work without demanding the appropriate compensation or rewards afforded to similarly positioned male leaders. Here, the books of feminist economists Linda Babcock and Sara Laschever still has salience: *Women Don't Ask: The High Cost of Avoiding Negotiations—and Positive Strategies for Change* (2007) and their sequel: *Ask for It: How Women Can Use the Power of Negotiations to Get What They Really Want* (2009).

There are three important aspects to this model (see table 10.2): First, in this schematic version, we disagree with Margaret Madden and others

Table 10.2. Model of Transactional and Transformational Leadership

Transactional leadership	Ethical, transformational leadership
Fear-based	Hope-affirming
Power and control	Empowerment, collaboration, and equity
Scarcity and deficit model	Abundance model (trust in creative process)
Egocentric	Sociocentric, altruistic
Information control and secrecy	Informational sharing, collegiality, and transparency
Rigid adherence to hierarchy	Flat hierarchy and service-leadership ideal
Risk management	Diversity leadership
Monochromatic, homogeneous culture	Commitment to intercultural competence
Academic excellence	Inclusive leadership: inclusive excellence and strategic mentoring/pipeline/bridge Initiatives
Cloaked in mantle of invincibility	Accountability and genuine peace-making culture

Source: Author provided.

who wish to synthesize the transactional with the transformational ideal of leadership. Some might wonder why academic excellence, a hallmark of most mission statements, should be attached to transactional leadership. Inclusive excellence in leadership involves the intentional strategies in higher education that are aimed at connecting diversity, inclusion, and equity variables, units, and programs to the vital educational vision and mission of any institution. Inclusive excellence leadership should be a value-laden, behavioral, attitudinal, and policy-goal attainment process in our daily undertakings. However, many other characteristics denote that a unity of opposites is not desirable. For instance, the sociocentrist, relational ideal of transformational leadership is starkly oppositional to the transactional model that is described as egocentric. So, rather than arguing for an integrative model, which adopts the best traits of transactional and transformational leadership, we argue for a defense of the transformational theory.

Secondly, the transactional model seems to have many of the features of toxic masculinity—a topic spearheaded by the popular Me Too movement, engendered by sexual assault survivor Tawana Burke and that rose to a global social justice movement after female Hollywood celebrities broke the Weinstein scandal in 2017. In fact, Weinstein's company excelled in secrecy, manipulation, and massive cover ups of sexual assault. Such practices are exemplified by legal nondisclosure agreements, and Harvey Weinstein amassed quite a few of them, but the majority of his accusers never even bothered to sue him, because his control over Hollywood was pervasive and his bullying was legendary.

It is important to note that we worry about gender essentialism when it comes to effective and ethical leadership. We speculate that it is quite possible that women who adopt the (masculinist) transactional leadership style do so as a coping mechanism or overcompensate in order to attain worth and credibility among peers and their direct reports. Furthermore, most white women who adopt transactional leadership styles are mentored and nurtured in the heteropatriarchal system similarly to white males. However, it is unclear whether this "iron lady" image works to their advantage. A Hillary Clinton who was perceived as "bossy" ended up losing to a Donald Trump, who seems to be a perfect archetype of toxic masculinity.

Third, we insist on describing the combined transformational and social change models as an ethical leadership model. Following Christine Allen (2018), ethical leadership has several traits: humility, role-modeling behavior that emphasizes giving credit to others and focusing on a culture of integrity, not compliance. Her sixth trait is crucial: "Senior leaders should focus on reinforcing integrity in lower-level management." This means (applied to our model) that it is quite meaningless if the CEO has high-minded visionary transformational commitments when their vision is not implemented throughout the organization or company, who, in fact, may just work in transactional, self-serving manner.

The social change model (SCM) of leadership challenges our diversity leaders to maintain congruence in their utterance and deeds, not just window dressing events. As diversity and inclusion advocates, we are tired of being tired of what our colleagues of color call "food, fun, and festival" and "organized happiness" to fulfill the institutional needs for the "appearance" of diversity, equity, and inclusion (DEI). Are our colleges and university presidents walking the talk? Collaboration is primary to the dynamics of producing social change. Diversity demands collaboration as stakeholders bring their agendas to the table—they must have a place at the table, but often the voices of minoritized groups and women are silenced by hegemonic powers at the table. Nonetheless, diversity leadership is human work, which is "grounded in relationships between people; in these relationships one develops the ability . . . to work collaboratively with others that is essential to the leadership process" (Komives et al., 2009, p. 195). Commitment enables transformational leadership to reach a point of sustenance. If college and university leadership is about stewardship, then commitment enables the leader to have a responsibility to serve, to be an advocate for all the people regardless of their minoritized status on campus, and common purpose trumps it all. Common purpose is an essential element for diversity leadership for a shared vision, inclusive meaning, democracy, and organizational success.

Next, we will explore what counts as ineffective risk leadership and decision-making when intercultural competence is lacking, and diversity leadership only means "managing diversity."

Failure in Diversity Management: What Happened to the Eagle and the Crow?

In researching and working in many colleges and on our own campus, we continue to explore the predictable administrative reactions to a sporadic campus crisis and develop a (cultural) competence analysis at the organizational level. With the intelligence of the crow, it is natural to respond to or defuse racist incidents. Yet the nurturing ability, humanity, strength, and endurance of the eagle in diversity and inclusion are missing in this leadership model. Crisis management modality means being stuck in the first two or three stages of denial, defense, and minimization. Similar to Bennett's (1993) model of cultural competence at the individual level is Terry Cross's (1988) model of the cultural competence continuum for systems analysis. We argue that the crow model alone corresponds to our transactional model, whereas the combined forces of the eagle and crow represent the ethical, transformational, and inclusive leadership paradigm.

Combining the social change leadership model and transformational leadership model for diversity leadership is the best approach for modern institutions that seriously make diversity and inclusion part of their modus operandi. In our previous work on diversity leadership, we proposed the following: "A core demand of diversity leadership, as opposed to diversity management, is to evaluate and validate the work of faculty of color [and women] as change agents in terms of inclusive academic excellence standards. The caged bird is indeed free to leave the cage and soar in community-engagement praxis, which will "count" towards valuable research, elevating the academy as a place that is accountable to its diverse residents" (Asumah, Nagel, & Rosengarten, 2016). Interestingly, while white women leaders in general are often called upon to serve and save a financially struggling company, Black and brown leaders are usually neglected (Bruckmüller et al., 2014; Cook & Glass, 2014). Cook and Glass use the concept of the glass cliff (instead of glass ceiling) to assert that women need to prove themselves in very stressful leadership roles, that is, managing organizations in crisis. In such moments, relying on the short-term semi-transformational approaches to "save" the organization seems a wise investment in organizational leadership, requiring such leaders to adopt a collaborative, nonagentic, nontransactional style. Eddy and VanDerLinden (2006) hold out hope for community colleges (i.e., two-year colleges) for leading the way on endorsing a transformative leadership style. When Harvard Business School starts adopting such leadership philosophy without any hint of racism and benevolent sexism (i.e., that women are naturally predisposed to a nonagentic style), perhaps we could say that the "crow paradigm" is being considered the dominant leadership theory. Until then, the road to diversity leadership is undulating, filled with obstacle courses for Black and brown people, white women, and minoritized groups in the academy.

Conclusion

In this chapter, we have argued that the traditional heteropatriarchal leadership models on our college and university campuses have failed to serve the needs of all women and Black and brown people and their aspiration for leadership roles in the academy. The transactional and situational theories are endowed with whiteness and heteropatriarchal orientation, and the changes that are needed based on the preponderance of evidence in the Me Too movement and Black Lives Matter movement require transformative and social change leadership. These two models require leaders who are ready to alter the dominant culture of society in order to effect institutional behavioral and procedural changes. Intentionality, pervasiveness, and human consciousness are inevitable in this leadership process. Educational leadership must be inclusive, hope-affirming, inextricably linked to our social responsibilities and civil rights in order for diversity leadership to be successful.

In the final part of this volume, part 3, titled "Visions/Second Sight," we take these insights for inclusive leadership back to the political, legal, and ethical realms of our institutions and the public sphere. We begin with the possibilities of rethinking whiteness, encourage the reader to engage in the Ubuntu ethic, and conclude with promises of a pedagogy of racial healing.

Part 3

Visions/Second Sight

Chapter 11

Racial Identity, the Danger of Being Too Comfortable, and Antiracist Decision/Policy-Making

Rethinking Whiteness

Race matters. Race matters in part because of the long history of racial minorities being denied access to the political process. . . . Race also matters because of persistent racial inequality in society—inequality that cannot be ignored and that has produced stark socioeconomic disparities

—Justice Sonya Sotomayor (2014)

Racial identity presented itself as a matter of trammels and impediments, as "tightening bonds about my feet." As I looked out into my racial world, the whole thing verged on tragedy. My "way was cloudy" and the approach to its high goals by no means straight and clear. I saw the race problem was not as I conceived, a matter of clear, fair competition, for which I was ready and eager. It was rather a matter of segregation, of hindrance and inhibition.

—W. E. B. Du Bois (1914)

A very different version of this chapter on racial identity was published in Asumah and Nagel, *Diversity, Social Justice, and Inclusive Excellence* (2014).

Introduction

In our daily interactions, we see different people around us all the time. There are people who look like us, in our families and inner circles, and some who look very different from us. Even though racial differences based on pigmentation should not matter, race is always the elephant in the room. It is an indefatigable fact that "race is a master category—a fundamental concept that has profoundly shaped, and continues to shape, the history, polity, economic structure, and culture of the United States" (Omi & Winant, 2015, p. 106). We think it is a well-founded conception that racial categories are not the only social constructs in any society. Race has an intersectional quality and agency or a high capacity to act with ethnicity, culture, gender, sexuality, class, geography, religion, earned ability, and other DEI categories. The concept of race is complex, and we cannot understand it well without dissecting the ability and capacity for racial structures to permeate the body politic. In the American polity, race has an agency in almost every policy-making process. Race matters in heterogeneous, capitalist societies, such as the United States. Race has been used as an instrument for acquiring different forms of results, whether positive or negative. Race will continue to secure a permanent domain in both our individual and institutional patterns of interaction. Consequently, denial of racial identities and race as an irrepressible agency in antiracist decision- and policy-making is an oxymoron that could only lead to grave public policy paralysis or decision myopia, a quagmire, with implications not only for subordinate races, but also for the superordinate ones.

Every time a subordinate group demands something of substance in the polity, let us say, power-sharing, resources, freedom, liberty, inclusion, and equity from the superordinate group, group political consciousness is at work, and identity politics remains the engine bloc of this action. Power differentials between superordinate and subordinate groups set the stage for demand-making, which involves identity politics. Without identity formation and group political consciousness, distribution of power and resources does not occur. Yet, as Frederick Douglass once informed us, "Power conceded nothing without a demand. It never did and it never will. Find out just what any people quietly submit to and you have found out the exact measure of injustice" (Douglass, 1857). The history of mostly oppressed groups demanding justice and equality is not a recent phenomenon. Since the genesis of the American polity was premised on gargantuan principles of injustice and inequality, minoritized groups and women have to engage in identity politics to receive a piece of the sociopolitical pie. The request for equal rights was based on Black folx making demands from white, heteropatriarchal, elite hegemons. Women's endeavors for securing voting rights was engineered by the women's right movements to demand civil, human, and political rights from white men, the major beneficiaries of heteropatriarchy. The demand and campaign by predominantly Black folx to make Juneteenth (Liberation Day, Emancipation Day, Freedom Day) a federal holiday, which started in Galveston, Texas, after 1865, did not materialize until the United States Congress passed the bill for such a holiday and when President Biden signed it into law on June 15, 2021. It was Black identity politics that propelled the demand for Juneteenth as a federal holiday, but it was also white identity politics that thwarted the long efforts and yet accepted the Black position on Juneteenth as a truthful and valuable demand for all Americans, despite the opposition of some white folx. White opposition against Juneteenth as a federal holiday is premised on hearsay and conspiracy theories that Juneteenth has been an attempt by Black folx to replace July Fourth (declaration of America's independence) with Juneteenth (liberation of Americans from the holocaust of enslavement). To this end, the discourse over race and racial identities, implicitly or explicitly, runs through every public policy and decision-making agenda, whether it is on the national or local level. Racial identity in America cannot be separated from identity politics.

Black feminist Barbara Smith and the Combahee River Collective propounded the term "identity politics" in 1974. The root of identity politics was about the politics of valuing differences when Smith and her organization provided us with the coinage (Garza, 2019). Without identity politics, the politics of sameness that perpetuates the crafts of white supremacy and white heteropatriarchal hegemony will remain unchallenged. If our attempt to make demands on the body politic comes from the "self" and the group and not from the other, then identity politics is the most natural and effective approach for organizing the political animal. Our racial identities and racialized selves shape our demands and desires, especially in a country whose beginnings were full of violence, enslavement, Jim Crow, segregation, and racial injustice. Identity politics and racial identity development are effective political instruments for organizing for civil rights, human rights, civic engagement, and racial justice. Minoritized groups have to come to terms in presenting their particular perspectives on critical issues that affect their raison d'être and mere existence. Garza asserts, "Racial identity is an invented series of social categories which have impacts on power and agency socially, economically, and politically" (2019, p. 4). So, these socially constructed categories, like race and racial identities, give meaning to our existence. We cannot deny their efficacy in decision-making and the policy process, especially in a racialized society.

Racialized politics and racism in America did not end with the Supreme Court ruling in *Brown v. the Board of Education of Topeka* (1954). And, over sixty years after *Brown*, a reexamination of the United States' national ethos today would indicate that Americans have made progress in some aspects of race relations, but metaracism, a white-dominated polity and decision machinery that supports and sustains whiteness and white privilege at the expense of people of color, still prevails. Racism and white supremacy did not end with the 1964 civil rights either. Racism is definitely ubiquitous, and it has permeated the fabric of the American polity, although many people feel "uncomfortable" talking about it. The brutal murder of a Black man in Jasper, Texas, in June 1998, in which the perpetrators of the crime tied and dragged the victim's body on the ground with their truck until his body was dismembered, and the knee lynching of George Floyd in Minneapolis by Derek Chauvin, a white police officer, in 2020 could not be termed aberrations. Nor could the numerous cases of racialized killings of people of color, but especially Black men in America by people of pallor (POP), predatory policing, infantilization of BIPOC folx, and racial profiling of Blacks, and Latinos, by mostly white police officers, white vigilantes, and immigration officers be characterized as anachronistic. Nonetheless, in the Jasper and Minneapolis cases, the citizens of those towns, and many people across the United States and the world, Blacks and whites alike, voiced their protestation against the acts of brutality and inhumanity of the murderers.

However, it is not the "Jasper-styled" racist terror and the "Minneapolis-styled" knee-lynching that destroy America the most. It is white supremacy and metaracism, the form of racism that is very prevalent in the marketplace, socioeconomic, and political institutions of power that consume Black bodies the most (Asumah & Johnston-Anumonwo, 2002). Iris Young affirms, "almost all traces of a commitment to race superiority have been removed, and only the grinding processes of a white-dominated economy and technology account for the continued misery of many people of color" (1990, p. 59). Thus, the standard in America is what is white. But whiteness is exhausting to both white and BIPOC folx. It derails hope in race relations and the realities of Black lifeworld. Austin Channing Brown captures the essence of whiteness: "I cannot hope in whiteness. I cannot hope in white people or white institutions or white America. I cannot hope in lawmakers or politicians, and I cannot even hope in pastors or ministries or mission statements. I cannot hope in misquoted wisdom from MLK, superficial ethnic heritage celebrations, or love that is aloof. . . . The longer this list gets, the more elusive hope becomes" (2018, p. 179).

Whiteness undermines identity politics and the politics of difference by dismissing the lived experiences, axiology, needs, and belief systems of BIPOC folx. False equivalences, Black Lives Matter vis-à-vis All Lives Matter, are designed to derail most of the conversation over race by whiteness. What is even more devastating is an attitude of complacent optimism by some Americans that we have reached racial equality and racism is not an issue in the post-Obama era. As Keeanga-Yamahtta Taylor carefully notes in her article, "The Obama Legacy: Barack Obama's Original Sin: America's Post-racial Illusion": "There was one moment when black America collectively came to terms with Barack Obama's refusal to use his position as president to intervene on behalf of African Americans. . . . In the end, the black president succumbed to states' rights. It was a moment of awakening for 'Generation O'—and of newfound understanding of the limits of black presidential power, not because Obama could not intervene, as his handlers insisted, but because he refused to do so" (2017). Obama understands American racial identity politics, and he was not ready to jeopardize his presidency to do the right thing or the "Black thing." Ironically, identity politics have helped the United States to make progress in some areas of civil rights, human rights, and in race relations.

New York Times columnist Anthony Lewis (1998), for instance, inculpated Stephen and Abigail Thernstrom of Harvard University and the Manhattan Institute in New York respectively, of believing that "America's race problem has been substantially solved" (p. 14). Though the Thernstroms claimed that was not their position, they still write "that the black condition, white attitudes and race relations have all improved dramatically" (Thernstrom & Thernstrom, 1997, p. 10). Yes, there has been progress, but the intensity and scope of racism in the United States, compared with other heterogeneous, multiracial nation states merit an ongoing dialogue on race. Ethnicity and racial heterogeneity in the United States place an irrepressible demand on policy-making and the body politic, which, in turn, makes racial identity a centripetal force in most political activities.

In this chapter, our primary argument is that, in heterogeneous, multiracial societies, such as the United States, where major decisions in the polity are made by predominantly white persons and leaders, the dominant group's acknowledgment of its whiteness as power instruments and group-phenomenologically sustained variables could enhance race relations and facilitate the decision-making and policy process. By consciously accepting race as an agency in every political activity, whites in America could use their white privilege positively in race relations and in the policy-making sphere. Hope-affirmingly, Cabrera et al. concur with our thesis above and statement of purpose for this chapter. They assert, "To truly support a society where 'all men [sic] are created equal,' it requires those in positions of systemic privilege to use those privileges toward undercutting the very systems that grant them these privileges in the first place" (2017, p. 85). Furthermore, we argue that the essentialization and episteme of "comfort" in racial conversations, difficult dialogues, and racialized decision-making are concomitant with dangers of illusion of resolve, solution, and closure, while racial identity issues and problems remain unresolved.

Many white policymakers, in particular, who often struggle with the feeling of guilt when a dialogue on race and racism emerges, will be more empowered to tackle racial problems if they develop a positive white racial identity. When whites become "comfortable" in discussing racism and white identity, considering their whiteness as both privilege and power statuses, they can be more effective in dealing with the American racial divide. Whites have both the economic and political resources to tackle America's racial problems, and to find solutions because the "race problem" is actually their own creation. Acknowledging white identity and white ownership of the generations of racism could lead to racial reconciliation—without recognition, there is no reconciliation. A positive, white, group identity is a first step toward racial harmony and reconciliation. Redefining whiteness involves dissecting white privilege, realistically and intentionally utilizing white unearned racialized benefits to facilitate decision making and changing racial narratives. Robin DiAngelo, a white, antiracist, critical race theorist, notes, "The identities of those sitting at the tables of power in this country have remained remarkably similar: white, male, middle- and upper-class, abled-bodied" (2018, p. xii). The decisions of these powerful white folx to shape the environment of all of us could go far if they consider their white privilege and those who are not privileged to count on their racial, ethnic, or gender identities. America's racial narrative has been mostly shaped by white heteropatriarchal hegemons who constantly deny their racial identity and their unearned privilege. It is indubitable that America's historical contradiction of freedom without liberated BIPOC folk disrupts the equation of freedom and justice for all. Those who profit from this racial arrangement have "The concrete benefits of access to resources and social rewards and the power to shape the norms and values of society which Whites receive, consciously or unconsciously: by virtue of their skin color in a racist society" (Wijeyesinghe et al., 1997).

In the discourse over racism and white privilege, if whites mostly see themselves as oppressors or the "bad guys," then the most logical thing for many of them to do is either to avoid such topics or deny the fact that they have the power and resources to do something about racism. Since very few people would like to be associated with the term "oppression" or "white supremacy," and since, historically, whites have utilized oppressive power in America for centuries, what approach can one take to convince white decision makers that they have power, as a group, to positively restructure racial dynamics and race relations to make antiracist decisions? This chapter is intended to explore the implications of positive white identity development in a racialized society and how to engage in antiracist policy-making without hiding behind the façade of comfortability and civility. This decision-making process should reflect the principle of inclusion, justice, and equity. Actually, it should be completely antiracist! Kendi maintains that "a racist policy is any measure that produces or sustains racial inequity between racial groups. An antiracist policy is any measure that produces or sustains racial equity between racial groups" (2019, p. 18). In Kendi's approach to a racism-free world, there should be no in-betweens. You are either a racist or an antiracist. Yet we believe that, since racial identity evolves and it is not a binary process, we submit to a racial identity development scheme that recognizes the reality of racial interaction. Furthermore, Kendi's definitions above are a bit hollow and circular. He uses racism in the definiendum and the definition becomes a philosophical fallacy. We will therefore use Janet Helms's (1990) conceptual framework for analyzing white racial identity development as a model for sustaining racial group power in decision-making and Ashley Jardina's work *White Identity Politics* (2019) for analyzing recent white identity politics. But first, a brief discussion of race and racism will serve as a sounding board for rethinking whiteness and guiding against the façade of comfortability in racial interactions.

Racial Identity, Race, and Racism Revisited: What of Ethnic Identity?

The literature on race and racism is impressive. Owing to the fact that the inception of the American polity was predicated on racial formation and the politics of race, many Americans could write books about race and racism with little trouble because of our personal and shared experiences with the agency of race. The social construction of race and texts of race and racism are deeply grounded in our cognitive structures and elicit racial groups' moral character. Americans have been put into racial categories for convenience since the first United States census of 1790 that used racial classifications, and yet Blacks (enslaved people) were only three-fifths of a person in that recorded history. Nevertheless, these categories of race have taken on forms of their own, shaping our precepts, norms, cultures, policy, decision-making, and patterns of political interactions. Therefore, in the American polity, race matters. Race plays a centripetal role in our polity. If the implications of race on public policy and decision-making remain unquestioned, the results could be overpowering and debilitating racial problems for the totality of the American populace and even with global implications. The knee-lynching of George Floyd by a white police officer, Derick Chauvin, not only affected the American public; it had a global effect and impact. To negate the adverse effects of race, one must understand the meaning of it as a social concept, by conditioning and problematizing race as a major category in American life. Omi and Winant define race as a "concept which signifies and symbolizes socioeconomic and political conflicts and interests by referring to different types of human bodies" (2015, p. 110). Though the human bodies referred to in this definition implore characteristics of humans associated with biological phenotypes, these organisms maintain sociohistorical and political properties as a result of their selection in any society. For instance, in American history, under the Supreme Court ruling of *Dred Scott v. Sanford* (1857), Blacks were only considered as pieces of property, not quite human during the times of enslavement. The status of Blacks in the American polity has been defined by the white society, and now Blacks are accepted as "somewhat coequal" of whites. If the definition and selection of race depend on a political process, then race itself is an "unstable" concept, constantly changing with the political process and it is concomitant with groups' competition to sustain their interests or resolve conflicts. Issues concerning racial categories, for the above-mentioned reason, will continue to be sociopolitical. Furthermore, racial categorization and the interaction of race and other diversity categories are inevitable: "There is a crucial and non-reducible visual dimension to the definition and understanding of racial categories" (Omi & Winant, 2015, p. 111). Race matters, race is a major category in our sociopolitical interaction, and racial identity politics shape the American polity.

The origins of white America's rejection of other peoples (races) could be traced from European racial reasoning, which Cornell West describes as "a division of deceptive consensual racial position based on the history of domination and subjugation of one race over another" (1994, p. 8). Prince Henry the Navigator's Portuguese racist chronicler, Gomes de Zurara, completed the first European racist book on Africa by his awful depiction of Black folx in 1453 (Kendi, 2019). Although, Zurara did not use the term race at that time, he still referred to the Africans as a group of people who were inferior to the European race and were predestined to remain at the bottom of the racial hierarchy. Another so-called race scientist, Carolus Linnaeus (1735), the Swedish botanist and European father of taxonomy, wrote his essay titled *Systema naturae*, by creating a racial position for whites in his hierarchy of human classification with the white race at the apogee of that pyramid and Blacks at the bottom (1735, pp. 5–60). Count Arthur De Gobineau, the French diplomat and scholar, maintained a similar sociopolitical position on the concept of race when he published his work *Essay on the Inequality of Race*. He was providing a synopsis and amplifying the ideas of the then Euro-American perception on race (1854, pp. 2–15).

Reginald Horsman correctly recapitulates: "In the first half of the nineteenth century many in the United States were anxious to justify the enslavement of the blacks and the expulsion and possible extermination of the Indian. The American intellectual community did not merely absorb European ideas; it also fed European racial appetites with scientific theories stemming from the supposed knowledge and observation of blacks and Indians" (1995, p. 3).

Yet, the science Horsman refers to in the citation above was nothing more than pseudoscience to justify white hegemonic thinking and attitude. In his work about moral and political philosophy, John Dewey quoted Thomas Jefferson, one of the authors of the declaration of American independence from Great Britain, who asserted, "In memory they are equal to whites, in reason much inferior. . . . I advance therefore . . . that the blacks, whether originally a different race, or made distinct by time and circumstances, are inferior to the whites" (Dewey, 1940, p. 52).

Such pseudoscientific characterization of race even by an American president was easily transformed into socioeconomic and political privilege for whites. Racial formations are therefore not natural. They are constructed by societies to affirm racial positions for decisions and public policy agendas. Race is currently understood as a sociohistorical and political concept. Many casual readers and students tend to confuse the concept of race with that of ethnicity. The English word "ethnic" is derived from the Greek *ethnikos*, the adjectival form of *ethos*, meaning "a nation." Later, the meaning of ethnos evolved to become paradigmatic for conceptualizing groups of different humans in the 1920s and 1930s (Asumah & Johnston-Anumonwo, 1999, p. 11). Ethnicity emerged as a conceptual challenge to the prevailing biological approach to race that made people of the Black race inferior. Ethnicity has been used as a tool for ethno-nationalism and ethnic cleansing in recent times. Ironically, in America, many whites refuse to associate themselves with the term "ethnicity." For some obscure reason, whites on most college campuses do not associate with the term "ethnic group." Whenever one hears the term "ethnic students," it is easy to associate it with Blacks, Latinos, Native Americans, or some groups other than white. Schaefer notes, "Ethnic minority groups are differentiated from the dominant group on the basis of cultural differences such as language, attitudes . . . and food habits. Ethnic groups are groups set apart from others because of their national origin or distinctive cultural patterns" (2019, p. 7). Theorization of ethnicity in America has its roots in Puritanism, the biological misunderstanding of race, religion, and white Anglo-Saxonism (Omi & Winant, 2015). This early twentieth-century theorizing of ethnicity can be easily associated to America's white ethnic identity crisis on steroids.

What then is ethnicity? Ethnicity is an affiliation or classification of a self-conscious group of people who share similar racial, kinship, cultural, and linguistic values (Barndt, 1991, p. 5). Ethnicity is a sociocultural phenomenon. Ethnic stratifications occur in multiethnic societies where a hierarchical arrangement of ethnic groups could emerge as one group establishes itself as a superordinate group, with power to shape the nature of ethic relation. Within both Black and white races there are different ethnic groups. Ethnic cleansing is an old practice and has gained currency in recent times. Schaefer notes, "Ethnic minority groups are differentiated from the dominant group on the basis of cultural differences such as language, attitudes toward marriage and parenting, and food habits. . . . Ethnic groups in the United States include . . . *Hispanics* or *Latinos*. Hispanics can be Black or White [race]. . . . The ethnic group category also includes White ethnic groups such as Irish Americans . . . and Norwegian Americans" (2019, pp. 7–8). Interestingly, many white folx do not believe they are part of the concept of ethnicity and many colleges and universities in the United States fail to include whites when the discourse over ethnic classification and campus climate emerges. White ethnic groups usually engage in an *ethnic paradox*, the ability to utilize one's ethnic tie to assimilate into the dominant culture, for example, Norwegian Americans becoming just white Americans. Ethnocentrism, the perception or misperception that one's ethnicity is superior and *ethnophaulisms*, the utilization of derogatory terms and ethnic slurs to demean an ethnic group are instruments in the America culture for sustaining the supereminence of whiteness and white supremacy.

Racism, the ability and power to enforce one's own prejudice or a group's, has had and continues to have grave impact on all races, although Blacks and other subordinate races have suffered much more of the effects of racism. Simply put, racism is group prejudice plus institutional power. Concerning individual and group prejudice, the social group that has institutional power and controls social capital maintains prejudgments to effect decision with the authority and power of the same group's sociopolitical systems. "Racism structures society so that the prejudices of one racial group are taught, perpetuated, and enforced to the benefit of the dominant group" (Barndt, 1991, p. 20). David Wellman succinctly characterizes racism as "a system of advantage based on race" (1977, p. 4). In America, the system of advantage is controlled and maintained by white folx.

A German physician and advocate of gay rights, Magnus Hirschfeld, gave currency to the concept and term racism in his book *Rassismus*. He provided the framework for studying racism and its history, and challenged the Nazi doctrine of racial formation (Hirschfeld, 1938). Many scholars have different characterizations, inflations, and deflations of the term racism to fulfill their academic, racial, and political interests. Omi and Winant refer to these political and cultural interests and activities associated with racism as racial projects. A racist racial project "creates or reproduces structures of domination based on racial significations and identities" (Omi & Winant, 2015, p. 128). By racial projects, scholars could redefine racism based on the racist activities involved. Racism and all other "isms" operate on a common premise. Most "isms," including racism, have a control group that exercises power and privilege, and a target group that is dominated, subjugated, and marginalized in resource and power distributions. Racism does not only rest on individual action and ignorance. Institutional powers make racism viable. From Main Street to Wall Street, whites control the institutional structures of power. From the village council to the national government, the same group has the marginal propensity to make most policies in America. Given these premises, and by making reference to racism as group prejudice plus institutional power, whites in America control and maintain the dominant structures of power to impose their will upon other groups and therefore benefit from racism. Certainly, not all whites are racists, but every white person implicitly or explicitly participates and benefits from the system that racism fosters. Furthermore, white supremacy harbors the most toxic forms of racism such as the knee-lynching of George Floyd, the Rodney King beating, and the Jasper, Texas, killing of Mr. Byrd.

Peggy McIntosh informs her readers about the historical "white privilege" that white America has over the rest of the general populace. McIntosh is particularly clear about this "unearned" privilege for whites in America (1988a, p. 2). With this privilege and power, whites are in a better position to solve America's racial problems by developing a positive white identity. This is not a crusade to push undue responsibility on white Americans and their image development. However, it is a truism that white Americans constantly fail to acknowledge their race as a group phenomenon, and that whites, as a group, maintain an "unearned privilege" to tackle America's racial problems. As we argue below, once whites have developed a unified, positive group identity, they can effectively shape public policy and decisions regarding racial issues.

Searching for White Racial Identity

Some proponents of democratic theory believe that racial identity politics could be antithetical to the basic principle of unification and oneness for a nation state (Gutmann, 2003). Nonetheless, the idea of a nation state itself is based on a broader principle of identity politics, the indivisibility of the nation state, and the questions of citizenship that have been vexing issues for the American polity. The irony of democracy is that minoritized groups have developed group identity politics because of the principle of freedom of association deeply ingrained in the American constitution. Yet most white Americans scrutinize racial identity politics when it comes to, especially, social justice, nationality, and immigration issues. But as Amy Gutmann notes, "The members of ascriptive groups of a particular race, gender, or nationality generally do not have a choice of being identified with the group" (2003, p. 24). Nevertheless, why are whites in America not engaged in racial identity politics or why do they have the luxury of not identifying as whites from a group phenomenological perspective? The process and state of defining for oneself and acknowledging the personal significance, responsibility, and social meaning of belonging to a particular group is referred to as racial identity development (Helms, 1990, p. 6). Although racial and ethnic identities are used interchangeably, and sometimes synonymously, they are different terms. As one can deduct from the earlier discussion in this chapter about race and ethnicity, racial identity and ethnic identity have clear distinctions. For instance, an Italian-American or a Jewish-American may identify themselves with a particular ethnic group, but may not consider themselves in racial terms as white. Similarly, one may acknowledge the personal linkage to a racial group, Black in this case, but not associate with the ethnicity of African American or Afro-Cuban. Nonetheless, racial and ethnic identities at times intersect.

At this juncture, one may pose a pressing and mind-boggling question: If racial categorization by Europeans were to serve a racist interest, then why must racial identity produce a positive effect on public policy and decisions? The response to the question lies in our approach to essentially planned sociopolitical constructs that give meaning to issues at a particular time in history. Racial identities prevail in many subordinate groups and if superordinate groups relegate their group responsibility as, perhaps, an individual, less important issues, then racial problems will not be effectively tackled. We must therefore discuss racial identity from a different perspective, with a shift in a paradigm, to effectively confront our racial problems in America. Hence, Beverly Tatum succinctly proclaims that "the concept of identity is a complex one, shaped by individual characteristics, family dynamics, historical factors, and social and political contexts" (1997, p. 18). The aggregate variables of individuals in a given entity become a group's identity. Tatum continues, "Dominant groups, by definition set the parameters within which the subordinates operate. The dominant group holds the power and authority in the society relative to the subordinates and determines how that power and authority may be acceptably used. Whether it is reflected in determining who gets the best jobs, whose history will be taught in school, or whose relationships will be validated by society, the dominant group has the greatest influences in determining the structure of the society" (p. 22).

Tatum's assertion supports the premise of the primary argument of this chapter. If the superordinate group has the most power and resources in shaping the dynamics of group interaction and policies, then, by not denying the fact that, as a group, it has the privilege of positively restructuring racial relationships, it can consciously produce public policy agendas and positive antiracist decisions with the subordinate group's interest in mind. The superordinate group in this aspect is a surrogate of political power and should use it positively to restructure race relations. But, as Frederick Douglass famously said, "Power concedes nothing without a demand."

The basic difference between white and Black racial identity development is that Blacks learn and understand "Blackness" very earlier on in life, while whites resist any association with "whiteness," especially when they are cognizant of the fact that there is a correlation between "whiteness" and privilege. This situation occurs because Blacks are socialized to be "Black" first, before anything else. Whites, on the other hand, are not socialized to be sociocentric; they are more egocentric in the process of their development. Tatum correctly notes in her work on racial identity that, "like many White people, this young woman had never really considered her won racial and ethnic group membership. For her, Whiteness was simply the unexamined norm. Because they represent the societal norm, Whites can easily reach adulthood without thinking much about their racial group" (1997, p. 95). Putting a normative value on whiteness for the rest of the society constrains subordinate groups in a condition of cultural imperialism. Here, the dominant group reinforces its position by bringing the other groups under the measure of its dominant norm (D. Young, 1990, p. 59). For this matter, white decision makers and policy advocates who fail to pay attention to their whiteness characterize their actions as only "normal," and "they are just doing their job."

Seldom do many whites stop to consider the benefits they accrue in belonging to their race. Nor does it surprise them that they possess such privilege. It is important to emphasize, however, that people who are not blind do not take time out to rave over their vision as a gift, for which they should be grateful. Certainly, having white skin does not grant one the immunity from failure or misfortune. Yet whites who fall to the bottom of the socioeconomic pile still have "white privilege" because of the color of their skin. One of the leading thinkers of identity politics, Amy Gutmann, believes that "group identity propels women and disadvantaged minorities to counteract inherited negative stereotypes, defend more positive self-images, and develop respect for membership of their group" (2003, p. 2). Is this the perception that explains why most white folx refrain from racial identity politics? Does white skin privilege play a part in disowning one's group identity? Why is this privilege so important in making public policy and in public decision making? To what extent can public policy and decision be more equitable if whites positively acknowledge their privilege as a group phenomenon? These questions will be tackled in the following sections of this chapter.

White Identity and Decision/Policy-Making

Human societies overall, including the American polity in particular, are complex. The social sciences have the Herculean task of making this complexity somewhat manageable. Public policy, besides examining what people do and why they develop series of steps to attain certain goals, is also concerned with the best thing to do and whether the best results could be attained through a given idea, approach, or technique. There is a plethora of literature addressing public policy and decision-making techniques, but almost none has taken account of the racial and ethnic identities of policy-makers and decision-makers in multiracial, diversity, and inclusive entities, and how that affects the process of decision, the policy-making, and a particular policy package. One cannot not comprehend the essence of group identity in the policy-making apparatus until they recognize the importance of benefits, representation, and the dynamics of alliance or accomplices in the process of policy- and decision-making. Legislators are directly involved in the policy process at all levels of government. Implicitly or explicitly, all branches of government—legislature, executive, and judiciary—have actions that result in some public policy and decision-making. Representation in these branches is regarded by political scientists as descriptive, symbolic, or substantive. Though Pitkin utilized these terms in association with the legislature, they are applicable to the other branches of government (1972, p. 5).

Descriptive representation is the degree to which institutions have the same demographic composition as those whom they represent. Symbolic representation is concerned with the extent to which a particular aspect of the general populace has confidence or trust in an institution charged with policy-making. Finally, substantive representation involves the process in which public policy agenda and the laws propounded by policy-makers reflect the preferences of the general populace (Pitkin, 1972, pp. 5–6). With reference to symbolic representation, Blacks, as well as whites, have relatively low levels of confidence and trust in the bureaucracy, Congress, or lawmaking bodies. In a PEW research study only 2 percent of the population say they trust the government always and 18 percent trust the government most of the time. A whopping 79 percent say they trust the federal government to do right sometimes but not all the time (PEW Research Center, 2020). Of course, this trust factor differs based on the president in power, party affiliation, political ideology, race, and ethnicity. For instance, Black (79 percent) and Latino (74 percent) prefer government that provides more public services vis-à-vis whites (41 percent) who prefer less government services. An overall historic low of trust levels for the federal government by Democrats was 12 percent under President Trump (PEW Research Center, 2020). In essence, both whites and Blacks have distrust for policy-makers, but it is much more so for Blacks, because whites, who spearhead the policy and decision processes, refuse to acknowledge their whiteness and privileged positions in the entire process, and yet they have remained too comfortable with the status quo.

The numerical preponderance of white policy/decision-makers at all levels of American society cannot be overemphasized. Even though the 117th Congress is historically more racially and ethnically diverse than all the previous years, whiteness still prevails in numbers, power, and privilege. Twenty-three percent of the House of Representatives and Senate is ethnically and racially minoritized groups. During the January 26, 2021, sitting of the Congress, of 532 voting members, 124 identifies as Black, Latino, Asian/Pacific Islanders, or Indigenous people. This is the highest level of progress we have witnessed in our law-making body (Schaeffer, 2021). Historically, the United States Congress has not been descriptively representative of Blacks in America. Of more than 12,415 persons who have served in that institution since 1789, only 163 have been Black (Schaeffer, 2021). Overall, the American Congress is not a representative body as far as subordinate races are concerned. Concomitant with white group identity denial, the policy-making process becomes even more elusive when the dominant group fails to incorporate identity politics of acknowledging its power dimension and the presence of race.

The United States Supreme Court has always been actively involved in judicial policy-making through the decisions of the court. The court is not only a legal institution; it is a political one, because it arrives at decisions on controversial questions of national policy. Chief Justice Roger B. Taney's infamous opinion in *Dred Scott v. Sanford* (1857) affected the lives of all Africans in America until the 1940s. He impugned:

> The question is simply this: can a Negro, whose ancestors were imported into this country, and sold as slaves, become a member of the political community formed and brought into existence by the constitution of the United States, and as such become entitled to all the rights, and privileges, and immunities, guaranteed by that instrument to be citizens. . . . We think they are not, and they are not included, were not intended to be included, under the word "citizen" in the Constitution, and can therefore claim none of the rights and privileges which that instrument provides for and secures to a citizen of the United States. On the contrary, they were at that time considered as a subordinate and inferior class of beings, who had been subjugated by the dominant race, and whether emancipated or not, yet remained subject to their authority, and had no rights or privileges. (Hall, Wiecek and Finkelman, 1991, p. 208)

Historically, the Supreme Court has, at times, been a racialized institution, refusing to support the universal freedom for Blacks. This is not 1857, and, yes, the court is changing with the times, yet it still maintains justices with similar racist ideas even in 2021. Chief Justice Rehnquist wrote this in a memorandum: "I realize it is an unpopular and unhumanitarian position, for which I have been excoriated by 'liberal' colleagues, but I think *Plessy v. Ferguson* was right and should be affirmed" (Liptak, 2005). In addition, the court is quite notorious in refusing to hire Black law clerks. Chief Justice Rehnquist has 99 percent white clerks; Scalia, 100 percent whites; Souter, 94 percent whites; and O'Connor, 91 percent whites. From 1972 to 1998, only 1.8 percent of the law clerks were Black, 1 percent were Latino, and 4.5 percent were Asian American. So, over twenty years ago, *USA Today* did a first ever study of the Supreme Court's racial composition of law clerks stated in the numbers above; a similar study in 2018 tells the same story, that since 2005, 85 percent of all the Supreme Court's clerks remain white (Mauro, 2018). When Chief Justice John Roberts became a member of the Supreme Court, white law clerks controlled the daily routine of the court. Eighty-five percent of all the law clerk for the justices were white and only 4 percent were Black and

1.5 percent Latino. While the white justices hired overwhelming white law clerks, Justice Sonia Sotomayor, a justice of color, hired 31 percent law clerks of color (Weiss, 2017). Therefore, racial identity politics are real even at the highest court of the land where some observers might think justice should be "blind." All these examples lead to the primary argument of this chapter, which holds that white decision/policy-makers indulge in actions that involve racial identity politics without accepting the preeminence of their privilege and whiteness. Once the positions of privilege and group identity are acknowledged and acted upon, reason will prevail in the decision/policy-making sphere and racist decisions/policies will be reduced, if not eliminated.

Even though the work of Ashley Jardina (2019) indicates that many whites are reclaiming their identity and we concur with Jardina's observations, we also argue that the recent resurgence of white identity politics, especially since the presidency of Barak Obama, the knee-lynching of George Floyd, the presidency of Donald Trump, the Black Lives Matter movement, and the irrepressibility of white comfort, is more in consilience with white nationalist and white supremacist ideology of racial superordination than an authentic claim to group political consciousness and racial identity. So, is recent white identity politics, epiphenomenal, episodic, or contextual? We will address these questions in the balance of this chapter.

In Weberian characterization, bureaucracy is a rule of officialdom, which maintains forms of power based on knowledge, rationality, and hierarchical structures (Weber, 1969, pp. 3–57). However, even though the primary function of bureaucracy is to execute the law and implement policy, it also serves quasi-legislative and quasi-judicial functions by administrative rule-making and adjudicating conflicts that arise under those rules in administrative courts and claims of agency beneficiaries. We live by bureaucratic decision/policy-making all the time, and they shape racial interactions. Indubitably, many more Blacks work in the federal bureaucracy, the Civil Rights Acts of 1957, 1960, and 1964 and Title VII of that act, which created the Equal Employment Opportunity Commission (EEOC), have all helped to ensure nondiscriminatory practices in federal employment and private companies holding federal contracts (Walton & Smith, 2000, p. 240). Yet the overall evaluation of the bureaucracy is that they have not been consistently useful in BIPOC and especially Black America's quest for universal freedom. Occasionally, the bureaucracy has been hostile to the African American quest (p. 241). The fact remains that most of the decision/policy-makers in the higher echelons of the federal, state, and local establishments are predominantly whites, who refuse to acknowledge any group identity and privilege.

In the racial structural functional model for decision/policy-making, all stages of the process are controlled primarily by white actors who have little consideration for affinity groups; only affiliation groups, such as political parties, are taken seriously. Decision/policy-makers in this model deal with the abstractions of decision/policy agenda, which are transformed into concrete goals without presumed consideration for race or ethnicity as an indicator of privilege, power, or powerlessness. Most of these decision/policy-makers and implementers who are white believe they are only "doing their jobs and race should not be a factor" (assuming the ideological mantle of race neutrality, colorblindness, race aversion, and post-racial reasoning). But as we all know, in America, race matters. DiAngelo puts it superbly well, "Because I haven't been socialized to see myself or to be seen by other whites in racial terms, I don't carry the psychic weight of race. Nor do I worry that my race will be held against me" (2018, p. 54). For a white woman (like DiAngelo) or any white decision/policy-maker, for that matter, they do not have to explain their racial "self" or their whiteness in the decision process. They are devoid of race and racial identity. They are comfortable in their skin and this comfortability has been carefully engineered and marketed to the American psyche and the mindset of the general populace. It is a camouflage, a façade behind which most people hide when difficult dialogues and crucial conversations around race and decisions emerge.

White Racial Comfort and the Danger of Being Too Comfortable

In our teachings, diversity, equity, and inclusion (DEI) workshops, and discourse over race, the word "comfort" finds a home in most difficult dialogues. "I am not comfortable talking about this" is a good way to avoid a discussion or participating in any reasonable exercise. "You don't have to say anything if you don't feel comfortable," many teachers will tell their students on conversations on race. Comfort is overpriced, over advertised, overused, and overvalued. Since the inception of this country and the emergence of racial awareness, discussions and actions involving racial matters in the academy and the polity can easily be tamed by invoking comfortability or adding the prefix "un-" to comfortable, and the deal is sealed. Everything has to be done in the comfort zone in order for it to be civil, and civility is defined from the perception of those who control the hegemonic power—mostly white males. What happened to the contact zone, where progress is usually made? The new code of silence and the process of infantilizing students over racial identity politics is the politics of avoidance, so that we can invoke the state of being "uncomfortable." Do our teaching places become "unsafe spaces" or does the United States Congress become an uncomfortable place when the holocaust of enslavement and reparation are brought into the discussion—for whites to own up to the process of reconciliation? As academics, we become disillusioned when critical race theory (CRT), critical whiteness studies, and conversations over anti-Black racism are characterized as divisive. Diversity and inclusion work truly is work about people. Thus, Michael Eric Dyson contends, "Yes, white privilege, white innocence, and white fragility are real and must be acknowledged and grappled with. But we must also confront white comfort, which is basically the arrangement of the social order for the convenience of white folk, one that offers them comfort as a noun, that is, ease and relief from pain or limits or constraints, and comfort as a verb, that is, taking action to console white grief or distress" (2020, pp. 184–185).

The career of comfort, just like race, has a balkanizing effect for those who enjoy comfort and those who work hard to provide comfort for those who control a particular social stratification. In the American major racial project, this country's foundation was established for the preservation of white comfort. Beginning from the holocaust of enslavement, Africans were forced to America in order to provide white Americans with colossal and immense comfort. These categories of comfort included but are not limited to free labor, plantation agriculture, finance through the sales of human capital, and the creation of wealth on the backs, sweat, blood, and tears of Black folk. What an expensive way to acquire comfort, but it worked for America. The laws of segregation, Supreme Court cases, such as *Plessy v. Ferguson* (1896), which strengthen the ideas of separation, segregation, and apartheid system in America, Jim Crow, school and housing segregation, white flight and Black encroachment, chocolate cites and vanilla suburbs, and the recent gentrification of the urban areas were all constructed for the nourishment of white comfort. Even de jure segregation should have ended with the court case of *Brown v. Board of Education of Topeka* (1954), yet de facto segregation still prevails to make whites comfortable. As we have mentioned in other areas in this book and in agreement with legal scholar and critical race theorist Professor Cheryl Harris's contention that whiteness must be seen as property, and it is one of the foundations of America's system of oppression, we express affirmatively that through American jurisprudence, property law trumps moral law and civil rights provisions. Whiteness is structured on property rights, instead of civil rights, to provide comfort to whites, and legal structures provide protection for those who maintain the comfort of whiteness in the use of their property just as it has "accorded holders of other types of property" (Harris, 1993, p. 1731).

Therefore, white comfort in identity politics paves the way for taming Black folx in their deeds, space, and communication styles. White comfort is disguised in terms of cross-cultural dialogue to appeal for "safe spaces" instead of brave spaces. White comfort is quick to examine the methods of exchange without paying attention to reasons why racial groups are engaging in policy decisions that they do not consider for the larger picture of structural racism. It is a grand tactic to change the narrative that America is not a racist country and things are not as bad as BIPOC folx think. White comfort submits to the bandage approach of dealing with racial problems without acknowledging white identity and denying that systemic racism exists. White comfort has adopted the sophistication and highest form of craftiness that even BIPOC folx have internalized white comfort to an extent that they invoke it in times of stress, situations of double bind, and settling for perceived peace (without justice)—just to make white people comfortable.

On many predominantly white university campuses, white comfort is uncontested in many cases during difficult dialogues about race and racial identity. In the interests of safe spaces and civility, white comfort prevails. Issues of comfort, fear, vulnerability, shame, blame, silence, and avoidance are cited by most white students and faculty in the discourse over race, racial identity, and racism. Nonetheless, we must not ignore the fact that BIPOC students or employees in especially predominantly white institutions do face challenges in interracial exchanges and dialogues. These instances occur when BIPOC students' experiences are put on public display for white students to learn from. When white students maintain their silence (in safe spaces) in the learning process on race and BIPOC students take the stage in educating their white classmates, BIPOC students carry an extra burden of racial education (Cabrera, 2012; Ford, 2012).

Whether it is intergroup or intragroup dialogue or a process of decision making with difficult racial dialogue based on the racialized society that we live in, personalized stories and experiences do come to the forefront and racial identities are indispensable in our interactions. No matter how trained facilitators or decision makers are, white comfort and BIPOC caution shape the nature of the discussion. In addition, the personal transcends individual experiences when the personal becomes political and systemic issue of exploitation, marginalization, and powerlessness. Maxwell and Chesler note, "The exploration of whiteness means going beyond matters of subjective identity and identification, to include understanding whiteness as a cultural and structural marker of privilege, entitlement, and supremacy" (2019, p. 251). Centuries of white comfort have reduced BIPOC folx to a state of nothingness, tiredness, exhaustion, existential threat, mental illness, and psychic disequilibrium—a total state of hermeneutic disorganization and homeostatic imbalance for BIPOC folx. The remedy for these debilitating states of toxic engagement for the benefit of white comfort is to demand our white brothers and sisters to reckon with the past and be intentional about being uncomfortable, leaving their comfort zones, actively engaging in the contact zone, confronting white fragility, and becoming an accomplice for social justice, and not just an ally.

White comfort has created a shield, bubble, a protective layer around white folx that dissuades them from acknowledging Black bodies in their truest forms. There is a disconnection between most white and Black folx in racial perceptions, the contumacy of race, and the agency of race in America. Group racial awareness has not been universal. While Black folx have remained aware—woke—on the American race project, whites are still suffering the effects of racial insomnia and myopia due to white comfort.

In her piece about the workplace and alerting white folx of the owning up to the dynamics and stress associated with white comfort, Jenae Holloway writes:

> It's time to prioritize the dire concerns of my Black community over the comfort of the white people around me, no matter the cost. . . . I'm undoing the conditioning that started when I was a kid, a survival method when I was one of only a few Black students in an all-white school in Indianapolis. If I made my white classmates comfortable, I thought, maybe they would forget that I didn't belong there. . . . . In the workplace, though I have always pushed for greater diversity both in the office and in our contents, I made sure to tread lightly when discussing race relations. . . . Sometimes I wondered, had I made my white

colleagues so comfortable that they had somehow forgotten I was Black? I realize now that prioritizing white comfort had actually had a numbing rather than a transformative effect. (Holloway, 2020)

For many years, in playing it safe, we have inadvertently strengthened the spaces of white supremacy by saying and doing things in America that would not upset fragile white folx and maintaining Black folx in survival modes. White comfort, whether it is in communication styles or building America from the scratch, has depended on Black survival. Whether in historical or contemporary times, Black folks are infantilized, validating white police officers' harassment by submitting to racial profiling and unreasonable actions, not talking back to a white superior, or teaching our students about the injustices perpetrated by many whites against Black folx. In this process of interaction, Black voices must be kept soft and calm, and Black body language "civil," with a fake smile so that, during contacts, Black folks can keep their little white students comfortable by showing their teeth as often. During the Obama presidency, his interaction and confrontation with the predominantly white hegemonic policy/decision-makers were so very well-orchestrated that he earned the nickname "No-Drama Obama" at a cost of not taking ownership of his Black "self." Thus, even in the White House, the Black commander-in-chief and leader of the free world had to control his soul, attitude, and behavior by making and keeping whites comfortable. It is ironic that a Black president of the United States could not utilize white comfort in the White House—his racial identity is Black!

The identities of those who control the power structures and decision-making apparatuses of our society remain remarkably similar, with white heteronormativity and heteropatriarchy maintaining the sociopolitical decision-making hegemony. In her interview with the *New Yorker*, when Isaac Chotiner (2019), the interviewer, asked the author of *White Identity Politics*, Ashely Jardina, "How much of a connection is there between strongly identifying with whiteness and racist attitudes?" Her response was:

> The connection is fairly weak, and that's for two reasons. One is that there are a lot of white people who are more racially prejudiced who do not identify as being white, and the converse is true. . . . One reason that we haven't talked a lot about whiteness in the past is because whites don't have to

confront their racial identity the way that people of color in the United States traditionally have. So we think about whiteness and white identity as being an invisible group identity because whites don't experience systemic subordination or discrimination. They have the lion's share of economic power and resources. A white person might not think about their own group. . . . They might not feel a sense of attachment to their group. But they still could go about their lives disliking people of color. (Chotiner, 2019)

In this perspective, whiteness, white identity politics, and white comfort have interlocking patterns of operation that strengthen hegemonic powers. In addition, people of pallor (whites) have the privilege of denying or accepting their group political consciousness of whiteness and racial identity as people of color do.

The fact remains that we can be disillusioned in "playing the game" of inclusion when we pretend white decision-makers do not think and act with the privilege of their whiteness when they are at the decision-making table. The illusion of inclusion prevails in most places where diversity and inclusion are the acceptable and expected norms of the game, but power differentials, implicit bias, unconscious bias, and identity politics are real in multicultural and multiracial societies. Ignoring that premise stands our ability to develop an antiracist society on its head. In her book *White Identity Politics*, Ashley Jardina (2019) asserts that whites in recent times have found new racial political identity not just among decision makers but also the working class that could be shaping racial conflicts in America for a long time. She recognizes the effects of white racial prejudice and behaviors and distinguishes them from white racial identity. Yet some white Americans, harboring the fear of losing their white comfort and power to minoritized groups in recent events, are mobilizing their own identity politics to maintain the status quo ante of the Black Lives Matter movement. Jardina argues that "today, whites' racial attitudes are not merely defined by prejudice; many whites also maintain a sense of racial identity and are motivated to protect their group's collective interests and to protect its status" (2019, p. 6). Nevertheless, the recent political landscape is dictating white identity politics without the affirmation of white racial identity. This intergroup dynamic might be misconstrued as a positive racial group phenomenon to improve race relations without the recent fear of losing white comfort and the perceived erosion of whiteness as our Make America Great Again (MAGA) proponents have been preaching.

Rethinking Positive White Identity in the Decision-Making Sphere

Racial identity development theory, according to Janet Helms, is concerned with the socio-psycho-cultural implication of racial group membership, which includes belief systems that evolve in reactions to different perceptions racial groups maintain (1990, pp. 3–25). Since in America racial group membership is emphasized, it is assumed that all groups, including white policy/decision-makers will form a racial identity at a certain time. However, whites have not come to terms with their whiteness. Helms asserts, "Concurrently, the person must become aware of her or his whiteness, learn to accept whiteness as an important part of herself or himself, and to internalize a realistically positive view of what it means to be White" (1990, p. 55).

Because of America's racial historical contradictions and the socialization processes in our homes and institutions, many whites continue to harbor animosity, dislike, negative biases, and resentment toward Black folx especially and BIPOC in general. Ironically, many of these white folx, who believe in their whiteness but would not talk about it, are also not in solidarity and group political consciousness with their white brothers and sisters. This white identity quagmire presents a confusing mixture of white antipathy and allophilia for "otherness" but at the same time not in identity with their own kind—white folx. In the era of diversity and inclusion, we cannot subscribe to what W. E. B. Du Bois challenged Booker T. Washington about over a hundred years ago, that the races in America need separate identities and institutions, like fingers on the hand. Du Bois had the perception that Black folx had to be part of all key institutions and decision-making process with strong Black identity. The United States is making progress and yet those who control most of the resources, power, and decision-making apparatuses, whites, have historically disassociated themselves from racial identity politics and white identity, and whiteness continues to be predominately instrumental and yet illusive.

Helms's (1990) classic work on white racial identity model remains persuasive. Helms's model can be bifurcated through, first, rejection of racism by whites, and, second, defining a positive white identity. That identity, theoretically, would result in white policy-makers making non-racist policy and seeing themselves as allies or accomplices to subordinate groups in the entire policy process. While several white allies and accomplices have resisted the role of oppressor, many of them, unfortunately, are political activists or educators who are not directly involved in the decision-making processes.

Helms's model consists of six stages: contact, disintegration, reintegration, pseudo-independent, immersion/emersion, and autonomy (1990, p. 58). At the contact stage, white decision-makers pay very little attention to their racial group membership. White decision-makers believe that it is "normal" for them to have white privilege. These individuals in this group seldom describe themselves as white. This is a universal humanist perspective. White decision-makers here always claim they are "just normal and doing their jobs" even if they engage in racist undertakings. White police officers engaged in racial profiling, unreasonable searches, and, more seriously, knee-lynching and chokehold are some of the examples at this stage, claiming for example, that racial profiling and even a chokehold (now banned in many states after the George Floyd murder case) are indispensable tools for police work.

The disintegration stage forces white policy-makers and implementers to begin to see how much their lives and the lives of subordinate groups have been affected by racist policies. Uncomfortable with this insight, they tend to deny the validity of information about racism, submerged in a state of cognitive dissonance and denial. White policy-makers and decision-makers at this stage make the case that racism ended in the 1960s, or they withdraw from discussing it (racism) at all. If policy-makers deny the premise of a racial problem at the input stage, there is every possibility that the policy will be devoid of any racial considerations, therefore failing to achieve the policy goal. For instance, it is common for white policy-makers to make the argument that there is no need to write new laws about hate crimes against Blacks and Asians or arson of Black churches and mosques, because there are already laws against crimes in general. What these policy-makers fail to acknowledge is the racial element to these crimes.

The third stage, reintegration, finds white policy-makers blaming the failure of the Black or BIPOC communities on Blacks and BIPOC folx themselves, or the victims. White policy-makers, at this juncture, instruct Blacks and minoritized groups to change their attitude and behavior in order to benefit from public policy or the decision reached. As Wellman (1977) correctly notes, such perception allows white individuals to relieve themselves of any guilt or responsibility for advocating social change. The "blame game" contributes to policy myopia: shortsightedness in policy making because of the misperceptions of policy-makers in examining problems carefully. They rather blame the problems on policy beneficiaries instead of going to the root-cause of the problem—racism.

Acknowledging racism, and understanding it, facilitates the reduction of "blaming the victim" by white policy-makers at the pseudo-independent stage. This is the stage at which the development of a positive white identity begins. White policy/decision-makers can easily recognize their hegemonic power in the decision/policy process and begin to form policy allies with Black policy-makers and beneficiaries. Lee Anne Bell characterizes hegemonic power as one in which "a dominant group can project a particular way of seeing social reality so successfully that its view is accepted as common sense, as part of the natural order even by those who are disempowered by it"—people of color (1997, p. 11). Here, white policy-makers will transcend the limits of thinking about racism as just an individual issue. They comprehend the sophistication of institutional racism in the American society and refrain from blaming subordinate groups for their own oppression. Furthermore, as Harris (1993) notes, whites will begin to understand that being white is not just about their racial self, but it is property with legacy and power in the American polity and that can help them to unmask the racialization and invisibility of white identity.

The next stage for white racial identity is the immersion/emersion stage. Here, white policy/decision-makers make efforts to create a positive white identity. Policy/decision-makers reexamine their own whiteness and find answers for their privilege. At this point, the feeling of guilt and shame are replaced with a newfound feeling of excitement and pride in whiteness. Policy-makers will become advocates for those who are oppressed because of their race. They can easily unlearn the racism that they learned at an earlier age. With this kind of a mindset, white decision/policy-makers will not remove themselves anymore from identity politics. They develop better techniques for using white privilege positively.

The final stage, autonomy, is concomitant with newfound whiteness. Policy-makers from the superordinate race interact with subordinate groups for positive policy goals. The positive aspect of this autonomy is an equitable policy package for the general populace. This is a stage of group self-consciousness and self-actualization. White policy-makers become more open-minded and are receptive to new information regarding racial dynamics. White policy-makers at this juncture become advocates for antiracist policy goals, but as Helms (1990) cautions, even at this point of self-actualization in race relations, white policy-makers must continue to work toward consciousness-raising for other whites for stronger alliances, just as Blacks continue to work for the achievement of a new Blackness. William Cross, *Shades of Black: Diversity in African American Identity* (1991), and Beverly Daniel Tatum, *Why Are All the Black Kids Sitting Together in the Cafeteria* (1997), have both concluded that white racial identity development has been neglected for too long and recognizing it and deliberately working on it could liberate white folx. Garza mentions that, "if whiteness is the standard, it is the criteria used to determine whether ideas, actions, or experience have worth, merit or value. Whiteness attempts to determine what is valid" (2019, p. 3). Nevertheless, realizing positive white identity development could mitigate the effects of the toxic and the invisibility of whiteness. The newfound whiteness could be liberating.

Conclusion

No nation state is as fertile a laboratory for studying the dynamics of racial identity, whiteness, race, and race relations as the United States. Nevertheless, owing to the sensitive nature surrounding the discourse on race, its centripetal force in racial interaction, decision-making, and the policy arena has been diluted or intentionally avoided by white policy-makers for the sake of comfort, convenience, and perhaps not knowing what to do because of the *longue durée* of race and racism in the American polity. The irony of this avoidance or cognitive dissonance is a resultant of even more racial tension, decision myopia, and racial policy paralysis. Since whites maintain the hegemonic power in the decision and policy sphere and hold socioeconomic and political power, and since racism is not only an individual but also institutional action or inaction, it is meaningful to examine whiteness, white privilege, and the decision/policy-making sphere through identity politics and positive white racial identity development. The goal in this approach is to redefine whiteness from a more positive perspective so that white leaders and policy-makers can use their privilege and power position to enhance the process of decision and policy-making for a better race relation. This is not to say that advocating the supereminence of white racial identity is a panacea for America's racial problems; it is one of the many approaches we can use in attaining concrete racial policy, program, and decision goals.

The hallmark of rethinking whiteness positively, though, is the sense of liberation from self-denial and an acknowledgment that whiteness is part of every white person's being in any multiracial and multiethnic polity, where whites are the superordinate group. Again, in a multiethnic and multiracial entity such as the United States, solutions to racial problems must be multiperspectival. It is indubitable that identity groups have many social markers such as gender, sexual orientation, ethnicity, class, religion, and more. Nonetheless, it is our contention in this chapter that the phenomenon of racial identity that has shaped the American polity and policy decision for centuries is not imaginary or illusionary. In a democracy, who gets what is wrapped in identity politics. In this sense, we offer this approach of reexamining whiteness not from a victimizer's point of view, but as accomplices to eradicate racism and produce antiracist decisions and policy goals. We must continue to dialogue, because our silence over the race question and America's racial identity project will only magnify the racial divide. As James Baldwin once eloquently said, "Not everything that is faced can be changed. But nothing can be changed until it is faced." In developing positive white racial identity, race will sustain an agency in the policy-making process and change will be possible. We must continue to keep hope for an antiracism American polity alive.

In the succeeding chapter, we rethink and reframe solutions in diversity, DEI leadership, and dealing with contemporary challenges for educational institutions and the nation state through a multicultural, inclusive, antiracist, accountability, and equity-minded framework. Coalition building, dismantling the system of oppression, commitments to courageous choices, and reaffirming our humanity involve recognition, reconciliation, and making these moments a movement for institutional change.

Chapter 12

Ubuntu Ethics

I Am Because We Are

A Cautionary Tale of Accountability Work and Punishment in the Era of Inclusion and Diversity Management

Our reflections in this book circle around the contexts and concepts of inclusive leadership, inclusive and equity-minded societies, Martin Luther King's beloved community, and the African philosophy that was made accessible by John Mbiti: "I am because we are, and, since we are, therefore I am." The individual's fate and sustenance are inextricably linked to those of the community and vice versa. In recent years, these concepts have evolved to encompass another powerful concept: Ubuntu ethics. First popularized by Archbishop Desmond Tutu of South Africa, Ubuntu conveys a deep sense of humanness, of shared value and humanity (Tutu, 1999). It is this indispensable context that sustains the human condition—I cannot recognize myself as human and a person of value to the community unless you see me as human. This dynamic relationship draws on *sociocentric ethics*, which is quite alien to the European Enlightenment project and Western sociopolitical concepts of individualism and egocentrism. In the era of Bacon and Descartes, it was important for white male Europeans to draw on an *egocentric, ethnosexual ideology*, culminating in the project of self-knowing: I think, therefore I am. Thus, Mbiti's (1990) response to the "self" is to remind us that the "self" cannot be devoid of the "other" and community—I am because We are.

What is less taught in the halls of (Western) academia and philosophy is that such a solipsistic framework of self-knowing and individualized discovery was convenient and instrumental for the imperialist conquest of the Americas and beyond, what is today referred to as the Global South. In his efforts to decolonize philosophy, Charles Mills (1997) would give the ideological project another important ascription, namely, the racial contract. Whites, specifically elite white men, engage in contractual agreements with other elite white men over women, indentured or enslaved humans, or cattle. Thus, contracts have the illusion of equality, in the way John Locke, Thomas Hobbes, or Jean-Jacques Rousseau postulate. Furthermore, Rousseauian civic religion punished vice for unbelievers and nonconformists and rewarded virtue for white cultural conformists and supporters of sovereign rights. In reality, those who invested in whiteness and capital get to have an unequal access to power over dominions. This is so well laid out in Hobbes's *Leviathan* where he discusses the finer points of differentiation between commonwealth and conquest. Those who agree amiably (and on equal terms of exchange) to join a social contract will be rewarded with citizenship. Those who object to having their land expropriated from them will be subdued into a compact by force as mere subjects or have their property seized via the principle of eminent domain that serves the purpose and wants of the power holder. Citizens are afforded the assets of whiteness, whereas subjects (or subalterns) are ontologically reduced to the Other, living beyond the pale (cf. Nagel, 2014).

A Call for Ubuntu Ethics

It is quite remarkable that a South African critic of apartheid would extoll the virtues of an Ubuntu ethics in the postapartheid era of the new South Africa. Ubuntu signifies shared humanity—the idea that my humanity is intertwined with yours. I am only human because you recognize me as human. As such, it stands out as an ethics of shared responsibility, a shared burden to do good and rectify or release harm. During the Truth and Reconciliation proceedings as well as in his subsequent books, Tutu championed Ubuntu as *shared humanity* above anything else, encouraging victimizers to speak the truth and victims' families to find the courage to forgive. However, at no point, was there pressure put on victimizers who sought amnesties for their atrocities to apologize to the victims or the commission. In the end, the Tutu Commission demanded material reparations paid to the thousands of victims of the apartheid regime and warned the government about the urgent need of addressing land claims, the grievance of systematic expulsions of millions of Black South Africans from their ancestral lands over a century ago by a white-minority government. So, Ubuntu ethics is a reparative ethics, recognizing that harms, whether systemic or individual, need to be addressed in symbolic and material ways. At the same time, whites who are enchanted by Ubuntu philosophy may be tempted to depoliticize the postcolonial moment by foregrounding the message of forgiveness and ignoring the fact that past grievances are not forgotten and must be addressed with care and compassion.

In the era of "Rhodes must fall!" and Black freedom cries for full access to free higher education ("Fees must fall!"), white South Africans still have to face their own racism, white privilege, specifically, how they reap the benefit of occupying stolen lands, being favored by credit institutions, schools, universities, embassies, and the criminal justice system, to name a few. The decolonizing process is an arduous, protracted struggle, as King (1967) echoed the abolitionist Theodore Parker's prophetic maxim: "The arc of the moral universe is long, but it bends towards justice." Former President Obama in 2009 puts this same quote in context for the American polity, as many social groups continue to struggle to acquire social justice and inclusive excellence.

Ubuntu practices are being emulated in contentious contexts the world over. However, reckoning with the historical record is obligatory before any earnest attempts at reconciliation. The United States' Smithsonian complex in the nation's capital finally added a museum devoted to the African American presence in the new world, showcasing their enormous contributions in building this nation state through blood, sweat, tears, and innovation. But the ghosting presence of a racial contract (e.g., chattel slavery, the convict lease system, lynching, Jim Crow, racist mass incarceration, and persistent microaggression) casts a long shadow, accounting for unspeakable atrocities over centuries committed under the white-washed guise of commonwealth, and Eurocentric and republican values. Criminologist Viviane Saleh-Hanna (2015) advocates for a Black feminist hauntology to account for historical and contemporary racist, sexist counterinsurgencies. In the South, a new museum documents the thousands of lynchings of Black people, extralegal killings by white supremacists who rarely faced punishment, not only in the South but all across the United States (Equal Justice Initiative, 2018). Also, some activists and scholars such as Joshua Inwood and Derek Alderman are bringing the idea of a Truth and Reconciliation Commission (TRC) to grassroots responses to local racial issues in Greensboro, North Carolina, and Detroit, Michigan (Inwood & Alderman, 2016).

Furthermore, other activists are calling upon lawmakers to increase TRC processes on pogroms or so-called race riots to the Southern states, specifically, Tulsa, Oklahoma, the collective trauma for descendants of Black Americans, demanding reparations. In fact, if apologies were sincere, they would be accompanied with material reparations. Congress apologized to Indigenous people of Hawaii for illegally deposing their queen and annexing the sovereign territory over a century ago. It was followed up with no remunerations, no reparations. Congress also apologized to Issei and Nissei (of Japanese descent) for incarcerating them in concentration camps during World War II. Survivors received a $20,000 settlement payment, a symbolic reparative gesture. Finally, Congress also apologized for enslaving people of African descent—again, *not* followed up with any promises of reparations. It is clear that such political apologies for crimes against humanity by themselves do not amount to a meaningful attempt of accountability cum reconciliation between perpetrators and victims as a class. Inwood and Alderman assert, "The US-based truth and reconciliation commission process represents an important departure point for questioning and thinking more closely about notions of transitional justice" (2016, p. 14). Yet, we believe that Congress has done enough talking and rendering apologies. There should be no statute of limitation on the atrocities and brutalities committed by this nation state against subordinate groups who have suffered the legacy of oppression and continue to suffer. Action is needed over the prolonged and protracted, sometimes meaningless conversations. Real change is attained through deliberate and intentional action!

Statue Wars and Tradition:
Giving Amazing Grace to the Disgraceful

How have racialized hierarchies and colonial processes of exclusion been addressed in the academy? In the wake of the global Black Lives Matter movement, symbolic insurgencies have occurred on college campuses and public spaces, such as toppling the statues of colonial and confederate overlords such as Cecil Rhodes at the University of Cape town in 2015 and Silent Sam at the University of North Carolina in 2018, and Lee Park, where the statue of Robert E. Lee was removed on September 8, 2021. The evil deeds that had been committed in yesteryears in the name of tradition, history, and white privilege cannot continue to haunt those who suffered oppression and dehumanization because of the characterization of statues, symbols, and colonial iconography as tradition or history. Americans, and especially our students, would only engage in convenient amnesia if we think we can ignore the trauma and toxic memories that the statues and colonial monuments emit on historically oppressed groups. Furthermore, these images tend to grant undeserving sympathy and greatness to superordinate cultures on the campuses of historically white colleges and universities. Even Marguerite Gardiner posed this question, "Who could look on these monuments without reflecting on the vanity of mortals in thus offering up testimonials of their respect for persons of whose very names posterity is ignorant?" (Gardiner, quoted in Ross, 2015). It is mind boggling that we can pose this same question in 2023.

Our institutions of higher learning are changing, but the mindset of the hegemony continues its grinding actions of cultural imperialism. Part of this problem is that we mostly spend time and money researching campus climate, which is not sufficient to make transformative change. Campus cultures and campus ecology (as we have argued earlier) continue to be neglected research and institutional endeavors in PWIs for producing change. Envisage Jewish students, who walk on campuses of German universities and colleges only to observe statues of Nazis and Nazi sympathizers who have slaughtered many Jews in the 1930s and 1940s? Imagine a learning community in Germany, where student centers could be named after Adolf Hitler, for his political leadership, or Josef Mengele, for his ability to experiment on defenseless Jews? What would the continuing trauma on these Jewish students be like? Flip the script for Black students in the United States and African students on the continent of Africa, where they have to encounter these images every day. We cannot give brutal history and tradition a pass because we live in a different era. The cacophony of voices of murderers and oppressive apparition scenes of long dreadful shadows of the statues of white supremacists negatively affect the mind, soul, and the very existence of minoritized groups, who, before enrolling in these institutions, think college is a safe haven for inclusive excellence. Why should fair-minded people or anybody resist changing the names of buildings or parks that honor wicked, dead, old white males?

Chumani Maxwele, a student at an elite South African university, began the "Rhodes Must Fall" campaign by emptying a bucket filled with excrement over the Rhodes statue, and, within weeks of continued defacement, the government removed the statue of the imperialist that stood there for some eighty years (Stiem, 2018). Maya Little, a student at the University of North Carolina, also took matters into her own hands by applying black paint and her own blood onto the century-old statute, a symbol of white supremacy and Jim Crow. Months later, at the beginning of the fall semester, hundreds of protesters pulled the statue down. However, Little, a PhD candidate in history, was convicted by the university's honor court for defacing. She walked out of the proceedings, because one of its members professed overt support for the Confederate cause and racist Southern statutes on his social media platform and therefore could not possibly be objective in understanding her political act and expression of moral outrage. To add insult to injury, a judge also found her guilty of a misdemeanor charge, in effect, she was convicted by two courts (see Stancill, 2018). At the University of Ghana (UG), Legon, lecturers and students petitioned and removed the statue of Mahatma Gandhi, who, ironically, is well-known for his nonviolent approach to fighting British colonialism and imperialism. Yet Gandhi internalized his racism against Black Africans (Afrophobia), when he lived in South Africa, calling them "kaffirs," a derogatory term like the "N-word." On one of our many visits to the University of Ghana, one of us witnessed the heroic activism of the students and faculty against the statue of the oppressive anti-Black racist, Gandhi. While the administrators and leaders were mostly silent about the Gandhi statue fiasco on the UG Legon campus, but had the audacity to explain why UG accepted the statue as a gift from India without sufficient research on the matter (the usual tactics for damage control), the persistency of the students and faculty generated enough political mobilization for the statue of Gandhi to be removed in December 2018. Racism and internalized racism can come in different shapes and colors, but, as we have learned in Racism 101, Blacks are always relegated to the lowest level of any racialized society.

While erecting statues, naming buildings, and streets on campuses around the world with the names/images of historical figures (usually dead white men) has a global appeal to glorify people (usually dead and white), and inspire others (the living) on especially PWI campuses, where Black and minoritized students were historically not allowed to share the same space as whites, the chances that one will find a statue of a Black person on campus is close to zero. Campus culture dictates whiteness! Thus, many minoritized folx walk on campus under the shadow, gaze, and traumatizing statues of oppression every day. Many of these university board of trustees and administrators have no idea or pretend they do not have the gumption to assess the impact of post-traumatic slave syndrome on our Black students. The constant reminders of how students of color who walk past these statues of dishonorable white men every day to classes or residence halls could negatively affect any student's college experience. There is always a feeling of psychic disequilibrium for our students of color, as if they were admitted to these institutions only to be reminded about the sins of the "beloved" institutions and the United States.

Ivy League universities and others in the South of the United States have to reckon with their shameful pasts beyond the usual accommodation of youthful protest of hateful symbols. Some are starting the process of redress. Georgetown University is giving legacy status to descendants of enslaved people who worked on their campus grounds some two hundred years ago. Legacy admission is the uncontested practice of giving preferential admission to children of alumni. Some of the descendants are also calling for tuition scholarship, a fitting measure of reparations. Nevertheless, students and faculty continue to petition the Georgetown administration to completely end legacy admissions (Moore-Carrillo, 2020).

Accountability work in the process of reconciliation has to embrace the difficult work of reparations. We have seen this play out with tremendous difficulty in the South African context. Whites, too often, demand a quick release from responsibility for the perpetration of apartheid and a war on African peoples by asking for forgiveness. However, how is it possible for a dispossessed people, deprived of educational advancement to forgive individual and state actors of brutal violence, when water resource wars and landless people are reduced to squatting illegally on white, colonial lands? The Truth and Reconciliation Commission was very clear in warning the Mbeki government that land rights ought to be a priority to foster the reconciliation process. The "Rhodes Must Fall" movement made it clear to the Zuma government that access to higher (and elite) education should not remain the privilege of the minority white population and the whitewashed curriculum needed a major overhaul so that African people could see themselves reflected in their pursuit of sciences, humanities, and other majors.

Are there lessons for American universities and colleges to learn in this process about curriculum development regarding marginalized disciplines such as inclusion and equity studies, ethnic studies, Africana studies, Latino studies, and women's studies? Lawrence Ross carefully notes in *Blackballed*, "Too often, schools reluctantly set up African American Studies offices, Multicultural Affairs departments, and Greek life offices that are woefully understaffed and underfunded, and then give the overworked administrators of the departments the thankless task of making sure students don't do anything racist. It is a hopeless mission, because no matter how many classes you force them to attend, white students see through the façade of concern" (2015, pp. 138–139). So, the window dressing continues, as most university administrators are more concerned about staying away from the media and legal challenges than tackling the critical issues that directly affect minoritized groups to make the campus climate conducive for all groups. Are the global human conditions different in different spaces, so that oppression and dehumanization of one group are meaningless to another group in the beloved community?

Ubuntu Ethics and Diversity Management

What would it look like if Ubuntu ethics made its mark in the everyday business of the academy? As we have noted in this book, diversity management has been treated to risk management with a sharp increase in funding for such entities as Title IX, human resources, and chief diversity and inclusion officers in the US academy during the Obama administration. However, today, at the federal level, support for marginalized citizens and immigrants of color is at a low point. Any feeble attempt to diversify the universities is counteracted with restrictive executive orders that smack of transphobia, xenophobia, and racism. It remains to be seen how historically Black colleges and universities and Tribal Colleges continue to survive the onslaught of white supremacists. Is it another mask on display that echoes the academic gatekeepers, whose practices solidified Jim Crow, antisemitism, misogyny, and misogynoir? Is it the ghost of the McCarthy era's purging of certifiable dangerous professors, because they were tainted by communist ideology?

Are the Me Too and Black Lives Matter movements on a collision course with First Amendment rights of free speech and academic freedom? Are numerical diversity and fluffy, window-dressing diversity and inclusion programs sufficient to mitigate the microaggressions and marginalization of students and faculty of color in historically white colleges and universities and predominantly white institutions? Racial microaggression—brief and commonplace daily verbal, behavioral, or environmental indignities, whether intentional or unintentional, that communicate hostile, derogatory, or negative racial slights and insults toward people of color (Sue et al., 2010)—is so rampant on our campuses that most people of color find it difficult to maneuver around it, and most whites students and administrators just cannot get it.

In this critical moment, universities are also facing the onslaught of a fundamentalism and white nationalism that are skeptical of the sciences, hostile to the humanities, anti-DEI, anti-immigration and migration, anti-CRT, and derisive of the social sciences that still worry about facts on the ground. It is as if fundamentalist bigots such as Steve Bannon and anti-DEI and anti-CRT crusader and Trumpublican Christopher Rufo have discovered postmodernism of a reactive kind and post-racialism as a Holy Communion. Alas, we are suspicious of post-anything that is associated with a post-racial America. All truths are perishable, with a twist—Bannon forges a truth that resonates with his base, hoi polloi, and it is a message of contempt and hate, and Rufo does not get tired of reminding us that we must turn everything about race/racism into CTR and sexuality or gender studies must become "grooming" as a strategy for attacking DEI.

Where does Ubuntu ethics come to the rescue? Self-help books and articles abound addressing the ideological divide since the 2016 presidential elections. How do we address the stranger and their ideological commitment, especially if the "stranger" is actually a family member? Perhaps Desmond Tutu's words are helpful here: "There is a bit of oppressor in me, as well." Ubuntu ethics has been interpreted to mean that "I am because we are, and because we are, I am." If Tutu is right, then I cannot be selective with respect to whose humanity I share, and whose I forgo (or imprison). It also means that microaggressions must be heard and accounted for, rather than simply deposited "as a narrative" in the college's crisis impact team annual reports.

A Note on Separatist Politics and Segregation

Other misguided campus cocurricular strategies that received pushback are the creation of "white groups" that wish to address racism. What might be wrong with white identity groups especially when most whites shy away from white group political consciousness? When white social groups are created by socially dominant stakeholders, these groups have an adverse impact, especially on minoritized students, faculty, and staff members.

Even if the intent of establishing such group is noble, such policy may feel to BIPOC folx as if "segregation (from above)" were imposed upon them. The impact of such policy matters more than the intent, due its harmful repercussions. Setting up a "whites-only" group certainly invites condemnation and ridicule, given the legacy and continuation of white supremacist practices, policies, and procedures, which are precisely the reasons why it was necessary for students of color to set up (separatist) organizations to reckon with historic discrimination and segregation. Separatist identity politics is a politics *from below*. Segregation follows a different logic from separation, but the two concepts get constantly conflated. Separatist politics may seem threatening or exclusionary to white students who feel entitled to all spaces as always already being white public or private (privatized) spaces. They simply belong (anywhere), such that a space becomes their marked place, with emotional associations of comfort and home. It will never dawn on them that white spaces may feel hostile, terrifying, or unwelcoming to students of color. A Latino student at a historically white campus may never quite get the sense of belonging, except, sporadically, at events organized by a Caribbean student organization or a carefully chosen residence hall floor. Bernice Reagon (1983) draws a pointed distinction between the need to (re)create home among self-chosen friends and the need of coalitional politics for solidarity purposes (e.g., with white accomplices).

The conflation of separatism with the self-segregation (which is a complete misnomer) runs deep in US society. It usually is along the lines of command language by outsiders (whites): "You ought not self-segregate!" This is the logic of white solipsism, because at stake is the absolute subordination of those who are "Othered" (by the oppressive system of white supremacy) to the psychic, emotional, material needs of those who are in dominant places and spaces. This logic is quite devastating to those who are experiencing its oppressive yoke, especially when its intents and purposes are internalized. Kristie Dotson (2011) calls such operational acquiescence *epistemic smothering*: a person of color smothers or suppresses consciously her testimony or the will to call somebody out because it feels unsafe to testify, call out, and so on.

It affects other areas that are not separatist per se, but that invite intellectual analysis, and/or cultural celebrations of specific ethnic and racial heritages. It is not uncommon that campus leaders must deal with irascible white students (often cis male students) who are outraged about the annual celebration of Black History Month. Where, after all, they charge, is the celebration of white studies? (This accusation is sometimes raised against Women's History Month, but usually not with the same kind of bigoted vehemence and hate speech). Often it falls upon Black faculty, especially those who organize the speakers' schedule of events and who already do more than a fair share of service, to respond with measured tone and respect to emails or angry phone messages. Most white students who characterize Black History Month as "racist" because "White History Month" is not widely celebrated on campus tend to forget that all the months of the year are technically and basically white months because people of color live by the experiences of white people every day. These young white college students also forget that Black history is America's history, told from the perception of the people's history. As a popular African proverb informs us, "Until the story of the hunt is told by the lion, the tale of the hunt will always glorify the hunter." So, until Black history is narrated by true Africanists and African Americanists, the story of greatness will persistently glorify the oppressor and cultural imperialists. Many of the mostly white faculty and students who protest against Black History Month come to us from a perception that "whiteness comes with a value, prestige, and reputation that can be eroded by blackness" (Ross, 2015, p. 72).

To these elements, Black History Month is a threat to white hegemonic power. These people usually tend to suffer from a convenient amnesia, an element of the fact that it was a predominantly white US Congress that supported President Gerald Ford's action in 1976 to institutionalize and nationalize Carter G. Woodson's 1925 vision of elevating the often-neglected Black accomplishments to elegance because of the racialized society of the United States. Nevertheless, there are a few Black folks who are not impressed by Black History Month. They believe that African American history should not be limited to the discussion of their achievements only in the month of February. Yet this camp of Black folks are usually Black conservatives (Shelby Steele, Thomas Sowell, and Allen West, to name a few), who are intoxicated with white conservative values. It is also ironic that successful Black History Month programs and the hard work of faculty and students of color who organize these events are sometimes ignored in the name of general institutional diversity efforts. Yet these same institutions and the marketing and publicity departments of especially predominantly white institutions are quick to claim most of the credits through their approach of reporting, sovereign ownership, and hegemonic power of disseminating information. Thus, these myopic racist invectives that contribute to a chilly campus climate not only reveal ignorance of history of struggle against settler colonialism, but also of white male solipsism, microassaults, microinsults, and microinvalidations.

Accountability Work: Carceral Feminism and the Run-Away Effects of Title IX

How do diversity stakeholders on a campus hold people accountable? Critical race theorists and feminist legal theorists have raised awareness about oppression that previously had no name—sexism, a common expression today, was a term coined by college student Pauline Leets in the 1960s, in explicit analogy to the term racism (Brogaard, 2020). As we wrote in an earlier chapter, misogynoir, created by Moya Bailey, is another term that engages with the framework of intersectional feminism, highlighting the enduring struggle of Black women in a white patriarchal polity. Is it possible to hold people accountable without shaming them? Much has been written about white guilt and how useless such emotion and stance is to mobilize whites to combat racism. Perhaps some lessons from effective peaceful communication is helpful to create purposeful intercultural dialogues. At the same time, the kind of communicative strategy pushed on campus leaves power relationships unchallenged. In the end, they are not conducive to concede to a progressive agenda of social justice that student groups in the Black Lives Matter era are demanding.

To what extent is the Me Too activist agenda wedded to a reactive policing philosophy akin to carceral feminism? It seems that, all too often, feminist activists and legal scholars defend policies of harsh punishment. In the 1990s, Hilary Clinton defended long sentences for young Black men, called "super-predators," endorsing the now-discredited, racist theory by John DiIulio, Jr. (West Savali, 2016). This demonization of young men as gangsters and waves of tough-on-crime legislation brought on mass incarceration. The concomitant war on drugs also ensnared Black women whose incarceration rate exploded (Davis, 2003). In fact, as many Black feminist critics, including Angela Y. Davis, have argued, the long-standing myth of the Black rapist still haunts the American polity to date. It certainly raised its ugly head with the unjust convictions of five young Black men in the Central Park jogger case in the 1990s. At that time, Donald Trump took out ads in the *New York Times*, demanding the death penalty for all of them. After a decade traumatized by the carceral system, they were freed, and a white man, convicted of serial rapes and murder, confessed to the crime.

In the past, some feminist scholars have proposed that the only way of stopping rampant sexual assault on college campuses involves the punitive measure of date rapists wearing distinctive clothing in order to raise consciousness about their offense as a clearly defined assault—instead of remaining an ambiguous, albeit problematic act of transgression and vile aggression (Baker, 1999). According to this logic of shaming the offender in a dramatic public way, toxic masculinity would fade away. Scarlett letters might be spectacularly effective. For instance, carceral feminists might demand that judges such as Brett Kavanaugh should face public humiliation and he could not be trusted to adjudicate and might even face criminal charges long after the fact of his youthful aggressive and sexual assaultive behavior. Instead, other forces prevailed, while the key witness Christine Blasey Ford has to take measures to safeguard her family from death threats. The senatorial fraternity's logic dictates that his shameless behavior is rationalized as a result of enjoying beer and the blame is put on women, who must endure dangerous or slut-shaming male behavior. Kavanaugh is now a sitting justice on the highest court of the United States, deciding the fate on death penalty cases, persons with addictions, youthful offenders, and millions of women and their right to reproductive health-care services.

Here again, we must reflect on the ideology of carceral feminism. Let us pause and think about due process when accusers face Title IX charges on college campuses, which steadfastly avoid mingling with off-campus criminal courts—for keeping the college's reputation intact, rather than serving fairly all involved in the process. Risk management is foremost about the college's liability, enrollments management, and saving face, so that alumni and donors will not be exposed to the realities on college campuses. What happens to the rights of the accused and the due process clause of the Fourteenth Amendment? This is acutely important, especially when the accused happen to be Black male students or faculty and the accusers are white women. This question is pursued in Emily Yoffe's multi-part series on research on criminalizing interracial sex in the *Atlantic*:

> Janet Halley, a professor at Harvard Law School and a self-described feminist, is one of the few people who have publicly addressed the role of race in campus sexual assault. Interracial assault allegations, she notes, are a category that bears particular

scrutiny. In a 2015 *Harvard Law Review* article, "Trading the Megaphone for the Gavel in Title IX Enforcement," she writes, "American racial history is laced with vendetta-like scandals in which black men are accused of sexually assaulting white women," followed eventually by the revelation "that the accused men were not wrongdoers at all." She writes that "morning-after remorse can make sex that seemed like a good idea at the time look really alarming in retrospect; and the general social disadvantage that black men continue to carry in our culture can make it easier for everyone in the adjudicative process to put the blame on them." She has observed the phenomenon at her own university: "Case after Harvard case that has come to my attention, including several in which I have played some advocacy or adjudication role, has involved black male respondents." (Yoffe, 2018)

Title IX officers are quick to reject such provocations following the logic of feminist jurisprudence, legal activism, and the FBI's analysis of sexual assault cases: false allegations are extremely rare, and, unlike other assault categories, there are high rates of underreporting. At the same time, they concede that most assaults are intraracial and most assailants are known to the victims. At the very least, it seems reasonable to collect demographic data to see if there are higher reports of false allegations in cases of interracial sexual assault. At the same time, we worry with Janet Halley about implicit bias and the long traumatic history of extralegal lynchings and "legal" capital punishment of Black men due to false reports made by white women. We will not forget about the Rosewood massacre, where a white woman lied about being raped by a Black man, causing whites in the neighboring town to burn down the entire Black township of Rosewood, Florida, in 1923. The 1950s Scottboro Nine case casts its evil shadow over the 1990s and 2000s. In the 1990s Central Park joggers' case, innocent Black men were framed for rape and locked up for years. We lock most Black folks up, but we don't lift them up.

Even former President Trump, during that incident, secured an advertisement in the *New York Times* to put those innocent young Black men on death row. Black people oftentimes are framed of rape and sexual assault by white women, and they end up in penitentiaries or cages for most of their lives. How can campus hearings be fair and provide due process for the accused? The respondent may retain a lawyer, but that legal counsel cannot speak up for the client during "trial." In fact, the criminal justice system provides more protections for the accused than campus judicial proceedings. An innocent student may be expelled from campus without appeal or other recourse, lose all scholarships, and be hard pressed to enroll at another university, because its admission office will inquire about previous criminal or expulsion records.

Laura Kipnis (2017) describes this new socio-legal jungle and administrative bullying in the academy succinctly: "I was introduced to an astonishing netherworld of accused professors and students, rigged investigations, closed-door hearings, and Title IX officers run amok. . . . And those in the know are too terrified to speak because the complaints typically arrive with demands for confidentiality and threats that speaking about the complaints will result in potential job loss or expulsion" (p. 6). Also, as Grace Kyungwon Hong (2018) points out in her excellent article "Intersectional and Anticarceral Approaches to Sexual Violence in the Academy," it is deeply problematic when punitive policies that focus on individualized punishment exacerbate existing structural inequities that reinforce racism, homophobia, and transphobia. With respect to Title IX enforcement, all too often, a myopic view of gender equality is enforced. She continues:

> At the same time, *impunity* is not the opposite of a culture of punishment but instead is its constitutive corollary. We can understand the universalizing, mandatory tendencies of more recent Title IX policies as a reaction to the pernicious culture of impunity that has allowed predatory sexual harassers and abusers, particularly those in positions of power as professors, administrators, and medical staff, to operate without consequence for years, sometimes decades. Impunity in this case is not the *lack* of action on the part of the university; the university is not *absent* when such conditions of impunity are allowed to occur. Rather, impunity is the policy that structures institutional response. The solution here is not simply to refortify the university as a punitive institution—particularly when such refortifications are implemented as a means of managing liability rather than in the pursuit of justice. (Hong, 2018)

What if we pursued justice in a nonpunitive way? A few colleges such as the College of New Jersey and Skidmore College have invested in restorative justice practices (Mangan, 2018). Such practices are more attuned to Ubuntu ethics and may help to transform lives. They bring about attitudinal shifts through education, reparations or restitution, and harm reduction measures; additionally, they show low recidivism rates, which is a hallmark of effectiveness (Karp & Conrad, 2005). It is interesting that so little attention and administrative resources are spent on such cheap and effective alternatives; instead, there is a focus on policing—risk management that checks the "Other" as stranger who might be out to kill me, not as somebody who might have a lot in common with me, at the very least being human. Those who critique restorative practices may implicitly favor risk management in securitization of the campus. It stems from a fear-based approach to punishment and "justice," and it suggests that severe, violent incidents can never be adjudicated or addressed in restorative ways.

In part, this has been driven by feminist analysis, which argues that women victims are disadvantaged in the process. This approach has been labeled as carceral feminism, that is, the reliance on criminal justice institutions to shame, punish, and incarcerate male perpetrators of sexual assault (cf. Law, 2014). They are also silent on the endemic racist, homophobic, and transphobic practices of police agencies, prosecutors, and so on. These feminists reject mediation and restorative practices, because they do not acknowledge power differentials, for example, intimidation practices by male perpetrators. However, it is clear that the enthusiastic (and monochromatic) reliance on the white supremacist police apparatus to gain justice for women who have been trafficked or have faced other forms of violence/violation ignores the power differential of these state actors, who may choose with impunity who are deserving victims.

Carceral feminism has been effectively critiqued by queer activists of color such as INCITE! Women, Gender Non-Conforming, and Trans people of Color against Violence or Brooklyn's Safe OUTside the System (SOS), affiliated with the Audre Lorde Project, which articulate a robust investment in harm reduction and empowerment, especially of cis women, trans, and gender nonbinary folx. They also insist on developing alternative justice structures outside violent, racist, heteropatriarchal institutions that control the risk-averse agenda in favor of reducing liability rather than favoring victims' needs and desire for restitution. SOS has created an imaginative de-escalation and safe party toolkit (https://alp.org/programs/sos). They also release alternative 9-1-1 phone numbers to members so that police do not have to be called for intervening at parties or domestic disputes.

These penal abolitionist organizations understand acutely that much violence emanates from institutional abuse of power, and they have invested in careful consciousness raising about institutional violence and strategies for addressing them. When systemic institutional violence is ill understood, it rears its ugly head—not only in corrupt police departments across the United States, but also in many universities and colleges, where no policing occurs—for decades, despite intricate reporting structures. It took a boy's mother over a decade to get "justice" when a public scandal broke Pennsylvania State University's top leadership. They tolerated a football administrator's sexual assault of boys. More recently, Michigan State University's administrators have been accused of cover up of the decades-long sexual abuse of students perpetrated by Larry Nasser, who was a celebrated doctor for the USA Olympic gymnastic teams.

Our focus here is on supporting students on and off campus. Investing in restorative justice makes also sense from an inclusive excellence framework of analysis. It includes pivoting focus not on how our students adapt to a college environment and assimilate all its values but putting the students *in the center* of the college universe, where students come first. Such student-centered and student-ready campus philosophy avoids hierarchical and silo thinking and creates caring and responsive communities across all stakeholders (McNair et al., 2016). While Tia Brown McNair's book on the student-centered campus does not address punitive campus policies, its analysis can be extended toward a student-centered restorative philosophy. It is not left to the division of student affairs to figure out how to make a student into a docile body so that they can be retained at minimal cost and make the college look good in terms of college ratings. A student-ready college philosophy steers clear of a deficit mindset which is mired in implicit bias: difference means deviance or deficiency. College leaders ask themselves how they can create an environment of compassion where risk management institutions and practices such as judicial boards and punishment would become obsolete. If college Title IX officers, human resources personnel, and judicial boards treat Black male students and faculty in a similar manner as they are treated by criminal justice system, namely, with suspicion and as proven guilty before being tried, it is clear that the vision of inclusive education has failed. So, restorative justice, when designed carefully with a stakeholders' framework, is only one piece of the puzzle of a student-ready college. It's a tool of last resort and used sparingly.

When diverse and underrepresented students see themselves reflected in the college curriculum; when the campus leadership investigates patterns of domination and invests in tackling them; when the minoritized students witness others investigating their privileges in the classroom, dorms, and intergroup dialogues; then they might begin to call their institution a home, rather than "the college I went to"—in the words of our former Provost Elizabeth Davis-Russell, describing her own experience with various institutions. She holds a PhD in psychology as well as another doctoral degree in education.

What would a student-centered approach that draws on principles of restorative justice and Ubuntu ethics look like? Students are given so many *mixed messages* when they arrive on campus: they are treated as customers (after all, they pay stiff tuition); as potentially delinquent minors (since many of the first-year students are below twenty-one years of age); as certified delinquents (whose criminal record continues to follow them into perpetuity), and as such they will be treated with great suspicion. German exchange students share that they are confused about the abstinence-only orientation, which led one student to exclaim: "I wasn't interested in taking drugs or drinking alcohol, but now I found my body and mind being curious about trying anything!" Clearly, the decades-old war on drugs has left its traces on college campuses. At the same time, it is well known (to police chiefs around the country) that campuses are a hotbed for illicit drug exchanges. Racial profiling and targeting of students and faculty of color also pervades the college campus, as it does the criminal justice system, noted by Black Lives Matter; in the poignant words of law professor Michelle Alexander (2010): the new Jim Crow. Much more scrutiny must occur about campus judicial board practices pertaining to suspensions and arrests.

More specifically, faculty as trusted advisors are given mixed messages: Are they beholden to the corporate messaging that demands that "the customer is always right"? Or, by contrast, do they need to follow the risk management paradigm, in the benign sense serving as parental surrogates, or, worse, as enforcers and mandated reporters? Of course, as the US society struggles with addictions from licensed pharmaceutical drugs and suicides by overdose, a college campus becomes a microcosmos of such struggles. Colleges cannot fill the demand for therapeutic counselors fast enough. In the spirit of Ubuntu ethics, we may want to validate the work of invisible people who exude empathy, not necessarily being licensed, who are able to mentor, reach, and engage vulnerable students. After all, if there are crisis moments, especially, when multiple students are affected, they tend to go to their faculty mentors, *not* to counseling professionals. And for students of color who mistrust historically oppressive institutional units such as counseling centers or infirmaries because of our historical contradictions (for instance, the Tuskegee Study of untreated syphilis of Black men in governmental institutions, 1932–1972), their trusted advisors or mentors are the main providers of support in an ironically predatory system where they cannot find a safe haven. Sometimes, it is the LGBTQ librarian, the local pastor, rabbi, or host family who give much-needed therapeutic support to other students. Those persons or organizations tend not to be on campus crisis resource lists but create a powerful albeit invisible web of life-sustaining energy. In addition, administrators are realizing that food insecurity as well as housing needs are *structural obstacles* that limit student well-being. Stopgap measures such as food pantries and providing housing during holidays, when parents are homeless, are important interventions.

However, public colleges, say in New York state, used to be free, as they are in many countries—even for international students. Nonetheless, New York decided to build up a costly prison industry to fight the drug war, costing over $100,000 per incarcerated person per year—a much higher cost than providing free tuition, room, and board for college-bound students. Even where it was proven that college education offered to prisoners lowers the recidivism rate drastically, a retributive Congress passed a crime bill in the 1990s, which shut down hundreds of thriving prison college education programs over night. To date, mass incarceration has had such a toll, touching almost every family, as some hundred million Americans now have a criminal record (Sentencing Project, 2014).

Ban-the-Box or Move-the-Box? Expansion of Carceral Surveillance in the Twenty-First Century

It is important to bring up the carceral context in our discussion of structural inequities on college and university campuses. Due to deadly mass shootings on college campuses (by people without prior criminal records), management divisions are preoccupied with unstable students and limit returning citizens' participation in civic life on campus. Across different sectors, including public employees, around the country, the initiative of "banning the box" is increasingly successful. This rallying cry refers to the demand that an applicant should not have to check a box if they have a felony record. In part, the success of political organizing has to do with the 1-in-3 statistic of felony records, and Black citizens have experienced the brunt of criminalization and incarceration. In the end, few Americans will remain eligible for any kind of public servant job, including janitorial staff. And we live in times, when immigrants are not facing a hearty welcome, especially if they arrive to the US from the Global South, so there are many vacancies that can't be filled. Public university systems such as SUNY have also welcomed the initiative of "banning the box" on the common application.

But, of course, this hard-fought victory comes with a serious catch: the box reappears, once the returning student is on campus and wants to live in the dorms or participate in study-abroad or internships. Even service-learning course activities may be affected. So, at each turn of committing themselves to high-impact learning, which is praiseworthy, those students with felony records will be reminded that they do not belong, and the campus continues to be suspicious about their "cleansed" record. Never mind, of course, that the research does not bear out such paranoid surveillance: returning citizens who pursue advanced degrees are a very low-risk group, and those who already pursued college credits while incarcerated have a recidivism rate of three percent or lower. They are very likely to make the honor roll and are the kinds of students professors dream of engaging in their classrooms. Because these are high-achieving students, they want to pursue high-impact, transformative education, civic engagement, study-abroad, meaningful internships with children, and so on. But exactly those opportunities are a pipe dream for returning citizens with felony records, because they will be quizzed at every opportunity; their parole officer, if they are kindly, will have to vouch for the parolee's good behavior in front of university committee, which is equally intimidating as a parole board. In fact, with the absurdity of the roulette game of "moving the box" (instead of banning it), ultimately, there is never a time when one is released from parole. Within the risk-adverse campus of today and the future, the criminal record will follow a student for decades to come. Continuously rejected as a productive citizen, these highly motivated students feel as despondent as Jean Valjean (of *Les misérables*), because they will never be good enough. Their felony is the modern scarlet letter—a "second chance" gesture (of legislative bills) becomes a hollow promise, and it surely takes a toll on their educational success.

Restorative justice and social justice must reach all people in the nation state. If justice does not reach the people, the people must demand it. Frederick Douglass (1857) cautioned us that "power concedes nothing without a demand. It never did and it never will." We, the people, must demand it! John Mbiti impressed upon us that the individual's humanity is inextricably linked to that of the community. We must not, therefore, characterize our differences as deficiencies but use our differences as assets to diversity, equity, and inclusion for institutional change in the beloved community. Martin Luther King (1964) championed the trope of societal change and the sword that heals. It is an uncomfortable juxtaposition. On the one hand, there was no greater champion of nonviolent direct action than King, who persisted at great cost to take down unjust laws and violent systems of control. King was an optimist who envisioned an expansive moral universe of the kind of Ubuntu ethics, where the children of those who hate today could be peace warriors and walk together tomorrow on the undulating terrain of social justice and inclusive excellence.

Conclusion

Sustaining an Inclusive Community of Learners—Recognition, Reconciliation, Accountability, and the Pedagogy of Healing

Our endeavors to conclude this exhausting work of attempting to dismantle the foundation and superstructure of injustice, racism, sexism, and other isms in the American polity reached fruition during the new threat of the Delta variant of COVID-19, the haunting heat, and unaccustomed conventional rainfalls of summer 2023. Diversity work is human work, and we must be intentional in our approaches and deliberations to secure any meaningful results. When we invoke the phenomenon of human work in inclusive literature, we make reference to the value that the human soul possesses—the freedom to be acknowledged, heard, respected, and treated as deserving of fairness and justice. The human soul wants to be connected and appreciated for the value it contributes to the community. It does not want to be fabricated, exploited, stigmatized, acculturized, or fixed because of the comfort of others.

Our work is still evolving as new questions are being asked about how to teach American history, Black studies, critical whiteness studies, transgender politics, diversity, equity and inclusion, and critical race theory. The contumacy over assaults on democracy and diversity, reemergence of xenophobia around immigration and migration issues, the effects of the SCOTUS's decision in tossing out *Roe v. Wade* (1973)—abortion rights and the right to privacy—and the recorded high cases of racial divisiveness since the era of Jim Crow have destroyed social trust and at the time increased the anathema for white supremacy. Nonetheless, new anti-Black voting laws to deny the sacred right and universal adult suffrage for especially BIPOC folx in the states of Georgia, Arizona, Florida, Texas, North

Carolina, Mississippi, and Alabama, and the unfortunate recent anti-Black and anti-Indigenous people racist campaign by Latino political leaders, especially the Los Angeles councilmembers' racist depiction of Blacks, Indigenous peoples, and immigrants as "monkeys," "accessories," and "He is with the Blacks" (Wick et al., 2022), which invokes "Otherness" and weakens the Black and brown coalition in America, tend to strengthen white supremacy. It seems the oldest democracy is racing toward an anocracy, dystopia, and some would even invoke Armageddon.

These assaults are premonition to the challenges ahead of all of us and not just for those of us in academia, and who are committed to doing human work. Regarding race and CRT, Tennessee, Oklahoma, Iowa, Idaho, and Texas are among thirty-six states that have passed laws forbidding the pedagogy of truth about enslavement, racism, feelings of discomfort for white students in DEI classes, and guilt around race, sex, religion, social justice classes, and other DEI categories (Foster et al., 2021). In other words, educators must not teach truth to power or anything that would make white students "uncomfortable." Therefore, our discussion of white comfort in this work is a precursory note to those who are engaged in new forms of social engineering to dismantle the pedagogy of healing. Thus, students and faculty of color, according to these acts of manipulation and the language of appeasement in the United States, should ironically continue to suffer from post-traumatic slave syndrome—the trauma associated with the brutality of American history—without healing. Is academic freedom dead in this era of cancel culture? As we continue to contemplate and envision the quest for inclusive excellence, social justice, and democratic principles in the American polity, we have not forgotten to keep the faith and make reference to religion and morality as diversity categories in this country. Perhaps God is too busy to be on constant call for humanity to do the right thing.

Conceivably, Friedrich Nietzsche (2006) was not incorrect in invoking Zarathustra—the power of the overman—to take charge of his/her/their own imperfection, idiosyncrasies, and destiny and declare the death of God. We can discern in Zarathustra that the person who is free from prejudice and discrimination might be the one to engage us in the process of institutional change. Nevertheless, Zarathustra may have not been successful in convincing the community to engage in a moral system and the energy and love to celebrate the essence of humanity with the value of diversity, inclusion, and social justice. The conspiracy of circumstances and historical contradictions in America's social fabric has dictated the difficult task of building bridges among communities of diverse cultures, precepts, and norms, yet it is our hope that, despite the turbulent diversity and inclusion voyage, our construction for a brighter and better future will prevail (perhaps not in our lives' time). We are hopeful, but not optimistic! Without igniting fire between interlocutors of Descartes's egocentric credo "I think; therefore, I am" and John Mbiti's sociocentric response "I am because we are; and since we are, therefore, I am" (Mbiti, 1990, p. 141), we remain transparent and hope-affirming in taking sides with the camp that is uncontroversially inclusive and community-centered—I am therefore *we* are. Mbiti and his vision for community considerations have shaped our perspectives, and we surrender with humility to that vision for an equitable and inclusive society.

In this era of the greatest pandemic that humanity has ever witnessed, there is concomitant suffering on our college campuses and in society because of the interlocking systems of oppression—social, political, economic systems—and matrices of domination. Nonetheless, we have not given up on the mantra for justice and liberation—*a luta continua, Vitória é certa* (the struggle continues, but victory is certain) and yet we are not ecclesiastically vested, but we are spiritual and have made reference to the scripture at times. In Ecclesiasticus, 4:30–31, "Be not as a lion in thy house, nor frantic among thy servants. Let not thine hand be stretched out to receive, and shut when thou shouldest repay" (King James Version with Apocrypha, 1962). We envision a community that is shaped by the principles of equity and reciprocity as noted in biblical literature many years before the modern edition of the holy book was written. There are times when one needs to invoke the adage, "Do unto others as you want it to be done to you." Alternatively, treat others as we want to be treated, as the Bible says. However, this statement went untested for too long. Members of the inclusive community would have to engage in continual soul searching for society. It is not an aberration that in modern society, the powerful in secular as well as religious institutions have organized liberation, freedom, and comfort mostly from the perception of the oppressor—white power holders in the American polity.

People of color and women's experiences and contributions to American society have been mostly inconsequential. Most of the time BIPOC and women's experiences have been that heteropatriarchy, capitalism, individualism, and whiteness see the American society as a possession and not as a process of relationship among humans, shaped by recognition of our values, unquestioned personhood, and justice. When will America in the post Gorge Floyd and Black Lives Matter era enlist the ennobling mind and action of the human spirit and the sociopolitical evolution of the totality of our humanness? The history of America's nation state, capitalism, individualism, meritocracy, and whiteness bears witness to the nature of the community we have today. Both BIPOC and POP (people of pallor) share the unfortunate legacy of the holocaust of enslavement, systemic racism, classism, homophobia, and the illusion of inclusion. America's diversity, inclusion, and social justice project must move from awareness to affirmation and from performative projects to transformative ones in order to acquire a sustainable and inclusive community. King was imbibed with the great idea of an inclusive and beloved community:

> The end is reconciliation; the end is redemption; the end is the creation of the beloved community. It is this type of spirit and this type of love that can transform opposers into friends. This type of love that I stress here is not eros, a sort of esthetic or romantic love; not philia, a sort if reciprocal love between personal friends; but it is agape which is understanding goodwill for all men. It is an overflowing love which seeks nothing in return. It is the love of God working in the lives of men. This is the love that may well be the salvation of our civilization. (King, 1957)

Most people in the world continue to find ways of building upon Martin Luther King's vision of the beloved community, searching for humanity, looking for love for society, seeking justice, and engaging in antiracism projects. However, while most reasonable people would agree that we have reached a point in American history where our humanity and that of all people should be inextricably linked—Ubuntu—unfortunately, "we the people" continue to witness evidence of dystopia, COVID-19 pandemic, sustenance of whiteness, white supremacy, white nationalism, xenophobia, neo-Nazism, misogynoir, anti-Black racism, new laws to reduce voting rights, attack on critical race theory, iconoclasm of civil rights ideas and images, and the destruction of human decency to promote dehumanization and selfish consciousness, instead of common consciousness.

Where is the love for humanity in American society when we have replaced our moral values with commodification and instrumentalization, where instrumentalization of life's meaning is measured in rigid risk assessment terms, without consideration of human value and quality of life? Here, our core values must move away from the maxim of "treating people as you want to be treated" to "treating people as they want to be treated." That gives a new meaning to self-love, reciprocity, appreciation for love, and our commitment to relational democracy. Our indebtedness to each other because of our membership to the community of soulful beings is concomitant with the obligation to respect and value people from their level and the human condition. This obligation to our humanity is observed not in linguistic violence, but in our language of showing appreciation in return—much obliged as we say in the English language, *obrigado* in Portuguese, or Ubuntu in Zulu—we are obliged to each other because of our personhood and humanness. However, why have we lost it? Where is the love? What kind of love defines the beloved community? When do we move from a society of microaggressions to one of microaffirmations?

It is what BIPOC folx in America have been saying for a long time. As Ta-Nehisi Coates chronicles in his *New York Times* bestseller book *Between the World and Me*, but most people are afraid to say about the American polity, "White America's progress, or rather the progress of those Americans who believe that they are white, was built on looting and violence. . . . But democracy is a forgiving God and America's heresies—torture, theft, enslavement—are so common among individuals and nations that none can declare themselves immune" (2015, p. 6). This is a depressing account of the beloved community, human relations, love, and premonition to Black babies unborn. Ceteris paribus, we must keep hope alive.

Austin Channing Brown (2018) would not have it differently. She interrogates America's love and what that means to the inclusive community. She questions the nature of love that is unfriendly and lazy, and that miseducates, diseducates, and transforms BIPOC folx and women into nonentities to serve capitalism's needs. And she dismisses that kind of love that disqualifies Black Lives Matter to make the context of the movement infinitesimally dilute. "I need a love that is troubled by injustice. A love that is provoked to anger when Black folks, including our children, lie dead in the streets. . . . A love that has no tolerance for hate, no excuse for racist decisions, no contentment in the status quo. I need a love that chooses justice" (Brown, 2018, p. 176). The qualities of the American polity and its membership are those that are shaped and shepherded by social justice, cultural awareness, empathy, respect, and values that will facilitate the unity of diverging viewpoints and systems for the sustenance of a true American inclusive democracy. Furthermore, as we write this conclusion around the celebration of Fourth of July, America's Independence Day, in 2023, we witness the vandalization of the images and statues of Martin Luther King, Jr., in different parts of the beloved nation state to send a message to the general populace that we are far from securing the vision of King for the beloved community. The Long Beach Police Department is still searching for those who defamed the statues of King with graffiti, swastika, and Nazi-related symbols (Good, 2021).

Many states are in the process of banning DEI programs, and many more are reviewing advanced placement African American studies courses to be banned (Meckler & Natanson, 2023). Parental rights movements, targeting inclusive education programs and banning, especially, books with woke, social justice, critical race theory, and transgender contents are dismantling structured and hidden curriculums. When Amanda Gorman's inspiring poem *The Hill We Climb* (2021), which calls for unity and was written specifically for the Biden-Harris inauguration, is seen as a threat to white supremacy and "uncomfortable" for white children to read, and is consequently banned by some states in America, there is a moment for soul-searching, a time for racial reckoning, and a juncture to recognize that there is something terribly wrong with the venoms of cancel culture and antiwokeism. Whether the vandals mentioned above are arrested or not, they made their case clear, and the states that are going after Black studies courses, literary works of BIPOC writers, and DEI programs are not ambiguous about their intentions. They are not interested in a beloved community that has a place for all Americans regardless of race, color, national origin, religion, class, disabilities, and sexual orientation.

Our work is not done yet, because without recognition, there is no reconciliation and reparations. We write on the land of the Indigenous people, whose lands were stolen and looted from them, and we have not reached closures as many unmarked graves of Indigenous people in the Indian boarding schools are being discovered in the United States and Canada. The process of Americanization and cultural genocide of the Indigenous people of the United States and the practice of General Pratt through the boarding school system have robbed the Indigenous people of their spaces, souls, and cultures up to today. The painful utterance of Pratt has not left any of us who dwell or teach on the land of our Indigenous people: "A great general has said that the only good Indian is a dead one. . . . I agree with the sentiment . . . that all the Indian there is in the race should be dead. Kill the Indian in him, and save the man" (1892/1973, pp. 46–59). The healing process in the beloved community starts from the acknowledgment of the sins of our white mothers and fathers—slavery, cultural genocide, and cultural imperialism of the Indigenous people—pave the way to the healing process.

The spirits of the Indigenous children murdered in the Indian boarding schools will not rest if the process of acknowledgment and reconciliation has to be completed. Canada has taken the lead in the recognition and reconciliation process as hundreds of unmarked graves of Indigenous residential schools have been found in 2021. The United States government participated in violent process of cultural imperialism through the dehumanization of Indigenous people in 1879. Daniella Zalcman of CNN reports, "Now, it's America's turn. Thanks to Haaland, one of the first Native women in Congress and the first ever Native Cabinet secretary, who fittingly now oversees the Bureau of Indian Education, the United States will finally have a chance to formally reckon with its own history on this issue. . . . In the US, Dartmouth scholar Preston McBride's research recently predicted that as many as 40,000 Indigenous students died during their time in boarding school" (Zelcman, 2021).

The lessons we learn from this process are that when governments and institutions work with people of color, who have suffered oppression and when they are genuinely put in a position of authority (not tokens), things could happen to address the injustice and inequity in American society and institutional change is inevitable. BIPOC folx must have a place at the table for change to come. The second lesson is that the principle of reconciliation begins with recognition of the role one played in any atrocity. Without recognition, there is no reconciliation. The third lesson is that no country or institution is too big or too arrogant to learn from BIPOC folx and countries such as South Africa and Canada that went through their own truth and reconciliation commissions. When white America starts listening—mindful listening—and becomes true accomplices and coconspirators to fight for justice, true change will occur in our institutions of higher learning and in society.

For more than a century, the United States' key institutions, corporations, agencies, and commissions have been set up to review America's problem with anti-Black racism, oppression, sexism, and other "isms." President Bill Clinton, for an example, set up a seven-member advisory board to start a "National Conversation on Race" in 1997. Many universities and colleges participated in the national conversation on race. On our own campus, as social justice advocates, we were appointed to lead and moderate the conversation on race for an entire academic year. The

Clinton's commission on race produced a report entitled *One America in the 21st Century*, which concluded that civil rights laws were not being enforced and there was widespread discrimination and systemic racism in America (Advisory Board on Race, 1998). Honestly, no serious congressional actions were taken after the report was submitted. The inaction in the US Congress has not been different from what has transpired in many institutions and communities in the United States for centuries.

Ironically, the American polity prides itself on an anti-oppression tradition and antiracist performative responses to major publicized racist events, and yet the country's approach to reaching the beloved community that Dr. King envisioned has not eclipsed the working theory and a pedagogy of healing fortified by sustainable, transformative race projects nation-wide. Antiracist theory, as Feagin mentions, contains the ideas, precepts, and norms that attempt to facilitate agency, the movement of human actors to bring change despite oppression in structures of racialized domination (2014, p. xii). The work of antiracism started many centuries before Ibram X. Kendi's book *How to Be an Antiracist* (2019) caught the eyes of many neophytes in race studies and diversity, equity, and inclusive studies across college campuses. Antiracist literature and programs in America could be traced as far back as 1688, where Quaker antiracist movements began (the second wave). The first wave of antiracist literature and programs could be assigned to Antonio de Montesinos in the 1500s, who challenged the racist intentions of Europeans, especially Spanish and Portuguese dehumanizing treatments of Africans and Taino Indians (Minster, 2019).

Abolitionist scholar activists, such as Frederick Douglass, Sojourner Truth, and Harriet Tubman, were among the third wave of antiracist activists. Then came the fourth wave composed of Ida B. Wells, Booker T. Washington, Oliver Cox, W. E. B. Du Bois, Malcolm X, Martin Luther King, and Kwame Ture. The current wave includes Angela Davis, Kimberleé Crenshaw, Cornel West, Michael Eric Dyson, Robin DiAngelo, Michael Omi and Howard Winant, Joe Feagin, and Ibram Kendi. Unfortunately, many college campuses, including our own campus, have joined the academic world in compounding antiracism events and programs on the backs of BIPOC folx as a *new* thing. Many of these programs become racialized *talk shows*—with the oppressed, BIPOC students, telling their traumatic stories to predominantly white audiences. These talk shows end without post-programming follow-ups or psychological processing. Many colleges are stuck at the awareness stage of diversity, equity, and inclusion programming. What most of these campuses, including our own, should be engaging in is a movement away from excessive lip services, window dressings, organized happiness, rhetorical exercises, and performative programming to a transformative stage of sustaining equity, policy restructuring, and DEI goals attainment. Furthermore, colleges and society must move beyond the old idea of tolerance, ally-ship, and comfort to a higher position of affirmation, microaffirmation, celebration of our humanity, and accompliceship. Thus far, we cannot forget the premonition Dr. King gave us in his Sunday sermon in 1955, when Rosa Parks was arrested for refusing to give up her seat to a white man in Montgomery: "Rarely do we find men [and women] who willingly engage in hard, solid thinking. There is an almost universal quest for easy answers and half-baked solutions. Nothing pains some people more than having to think." When it comes to DEI work, too many people take it for granted. They forget it is human work and the complexity of human work requires hard cognitive and visceral projects and engagements.

We are not arguing that *none* of the antiracism projects and programs yield results. Yet the scramble for performative antiracism programs on college campuses and in society in recent times are filled with rhetorical and sloganeering antics for antiracism campaigns, which create backlashes that tend to empower white supremacists and DEI impostors to disrupt the movement for racial justice. Witness to date Cornell Law School professor William Jacobson and his attack on critical race theory ("Cornell Daily Sun Interviews Professor William Jacobson," 2021). What we advocate are transformative and not just performative programs of food, fun, festivals, and "organized happiness," in the words of a colleague. As Frederick Douglas (1849) insists, "The white man's happiness cannot be purchased by the black man's misery."

Hitherto, we acknowledge modicums of progress in the trajectory of racial and gender equity in American society—from singing "Kumbaya" during the holocaust of enslavement, to appealing to the world with "We shall Overcome," to group political consciousness during the Black Power, civil rights, and women's rights movements, and now back to the reaffirmation of the humanity of the oppressed—Black Lives Matter. There are new demands for gender and racial justice in the American polity for the beloved community and the Biden administration has taken serious steps for dismantling systemic racism. This is one of the first times in recent years that the intensity and scope of injustice in America has tickled the moral consciousness of our leaders at the federal level for them to make racial justice a priority. The United States' ambassador to the United Nations, Linda Thomas-Greenfield, made this statement about the United States' endeavors during the United Nation's International Day for Elimination of Racial Discrimination: "The prevalence, and pervasiveness, of racial discrimination might make the situation look hopeless, but we remain hopeful. Let us expose the racism and racial discrimination endemic to every society, around the globe. Let us press forward, to root out that discrimination and remove the rot from our foundations. And on this day dedicated to ending racial discrimination, let us leave our children a less hateful, more hopeful world" (Thomas-Greenfield, 2021). It seems to be an important step in the right direction. Twenty years ago, the US delegation walked out of the World Conference against Racism in Durban, South Africa, and continued to withhold support for it under the Obama administration in 2009. While condemning racism domestically and abroad, the US government again has refused to acknowledge the Durban Declaration and Program of Action (DDPA) and refuses to attend any events related to the Durban anniversary in 2021 (Engelman, 2021).

Among the policy targets for the Biden administration is Executive Order 13985, which was established to advance racial equity in the federal government. The federal government has become partners with most colleges and universities in creating an office of chief diversity and inclusion officer (CDIO) at the US State Department. The United States government is incorporating racial justice into the country's foreign policy goals. Hopefully, this endeavor would help tweak US immigration policy toward Black and brown people around the world and it would improve relations with the developing world. In addition, the United States will support historically marginalized populations around the world. These countries include those whose ancestors built the White House and America with their free labor—African and the Caribbean. Finally, the Biden administration has nominated Professor Gay McDougall to the Committee on the Elimination of Racial Discrimination, a cadre of eighteen experts that will monitor and advise the president on racial issues and problems (Thomas-Greenfield, 2021). If the change to sustain a just society begins from the top, the rest might follow.

In similar vein, the long fight to recognize June 19, 1866, Juneteenth, and Freedom Day, the commemoration of the ending of enslavement (for Blacks and America) as a national holiday came to fruition when President Biden signed into law Juneteenth (June 19, 2021) as the newest federal holiday—at long last! We commend the ancestors and the Black community in Galveston, Texas, in fighting a good fight for the country. When we fight as a beloved community, we win! Also, the five-year fight over what to do with the statue of Confederate General Robert E. Lee in Charlottesville, Virginia, where in 2017 white nationalists and neo-Nazis, in their despicable rally, killed Heather Heyer and injured several as one of them used their car as a weapon of destruction, came to an end. The statue was dismounted from its pedestal in Market Street Park on July 10, 2021 (Good, 2021). Is systemic change finally coming to America? Is change coming to our institutions of power? The change for diversity and inclusive leadership must also incorporate changing the "self," the soul, and what makes us tick.

Too often, we see political change situated firmly in symbolic or performative gestures. Yes, removing statutes and statues is important, but how will the historical context be analyzed in school textbooks? Black educators are beginning to leave the profession en masse, as the backlash vitriol of school boards demands loyalty oaths to adhering to a "patriotic" curriculum, not seen since the McCarthy era. Meanwhile, the need for abolitionist teaching, as the visionary educator Bettina Love (2019) calls for, and the need for cultivating genius, coined by another influential voice, Gholdy Muhammad (2020), could not be greater. How is the demand for equity, equity-minded educators, equity-minded politicians, and antiracist learning being realized in an age that is threatened by such sobering analysis?

Our (white) students often opine that there will be racial progress with the younger generation self-actualizing and college students taking up diversity studies infused in their curriculum. College administrators have long been complacent and comforted by such naive self-assessment, and, certainly, white teachers' attitudes, as Love and Muhammad point out, show all too often that no racial progress is on the horizon. Colleges that offer teacher education programs must do better in preparing the next generation of leaders. It is not enough to sprinkle a few diversity themes into one of dozens of courses of a four-year educational program. It is not good enough to reduce the protracted freedom struggle to Rosa Park's fatigue on a bus or King's dream speech in Washington, DC.

Great care must go into syllabus preparation and course delivery that is true pedagogy for transgression, abolitionist teaching, and giving all college students tools to overcome deficit assumptions and truly cultivate genius in BIPOC students in pre-K through 12 school settings. In fact, it is the culturally responsive courses offered at colleges and universities that may create great harm by perpetuating bias and stereotypes through microaggressions unleashed in the college classroom. BIPOC college students then find themselves in the burdensome role of undoing miseducation and guiding white professors who get defensive rather than become responsible. One such faculty claim may be that their graduate programs did not prepare them for navigating such spaces and listening to all voices empathetically. Of course, we note in our combined thirty years–plus of teaching critical whiteness studies, race and racism, and DEI careers that we all must engage in life-long learning. What is most troubling is that our BIPOC students have been making the *same* carefully crafted demands for structural change over a span of thirty years. Every decade engenders its own student protest, and thirty years ago, it was prompted by the nation-wide protests surrounding the acquittal of police officers for severely assaulting Rodney King.

Embracing authentic diversity and inclusive leadership entails a deep, financial commitment to inclusive excellence. It cannot be simply realized with installing a CDIO responsible for everything related to inclusion efforts, including asking CDIOs to "police" those faculty or staff who go astray with careless comments and serious microaggressions or to keep in line BIPOC faculty and accomplices who are not satisfied with diversity management plans.

The call for an abolitionist democracy, as first articulated by W. E. B. Du Bois, will need to be retooled to accommodate today's demands, as the settler colonial nation state undergoes a reckoning of past wrongs. However, Du Bois's assessment of the twentieth century still remains prescient for the twenty-first century—that the main challenge is anti-Black racism. Perhaps the US nation state will adopt and create a systematic infrastructure for transitional justice mechanisms, South African–style, or perhaps it will occur with terse apologies and reparations, German-style. But one thing is clear: the past is never past nor dead. And a mere apology for enslavement or for deposing a king and colonizing territories will no longer suffice. Defunding the police might be one popular rallying cry of 2020 with some police departments facing reorganization as a result. But it is another thing altogether to defund the Catholic Church over its history of cover ups of sexual assaults of tens of thousands of children and teenagers. The church has more reckoning to do considering its long imperial history, and 1492 may just be an arbitrary historical starting point for such significant soul-searching conversations and tribunals. The Crusades are another point of contention. Certainly, Canada is currently haunted by the church's crimes targeting Indigenous families, and, sooner than later, other crimes against Indigenous peoples enslaved in its "mission system" in the territory of the United States, the "boarding school" experience, and so on, will have to be dealt with.

Higher education institutions must face their past ghosts as well, including Ivy League universities, Harvard, Yale, Brown, and Princeton. A few are starting to pay restitution to descendants of people enslaved on their campus "plantations," but "Hidden Ivy Leagues" such as Georgetown in Washington, DC, a Jesuit institution, prefer to tie reparations to tuition scholarships. As many institutions are undergoing an internal reckoning and launching multi-million-dollar campaigns to attract "the talented tenth" of BIPOC faculty taking coveted tenure-track positions, they still have to ask themselves, Will these gifted faculty of color actually stay? Even super star faculty such as Nikole Hannah-Jones or Cornel West are being denied tenure, reversed in Hannah-Jones's case, after a public outcry within and beyond the university of North Carolina. Hannah-Jones fought hard the politics of misogynoir of donors' interference in the tenure process. With the assistance of her NAACP legal team, she took on the naysayers who misjudge BIPOC women of color as incompetent and prevailed as the board of trustees had to vote again. With the power of the pen, she stirred up academia's conscience that would make the ancestors Ida B. Wells-Barnett and Toni Morrison proud. Thus, Hannah-Jones turned her back on the historically white institution and joined Howard University, where she is starting a Knight Center of Journalism, inspiring the next generation of BIPOC journalists, sorely missing in mainstream media.

The beloved society, as realized by a liberated people during the brief era of Black Reconstruction, will rise again when all stakeholders for diversity, equity, and inclusion are engaged in an enterprise that fulfils the expectation of the human condition—for who we are—and the affirmation of social justice will be secured as the guiding principle for each other's existence. The ignoble practice of injustice, prejudice, and discrimination would be nailed in the coffin of oppression, as we continue to confront our historical contradictions, making inclusive leadership and institutional change a priority, and rediscovering our future possibilities by maintaining the centrality of our lives through the halls of social justice.

References

Achebe, C. (1958). *Things fall apart.* William Heinemann.

Acker, J. (2006). *Class questions, feminist answers.* Rowman and Littlefield.

Adams, B. (2020, May 27). Additional video shows George Floyd was not resisting arrest as police claimed. *The Grio.* https://thegrio.com/2020/05/27/video-shows-george-floyd-not-resisting/

Advisory Board on Race. (1998). *One America in the 21st century: Forging a new future.* US Government Printing Office.

African American Policy Forum. (2020). *Say her name.* https://aapf.org/sayhername

After COVID-19 outbreak, SUNY Oneonta president departs. (2020, October 15). *AP News.* https://apnews.com/article/virus-outbreak-new-york-oneonta-0b43f0aee1a1e2a2c372b1f2ade8d67e

After racist encounter, Chris Cooper takes us birding in Central Park. (2020, June 17). *Good Morning America* (ABC News). https://www.youtube.com/watch?v=-qd2XyGFTzk

Ahmed, S. (2012). *On being included: Racism and diversity in institutional life.* Duke University Press.

Ahmed, S. (2016, May 30). Resignation. *Feminist killjoys* (Blog). https://feministkilljoys.com/2016/05/30/resignation/

Aizenman, N. (2018, January 12). Trump wishes we had more immigrants from Norway—turns out we once did. *NPR.* https://www.npr.org/sections/goatsandsoda/2018/01/12/577673191/trump-wishes-we-had-more-immigrants-from-norway-turns-out-we-once-did

Alcoff, L. M. (2006). *Visible identities: Race, gender and the self.* Oxford University Press.

Alexander, M. 2010. *The new Jim Crow: Mass incarceration in the age of colorblindness.* New Press.

Allen, C. (2018, January 27). *Keys to ethical leadership in corporate culture.* Insight Business Works. https://insightbusinessworks.com/keys-to-ethical-leadership-in-corporate-culture-a-critical-opportunity-in-enterprise-risk-management/

References

Alvarado, M., & Gomez, A. (2020, February 25). New Trump immigration policy could ban thousands of African immigrants from US. *USA Today*. https://www.usatoday.com/story/news/politics/elections/2020/02/24/new-trump-travel-ban-could-keep-african-immigrants-out-us/4861122002/

American Association of Colleges and Universities (AAC&U). (1994). *Diversity, and democracy in higher education*. AACU Press.

American Association of Colleges and Universities (AAC&U). (1995). *The drama of diversity and democracy: Higher education and American commitments*.

American Association of Colleges and Universities (AAC&U). (1998). *The drama of diversity and democracy*.

American Association of Colleges and Universities (AAC&U). (n.d.). *Making excellence inclusive*. http://www.aacu.org/making-excellence-inclusive

American Civil Liberties Union. (2020). *Block the vote: Voter suppression in 2020*. https://www.aclu.org/news/civil-liberties/block-the-vote-voter-suppression-in-2020/

American Council on Education (ACE). (2017). *Annual report, 2017*. https://www.acenet.edu/Documents/Annual-Report-2017-final.pdf

Anderson, M. (2017a, February 14). *African immigrant population in U.S. steadily climbs*. Pew Research Center. https://www.pewresearch.org/fact-tank/2017/02/14/african-immigrant-population-in-u-s-steadily-climbs/

Anderson, M. (2017b, February 14). *Key facts about Black immigrants in the U.S.* Pew Research Center. http://www.pewresearch.org/fact-tank/2018/01/24/key-facts-about-black-immigrants-in-the-u-s/

Anderson, M. (2018, January 24). *Facts about Black immigrants*. Pew Research Center http://www.pewresearch.org/fact-tank/2018/01/24/key-facts-about-black-immigrants-in-t

Anderson, M., & Lopez, A. (2018, January 24). *Facts about Black immigrants*. Pew Research Center. http://www.pewresearch.org/fact-tank/2018/01/24/key-facts-about-black-immigrants-in-the-u-s/.

Applebaum, B. (2010). *Being white, being good: White complicity, white moral responsibility and social justice pedagogy*. Lexington Books.

Archias, E., & Stimson, B. (2023, May 10). The labor of teaching and administrative hysteria: When leaders usurp faculty expertise with kitsch social justice, students suffer. *Chronicle of Higher Education*.

Asante-Muhammad, D., & Gerber, N. (2018, January 12). African immigrant: Immigrating into a racial wealth divide. *HuffPost*.

Asumah, S. N. (2015). Race immigration reform, and heteropatriarchal masculinity: Reframing the Obama presidency. *Wagadu*, 13, 9–41.

Asumah, S. N. (2022). *Knowing who we are*. Keynote address, 9th Annual Watertown Juneteenth, Watertown, New York. https://www.wwnytv.com/2022/06/14/9th-annual-watertown-juneteenth-coming-up-saturday/

Asumah, S. N., and Johnston-Anumonwo, I. (1999). *Issues in multiculturalism: Cross-national perspectives* (2nd ed.). Whittier.

Asumah, S. N., and Johnston-Anumonwo, I. (2002). *Diversity, multiculturalism and social justice*. Global Academic.

Asumah, S. N., & Nagel, M. (eds.). (2014). *Diversity, social justice, and inclusive excellence: Transdisciplinary and global perspectives*. State University of New York Press.

Asumah, S. N., & Nagel, M. (2020). An American kaleidoscope: Rethinking diversity and inclusion leadership through the prism of gender and race. In J. Marques (Ed.), *The Routledge companion to inclusive leadership*. Routledge.

Asumah, S. N., Nagel, M., & Rosengarten, L. (2016). New trends in diversity leadership and inclusive excellence. *Wagadu, 15*, 139–161.

Asumah, S. N., & Perkins, V. C. (2001). *Educating the Black child in the Black independent school*. Global.

Aurdal, M. (2018, January 15). Norwegian: No thank you, President Trump. *CNN*. https://www.cnn.com/2018/01/13/opinions/norway-says-no-thanks-to-trump-aurdal-opinion/index.html

Ayim, M., Oguntoye, K., & Schultz, D. (1986). *Farbe bekennen: Afrodeutsche Frauen auf den Spuren ihrer Geschichte*. Orlando Verlag.

Ayim, M., Oguntoye, K., & Schultz, D. (1992). *Showing our colors: Afro-German women speak out* (A. Adams, Trans.). University of Massachusetts Press.

Babcock, L., & Laschever, S. (2007). *Women don't ask: The high cost of avoiding negotiations—and positive strategies for change*. Bantam.

Babcock, L., & Laschever, S. (2009). *Ask for it: How women can use the power of negotiations to get what they really want*. Bantam.

Bailey, I. (2017, June 3). The disrespect shown to Obama still rankles. *CNN*. https://www.cnn.com/2017/06/03/opinions/disrespect-for-obama-still-upsetting-bailey/index.html

Bailey, M., & Trudy. (2018). On misogynoir: Citation, erasure, and plagiarism. *Feminist Media Studies, 18*(4), 762–768.

Baker, K. (1999). Sex, rape and shame. *Boston University Law Review, 79*, 663–716.

Banks, J. A. (2016). *Cultural diversity and education: Foundations, curriculum, and teaching* (6th ed.). Routledge. (Original work published 1981)

Banning, J. H., & Kuk, L. (2005, November). Campus ecology and student health. *Spectrum*, 9–15.

Barndt, J. (1991). *Dismantling racism in America: The continuing challenge to white America*. Augsburg Fortress.

Bart, M. (2016). *Diversity and inclusion in the college classroom* (Special report). Faculty Focus. https://www.facultyfocus.com/free-reports/diversity-and-inclusion-in-the-college-classroom

Bauer, K. W. (1998). *Campus climate: Understanding the critical components of today's colleges and universities*. Jossey-Bass.

Bauer-Wolf, J. (2021, January 13). More Black students enroll in HBCUs following hate crime reports, study. *Higher Ed Dive*. https://www.highereddive.com/news/more-black-students-enroll-in-hbcus-following-hate-crime-reports-study/593247

Bell, L. A. (1997). Theoretical foundation of social justice education. In M. Adams, L. A. Bell, & P. Griffin (Eds.), *Teaching for diversity and social justice: A sourcebook* (pp. 3–15). Routledge.

Belson, K., & Capuzzo, J. P. (2007, September 26). Towns rethink laws against illegal immigrants. *New York Times*. https://www.nytimes.com/2007/09/26/nyregion/26riverside.html?_r

Bennett, M. J. (1993). Towards ethnorelativism: A developmental model of intercultural sensitivity. In R. M. Paige (Ed.), *Education for the intercultural experience* (2nd ed., pp. 21–71). Intercultural Press.

Bensemon, E. M. (2016). *Protocol for assessing equity-mindedness in state policy*. Center for Urban Education, University of Southern California. https://cue.usc.edu/files/2017/02/CUE-Protocol-Workbook-Final_Web.pdf

Berkowitz, D. S. (1948). *Inequality of opportunity in higher education: A study of minority group and related barriers to college admission*. Williams.

Berry, M. F. (1995). *Black resistance/white law: A history of constitutional racism in America*. Penguin.

Biden addresses threats to American democracy in "soul of the nation" address. (2022, September 1). MSNBC (YouTube channel). https://www.youtube.com/watch?v=fASIvWtHHkg

Bigelow, B., & Peterson, B. (2003). *Rethinking Columbus: The next 500 years* (2nd ed.). Rethinking Schools.

Biggers, J. (2012, December 13). Why federal intervention matters: Will Mexican American studies fiasco in Tucson end in 2013? *Huffington Post*. https://www.huffpost.com/entry/why/-federal-intervention_b_2296093

Binkley, C. (2021, January 21). Biden "revokes Trump report promoting" patriotic education. *Associated Press*. https://apnews.com/article/biden-revoke-trump-patriotic-education-259b9302ab24bac55fa14676a1a9d11e

Biondi, M. (2012). *The Black revolution on campus*. University of California Press.

Black Justice League. (2020, June 29). *A statement from the Black justice league in response to the removal of the Wilson name*. Medium. https://medium.com/@blackjusticeleague15/a-statement-from-the-black-justice-league-in-response-to-the-removal-of-the-wilson-name-853153b6c12f

Black Liberation Collective (BLC). (2015). *Our principles*. https://blacklibco.squarespace.com/our-beliefs

Black Lives Matter. (2020). https://blacklivesmatter.com

Boeckenstedt, J. (2014, December 17). Why the admissions office may be part of the problem of college access. *Chronicle of Higher Education*. http://chronicle.com/article/Why-the-Admissions-Office-May/150883/

Boeckenstedt, J. (2020). Some final thoughts on SAT and ACT. https://jonboeckenstedt.net

Bona, E. (2020, June 14). Liverpool's shameful history and why we must never forget it. *Echo*. https://www.liverpoolecho.co.uk/news/liverpool-news/anti-slavery-day-liverpools-shameful-15288358

Brennan, D. (2018, September 19). Serena and Venus Williams blackface impersonators draw scorn and racism accusations across internet. *Newsweek*. https://www.newsweek.com/serena-venus-williams-blackface-impersonators-draw-scorn-and-racism-1127427

Brockes, E. (2018, January 15). #MeToo founder Tarana Burke: "You have to use your privilege to serve other people." *Guardian*. https://www.theguardian.com/world/2018/jan/15/me-too-founder-tarana-burke-women-sexual-assault

Brogaard, B. (2020, August 20). Beware of these 10 sexist fallacies. *Psychology Today*. https://www.psychologytoday.com/us/blog/the-mysteries-love/202008/beware-these-10-sexist-fallacies

Brown, A. C. (2018). *I'm still here: Black dignity in a world made for whiteness*. Convergent Books.

Brown, C. R., & Mazza, J. (1991). *Peer training strategies for welcoming diversity* (Unpublished paper). National Coalition Building Institute, Arlington, Massachusetts.

Bruce-Jones, E. (2017, April 17). Police brutality and racism in Germany. *Black Perspectives*. https://www.aaihs.org/police-brutality-and-racism-in-germany/

Bruckmüller, S., Ryan, M. K., Rink, F., & Haslam, S. A. (2014). Beyond the glass ceiling: The glass cliff and its lessons for organizational policy. *Social Issues and Policy Review*, 8(1), 202–232.

Brutus. (1787). *To the citizens of the state of New York* (Brutus no. 1). https://www.khanacademy.org/humanities/us-government-and-civics/us-gov-primary-documents/primary-documents-in-us-government-and-civics/a/brutus-no-1

Burke, L. (2020, October 27). Black workers and the university. *Inside Higher Ed*. http://www.insidehighered.com/new/2020/10/27/black-workers-universities-often-are-left-out-conversations-about-race-and-higher

Butler, P. (2017). *The chokehold: Policing Black men*. New Press.

Cabrera, N. (2012). Working through whiteness: White, male college students challenging racism. *Review of Higher Education*, 35(3), 375–401.

Cabrera, N. L., Franklin, J. D., & Watson, J. S. (2017). *Whiteness in higher education: The invisible missing link in diversity and racial analysis* (Association for the Study of Higher Education Report, vol. 42, no. 6). Wiley.

Cabrera, N. L., Watson, J. S., & Franklin, J. D. (2016). Racial arrested development: A critical whiteness analysis of campus ecology. *Journal of College Student Development, 57*(2), 119–134.

Call, C. T. (2021, January 8). No, it's not a coup—it's a failed self-coup that will undermine US leadership and democracy worldwide. *Brookings.* https://www.brookings.edu/blog/order-from-chaos/2021/01/08/no-its-not-a-coup-its-a-failed-self-coup-that-will-undermine-us-leadership-and-democracy-worldwide/

Capps, R., McCabe, K., & Fix, M. (2011). *New streams: Black African migration to the United States.* Migration Policy Institute.

Capps, R., McCabe, K., & Fix, M. (2012). *Diverse streams: Black African migration to the United States.* Migration Policy Institute.

Carlyle, T. (1888). *On heroes, hero-worship and heroic in history.* Frederick A. Stokes.

CCA. (2015). Educational field trips. https://ccaeducate.me/educational-field-trips/

Center for Community Alternatives. (2015, March). *Boxed out: Criminal history screening and college application attrition.* https://communityalternatives.org/pdf/publications/BoxedOut_FullReport

Centers for Diseases Control and Prevention (CDC). (2022). Investigate the rate of COVID-19 in the United States. https://data.cdc.gov/Case-Surveillance/COVID-19-Case-Surveillance-Restricted-Access-Detai/mbd7-r32t

Chapman, M. W. (2014, September 5). White unemployment 5.3%—Black unemployment 11.4%. *CNSNews.com.* https://cnsnews.com/news/article/michael-w-chapman/white-unemployment-53-black-unemployment-114

Chertoff, M. (2008). Laws to be waived for border fence. CNN. https://edition.cnn.com/2008/POLITICS/04/01/border.fence/index.html

Chikanda, A., & Morris, J. S. (2020). Assessing the integration outcomes of African immigrants in the United States. *African Geographical Review, 40*(1), 1–18.

Chimbelu, C. (2020, June 1). Opinion: George Floyd killing opens racism wounds for European Blacks. *DW.* https://www.dw.com/en/opinion-george-floyd-killing-opens-racism-wounds-for-european-blacks/a-53648169

Chotiner, I. (2019, January 19). The disturbing, surprisingly complex relationship between white identity politics and racism. *New Yorker.* https://www.newyorker.com/news/q-and-a/the-disturbing-surprisingly-complex-relationship-between-white-identity-politics-and-racism

Cineas, F. (2020, September 24). "Critical race theory, and Trump's war on it, explained." *Vox.* https://www.vox.com/2020/9/24/21451220/critical-race-theory-diversity-training-trump

Clark, J. B., Leslie, W. B., & O'Brien, K. P. (2010). *SUNY at sixty: The promise of the State University of New York.* State University of New York Press.

Cluster, D. (1979). *The borning struggle: An interview with Bernice Johnson Reagon.* http://civilrightsteaching.org/resource/the-borning-struggle-bernice-johnson-reagon/

Coates, T. (2015). *Between the world and me.* Random House.

Cole, E. R., & Harper, S. (2017). Race and rhetoric: An analysis of college presidents' statements of campus racial incidents. *Journal of Diversity in Higher Education, 10*(4), 318–333.

Collier, P. (2007). *The bottom billion: Why the poorest countries are failing and what can be done about it.* Oxford University Press

Collinson, D., & Hearn, J. (1996). Breaking the silence: On men, masculinities and management. In D. Collinson and J. Hearn (Eds.), *Men as managers, managers as men.* Sage.

Combahee River Collective (CRC). (1977). *The Combahee River Collective statement.* Black Past. https://www.blackpast.org/african-american-history/combahee-river-collective-statement-1977/

Congressional Quarterly. (2011). *Issues in race and ethnicity.* Washington, DC: CQ Press.

Cook, A., & Glass, C. (2014). Women and top leadership positions: Towards an institutional analysis. *Gender, Work and Organization, 21*(1), 91–103.

Cooper, A. (2020, May 26). Statement from Amy Cooper on Central Park incident. *PR Newswire.* https://www.prnewswire.com/news-releases/statement-from-amy-cooper-on-central-park-incident-301065492.html

Cornell Daily Sun interviews Professor William Jacobson on CRT site. (2021, February 24). *Cornell Review.* https://www.thecornellreview.org/full-interview-cornell-daily-sun-interviews-professor-william-jacobson-on-crt-site/

Cornell University. (2021). *The takeover of Willard Straight Hall (1969).* https://assembly.cornell.edu/tools-tabs-resources/history-shared-governance/takeover-willard-straight-hall-1969

Coronavirus in the U.S.: Latest map and case count. (January 8, 2021). *New York Times.* https://www.nytimes.com/interactive/2020/us/coronavirus-us-cases.html

Couloute, L. (2011). Student diversity sit-in. *radicalumass's blog.* https://blogs.umass.edu/radicalumass/histories-of-radical-actions-at-umass/99-2/

Cox, T., Jr. (1991). The multicultural organization. *Academy of Management Executive, 5*(2), 34–47.

Crawford, B. (2021, December 12). Ranking college football's most valuable programs. *247 Sports.* https://247sports.com/LongFormArticle/Ranking-college-footballs-most-valuable-programs-Alabama-Michigan-Texas-Georgia-Ohio-State-Oklahoma-178007658/#178007658_1

Crawford, F. (2013, May 4). Africana Studies and Research Center is on the ascendant. Cornell News Service. http://archive.is/Mr5R

Crenshaw, K. (1989). Demarginalizing the intersection of race and sex: A Black feminist critique of antidiscrimination doctrine, feminist theory and antiracist politics. *University of Chicago Legal Forum, 1989*(1): 139–167.

Crenshaw, K. (2018, September 27). We still haven't learned from Anita Hill's testimony. *New York Times.* https://www.nytimes.com/2018/09/27/opinion/anita-hill-clarence-thomas-brett-kavanaugh-christine-ford.html

Cross, T. (1988). Services to minority populations: Cultural competence continuum. *Focal Point*, *3*(1), 1–4.

Cross, T. L., Bazron, B. J., Dennis, K.W., & Issacs, M. R. (1989). *Towards a culturally competent system of care: A monograph on effective service for minority children who are severely emotionally disturbed*. CASSP Technical Center, Georgetown University Child Development Center.

Cross, W. E. (1991). *Shades of Black: Diversity in African American identity*. Temple University Press.

CUNY History. (n.d.). The history of the City College of New York, 1969–1999. http://cunyhistory.tripod.com/thehistoryofcitycollege19691999/id1.html

Cuomo, A. (2016, March 29). Governor Cuomo bans non-essential state travel to North Carolina. Governor A. Cuomo website. https://www.governor.ny.gov/news/governor-cuomo-bans-non-essential-state-travel-north-carolina

Daniels, R. (1993). United Sates policy towards Asian immigrants: Contemporary developments in historical perspective. *International Journal*, *48*(2), 310–334.

Darwish, R. (2018, July 31). #MeTwo floods internet revealing the ugly truth about racism in Germany. *Al Bawaba*. https://www.albawaba.com/loop/metwo-floods-internet-revealing-ugly-truth-about-racism-germany-1166890

Davis, A. Y. (1981). *Women, race and class*. Random House.

Davis, A. Y. (2003). *Are prisons obsolete?* Seven Stories.

Dawsey, J. (2018, January 12). Trump derides protections for immigrants from "shithole" countries. *Washington Post*. https://www.washingtonpost.com/politics/trump-attacks-protections-for-immigrants-from-shithole-countries-in-oval-office-meeting/2018/01/11/bfc0725c-f711-11e7-91af-31ac729add94_story.html?noredirect=on&utm_term=.7b6b004b6010

de Gobineau, A. (1915). Essay on the inequality of the human races (A. Collins, Trans.). Putman's. (Original work published 1854)

Delgado, R. (1996). *The coming race war? And other apocalyptic tales of America after affirmative action and welfare*. New York University Press.

Dewey, J. (1940). *The living thoughts of Thomas Jefferson*. Longman.

DiAngelo, R. (2018). *White fragility: Why it is so hard for white people to talk about racism*. Beacon Press.

DiTomaso, N. (2013). *The American non-dilemma: Racial inequality without racism*. Russell Sage Foundation.

DiversityInc. (2018, September 21). Homeland security office supervisor calls Black and Latino workers "monkeys." https://www.diversityinc.com/homeland-security-norfolk-racist

Dix, A. (2018). "And 1" more piece of evidence of discrimination against black basketball players. *Howard Journal of Communications*, *30*(3), 1–19.

Dixon, E., & Piepzna-Samarasinha, L. L. (Eds.). (2020). *Beyond survival: Strategies and stories from the transformative justice movement*. AK Press.

Doherty, M. (2019, November 13). The philosopher of #MeToo: Kate Manne and the fight against misogyny. *Chronicle of Higher Education.* https://www.chronicle.com/article/the-philosopher-of-metoo/

Dominici, F., Fried, L. P., & Zeger, S. L. (2009). So few women leaders—it's no longer a pipeline problem, so what are the root causes? *Academe, 95*(4), 25–27.

Dotson, K. (2011). Tracking epistemic violence, tracking practices of silencing. *Hypatia, 26*(2), 236–257.

Dotson, K. (2014). Conceptualizing epistemic oppression. *Social Epistemology, 28*(2), 115–138. https://newdiscourses.com/tftw-epistemic-oppression/

Douglass, F. (1849, November 16). *The destiny of colored Americans.* New York Historical Society. https://teachingamericanhistory.org/library/document/the-destiny-of-colored-americans/

Douglass, F. (1857). *West India emancipation—if there is no struggle, there is no peace* (Speech). https://www.blackpast.org/african-american-history/1857-frederick-douglass-if-there-no-struggle-there-no-progress/

Drucker, D. (2010, January 27). Obama talking points: Rescue, rebuild, restore America. https://rollcall.com/2010/01/27/obama-talking-points-rescue-rebuild-restore-america/

Du Bois, W. E. B. (1914, July 19). Does Race Antipathy Serve Any Good Purpose? *Boston Globe.*

Dunbar-Ortiz, R. (2014). *An Indigenous people's history of the United States.* Beacon Press.

DuVernay, A. (Dir.). (2019). *When they see us.* Harpo Films.

Dyson, M. E. (2014, August 19). Obama failed us, not only Black people but he failed the nation. *Real Clear Politics.* https://www.realclearpolitics.com/video/2014/08/19/michael_eric_dyson_obama_failed_us_not_only_as_black_people_but_he_failed_the_nation.html

Dyson, M. E. (2017*). Tears we cannot stop: A sermon to white America.* St. Martin's.

Dyson, M. E. (2020). *Long time coming: Reckoning with race in America.* St. Martin's.

Eagly, A. H., & Karau, S. J. (2002). Role congruity theory of prejudice toward female leaders. *Psychological Review, 109*(3), 573–598.

Eddy, P. L., & VanDerLinden, K. E. (2006). Emerging definitions of leadership in higher education: New visions of leadership or same old "hero" leader? *Community College Review, 34*(1), 5–26.

Edward Coston statue pulled out of Bristol Harbour. (2020, June 11). BBC News. https://www.bbc.com/news/uk-england-bristol-53004748

Elflein, J. (2023). Total number of cases and deaths from COVID-19 in the United States as of April 26, 2023. *Statista.Com.* https://www.statista.com/statistics/1101932/coronacirus-civid19-cases-and-deaths-number-us-america

Ellemers, N., Rink, F., Derks, B., & Ryan, M. K. (2012). Women in high places: When and why promoting women into top positions can harm them individually or as a group (and how to prevent this). *Research in Organizational Behavior, 32*, 163–187.

Elshtain, J. B. (1980). *Public man, private woman*. Princeton University Press.

Eltis, D. (2001). The volume and structure of the transatlantic slave trade: A reassessment. *William and Mary Quarterly, 58*(1), 17–46.

Engelman, S. (2021). *Biden administration announces it will not participate in Durban IV conference*. Brandeis Center.

Equal Justice Initiative. (2017). *Lynching in America: Confronting the legacy of racial terror*. https://lynchinginamerica.eji.org

Equal Justice Initiative (2018). *The national memorial for peace and justice*. https://museumandmemorial.eji.org/memorial

Fanon, F. (1967). *Black skin, white mask*. Grove.

Fanon, F. (2004). *The wretched of the earth* (R. Philcox, Trans.). Grove. (Original work published 1961)

Farley, J. C. (2012). *Majority-minority relations* (6th ed.). Prentice Hall.

Feagin, J. (2010). *Racist America: Roots, current realities, and future reparations*. Routledge.

Feagin, J. (2014). *Racist America: Roots, current realities, and future reparations*. Routledge.

Feagin, J. (2018). *Racist America: Roots, current realities, and future reparations* (3rd ed.) Routledge.

Feagin, J., & O'Brien, E. (2003). *White men on race*. Beacon.

Fernandez, M., & Hauser, C. (2015, October 5). Texas mom teaches text book company a lesson on accuracy. *New York Times*. https://www.nytimes.com/2015/10/06/us/publisher-promises-revisions-after-textbook-refers-to-african-slaves-as-workers.html

Flaherty, C. (2016). Tenure denied. *Inside Higher Education*. https://www.insidehighered.com/news/2016/05/17/campus-unrest-follows-tenure-denial-innovative-popular-faculty-member-color

Flaherty, C. (2020, November 10). Against face-to-face teaching mandates: Professors and graduate students urge caution on spring plans for in-person instruction. *Inside Higher Ed*. https://www.insidehighered.com/news/2020/11/10/professors-fight-face-face-spring-teaching-mandates

Florvil, T. (2017, July 5). From ADEFRA to Black lives matter: Black women's activism in Germany. *Black Perspectives*. https://www.aaihs.org/from-adefra-to-black-lives-matter-black-womens-activism-in-germany/

Ford, K. (2012). Shifting white ideological script: The educational benefits of inter- and intraracial curricular dialogues on the experiences of white college students. *Journal of Diversity in Higher Education, 5*(3), 138–158.

Foster, K., French, D. Stanley J., & Williams T. C. (2021, July 5). We disagree on a lot of things, except the danger of anti-critical race theory laws. *New York Times*. https://www.nytimes.com/2021/07/05/opinion/we-disagree-on-a-lot-of-things-except-the-danger-of-anti-critical

Foster-Frau, S., Melinik, T., & Bianco, A. (2021, October 8). "We're talking about a big, powerful phenomenon": Multiracial Americans drive change. *Washington Post*. https://www.washingtonpost.com/nation/2021/10/08/mixed-race-americans-increase-census/

Fox, K. (2018, January 12). Norwegians aren't likely to move to the US, even if they're welcome. *CNN*. https://www.cnn.com/2018/01/12/european/norway-trump-reaction-intl/index.html

Franklin, J. H. (1993). *The color line: Legacy for the twenty-first century*. University of Missouri Press.

Fraser, N. (1998a). From redistribution to recognition? Dilemmas of justice in a "post-socialist" age. In C. Willett (Ed.), *Theorizing multiculturalism: A guide to the current debate*. Blackwell.

Fraser, N. (1998b). Social justice in the age of identity politics: Redistribution, recognition, and participation. In G. Peterson (Ed.), *The Tanner lectures on human values XIX*. University of Utah Press.

Frey, W. H. (2021a). New 2020 census results show increased diversity countering decade-long declines in America's white and youth population. *Brookings Institute*. https://www.brookings.edu/research/what-the-2020-census-will-reveal-about-america-stagnating-growth-an-aging-population-and-youthful-diversity/

Frey, W. H. (2021b). What the 2020 census will reveal about America: Stagnating growth, an aging population, and youthful diversity. *Brookings Institute*. https://www.brookings.edu/research/what-the-2020-census-will-reveal-about-america-stagnating-growth-an-aging-population-and-youthful-diversity/

Fricker, M. (2007). *Epistemic injustice: Power and ethics of knowing*. Oxford University Press.

Fryberg, S.A., & Martínez, E. J. (2014). Constructed strugglers. In S. A. Fryberg & E. J. Martínez (Eds.), *The truly diverse faculty: New dialogues in American higher education* (pp. 3–25). Palgrave Macmillan.

Frye, M. (1983). Oppression. In *The politics of reality* (pp. 1–17). Crossing Press.

Gallagher, S. (2013). *Brothers of the Black list*. Passion River Films.

Garrigan, L. (2010, March 5). Nothing funny about this monkey mail. *Nashville Scene*. https://www.nashvillescene.com/news/nothing-funny-about-this-monkey-mail/article_42a81022-feb2-5341-a775-3b6642b96e2d.html

Garza, A. (2014, October 7). A herstory of the #BlackLivesMatter movement. *Feminist Wire*. http://www.thefeministwire.com/2014/10/blacklivesmatter-2/

Garza, A. (2019). *Identity politics: Friend or foe?* Othering and Belonging Institute, UC Berkley.

Gay, R. (2020, May 30). Remember, no one is coming to save us. *New York Times* https://www.nytimes.com/2020/05/30/opinion/sunday/trump-george-floyd-coronavirus.html

Geiger, R. L. (2005). Ten generations of American higher education. In P. G. Artbach, R. O. Bardahl, & P. J. Gumport (Eds.), *American higher education in the twenty-first century: Social, political, and economic challenges* (2nd ed., pp. 38–70). Johns Hopkins University Press.

Germany gripped by #MeTwo racism debate. (2018, July 30). *BBC News.* https://www.bbc.com/news/world-europe-45006340

Gladney, J. (2015, November 20). Black students who demand equality aren't impinging on your rights. *Occupy.com.* http://www.occupy.com/article/black-students-who-demand-equality-arent-impinging-your-rights

Glazer, N., & Moynihan, D. P. (1963). *Beyond the melting pot: The Negroes, Puerto Ricans, Jews, Italians, and Irish of New York City.* MIT Press.

Gonzalez, M. (2016, February 3). Finally, Europe is waking up to dangers of multiculturalism. *Daily Signal.* http://dailysignal.com/2016/02/03/finally-europe-is-waking-up-to-dangers-of-multiculturalism/

Good, B. (2021, July 8). Vandalization of MLK statue in Long Beach, California leads to hate crime investigation. Diversity Inc. https://www.diversityinc.com/vandalization-of-mlk-statue-in-long-beach-california-leads-to-hate-crime-investigation/

Gorman, A. (2021, January 20,). *The hill we climb.* Poem presented at presidential inauguration, Washington, DC.

Green, D. (2019, February 6). Hearing the queer roots of Black Lives Matter. *Medium.* https://medium.com/national-center-for-institutional-diversity/hearing-the-queer-roots-of-black-lives-matter-2e69834a65cd

Greenleaf, R. K. (1977). *Servant leadership: A journey into the nature of legitimate power and greatness.* Paulist Press.

The Grio. (2020, June 5). The death of George Floyd. https://flipboard.com/@thegrio/the-death-of-george-floyd-d6o6sav0r2lrtfe7

Gutmann, A. (2003). *Identity in democracy.* Princeton University Press.

Hall, K., Wiecek, W., & Finkelman, P. (Eds.). (1991). Dred Scott v. Sanford 60 US 393,1857. In *American Legal History: Cases and Materials.* Oxford University Press.

Hannah-Jones, N. (2019, August 18,). The 1619 Project. *New York Times Magazine.* https://pulitzercenter.org/sites/default/files/full_issue_of_the_1619_project.pdf

Hanson, H. (2017, January 3). Nixon aide reportedly admitted drug war was meant to target black people. *HuffPost.* https://www.huffpost.com/entry/nixon-drug-war-racist_n_56f16a0ae4b03a640a6bbda1

Harding, V. (2007). *Is America possible? A letter to my young companions on the journey of hope.* Fetzer Institute

Harris, A. P. (2011). Heteropatriarchy kills: Challenging gender violence in a prison nation. *Washington University Journal of Law and Policy, 37*(1.3). http://openscholarship.wustl.edu/law_journal_law_policy/vol37/iss1/3

Harris, C. I. (1993). Whiteness as property. *Harvard Law Review, 106*(8), 1707–1791.

Harris, J. C., Barone, R. P., & Davis, L. P. (2015, Winter). Who benefits? A critical race analysis of the (d)evolving language of inclusion in higher education. *Thought and Action*, 21–38.

Harris-Perry, M. (2013, August 31). A letter to the Montana judge who went easy on a child rapist. *NBC News*. https://www.nbcnews.com/id/wbna52892752

Hayes, C. (2017). *A colony in a nation*. Norton.

Helm, A. (2018, January 17) "African Immigrants to U.S." *The Root*. https://www.theroot.com/africans-are-the-most-educated-immigrants-in-u-s-repo-1822169956

Helms, J. (1990). *Black and white identity: Theory, research and practice*. Greenwood.

Henderson, N. (2014, December 3). Black respectability politics are increasingly absent from Obama's rhetoric. *Washington Post*. http://www.washingtonpost.com/blogs/the-fix/wp/2014/12/03/black-respectability-politics-are-increasingly-absent-from-obamas-rhetoric/

Hesson, T., & Rosenberg, M. (2021, March 18). Explainer: Why more migrant children are arriving at the U.S.-Mexico border. *Reuters*. https://www.reuters.com/article/us-usa-immigration-children-explainer/explainer-why-more-migrant-children-are-arriving-at-the-u-s-mexico-border-idUSKBN2BA11B

Hill Collins, P. (1993). Toward a new vision: Race, class, and gender as categories of analysis and connection. *Race, Sex and Class*, *1*(1), 25–45.

Hiler, T., Fishman, R., & Nguyen, S. (2021, January 21). *One semester later: How prospective and current college students' perspectives of higher ed have changed between August and December 2020*. Third Way. https://www.thirdway.org/memo/one-semester-later-how-prospective-and-current-college-students-perspectives-of-higher-ed-have-changed-between-august-and-december-2020

Hirschfeld, M. (1938). *Racism* (E. Paul & C. Paul, Trans.). (1973). Gollancz.

Hoagland, S. L. (2007). Heterosexualism and white supremacy. *Hypatia*, *22*, 166–185.

Hoagland, S. L., & Penelope, J. (1980). Lesbianism, sexuality, and power: The patriarchy, violence, and pornography. *Sinister Wisdom*, *15*.

Hollinger, D. A. (1997). The disciplines and the identity debates, 1970–1995. *Daedalus*, *126*(1), 333–351.

Holloway, J. (2020, June 11). White people: Your comfort is not our problem. *Vogue*. https://www.vogue.com/article/white-people-your-comfort-is-not-my-problem-black-lives-matter

Holmes, K., & Murray, S. (2021, January 15). Despite Trump administration promise, government has no more "reserve" 2nd vaccine doses. *CNN*. https://www.cnn.com/2021/01/15/politics/coronavirus-vaccine-reserve-dose/index.html

Holmes, T. (2018, September 20). Serena Williams' US Open punishment a case of double standards. *ABC News*. http://www.abc.net.au/news/2018-09-11/is-serena-williams-us-open-punishment-double-standards/10222688?pfm=ms

Honan, E. (2019, June 28). "That little girl was me": Kamala Harris, Joe Biden spar over desegregation at Democratic debate. *ABC News*. https://abcnews.

go.com/Politics/girl-senator-harris-vice-president-biden-spar-desegregation/story?id=64007842

Honeysett, S. (2018, September 18). Serena Williams cartoon was sexist, not racist says Germaine Greer. *Nine.* https://wwos.nine.com.au/tennis/serena-williams-us-open-cartoon-sexist-not-racist-says-germaine-greer/9141c093-bf0a-4a1c-a7e3-95c07be0adb6?ref=BP_RSS_ninesport_5_serena-cartoon-not-racist-but-meltdown--repellent-_180918

Hong, G. K. (2018, November–December). Intersectional and anticarceral approaches to sexual violence in the academy. *Academe.* https://www.aaup.org/article/intersectional-and-anticarceral-approaches-sexual-violence-academy#.YYiGWL3MJoI

hooks, b. (1981). *Ain't I a Woman? Black women and feminism.* Southend Press.

hooks, b. (1994). *Teaching to transgress: Education as the practice of freedom.* Routledge.

Horsmann, R. (1995). *Race and manifest destiny: The origins of American racial Anglo-Saxonism.* Harvard University Press.

Hubbard, D. W. (2020). *The failure of risk management: Why it is broken and how to fix it.* Wiley.

Hughes, L. (1935). Let America be America again. https://poets.org/poem/let-america-be-america-again

Hull, A. G., Bell-Scott, P., & Smith, B. (1982). *All the women are white, all the Blacks are men, but some of us are brave: Black women's studies.* Feminist Press.

Huntington, S. (1993, Summer). The clash of civilizations? *Foreign Affairs.* https://www.foreignaffairs.com/articles/united-states/1993-06-01/clash-civilizations

Hurtado, S., Milem, J. F., Clayton-Pedersen, A. R., & Allen, W. R. (1998). Enhancing campus climates for racial/ethnic diversity: Educational policy and practice. *Review of Higher Education, 21*(3), 279–302.

Ignatiev, N. (1994, November–December). Treason to whiteness is loyalty to humanity. *Utne Reader.*

INCITE! Women of Color against Violence. (2006). *The color of violence: The INCITE! anthology.* South End Press.

Inwood, J. F., & Alderman, D. (2016). Taking down the flag is just a start: Towards the memory-work of racial reconciliation in white supremacist America. *Southern Geographer, 56*(1), 9–15.

Ivanov, D. (2021, January 13). Some UF faculty outraged over tattle Button. *Gainesville Sun.* https://www.gainesville.com/story/news/education/2021/01/13/some-uf-faculty-upset-app-change-lets-students-report-virtual-classes/6640263002/

Jardina, A. (2019). *White identity politics.* Cambridge University Press.

Johnson, B. N. (2023, February 7). 10 Things to never say to a coworker just because they're Black. *Builtin.com.* http://builtin.com/diversity-inclusion/things-never-to-say-to-Black-coworkers

Johnson, R., Anya, U., & Garces, L. M. (Eds.). (2022). *Racial equity on college campuses: Connecting research and practice*. State University of New York Press.
Johnston, D. C. (2016). *The making of Donald Trump*. Melville House.
Jones, N., Marks, R., Ramirez, R., & Rios-Vargas, M. (2021, August 12). *2020 census illuminates racial and ethnic composition of the country*. United States Census Bureau. https://www.census.gov/library/stories/2021/08/improved-race-ethnicity-measures-reveal-united-states-population-much-more-multiracial.html#:~:text=In%202020%2C%20the%20percentage%20of,33.8%20million%20people)%20in%202020
Joyner, C. (n.d.). The Middle Passage. *PBS*. www.pbs.org/wgbh/aia/part1/1i3067.html
June, A. W. (2015, July 20). When activism is worth the risk. *Chronicle of Higher Education*. http://chronicle.com/article/When-Activism-Is-Worth-the/231729/
Kadi, J. (1996). *Thinking class: Sketches from a cultural worker*. South End Press.
Kafka, A. C. (2022). Does administrative diversity matter? In *Diverse leadership for a new era: How to recruit and support an inclusive administration*. Chronicle of Higher Education.
Karenga, M. (2010). *Introduction to Black studies* (4th ed.). Sankore University Press.
Karaim, R. (2008). America's border fence. *Congressional Quarterly Researcher*, 18(32), 745–768.
Karp, D., & Conrad, S. (2005). Restorative justice and college student misconduct. *Public Organization Review*, 5(4), 315–333.
Kelley, R. (2016, March 1). Black study, Black struggle: The university is not an engine of social transformation—activism is. *Boston Review*. https://www.bostonreview.net/forum/robin-kelley-black-struggle-campus-protest/
Kendi, I. X. (2016). *Stamped from the beginning: The definitive history of racist ideas in America*. Bold Type Books.
Kendi, I. X. (2019). *How to be an antiracist*. One World.
Kessler, G (2020, May 8). The "very fine people" at Charlottesville: Who were they? *Washington Post*. https://www.washingtonpost.com/politics/2020/05/08/very-fine-people-charlottesville-who-were-they-2/
Khan, A. (2017, September 26). In New York, major crime complaints fell when cops took a break from "proactive policing." *LA Times*. https://www.latimes.com/science/sciencenow/la-sci-sn-proactive-policing-crime-20170925-story.html
Khapoya, V. (2013). *The African experience: An introduction* (4th ed.). Pearson Education.
Kim, E. (1993). Between black and white: An interview with Korean American community activist Bong Hwan Kim. In K. Aguilar-San Juan (Ed.), *The state of Asian America: Activism and resistance in the 1990s* (pp. 71–100). South End Press.
King James Version with Apocrypha (American ed.). (1962). https://www.bible.com/bible/546/SIR.4.KJVAAE

King, M. L. (1957). Quotes about the "Beloved Community." https://www.wearethe-belovedcommunity.org/bcquotes.html
King, M. L. (1963). *I have a dream speech.* http://www.let.rug.nl/usa/documents/1951-/martin-luther-kings-i-have-a-dream-speech-august-28-1963.php
King, M. L. (1964). *Why we can't wait.* Beacon.
King, M. L. (1966). *The King philosophy.* https://thekingcenter.org/king-philosophy/
King, M. L. (1967). *Where do we go from here: Chaos or community?* Beacon.
King, M. L. (2014). *In a single garment of destiny: A global vision of global justice.* Beacon Press. (Original work published 1963)
Kipnis, L. (2017). *Unwanted advances: Sexual paranoia comes to campus.* Harper Collins
Kluger, R. (1977). *Simple Justice: The history of Brown v. Board of Education.* Vintage.
Komives, S. R., Wagner, W. E., & associates. (2009). *Leadership for a better world: Understanding the social change model of leadership development.* Jossey-Bass.
Kotter, J. P. (1990). *A force for change: How leadership differs from management.* Free Press.
Kovel, J. (1984). *White racism: A psychohistory* (2nd ed.). Columbia University Press.
Kozol, J. (1991). *Savage inequalities: Children in America's schools.* Random House.
Krehbiel, R. (2011, August 18). Coburn sour on the economy. *Tulsa World.* http://www.tulsaworld.com/news/article.aspx?subjected=336&articleid=20110818_16_A14CUTLIN4971225
Kuh, G. D., and Whitt, E. J. (1988). *The invisible tapestry: Culture in American colleges and universities* (ASHE-ERIC Higher Education Report 1). Josey-Bass
Kunjufu, J. (1995). *Countering the conspiracy to destroy Black boys.* African American Images.
Latino leaders throw support behind Newt Gingrich. (2016, December 12). *Fox News.* https://www.foxnews.com/politics/latino-leaders-throw-support-behind-newt-gingrich
Law, V. (2014, October 17). Against carceral feminism. *Jacobin Magazine.* https://www.jacobinmag.com/2014/10/against-carceral-feminism/
Leadership Conference: The Nation's Premier Civil and Human Rights Coalition. (1997). President Clinton Announces Race Initiative. *Civil Rights Monitor,* 9, 2–3.
Leary, J. D. (2005). *Post traumatic slave syndrome: America's legacy of enduring injury and healing.* Upton Press.
Leary, J. D. (2017). *Post traumatic slave syndrome: America's legacy of enduring injury and healing* (Rev. ed.). Joy DeGruy Publications.
Leonardo, Z. (2009). *Race, whiteness, and education.* Routledge.
Leonardo, Z., & Porter, R. K. (2010). Pedagogy of fear: Toward a Fanonian theory of safety in race dialogues. *Race, Ethnicity, and Education, 13*(2), pp. 139–157.
Lewis, A. (1998, August 13). The case of Lani Guinier. *New York Review of Books.*

Linkova, M. (2017). Academic excellence and gender bias in the practices and perceptions of scientists in leadership and decision-making positions. *Gender and Research, 18*(1), 42–91.

Linnaeus, C. (1735). *Systema naturae*. Amsterdam.

Lipsitz, G. (1998). *The possessive investment in whiteness: How white people profit from identity politics*. Temple University Press.

Lipsitz, G. (2011). *How racism takes place*. Temple University Press.

Liptak, A. (2005, September 11). The Memo that Rehnquist wrote and had to disown. *New York Times*. https://www.nytimes.com/2005/09/11/weekinreview/the-memo-that-rehnquist-wrote-and-had-to-disown

Loewen, J. (2007). *Lies my teacher told me: Everything your American history textbook got wrong* (Rev. ed). Atria Books. (Originally published 1995)

Long, C. (2018, June 15). Sessions cites Bible to defend separating immigrant families. Associated Press. https://apnews.com/0bcc5d5d077247769da065864d215d1b

Lorde, A. (1983). *There is no hierarchy of oppressions*. http://womenscenter.missouri.edu/wp-content/uploads/2013/05/THERE-IS-NO-HIERARCHY-OF-OPPRESSIONS.pdf

Love, B. L. (2019). *We want to do more than survive: Abolitionist teaching and the pursuit of educational freedom*. Beacon.

Lu, A. (2023, June 6). Race on campus: Catch up on the roiling debate over diversity statements. *Chronicle of Higher Education*. https://www.chronicle.com/newsletter/race-on-campus/2023-06-06

Madden, M. (2011). Gender stereotypes of leaders: Do they influence leadership in higher education? *Wagadu, 9*, 55–88.

Mangan, K. (2018, September 18). How restorative justice works in sex-assault cases. *Chronicle of Higher Education*.

Manne, K. (2017). *Down girl: The logic of misogyny*. Oxford University Press.

Manne, K. (2020). *Entitled: How male privilege hurts women*. Penguin.

Mark, M. (2017, December 23). Trump reportedly said Haitians "all have AIDS" and Nigerians live in "huts" during outburst on immigration. *Business Insider*. https://www.businessinsider.com/trump-reportedly-said-haitians-have-aids-nigerians-live-in-huts-in-immigration-outburst-2017-12

Marques, J. (2020). *The Routledge companion to inclusive leadership*. Routledge.

Martinez, E. (2010). Seeing more than Black and white. In M. Andersen & C. Hill Collins (Eds.), *Race, class and gender: An anthology*. Wadsworth.

Massey, D., & Denton, N. (1993). *American apartheid: Segregation and the making of the underclass*. Harvard University Press.

Massey D. S., Mooney, M., Torres, K. C., & Charles, C. Z. (2007). Black immigrants and Black natives attending selective colleges and universities in the United States. *American Journal of Education, 113*(2), 243–271.

Matthews, C. (2010, January 27). MSNBC's Matthews on Obama: "I forgot he was Black tonight." http://www.realclearpolitics.com/video/2010/01/27/msnbcs_matthews_on_obama_i_forgot_he_was_black_tonight.html

Mauer, M. (2006). *Race to incarcerate* (2nd ed.). New Press.

Mauro, T. (2018, January 8) Supreme Court clerks are overwhelmingly white and male—just like 20 years ago. *USA Today*. https://www.usatoday.com/story/opinion/2018/01/08/supreme-court-clerks-overwhelmingly-white-male-just-like-20-years-ago-tony-mauro-column/965945001/

Maxwell, K., & Chesler, M. (2019). White student comfort and conflict in experiential racial dialogues. *Journal of Experiential Education*, *42*(3), 249–263.

Mayer, J., & Farrow, R. (2018, May 17). Four women accuse New York's attorney general of physical abuse. *New Yorker*. https://www.newyorker.com/news/news-desk/four-women-accuse-new-yorks-attorney-general-of-physical-abuse

Mayeri, S. 2011. *Reasoning from race: Feminism, law, and the civil rights revolution*. Harvard University Press.

Mbiti, J. (1990). *African religions and philosophies* (2nd ed.). Heinemann.

McGlauflin, P. (2022, May 23). The number of Black Fortune 500 CEOs returns to record high—meet the 6 chief executives. *Fortune*. https://fortune.com/2022/05/23/meet-6-black-ceos-fortune-500-first-black-founder-to-ever-make-list/

McGrirt, E. (2018, March 1). RaceAhead: Only three Black CEO's in Fortune 500. *Fortune*. http://fortune.com/2018/03/01/raceahead-three-black-ceos/

McIntosh, P. (1988a). *White privilege and male privilege* (Working papers, 189). Wellesley College, Center for Research on Women.

McIntosh, P. (1988b). *Unpacking the invisible knapsack of white privilege*. Racial Equity Tools. https://www.racialequitytools.org/resourcefiles/mcintosh.pdf

McIntosh, P. (1998). White privilege, color and crime: A personal account. In C. R. Mann & M. S. Zatz (Eds.), *Images of color, images of crime: Readings*, pp. 207–216. Roxbury.

McNair, T. B., Albertine, S., Cooper, M. A., McDonal, N., & Major, T. (2016). *Becoming a student-ready college: A new culture of leadership for student success*. Jossey-Bass.

McNair, T. B., Bensimon, E. M., & Malcom-Piqueux, L. (2020). *From equity talk to equity walk: Expanding practitioner knowledge for racial justice in higher education*. Jossey-Bass.

Meckler, L., & Natanson, H. (2023, February 18). More states scrutinizing AP Black studies after Florida complaints. *Washington Post*. https://www.washingtonpost.com/education2023/02/18/states-review-ap-african-american-studies-classes/

Medina, E. (2012). *The epistemology of resistance*. Oxford University Press.

Messner, M. A. (1997). *Politics of masculinities: Men in movements*. Sage.

Me Too Movement. (2020). https://metoomvmt.org

Meyer, M. (2019). *White lives matter most and other "little" white lies*. PM Press.

Miller, C. C. (2018, May 16). How same-sex couples divide chores, and what it reveals about modern parenting. *New York Times*. https://www.nytimes.com/2018/05/16/upshot/same-sex-couples-divide-chores-much-more-evenly-until-they-become-parents.html

Miller, L. S., Ozturk, M., & Chavez, L. (2005). *Increasing African American, Latino, and Native American representation among high achieving undergraduates at selective colleges and universities*. Consortium for High Academic Performance Institute for Social Change, UC Berkeley. https://escholarship.org/uc/item/10s3p1xt

Mills, C. (1997). *The racial contract*. Cornell University Press.

Minster, C. (2019, August 20). Biography of Antonio de Montesinos, defender of Indigenous rights. *ThoughtCo*. https://www.thoughtco.com/antonio-de-montesinos-2136370

Mitchell, C. (1992). *Western hemisphere immigration and United States foreign policy*. Pennsylvania State University Press.

Moller, L. (2020, June 15). MIT study: Race an important factor in determining who dies from Covid-19. *CBS News Boston*. https://boston.cbslocal.com/2020/06/15/coronavirus-study-mit-race-deaths/

Moore, B. V. (1927). The May conference on leadership. *Personnel Journal, 6*(124), 124–128.

Moore-Carrillo, J. (2020, July 6). Students call for an end to legacy admissions. *The Hoya*. https://thehoya.com/students-call-for-an-end-to-legacy-admissions-at-georgetown/

Mor-Barak, M. E. (2014). *Managing diversity: Toward a globally inclusive workplace* (3rd ed.). Sage.

Morris, M. (2018). *Pushout: The criminalization of Black girls*. New Press.

Moser, L. (2015, October 15). How did a Texas textbook end up describing slaves as "workers from Africa"? *Slate*. http://www.slate.com/blogs/schooled/2015/10/06/texas_textbook_controversy_roni_dean_burren_finds_omission_in_son_s_geography.html

Mudede, C. (2017, September 25). Why the overrepresentation of Black Americans in professional sports is not a good thing. *The Stranger*. https://www.thestranger.com/slog/2017/09/25/25432524/why-the-over-representation-of-black-americans-in-professional-sports-is-not-a-good-thing

Muhammad, G. (2020). *Cultivating genius: An equity framework for culturally and historically responsive literacy*. Scholastic.

Mull, R. C. (2020, July 15). Colleges are in for a racial reckoning—name changes are only the beginning. *Chronicle of Higher Education*. https://www.chronicle.com/article/Colleges-Are-in-for-a-Racial/249116?utm_source=at&utm_medium=en&utm_source=Iterable&utm_medium=email&utm_campaign=campaign_1337846&cid=at&source=ams&sourceId=381021

Nagel, M. (2008). Prisons as diasporic sites: Liberatory voices from the diaspora of confinement. *Journal of Social Advocacy and Systems Change, 2008*, 1–31.

Nagel, M. (2014). Teaching feminist philosophy on race and gender: Beyond the additive approach? In S. N. Asumah & M. Nagel (Eds.), *Diversity, social justice, and inclusive excellence: Transdisciplinary and global perspectives* (pp. 55–67). State University of New York Press.

Nagel, M., & Asumah, S. N. (2014). Diversity studies and managing differences: Unpacking SUNY Cortland's case and national trends. In Gudrun Hentges, Kristina Nottbohm, Mechtild M. Jansen, & Jamila Adamou (Eds.), *Sprache, Macht, Rassismus* (pp. 349–466). Metropol Verlag.

Nagel, M., & Asumah, S. N. (2016). Pitfalls of diversity management within the academy. *Wagadu, 16*, 2016, 40–76.

Nguyen, V. T. (2018, June 11). Call me a refugee, not an immigrant (Interview by J. Wiener). *The Nation.* https://www.thenation.com/article/archive/call-refugee-not-immigrant-viet-thanh-nguyen/

Nieto, S. (1992). *Affirming diversity: The sociopolitical context of multicultural education.* Longman.

Nietzsche, F. (2006). *Thus spoke Zarathustra: A book for all and none* (A. Del Caro & R. Pippin, Eds.; A. Del Caro, Trans.). Cambridge University Press.

Nittle, N. K. (2020, October 30). The history of the three-fifths compromise. *ThoughtCo.* https://www.thoughtco.com/three-fifths-compromise-4588466

Northouse, P. (2018). *Introduction to leadership: Concepts and practice.* Sage.

Northouse, P. G. (2013). *Leadership: Theory and practice* (6th ed.). Sage.

Obama, B. H. (2020). *A promised land.* Diversified Publishing.

Obama, M. (2018). *Becoming.* Crown.

Obama on Garner decision. (2014, December 3). *CNN.* https://www.youtube.com/watch?v=fsWUS9gcCHU#t=64

Olsen, J. E., & Martins, L. L. (2012). Understanding organizational diversity management programs: A theoretical framework and directions for future research. *Journal of Organizational Behavior, 33*(8), pp. 1168–1187.

Omi, M., and Winant, H. (2015). *Racial formation in the United States* (3rd ed.). Routledge.

Orgeret, K. S. (2016). The unexpected body: From Sara Baartman to Caster Semenya. *Journal of African Media Studies, 8*(3), 281–294.

Osamu, N. (2006). Humanitas and anthropos: Two western concepts of "human being." In N. Sakai & J. Solomon (Eds.), *Translation, biopolitics, colonial difference* (pp. 259–273). Hong Kong University Press.

Outlaw, L. (2016). Philosophy, ethnicity, and race. In F. L. Hord & J. S. Lee (Eds.), *I am because we are: Readings in Black philosophy* (pp. 412–436). University of Massachusetts Press. (Originally published 1988)

Padgett, D. (2021, January 12). Betsy DeVos takes last swipe at trans youth on way out of office. *Out.* https://www.out.com/news/2021/1/12/betsy-devos-takes-last-swipe-trans-youth-way-out-office

Pager, D. (2004). The mark of a criminal record. *Focus*, *23*(2), 44–46.
Paulson, A. (2010, May 19). Texas textbook war: "Slavery" or "Atlantic-triangular trade"? *Christian Science Monitor*. http://www.csmonitor.com/USA/Education/2010/0519/Texas-textbook-war-Slavery-or-Atlantic-triangular-trade
Peagler, R. (2000). *Report: Recruitment and retention of ethnic minority students*. SUNY Cortland. (On file with author)
Penner, R. H. (2013). *Cornell University: The campus history series*. Arcadia.
Perez, M., & Saldaña, J. (2016, June 22). Before we say "no more drug war," we need to say black lives matter" and "not one more." *Huffington Post*. http://www.huffingtonpost.com/maritza-perez/no-more-drug-war-racism_b_10616636.html
Perez-Pena, R. (2012, February 24). U.S. bachelor degree rate passes milestone. *New York Times*. https://www.nytimes.com/2012/02/24/education/census-finds-bachelors-degrees-at-record-level.html
PEW Research Center. (2007). *Americans and social trust: Where and why*. https://www.pewsocialtrends.org/2007/02/22/americans-and-social-trust-who-where-and-why/
PEW Research Center. (2020, September 14). *Americans' views of government: Low trust, but some positive performance rating*. https://www.pewresearch.org/politics/2020/09/14/americans-views-of-government-low-trust-but-some-positive-performance-ratings/
Philbrick, S. (2018, September 16). *Understanding the three-fifths compromise*. Constitutional Accountability Center. https://www.theusconstitution.org/news/understanding-the-three-fifths-compromise/
Pierce, C. M. (1975). The mundane extreme environment and its effect on learning. In S. G. Brainard (Ed.), *Learning disabilities: Issues and recommendations for research* (pp. 111–119). National Institute of Education, US Department Health, Education, and Welfare.
Pitkin, H. (1972). *The concept of representation*. University of California Press.
Pitts, L. (2021, April). No, it's not the economy, stupid—Trump supporters fear a black and brown America. *Miami Herald*. https://www.miamiherald.com/opinion/opn-columns-blogs/leonard-pitts-jr/article211963789.html
Police who arrested professor "acted stupidly." (2009, July 22). *CNN*. http://edition.cnn.com/2009/US/07/22/harvard.gates.interview/
Porter, N. (2016). Unfinished project of civil rights in the era of mass incarceration and the movement for Black lives. *Wake Forest Journal of Law and Policy*, *6*(1), 1–34.
Pratt, R. H. (1973). The advantages of mingling Indians with whites. In F. P. Prucha, *Americanizing the American Indians*. Harvard University Press. (Original work published 1892)
Prewitt, K. (2013). *What is your race? The census and our flawed efforts to classify Americans*. Princeton University Press.

Prinster, R. (2016, May 23). University of Tennessee forced to shutter its diversity office. *Insight Into Diversity*. http://www.insightintodiversity.com/university-of-tennessee-forced-to-shutter-its-diversity-office/

Putnam, R. D. (1993). *Making democracy work: Civic traditions in modern Italy*. Princeton University Press.

Ralston, M. (2019). Why there aren't more Black quarterbacks in the NFL. *Matt Ralston's Blog*. http://mattralston.net/sports/the-unimpressive-rise-of-black-quarterbacks-in-the-nfl/

Ralstone, L. (1991). *Cortland College: An illustrated history*. Alumni Association of Cortland College.

Rankine, C. (2014). *Citizen*. Graywolf.

Rankine, C. (2015, August 25). The meaning of Serena Williams. *New York Times Magazine*. https://www.nytimes.com/2015/08/30/magazine/the-meaning-of-serena-williams.html

Ransom. J. (2020). Amy Cooper faces charges after calling police on black birdwatcher. *New York Times*. https://www.nytimes.com/2020/07/06/nyregion/amy-cooper-false-report-charge.html

Reagon, B. J. (1983). Coalition politics: Turning the Century. In B. Smith (Ed.), *Home girls* (pp. 356–368). Kitchen Table Press.

Redden, E. (2020, October 8). How transparent is your college's COVID dashboard? *Inside Higher Ed*. https://www.insidehighered.com/news/2020/10/08/many-colleges-publish-covid-dashboards-theres-no-uniform-standard-public-reporting

Reid, R., and Curry, T. (2019, April 12). The white man template and academic bias: Legitimate pursuit of knowledge are expression of power. *Inside Higher Ed*. https://www.insidehighered.com/advice/2019/04/12/how-white-male-template-produces-barriers-minority-scholars-throughout-their

Reingold, J. (2015, January 21). Everybody hates Pearson. *Fortune*. http://fortune.com/2015/01/21/everybody-hates-pearson/

Remnick, D. (2014, January 27). Annals of the presidency: Going the distance—on and off the road with Barack Obama. *New Yorker*.

Renfro, S., & Armour-Garb, A. (1999). *Report: Open admissions and remedial education at the City University of New York*. Archives of Rudolph Giuliani. http://www.nyc.gov/html/records/rwg/cuny/pdf/history.pdf

Rich, A. (1986). Invisibility in academe. *Blood, bread, and poetry*. Norton.

Richardson, D. (2012, September 4). SUNY Oneonta looks past Black List. *Daily Star*. http://thedailystar.com/localnews/x1884284282/SUNY-Oneonta-looks-past-Black-List

Riggs, M. (1987). *Ethnic notions* (film). California Newsreels. https://newsreel.org/video/ethnic-notions

Ringer, F. (1969). *The decline of the German mandarins: The German academic community, 1890–1933*. Wesleyan University Press.

Robinson, R. (2000). *The debt: What America owes to blacks.* Dutton.
Roithmayr, D., Gonsalves, G., Farley, A. P., Taylor K, & Bonilla-Silva, E. (2020, June 25). Insight: Universities should stay closed to protect workers of color. *Bloomberg Law.* https://news.bloomberglaw.com/us-law-week/insight-universities-should-stay-closed-to-protect-workers-of-color
Rosaldo, R. (1993). Introduction. In *Culture and truth: The remaking of social analysis.* Beacon.
Ross, L. (2015). *Blackballed: The Black and white politics of race on America's campuses.* St. Martin's.
Ross, L. (2019, August 17). I am a black feminist. I think call-out culture is toxic. *New York Times.* https://www.nytimes.com/2019/08/17/opinion/sunday/cancel-culture-call-out.html?fbclid=IwAR2MYHpdeZo68G5_hixYKi6rC2KWqrHA1zqH_B5EBxi3yousGWRdG7fKPjY
Rost, J. C. (1991). *Leadership for the twenty-first century.* Praeger.
Rothwell, J. (2016, Jun 29). *Black and Hispanic kids get lower quality pre-K.* Social *Mobility Memos* (Blog). https://www.brookings.edu/blog/social-mobility-memos/2016/06/29/black-and-hispanic-kids-get-lower-quality-pre-k/
Rudman, L. A., & Glick, P. (2001). Prescriptive gender stereotypes and backlash toward agentic women. *Journal of Social Issues, 57*(4), 743–762.
Russell-Brown, K. (1998). *The color of crime.* New York University Press.
Russell-Brown, K. (2008). *The color of crime: Racial hoaxes, white fear, Black protectionism, police harassment, and other macroaggressions* (2nd ed.). New York University Press.
Safe OUTside the System Collective (SOS). Programs. https://alp.org/programs/sos
Saleh-Hannah, V. (2015). Black feminist hauntology: Rememory the ghosts of abolition? *Champ Pénal/Penal Field, 12.* https://doi.org/10.4000/champpenal.9168
Samuel Johnson (1709–1784). (2014). In *History—historical figures.* BBC. http://www.bbc.co.uk/history/historic_figures/johnson_samuel.shtml
Sawyer, D. (1991). *True colors.* ABC Prime Time News.
Sawyer, D. (1993). *The fairer sex.* ABC Prime Time News.
Sawyer, W., and Wagner, P. (2022). *Mass incarceration: The whole pie 2022.* Prison Policy Initiative. https://www.prisonpolicy.org/reports/pie2022.html
Schaefer, R. T. (2019). *Race and ethnicity in the United States* (9th ed.). Pearson.
Schaeffer, K. (2021, January 28). *Racial, ethnic diversity increases yet again with the 117th Congress.* Pew Research Center. https://www.pewresearch.org/fact-tank/2021/01/28/racial-ethnic-diversity-increases-yet-again-with-the-117th-congress/
Schlesinger, A. (1991). *The disuniting of America: Reflections on a multicultural society.* Whittle Books.
Schmidt, C. K., Earnest, D. R., & Miles, J. R. (2020). Expanding the reach of intergroup dialogue: A quasi-experimental study of two teaching methods

for undergraduate multicultural courses. *Journal of Diversity in Higher Education, 13*(3), 264–273.

Scott, M. (2012). *Think race and ethnicity*. Pearson.

Sentencing Project. (2014). *Half in ten: Americans with a criminal record*. https://www.sentencingproject.org/wp-content/uploads/2015/11/Americans-with-Criminal-Records-Poverty-and-Opportunity-Profile.pdf

Sertima, I. V. (1976). *The African presence in ancient America: They came before Columbus*. Random House.

Shafer, J. (2013). Column. Facebook and the outer limits of free speech. *Reuters*. https://www.reuters.com/article/us-shafer-facebook/column-facebook-and-the-outer-limits-of-free-speech-idUKBRE94T0O920130530

Sharma, R. S. (1997). *The monk who sold his Ferrari: A fable about fulfilling your dreams and reaching your destiny*. Harper Collins.

Shermer, E. T. (2015). *Nelson Rockefeller and the State University of New York's rapid rise and decline* (Rockefeller Archive Center Research Reports Online). https://rockarch.issuelab.org/resources/27918/27918.pdf

Siegel, R. B. (2003). Introduction: A short history of sexual harassment. In C. A. MacKinnon & R. B. Siegel (Eds.), *Directions in sexual harassment law* (pp. 1–42). Yale University Press.

Silva, C. (2018, January 11). Trump's full list of "racist" comments about immigrants, Muslims and others. *Newsweek*. https://www.newsweek.com/trumps-full-list-racist-comments-about-immigrants-muslims-and-others-77

Silverstein, H. (2016, January). Faculty panel discusses the teaching of "Black lives matter." *Dartmouth Now*. http://now.dartmouth.edu/2016/01/faculty-panel-discusses-teaching-black-lives-matter

Simmons, A.M. (2018, January 12). African immigrants are more educated than most—including people born in U.S. *Los Angeles Times*. https://www.latimes.com/world/africa/la-fg-global-african-immigrants-explainer-20180112-story.html

Smith, A. (2008). *Heteropatriarchy and the three pillars of white supremacy: Rethinking women of color organizing*. http://www.cpt.org/files/Undoing%20Racism%20-%20Three%20Pillars%20-%20Smith.pdf

Smith, D. (1998, November 7). The enigma of Jefferson: Mind and body in conflict. *New York Times*.

Smith, D. G. (1995). Organizational implications of diversity in higher education. In M. Chemers, S. Oskamp, & M. Costanza (Eds.), *Diversity in Organizations* (pp. 220–244). Sage.

Smith, R. C. (2010). *Conservatism and racism and why in America they are the same*. State University of New York Press.

Sotomayor, S. (2014, April 22). Sonia Sotomayor wrote an epic dissent against the Supreme Court decision upholding Michigan's affirmative action ban. *New*

York Magazine. https://nymag.com/intelligencer/2014/04/sotomayor-epic-affirmative-action-ban-dissent.html

Souza, P. (2009). *The beer summit* (Photo by chief official White House photographer). http://www.nydailynews.com/news/politics/post-beer-summit-advocates-hope-president-obama-begins-real-discussion-racial-profiling-article-1.396509

Spitzer, R. J. (2014, November 18). Obama's executive orders: Can we talk? *Huffington Post*. http://www.huffingtonpost.com/robert-j-spitzer/obamas-executive-orders-c_b_6167636.html

Spivak, G. (1993). *Outside in the teaching machine*. Routledge.

Stancill, J. (2018, October 26). Fellow students punish protester who poured blood and ink on Silent Sam statue. *News Observer*. https://www.newsobserver.com/news/local/article220687340.html

Steck, H. (2012). Higher education in New York State. In G. Benjamin (Ed.), *The Oxford handbook of New York state government and politics* (pp. 662–711). Oxford University Press.

Steck, H., et al. (1992). *Report: Toward a more equitable, inclusive, and diverse academic community*. SUNY Cortland. (On file with author)

Steele, C. M. (2010). *Whistling Vivaldi and how other stereotypes affect us*. Norton.

Stiem, T. (2018, September 26). Statue wars: What should we do with troublesome monuments? *Guardian*.

Stripling, J. (2021, July 6). How Chapel Hill bungled a star hire: In the Nikole Hannah-Jones tenure case, leaders settled for less and wound up with nothing. *Chronicle of Higher Education*. https://www.chronicle.com/article/how-chapel-hill-bungled-a-star-hire

Sue, D. W. (2010). *Microaggressions in everyday life: Race, gender, and sexual orientation*. Wiley.

Sue, D. W., Capodilupo, C. M., &. Holder, A. M. B. (2008). Racial microaggressions in the experience of Black Americans. *Professional Psychology: Research and Practice*, 39(3), 329–336.

Sue, W. D., Capodilupo, C. M., Torino, G. C., Bucceri, J. M., Holder, A. M. B., Nadel, K. L., & Esquilin, M. (2007). Racial microaggression in everyday life: Implications for clinical practice. *American Psychologist*, 62(4), 271–286.

Sue, D. W., Rivera, D. P., Capodilupo, C. M., Lin, A. I., & Torino, G. C. (2010). Racial dialogues and white trainee fears: Implications for education and training. *Cultural Diversity and Ethnic Minority Psychology*, 16(2), pp. 206–214.

Sunstein, C. (1992). Free speech now. In G. R. Stone, R. A. Epstein, & C. Sunstein (Eds.), *The Bill of Rights in the modern state*. University of Chicago Press.

SUNY PRODiG 2019–2020 Cohort Data and Analytics Dashboard. (2021). https://www.suny.edu/prodig/resources/data/

Supiano, B. (2020, March 20). Nobody signed up for this: One professor's guide for an interrupted semester. *Chronicle of Higher Education*. https://www.

chronicle.com/article/nobody-signed-up-for-this-one-professors-guidelines-for-an-interrupted-semester/

Swarns, R. (2019, October 30). Is Georgetown's $400,000-a-year plan to aid slave descendants enough? *New York Times.* https://www.nytimes.com/2019/10/30/us/georgetown-slavery-reparations.html

Swiffen, A. (2018). New resistance to hate crime legislation and the concept of law. *Law, Culture and the Humanities, 14*(1): 121–139.

Takaki, R. (1993). *A different mirror: A multicultural history of the United States.* Little, Brown.

Takenaga, L. (2019, November 8). "I will never be German": Immigrants and mixed-race families in Germany on the struggle to belong. *New York Times.* https://www.nytimes.com/2019/11/08/reader-center/german-identity.html

Talbot, M. (2018, October 8). On the attack: Christine Blasey Ford's experience was just as bad as Anita Hill's—maybe worse. *New Yorker.* https://www.newyorker.com/magazine/comment/on-the-attack

Tamir, C., & Anderson, M. (2022, January 20). *A growing share of Black immigrants have a college degree or higher. Pew Research Center.* https://www.pewresearch.org/race-ethnicity/2022/01/a-growing-share-of-black-immigrants-have-a-college-degree-or-higher

Tatum, B. (1997). *Why are all the Black kids sitting together in the cafeteria?* Basic Books.

Tauriac, J., & Liem, J. (2012). Exploring the divergent academic outcomes of U.S.-origin and immigrant-origin Black undergraduates. *Journal of Diversity in Higher Education, 5*(4), 244–258.

Taylor, K. Y. (2017, January 13). Barack Obama's original sin: America's post-racial illusion. *Guardian.* https://www.theguardian.com/us-news/2017/jan/13/barack-obama-legacy-racism-criminal-justice-system

Thernstrom, S., and Thernstrom, A. (1997). *America in Black and white: One nation indivisible—race in modern America.* Simon and Schuster.

Thomas, H. (1997). *The shame response to rejection.* Albanel.

Thomas-Greenfield, L. (2021, March 21). *Fact sheet: U.S. efforts to combat systemic racism.* White House Briefing Room. https://www.whitehouse.gov/briefing-room/statements-releases/2021/03/21/fact-sheet-u-s-efforts-to-combat-" systemic-racism/

Thompson, V. (2022). "There is no justice, there is just us!" Towards a postcolonial feminist critique of policing using the example of racial profiling in Europe. In M. J. Coyle & M. Nagel (Eds.), *Contesting carceral logic.* Routledge.

Time's Up. (2020). https://www.timesupnow.com

Traub, J. (1994). *City on a hill: Testing the American dream at City College.* Addison-Wesley.

Tutu, D. (1999). *No future without forgiveness.* Doubleday.

Unzueta, M. M., Gutiérrez, A. S., & Ghavami, N. (2010). How believing in affirmative action quotas affects white women's self-image. *Journal of Experimental Psychology*, *46*, 120–126.
US Census Bureau. (2004). US population projections. https://www.census.gov/population/www/projection/2009projections.html
US Census Bureau. (2010). US population projections. https://www.census.gov/population/www/projection/2009projections.html
US Census Bureau. (2015). The Black alone population in the United States. https://www.census.gov/data/tables/2015/demo/race/ppl-ba15.html
US Holocaust Memorial Museum. (n.d.). *Herero and Nama genocide*. https://www.ushmm.org/collections/bibliography/herero-and-nama-genocide
Vallas, R., & Dietrich, S. (2014). *One strike and you're out!* Center for American Progress. https://www.americanprogress.org/issues/poverty/report/2014/12/02/102308/one-strike-and-youre-out/
van Dam, A. (2014). *I can't breathe: A better America—a political cartoon*. https://www.cagle.com/arand-van-dam/2014/12/i-cant-breathe-3
Vertovec, S. (2014). Introduction: Formulating diversity studies. In S. Vertovec (Ed.), *Routledge international handbook on diversity studies* (pp. 1–20). Routledge.
Vidal, G. (2004, September 13). The state of the union. *The Nation*.
Visconti, M. (2014, November 19). Ask the white guy: Should President Obama and AG Holder ask for calm in Ferguson? DiversityInc. http://www.diversityinc.com/ask-the-white-guy/ask-white-guy-president-obama-ag-holder-ask-calm-ferguson/
Vollman, A. (2016, May 26). Pomona adds diversity requirement to tenure-review process. *Insight into Diversity*. http://www.insightintodiversity.com/pomona-college-adds-diversity-requirement-to-tenure-review-process/
Walker, K. (1998, April 9). 60 Minutes reports "queer studies" supported at leading universities. *Baptist Press*. https://www.baptistpress.com/resource-library/news/60-minutes-reports-queer-studies-supported-at-leading-universities/
Wallis, V. (2015). Intersectionality's binding agent: The political primacy of class. *New Political Science*, *37*(4), 604–619.
Walton, H., & Smith, R. C. (2000). *American politics and the African American quest for universal freedom*. Longman.
Ward, E. K. (2022). You're my inspiration: How I came to understand racism in America—and what we can do about it. *American Educator*, *46*(1), 4–11.
Washington Post/Kaiser Family Foundation/Harvard University Survey Project (1996).
Watkins, D. (2019). *We speak for ourselves: How woke culture prohibits progress*. Simon and Schuster.
Watkins, E., & Phillip, A. (2018, January 12). Trump decries immigrants from "shithole countries" coming to US. *CNN*. https://www.cnn.com/2018/01/11/politics/immigrants-shithole-countries-trump/index.html

Weber, M. (1969). *Essays in sociology*. Oxford University Press.
Weiner, R. (2009, August 30). Obama beer summit: President "fascinated with the fascination" (video). *Huffington Post*. https://www.huffpost.com/entry/obama-beer-summit-discuss_n_248116
Weiss, D. C. (2017, December 12). Supreme court law clerks are still mostly white men; which justices had most diverse clerks? *ABA Journal*. https://www.abajournal.com/news/article/supreme_court_law_clerks_are_still_mostly_white_men_which_justices_had_the
Wellman, D. (1977). *Portraits of white racism*. Cambridge University Press.
West Savali, K. (2016, September 30). For the record: "Superpredators" is absolutely a racist term. *The Root*. https://www.theroot.com/for-the-record-superpredators-is-absolutely-a-racist-t-1790857020
West, C. (1994). *Race matters*. Vintage.
When tuition at CUNY was free, sort of. (2011, October 12). *CUNY Matters*. https://www.cuny.edu/wp-content/uploads/sites/4/page-assets/publications/cm-fall2011.pdf
White House, Office of the Press Secretary. (2016, June 10). *Fact sheet: White House launches the fair chance higher education pledge*. https://obamawhitehouse.achieves.gov/the-press-office/2016/06/10/fact-sheet-white-house-launches-fair-chance-higher-education-pledge
Wick, J., Meek, R., & Lizarraga, J. R. (2022, October 10) Breaking down crucial moments in the racist leaked recording of L. A. councilmembers. *Los Angeles Times*. https://www.latimes.com/california/story/2022-10-10/listen-audio-excerpts-of-leaked-recording-of-l-a-council-members
Wijeyesinghe, C. L., Griffin, P., & Love, B. (1997). Racism curriculum design. In M. Adams, L. A. Bell, & P. Griffin (Eds.), *Teaching for Diversity and Social Justice* (1st ed., pp. 82–109). Routledge.
Wildavsky, A. (1988). *The new politics of the budgetary process*. Scott, Foresman.
Wilhelm, I. (2016, April 17). Ripples from a protest past. *Chronicle of Higher Education*. http://chronicle.com/article/Why-an-Armed-Occupation-of/236133
Williams, A. (2015, November 8). The invisible labor of minority professors. *Chronicle of Higher Education*.
Williams, C. L. (2014, September/October). Darlene Clark Hine. *Humanities*.
Wilson, J. (2015, December 31). How Black Lives Matter saved higher education. *Al Jazeera America*. http://america.aljazeera.com/opinions/2015/12/how-black-lives-matter-saved-higher-education.html
Wilson, M., & Russell, K. (1996). *Divided sisters: Bridging the gap between black women and white women*. Anchor.
Wong, A. (2018, August 10). The Common App will stop asking about students' criminal histories. *Atlantic*. https://www.theatlantic.com/education/archive/2018/08/common-app-criminal-history-question/567242/
Worldometer. (2022). *Coronavirus cases USA*. https://www.worldometers.info/coronavirus/country/us/

Worthington, R., Stanley, C., & Lewis, W. (2014). *Standards of professional practice for chief diversity officers*. National Association of Diversity Officers in Higher Education.

Wrench, J. (2014). Diversity management. In S. Vertovec (Ed.), *Routledge international handbook on diversity studies* (pp. 254–262). Routledge.

Wu, F. H. (2002). *Yellow: Race in America beyond black and white*. Basic Books.

Wuerker, M. (Cartoonist). (2014, November). *What is your color of justice*. In Michael Cavna, 15 of the most striking #Ferguson cartoons so far. *Washington Post*. https://www.washingtonpost.com/news/comic-riffs/wp/2014/11/28/see-some-of-the-most-striking-ferguson-cartoons-so-far/

Yoffe, E. (2017, September 11). The question of race in campus sexual-assault cases: Is the system biased against men of color? *Atlantic*. https://www.theatlantic.com/education/archive/2017/09/the-question-of-race-in-campus-sexual-assault-cases/539361/

Young, D. (2019). *What doesn't kill you makes you blacker: A memoir in essays*. HarperCollins.

Young, G., & Davis-Russell, E. (2002). The vicissitude of cultural competence: Dealing with difficult classroom dialogue. In E. Davis-Russell (Ed.), *California School of Professional Psychology handbook of multicultural education, research, intervention, and training*. Jossey-Bass.

Young, I. M. (1990*). Justice and the politics of difference*. Princeton University Press.

Young, I. M. (1998). Unruly categories: A critique of Nancy Fraser's dual systems analysis. In C. Willett (Ed.), *Theorizing multiculturalism: A guide to the current debate*. Blackwell.

Zakaria, F. (2020, October 6). The pandemic upended the present: But it's given us a chance to remake the future. *Washington Post*. https://www.washingtonpost.com/opinions/2020/10/06/fareed-zakaria-lessons-post-pandemic-world/?arc404=true

Zelcman, D. (2021, July 13). US begins its reckoning on Native American children. *CNN*. https://www.cnn.com/2021/07/13/opinions/native-american-children-united-states-reckoning-zalcman/index.html

Zimpher, N. (2015, September 10). Memorandum (re: Diversity, Equity, and Inclusion Policy). Office of the Chancellor, State University of New York. https://www.suny.edu/about/leadership/board-of-trustees/meetings/webcastdocs/Reso%20Tab%2005%20-%20Diversity,%20Equity,%20and%20Inclusion%20Policy.pdf

Zimpher, N. (2016). State of the university address. https://www.suny.edu/about/leadership/chancellor-nancy-zimpher/speeches/2016-sou/

Zinn, H. (1980). *A people's history of the United States*. HarperCollins.

Zong, J., & Batalova J. (2017, May 3). Sub-Saharan African immigrants in the United States (Spotlight). Migration Policy Institute. https://www.migrationpolicy.org/article/sub-saharan-african-immigrants-inited-states-2015

Index

1619 project, 64, 104
1776 Commission, 64, 104

AAC&U. *See* Association for American Colleges and Universities
ableism, 109, 179
abolitionism, xvii, 226–228
abolitionist democracy, 322–323
abortion, 21, 311–312
academic advising, 93–95
access, equity and, 99–105
accountability work, 300–307
activism, 65, 91, 113–114, 181–183, 235
administration. *See specific topics*
admissions offices, 92–93
affirmative action, 5, 40–42, 102–103, 108–111
Africa
   African diaspora, 193–194
   Caribbean and, 10–11
   Europe and, 164–165
   genocide in, 234–235
   immigration and, 161, *162*, 163, 167–169
   slavery and, 157–158
   study abroad in, 72–75
   US and, 245, 293

African American diaspora studies, 196
African Americans. *See* Blacks
Africana studies, 65–72, 91–92, 96, 113
Africans, 155–157
Africology, 65–73, 197
Afro-Germans, 233–236
Afrophobia, xxvi, 77, 157–161, 209, 225
Ahmed, Sara, 116, 120
Alcoff, Linda, 123, 137
Alderman, Derek, 291–292
Alexander, Michelle, 102, 110, 306
All Lives Matter, 172–178
All the Women Are White (Hull, Scott & Smith), 17, 119
Allen, Christine, 253–254
Allen, Theodore, 186
allophilia, xxvi, 172, 179
America. *See* United States
American Association of Colleges and Universities, xv, 15–16, 34, 94
American Colonization Society, xvi–xvii
American Dream, 143–144, 156, 179
American Revolution, 226–227
Americans with Disability Act, 58
Angola, 66

anocracy, 13–14
Anthony, Susan B., xvii
anti-Black racism
　in Europe, 10
　history of, 182
　oppression and, 181, 317–318
　in politics, 311–312
　psychology of, xxvi
　racial despotism and, 13
　in society, 171–172
　to United Nations, 234–235
　white feminism and, 225–232
anti-politics, 207
antiracism
　education, 48
　guides to, 183
　in higher education, 48–49
　in institutions, 2
　Me Two for, xxvii
　policy, 259–265
　social alexithymia and, xxii–xxiii
　at SUNY Cortland, 27
Anzaldúa, Gloria E., 119
Arbery, Armaud, 210
Archias, Elise, 56
Aristotle (Stagiritis), 243, 249
Asantewaa, Yaa, 250
Ashley, Larry, 31
Asians, 153, 155, 167, 183, 200–201, 221
asphyxiation (political), xxv, 128, *129*, 140–141
Association for American Colleges and Universities (AAC&U), 5–6, 31–32, 35, 51, 61
assumptions, 88
Asumah model, 37
Auxiliary Service Corporation, 184
Azamati, Vindra, 61

Baartman, Sara, 225. *See also* Hottentot, Venus

Bacon, Francis, 289
Bahng, Aimee, 117
Bailey, Moya, 218, 300
Bakke v. Regents of the University of California, 241, 247–248
Banks, James A., 97, 103–104
Bannon, Steve, 297
Barber, Francis, 226–227
Bauer, Karen W., 28
Beck, Glenn, 142
Bell, Derrick, 43
Bell, Lee Anne, 285
Bello, Akil, 92
beloved community, xxviii, 75–77
Belson, Ken, 144
Bennett, Milton J., 255
Berkowitz, David, 100
Berry, Mary Frances, 137
Bethune, Mary McCloud, xvii
Between the World and Me (Coates), 196, 315
Biden, Joe
　DeSantis and, 152
　Harris, K., and, 100, 209
　inclusive leadership by, 14
　for Juneteenth, 261, 320–321
　loan forgiveness by, 93
　McConnell against, xxv
　racial justice to, 9
　Trump and, 56–57, 104, 157
Bigelow, Bill, 104
Binghamton University, 75
BIPOC. *See* Black, Indigenous, and People of Color
Birth of a Nation (film), 174
Black, Indigenous, and People of Color (BIPOC)
　administration and, 80
　BLM for, 106
　Civil Rights Acts for, 276–277
　during COVID-19, 18–19
　DEI for, 52–53

double binds for, 117–120
education for, 321–322
faculty, 6, 89, 117, 198, 207–208
faculty of color and, 55
in group dialogue, 279–280
hate crimes against, 233
hegemony for, 75
in heteropatriarchy, 313–314
in higher education, 311–312
LGBTQ and, xxx
mortality rate of, 194–195
multicultural education for, 95
people of pallor and, 314
poverty and, 201–202
PRODiG for, 113
reconciliation for, 316–323
reform to, 213–214
students, 4–5, 19–20, 28–29, 47, 83, 100, 105, 202–203
systemic racism against, xxvii, 15
in US, 59
white institutional presence for, 18
white supremacy against, 194
whiteness for, 94–95, 195–196, 279
women of color and, 323
Black Africans, xxv–xxvi, 110–111, 154–161, *162*, 163
Black bodies movement, 10–12, 197, 205, 209
Black children, 100, 248
Black faculty, 58
Black feminism, 17, 291–292
Black girls, 224–225, 248–249
Black History Month, 298–300
Black Liberation Collective, 107
Black Lives Matter (BLM)
  allophilia and, xxvi
  for BIPOC, 106
  Black bodies movement and, 209
  Black Power and, 319–320
  Black Student Union for, 71
  campus climate with, 70

Civil Rights Movement and, 13
demonstrations, 9
in Europe, xxvii
feminism and, 119–120
George Floyd murder and, 125, 232, 246, 314
global, 292–293
Me Too and, 1, 65–66, 232–235, 238, 296–297
for people of color, 117–118
police to, 140
politics of, 171–178, 191–192
protests for, 181–183
in society, 178–181
to Trump, 102
in US, 98
whiteness and, 263
Black negativity, 131
Black Panther Party, 106
Black Power, 98, 101
Black Power movements, 13, 66, 319–320
Black racism, 209
Black Reconstruction, xxix, 323
Black Student Union, 70–72, 98, 114, 118, 172, 184–185, 190
Black studies, 40, 69
Black Wall Street, xvii
Black women, xvii, xxvii–xxviii, 235–236, 248–249
Blackballed (Ross), 60, 70–71, 185, 190, 295–296
Blackness, 171–178, 272
Blacks. *See also specific topics*
  activism by, 65
  Black Africans and, 110–111
  Black vulnerability, 204
  brown bodies and, 143–144
  campus climate for, xxx
  as CEOs, 246
  in Constitution, 38
  in COVID-19, 202

Blacks *(continued)*
  crime and, 141
  discrimination against, 40–41, 108–109
  Dred Scott v. Sanford for, 130
  feminism and, 181
  in Germany, 234–235
  in higher education, 70–71, 74
  identity of, 150
  in institutions, 137–138
  Jim Crow against, 171, 244, 247
  Latinos and, 19, 71, 101–102, 147, 160
  in monoculturalism, 106–107
  Obama, B., to, 263
  oppression against, 60
  police and, 125–128, 138–140
  in prison, 109, 307–308
  Puerto Ricans and, 101
  racism against, 311–312
  social asphyxiation of, 209–210
  in society, 173–176
  stereotypes of, 69, 221, 243–245
  in Tuskegee study, 214, 307
  in US, xv–xviii, 266
  white leadership and, 76–77
  white supremacy to, 225
  youthification and, 163, *164*
Black/white binary model, 137–142, *138, 139*
Black-white paradigm, 124, 137–142, *138–139*
BLM. *See* Black Lives Matter
blue fragility, 211–212
Booker, Cory, 229
Bridge, Edmund Pettus, 177
Brothers of the Black List (Gallagher), 112
Brown, Austin Channing, 262–263, 315–316
Brown, John, 189
Brown, Michael, 106, 125, 133, 140–141, 172–173, 232

brown bodies, 143–144
Brown v. Board of Education, 100, 242, 262, 278–279
Brutus, Marcus J., 37–38
Buchanan, James, 148
Burke, Lilah, 193
Burke, Tarana, 217
Bush, George H. W., 134, *135*
Bush, George W., 42, 134, *135*
Butler, Paul, 212
Byrd, James, 133, 270

Cabrera, Nolan L., 6, 29, 53, 59, 62, 99, 264
callout culture, 56–57, 173–175
campus climate
  AAC&U on, 51
  avoidance in, 85–86
  for Blacks, xxx
  with BLM, 70
  with carceral surveillance, 307–309
  with CIDOs, 75
  diversity studies and, 42–45
  for people of color, 19–20
  at predominantly white institutions, 294–295
  for racial justice, 57–58
  with safe spaces, 42–43
  sexual orientation and, 32
  social media and, 117–118
  students and, xxiii
  at SUNY, 28
Can, Ali, 233
Canada, 233, 316–317, 322–323
cancel culture, xxii
Capps, Randy, 157–158
Capuzzo, Jill P., 144
Carafano, James, 145
carceral feminism, 300–307
carceral surveillance, 307–309
Caribbean, 10–11, 110–111
Carlyle, Thomas, 250
Carmichael, Stokely, 66

Index | 359

Cassanello, Robert, 199
Castilo, Philando, 210
CDIOs. *See* chief diversity and inclusion officers
CDOs. *See* chief diversity officers
census data, 25–26, 165–166
Center for Community Alternatives, 90
Center for Disease Control, 199, 202–203
Center for Energy and Environmental Policy Research, 208
Central America, 156–157
Central Park Five, 177
Charles III (king), 11
Chauvin, Derek, xxvii, 128, 132–133, 140, 195, 211–213. *See also* George Floyd murder
Chicana/os, 104, 124, 134, 183
chief diversity and inclusion officers (CIDOs)
  BLM to, 178
  campus climate with, 75
  in higher education, 55, 57, 296, 320
  intersectionality and, 240
  microaggressions by, 63–64
  as police, 322
  at SUNY, 238–239
chief diversity officers (CDOs), 40–41, 99, 111–113
Child, Lydia Maria, 189
Chinese Exclusion Act (1882), 155
The Chokehold (Butler), 212
Chotiner, Isaac, 281–282
"Christine Blasey Ford's Experience Was Just as Bad as Anita Hill's" (Talbot), 228–229
Citizen (Rankine), 223
City University of New York (CUNY), 98–99, 101, 107–108, 110
civil discourse, 113–116
Civil Rights Movements
  BLM and, 13
  Civil Rights Acts, 38, 156, 276–277

DEI and, xxi
history of, xx
Kaepernick in, 11
during Vietnam War, 39–40
Voting Rights Act, 38
Civil War, xx
Clark, Stephon, 210
"The Clash of Civilizations?" (Huntington), 103
class, xxvii–xxviii, 9–10, 109, 166–167, 217–218, 239–240, 272–273
Clinton, Hillary, 253, 300
Clinton, William ("Bill"), 33, 317–318
Coates, Ta Nehisi, 196, 315
Coburn, Tom, 141
cognitive inquiry, 86
COINTELPRO, 106
College Crisis Initiative, 207
Collier, Paul, 53
Collins, Patricia Hill, 220
colonialism, 66, 75, 118
  cultural imperialism in, 164–165, 293–294
  settler, xxii, 119, 189, 221, 225, 300, 322
color neutrality, xxviii, 6, 54
The Color of Violence (INCITE!), 119
colorblindness, xxviii, 54, 203–208
Columbus, Christopher, 158
Combahee River Collective, 106–107, 221–222, 261
comfortableness, 277–283
Cook, Alison, 255
Cooper, Amy, 173–177, 178
Cooper, Christian, 173–177
Cornell University, 40, 98, 105–106, 184, 319
corporate social media, 225
corporations, xvi, 11, 238–240, 243, 246, 253–254
COVID-19. *See specific topics*
Crenshaw, Kimberlé, 17, 43, 222, 228, 230

crime, 90–91, 141
critical race theory (CRT), xx, 5–6,
    43, 278, 312
  anti-CRT, 297
  difficult dialogue and, 29
  discourse, 119–120
  politics of, 124–125, 319
  slavery and, xv–xvi
  socioeconomics, 95–96
  white supremacy against, xxix
critical whiteness studies (CWS), xx,
    5–6, 29, 172, 278
Cross, Terry L., 55, 255
Cross, William, 286
Crowley, James, 138–139
CRT. *See* critical race theory
Cullors, Patrisse, 119–120, 232
cultural competence, xxi, 26–27, 181,
    254–255
Cultural Diversity and Education
    (Banks), 97
cultural genocide, 316–317
cultural imperialism
  in colonialism, 164–165, 293–294
  history of, 65–66
  immigration and, 156
  in US, xxii, 10–12
  violence from, 120, 317
  whiteness and, 244, 272
CUNY. *See* City University of New
    York
Cuomo, Andrew, 105
CWS. *See* critical whiteness studies

Dam, Arend van, 128, *129*
Dartmouth College, 117–118
Darwinism, 13
Davidson College, 207
Davis, Angela Y., 104, 227, 230, 235,
    249, 300–301
Davis-Russell, Elizabeth, 35–37, 86,
    306

De Gobineau, Arthur, 130, 267
Declaration of Independence, 9
dehumanization, 65–66
DEI. *See* Diversity, Equity, and
    Inclusion
Delgado, Richard, 43, 137
democracy, 13–14, 51–52, 322–323
  diversity and, xvi, 6–9, 87
  multicultural, 7, 15, 34–35, 39
DeRussy, Candice, 64
DeSantis, Ron, xxiii–xxiv, 2–3, 57, 152
Descartes, René, 289, 313
DeVos, Betsy, 8
Dewey, John, 131
Diallo, Amadou, 210
DiAngelo, Robin, 211–212, 264, 277
difficult dialogue, xxviii–xxiv, 29
  civil discourse and, 113–116
  inclusive excellence with, 85–87
  listening to, 42–49
  whiteness and, 188–191
DiIulio, John, Jr., 300
diverse students, 91–95
diversity. *See specific topics*
Diversity, Equity, and Inclusion (DEI),
    xx–xxiv
  activities, 6
  for administration, 61–62, 67–68,
    93
  anti-DEI, 297
  for BIPOC, 52–53
  categories, 260
  to CDOs, 99
  equity-minded approaches for, 18
  gender and, 238–240
  graduation rates with, 93–94
  heteropatriarchal leadership and, 22
  as inclusive curriculum, 312,
    321–322
  making excellence inclusive and, 94
  for marginalized citizens, 4
  politics of, xix, 2, 316

social change model and, 254
social justice and, 21
in society, 81
for students, 318–319
testing, 195
in US, 25–26
workshops, 277–278
at WU, 49
Diversity, Social Justice, and Inclusive Excellence (Asumah & Nagel), xix–xxii
diversity discourse, 97, 113–116
diversity education. *See* diversity studies
diversity management
  affirmative action and, 40–42, 108–111
  in corporations, 11
  diversity leadership and, 81–85, *84*
  double standards in, 89–90
  equity-minded approaches after, 95–96
  faculty and, 80
  failures in, 254–255
  in higher education, 81–85, *84*, 238–239
  to National Association of Diversity Officers in Higher Education, 112–113
  Ubuntu ethics and, 296–297
  in US, 116
diversity studies
  campus climate and, 42–45
  in higher education, 25–27, 37–42
  history of, 27–34
  at SUNY Cortland, 34–37, 45–49
  in US, 37–40
Divided Sisters (Russell and Wilson), xviii
Dix, Andrew, 224
Dotson, Kristie, xxvii, 218, 220, 229–230
double binds, 87–91, 117–120, 127
double standards, 87–90, 117–120
Douglass, Frederick, xvii, 66, 219, 250, 260–261, 272, 283, 308–309
Down Girl (Manne), 231
DREAMers, 98, 144
Dred Scott v. Sanford, 130, 155, 244, 266–267, 275
drugs, 101
Du Bois, W. E. B., 16–17, 21, 43, 259, 322
Dunbar-Ortiz, Roxanne, 183
Durban Declaration and Program of Action, 320
DuVernay, Ava, 177
Dyson, Michael Eric, 141, 186–187, 196, 204, 212
  racism to, 69, 72, 278
  on whiteness, 58, 64–65

East Africa, 73
Eddy, Pamela L., 255
education. *See specific topics*
effective dialogue, 87
Electoral College system, 7–8
Elizabeth II (queen), 11
Ellison, Treva C., 117–118
Elshtain, Jean Bethke, 243
Emancipation Proclamation, 13
England, 10–11
enslavement. *See* slavery
Entitled (Manne), 231
epistemic oppression, xxvii, 225–226
Equal Employment Opportunity Commission, 276
equal opportunity, 247–248
Equal Rights Amendment, 228
equity, xxii–xxiii, 1–6, 18, 21–22, 45–46, 95–96, 99–105. *See also specific topics*
Erdogan, Recep Tayyip, 233

Essay on the Inequality of Race (de Gobineau), 130, 267
ethnic diversity, 54–55
Ethnic Notions (Riggs), 177–178
ethnic paradox, 269
ethnicity, 132, 263, 266–271, 287
eugenics, 156
Europe
 Africa and, 164–165
 anti-Black racism in, 10
 BLM in, xxvii
 Eurocentricism, 106
 European racial reasoning, 267
 higher education in, 72
 history of, 104, 130
 philosophy from, 289–290
 police in, 234–235
 racism in, 318
 stereotypes of, 160–161
 US and, 13, 235
 white supremacy in, 233–234

faculty. *See specific topics*
Fair Access to Education Act, 91
The Fairer Sex (documentary), 224
Fanon, Frantz, xxvi, 43, 75, 172, 180
Farley, John E., 124
Farley, Lin, 230
Feagin, Joe
 research from, 43–44, 57, 74, 130, 159, 177–178
 on WRF, 188–189, 212–213, 244–245
Federal Bureau of Investigation, 106, 173
Federalists Papers, 6–7
feminism
 Black, 17, 291–292
 Blacks and, 181
 BLM and, 119–120
 cages in, 87–88
 carceral, 300–307

Combahee River Collective for, 106–107
Me Too and, 217–218, 235–236
racism in, 191
white, 220, 225–232
women of color, 119
Floyd, George. *See* George Floyd murder
Ford, Christine Blasey, 228–231, 301
Ford, Gerald, 134, *135*, 299
Ford Foundation, 5–6
Franklin, Ben, 226
Franklin, John Hope, 137–138
Fraser, Nancy, 98–99, 136–137
Frazier, Darnella, 209
Frey, William, 25
From Equity Talk to Equity Walk (McNair), 35–36
Fryberg, Stephanie A., 88–90, 117–119
Frye, Marilyn, 87–88
Fuchs, Kent, 199
full-time faculty, 68–69
funnel for diversity leadership, *84*

Gallagher, Sean, 112
Gandhi, Mahatma, 294
Gardiner, Marguerite, 293
Garner, Eric, 125, 128, 133, 140–141, 210, 212
Garza, Alicia, 119–120, 232, 261–262, 286
Gates, Henry Louis, Jr. ("Skip"), 125, 138–141
Gay, Roxane, 193, 213–214
gender. *See also specific topics*
 class and, 166–167
 DEI and, 238–240
 in intersectionality, 10
 Marx on, 16–17
 multiculturalism and, 32
 oppression of, 62–63

politics, xxii
race and, xxviii, 148, 240–249, *241*, 256
stereotypes, *241*, 241–242, 251–253, *252*
studies, 91–92
tenure and, 89–90
whiteness and, 173–174
Generation Z, 58
genocide, 234–235
George (king), 226
George Floyd murder
  BLM and, 125, 232, 246, 314
  Chauvin and, 128, 132–133, 140, 195
  during COVID-19, xxvi–xxvii
  COVID-19 and, 67, 213–215
  in media, 48–49
  police in, 266
  politics of, 208–213, 270
  protests after, xxi–xxii
  racial justice after, 10–11, 113
  systemic racism and, xxiii, 53–54, 193–197, 234
  Trump and, 276
Georgetown University, 295
Germany, 233–236, 293
Gettysburg Address (Lincoln), 15
Gingrich, Newt, 143
Glass, Christy, 255
Glazer, Nathan, 136
global diversity, 72–75
Global North, 205, 234
Global South, 205
Gorman, Amanda, 316
graduation rates, 93–94, 99–100, 111
Graham, Lindsey, 231
Gratz v. Bollinger, 5
Gray, Freddie, 210
Great Man theory, 237–240, 250
Great Migration, 13
Greenleaf, Robert K., 250–251
Greer, Germaine, 220–221

Grimke, Angelina, 227
group dialogue, 279–280
group identity, 272–273
group politics, 271–272
Grutter v. Bollinger, 41–42
Gutmann, Amy, 271–273

Halley, Janet, 301–302
Hamilton, Alexander, 7
Hamilton, Charles, 66
Hannah-Jones, Nikole, xxix–xxx, 64, 104, 154–155, 323
Harding, Vincent, xxi
Hare, Nathan, 69
Harlem rebellion, 107
Harris, Cheryl, 279, 285
Harris, J. C., 4
Harris, Kamala, 16, 93, 100, 209
Harvard University, 182, 246–247, 255
hate crimes, 233
hate speech, 183–187
Hayes, Chris, 65
HBCUs. *See* Historically Black Colleges and Universities
health insurance, 204–205
hegemonic masculinity. *See* heteropatriarchal hegemony
hegemony, 5, 56, 75, 106, 281
  oppression and, 113–114
  risk management and, 97–99
  of tradition, 293
  in US, 80–81
  at WU, 65–72
Helm, Angela, 153
Helms, Janet, 265, 283–286
Hemings, Sarah, 244
heteronormativity, xxii, 17, 149, 188–189, 231, 241, 281–282
heteropatriarchal hegemony, xxvii–xxviii, 8, 123–128, 133, 166–167
  Obama, B., and, 135–137, 141–142, 147–150, 159

heteropatriarchal hegemony *(continued)*
  whiteness and, xxv, 12–13, 76,
    85–86, 245, 256
heteropatriarchal leadership, xxviii, 3,
    22, 238, 255–256
heteropatriarchy, xxv, 313–314
heterosexism, *241*, 241–242
Heyer, Heather, 321
hidden double binds, 87–90
higher education. *See specific topics*
Hill, Anita, 228–231
The Hill We Climb (Gorman), 316
himpathy, 231
Hine, Darlene Clark, 89–90
Hirschfeld, Magnus, 269–270
Hispanics, 268–269
Historically Black Colleges and
    Universities (HBCUs), xxix, 93,
    185, 296
historically white colleges and
    universities, 54, 66–67, 88, 117
Hitler, Adolf, 293
Hobbes, Thomas, 290
Hochschild, Arlie, 242–243
Holder, Eric, 140
Hollinger, David A., 136
Holloway, Jenae, 280–281
Holocaust, 21
holocaust of enslavement, 10–13, 65–
    66, 154, 158, 194–195, 209–210,
    319–320
homophobia, 17, 77
Hong, Grace Kyungwon, 303
hooks, bell, 180, 191
Hopkins, Samuel, 226
Horsman, Reginald, 130–131, 267
Hottentot, Venus, 225. *See also*
    Baartman, Sara
How Racism Takes Place (Lipsitz),
    188–189
How to Be an Antiracist (Kendi), 318
Howard University, xxx, 69, 323

HSS. *See* Department of Health and
    Human Services
Hughes, Langston, xxi, 39, 156
Hull, Akasha, 17, 119
human resources departments, 73–74,
    82
humanity. *See* Ubuntu ethics
Huntington, Samuel, 103
Hurricane Katrina, 201–202

identity. *See also* racial identity
  of Blacks, 150
  group, 272–273
  of heteropatriarchal hegemony, 133
  mixed-race, 245
  politics, xx, 135–137, 260–265
  sexual orientation and, 85
  social, 112–113, 124
  white, 273–277
  white racial, 270–273, 283–286
Ignatiev, Noel, 133
immigration. *See also* racial exclusion
  Africa and, 161, *162*, 163, 167–169
  American Dream and, 143–144
  Black Africans in, xxv–xxvi, 160–
    161
  cultural imperialism and, 156
  heteropatriarchal hegemony and,
    166–167
  immigrant bodies, 123–128, 142–
    143
  immigrants of color, 155–157
  Immigration and Naturalization
    Act, 156
  laws, 143–144
  to Obama, B., 145–147
  policy, xxv–xxvi, 125–126, 145–147,
    150–153
  research on, 158–159, 161, *162*, 163
  Secure Fence Act, 160
  taxation and, 167–168
  in US, 123–124

white supremacy and, 156
  xenophobia and, 13–14
imperialism, 66, 183
implicit bias, 224, 246–247
imposters, 63–65
INCITE!, 119
inclusion. *See specific topics*
inclusive curriculum, xix–xx, 312, 321–322
inclusive excellence, xxi, 5–6, 79–81, 85–87
inclusive leadership
  by Biden, 14
  democracy and, 7–9
  diversity and, 17–18
  for equity-minded policy, 1–6
  Great Man theory and, 237–240
  for institutional change, 13
  policy for, 82–83
  professional development and, 48
  against systemic oppression, xxiv–xxv
  transactional leadership and, 2–3
  in US, 2–3, 240–249, *241*, 256
Indigenous people, 107, 109, 316–317, 322–323
An Indigenous People's History of the United States (Dunbar-Ortiz), 183
Initiative of Black people in Germany, 236
institutional change, 6, 13, 91–92, 291–292, 315–316. *See also specific topics*
institutional racism, 30–31
institutions
  antiracism in, 2
  Blacks in, 137–138
  descriptive representation of, 273–274
  heteropatriarchal hegemony in, xxvii–xxviii
  of higher education, 17–18

human resources departments in, 73–74
numerical diversity at, 16
predominantly white, 22, 28, 54, 62, 294–295
risk management in, xvi
social justice in, 81–82
transactional leadership in, 82–83
intergroup dialoguing, 186
Internal Security Act (1950), 156
internalized colonialism, 66
international curriculum, 72–75
International Monetary Fund, 53
intersectionality, 10, 222, 228–229, 240
"Invisibility in Academe" (Rich), 47
Inwood, Joshua, 291
Islamophobia, 77, 144, 234–235
Ithaca College, 60, 75

Jacobson, William, 319
Jalloh, Oury, 234
January 6th insurgency, 8–9, 14, 48–49, 209
Japan, 155–157, 219, 292
Japanese Exclusion Act (1907), 155
Jardina, Ashley, 136–137, 265, 276, 281–283
Jay, John, 7
Jefferson, Thomas, 131, *135*, 143, 154, 226–227, 244
Jews, 21, 99–100, 293
Jim Crow, 13, 60, 102–103, 171–176, 190, 244, 247. *See also specific topics*
job retention, 112
job security, 88–89
Johnson, Brennan Nevada, 116
Johnson, Samuel, 226–227
Joyner, Charles, 154
June, Audrey Williams, 249
Juneteenth, 261, 320–321

K-12 education, 110
Kaepernick, Colin, 11
Karens, 173–176
Kavanaugh, Brett, 229–231, 301
Kelley, Robin, 107, 113–114
Kendi, Ibram, 226, 265, 318
Kennedy, John, 102–103, 108–110
Kim, Elaine, 137
King, Martin Luther, Jr. (MLK), xix, xxi, 76, 126, 309, 314–319
King, Rodney, 41, 133, 270
Kipnis, Laura, 303
Knittel, Christopher R., 208
knowledge production, 64
Komives, S. R., 83–84
Kotter, J. P., 82
Kovel, J., 12
Kozol, Jonathan, 102, 104
Ku Klux Klan, xvii, 44–45, 156, 173–174
Kueng, Alex, 211
Kuh, George D., 27–28
Kumbaya sessions, 203–208, 319–320
Kunjufu, Josey-Bass, 248

Lane, Thomas, 211
language barriers, 92
Latin Americans, 8, 153, 167
Latinos
  activism by, 65
  Blacks and, 19, 71, 101–102, 147, 160
  in border states, 146–147
  Chicana/os and, 124
  in COVID-19, 202
  ethnicity of, 132
  in higher education, 184
  Hispanics and, 268–269
  Latino studies, 295–296
  in media, 145
  in US, 143
Law, Victoria, 233
Lawore, Jide, 168–169

Lazarus, Emma, 156
leadership. *See specific topics*
leadership models, 237–240, 250–251
learned racism, 56–57
Leary, Joy DeGruy, 180, 249
Lee, Robert E., 182–183, 293, 321
legacy admissions, 295
Leonardo, Zeus, 59
"Let America Be America Again" (Hughes), 156
Lewandowski, Corey, 167
Lewis, Anthony, 263
Lewis, John Robert, 209
LGBTQ, xxx, 17, 21, 307
liberal arts, 94–95
Liberia, 35–36
Lies My Teacher Told Me (Loewen), 104
Lincoln, Abraham, 15, 134, *135*
Linkova, Marcela, 243
Linnaeus, Carolus, 130, 267
Lipsitz, George, 188–189
Lissanu, Abyssinia, 181
Little, Maya, 294
loan forgiveness, 93
local government, 13–14
Locke, John, 290
Loewen, James, 104
Lorde, Audre, xxii, 17, 109, 229, 235–236
Love, Bettina, 321

Maafa, 12–13, 154, 194–195, 210–211
Machel, Somora, 66
MacKinnon, Catharine, 230
Madison, James, 7
Major League Soccer, 12
Make America Great Again, 14–15, 39, 152, 283
making excellence inclusive, 94
Making Face/Making Soul (Moraga & Anzaldúa), 119

Malatras, Jim, 205–206
management leadership, 82
Mandela, Nelson, 250
Manne, Kate, 231
Manning, Deborah, 31
marginalization, xxviii–xxix, 4, 10–11, 16, 80, 297–298
Marques, Joan, 3
Marshall, Thurgood, 229
Martin, Trayvon, 106, 125, 141, 210, 232
Martinez, Elizabeth, 137, 228–229
Martínez, Ernesto J., 88–90, 117–119
Martins, Luis L., 82
Marx, Karl, 16–17
Matel v. Tam, 185
Matthews, Chris, 125
Maxwele, Chumani, 293–294
Mbiti, John, 289, 313
McConnell, Mitch, xvi–xvii, xxv, 127
McDonald, Laquan, 210
McDougall, Gay, 320
McEnroe, John, 223
McIntosh, Peggy, 133, 186, 189–191, 270
McKinley, William, 134, *135*
McNair, Tia Brown, 35–36, 305
Me Too
  BLM and, 1, 65–66, 232–235, 238, 296–297
  feminism and, 217–218, 235–236
  Ford and, 230–231
  gender trouble in, 16–17
  misogynoir and, xxvii
  police and, 300–301
Me Two, xxvii, 217–218, 232–236
media, 14–15, 48–49, 64, 145, 194–195, 306–307
Mengele, Josef, 293
Messner, Michael, 123
metacognition, 48
Mexican-American studies, 104

Mexico, 145–146, 152
Meyer, Matt, 173
Michigan State University, 305
microaggressions
  by CDIOs, 63–64
  in education, 43
  intent and, 43–44
  microaffirmations and, 315
  microinsults as, 73
  against Obama, B., xxv
  against people of color, 29
  somatopolitics from, 224–225
  in sports, 223–224
  subcategories of, 62
microinvalidation, 55–56, 63–65
migration, 157–160
Mill, John Stuart, 185
Mills, Charles, xxvi, 220, 290
mindful listening, 86
minorities, 72–75. *See also specific minorities*
misogynoir
  examples of, 218–225, 300
  Me Too and, xxvii
  Me Two and, 217–218, 235–236
  politics and, 228–232, 323
  on social media, xxvii
misogyny, 228–232
mixed-race identity, 245
MLK. *See* King, Martin Luther, Jr.
model minorities, 72–75
Moderna, 194
Mohanty, Chandra Talpade, 34
monoculturalism, 37–38, 106–107
Moraga, Cherríe, 119
Mor-Barak, Michàlle E., 82
Morris, Barbara Jean, 205–206
Morris, Monique, 172, 180–181
Morrison, Toni, 323
Moynihan, Patrick, 136, 248–249
Mozambique, 66
Muhammad, Gholdy, 321

Mull, Rachel Cieri, 51
multicultural education, xxx, 22, 95, 104
multiculturalism, xxiv, 7, 15, 26–27, 32–35, 39, 97, 98–99
Murray, Pauli, 222, 228

Nagel, Mechthild, 36–37, 46
Namibia, 234
National Association for the Advancement of Colored People, 70, 323
National Association of Diversity Officers in Higher Education, 111–113
National Coalition Building Institute, 30–32, 35, 61
National Diversity Institute, 61
National Football League, 11–12, 246
National Origin Act (1924), 155–156
Native Americans, 103, 183
neocolonialism, 118
neoliberal higher education, 111–113
neo-Nazis, 44–45, 62, 235–236, 321
The New Jim Crow (Alexander), 102, 110
New York. *See specific topics*
Nguyen, Viet Thanh, 157
Nieto, Sonia, 181
Nietzsche, Friedrich, 312–313
Nigeria, 2, 152, 161, *162*, 165–166, 168–169
Nixon, Richard, 101, 134
Noah, Trevor, 233
numerical diversity, 16
Nyong'o, Lupita, 217–218

Obama, Barack
to Blacks, 263
Brown, M., and, 172–173
election of, 102
heteropatriarchal hegemony and, 135–137, 141–142, 147–150, 159
immigrant bodies and, 142–143
immigration to, 145–147
for marginalized citizens, xxviii–xxix
McConnell and, xvi–xvii
microaggressions against, xxv
race relations under, 137–142, *138*, *139*
racism after, 276
reform under, 7–8
SUNY and, 110
Trump and, 3–4, 39
US with, 123–128, 245
white hegemony to, 281
Obama, Michelle, 94, 141–142, 149
O'Brien, Eileen, 74
Occupy Wall Street, xxiii, 27
O'Connor, Sandra Day, 275
Olsen, Jesse E., 82
Omi, Michael, 10, 57, 123, 129–130, 240, 266–270, 318
On Liberty (Mill), 185
One America in the 21st Century (race report), 318
Opal, Tometi, 232
open universities, 99–105
oppression
anti-Black racism and, 181, 317–318
against Blacks, 60
cycles of, 115
from double binds, 88
epistemic, xxvii, 225–226
against faculty of color, 74–75
of gender, 62–63
hegemony and, 113–114
of heteropatriarchal leadership, xxviii
from language barriers, 92

narratives of, 89
Olympics, 74–75, 138, 167, 197–198, 228–232
policy for, 189
systemic, xxiv–xxv, 189
Oregon State University, 75
Ōsaka, Naomi, 219, 221
ouch and educate, 46
Outlaw, Lucius, 202
Ozaltuna, Bora, 208
Özil, Mesut, 233–234

Pan African Student Coalition, 70
pansexuality, 126
Parameswaran, Gowri, 48
Parker, Theodore, 291
Parks, Rosa, 319
partisan politics, 146–148
paternalism, 244
patriotism, 104
Patterson, Orlando, 229–230
Paul, Alice, 228
Pearson Corporation, 105
Pennsylvania State University, 305
people of color. *See also specific topics*
   BLM for, 117–118
   brown bodies, 143–144
   campus climate for, 19–20
   education for, 96
   ethnic diversity and, 54–55
   graduation rates for, 111
   microaggressions against, 29
   in politics, 39
   racial exclusion for, 155–157
   as students, 46
   at SUNY Cortland, 114–115
   whiteness to, xv–xviii
   women and, 16, 313–314
people of pallor, 262, 314
A People's History of the United States (Zinn), 104

perception research, 116
Peterson, Bob, 104
Pfizer, 194
Phillip, Abby, 14
Pittinsky, Todd, xxvi, 172, 179
plantations, xvii–xviii, 196
Plato (Aristocles), 76
Plessy v. Ferguson, 100, 155, 242, 275, 278
police. *See also specific topics*
   All Lives Matter for, 172–178
   Blacks and, 125–128, 138–140
   defunding, 322–323
   in Europe, 234–235
   in George Floyd murder, 266
   Me Too and, 300–301
   Trump and, 172–173
   violence, 208–213
policy
   antiracism, 259–265
   immigration, xxv–xxvi, 125–126, 145–147, 150–153
   for inclusive leadership, 82–83
   for institutional change, 6
   for oppression, 189
   policy-making, 263–264, 273–277
   racialized, 196–197
   racism and, 264–265
   racist, 284
   for STEM education, 21
   at SUNY Cortland, 33–34
   white identity and, 283–286
political asphyxiation, 128, *129*, 140–141
political decapitation, 63
political science, 33–34, 133–134
politics
   affirmative action in, 102–103
   of Africana studies, 96
   anti-Black racism in, 311–312
   of anti-politics, 207

politics (continued)
  asphyxiation in, xxv
  of Black Power movements, 101
  of BLM, 171–178, 191–192
  campus, 63–65
  in Canada, 322–323
  of CRT, 124–125, 319
  of DEI, xix, 2, 316
  in Federalists Papers, 6–7
  gender, xxii
  of George Floyd murder, 208–213, 270
  group, 271–272
  of hate speech, 183–187
  heteropatriarchal hegemony in, 8
  of higher education, 18–19
  identity, xx, 135–137, 260–265
  of local government, 13–14
  misogynoir and, 228–232, 323
  of multicultural education, xxx, 104
  partisan, 146–148
  people of color in, 39
  racial, 9–13
  of racial exclusion, 145–147, 151–153, 161, 162, 163, 166–169
  of *Roe v. Wade*, 21
  separatist, 297–300
  sociopolitics, 32–33, 81–82
  somatopolitics, 224–225
  in US, 71
Pomona College, 96
positive psychology, xxvi
The Possessive Investment in Whiteness (Lipsitz), 188–189
post-traumatic slave syndrome, 60, 180
poverty, 201–202
predominantly white institutions, 22, 28, 54, 62, 294–295
Premier League, 10–12
presidents, 134–135, 135, 149–150.
  See also specific presidents

Princeton University, 2, 69, 94, 181–182, 323
prison, 90–91, 101, 109, 307–308
PRODiG. See Promoting Recruitment, Opportunity, Diversity, Inclusion, and Growth
professional development, 48
progressivism, 156
A Promised Land (Obama, B.), 127
Promoting Recruitment, Opportunity, Diversity, Inclusion, and Growth (PRODiG), 4, 67, 113
public education, 307
Puerto Ricans, 101, 154–155
Pushout (Morris, M.), 180–181

quota systems, 240–241

R1. See Research 1
race. See also specific topics
  to Black Student Union, 70–72, 98, 114, 184–185
  Black/white binary model, 137–142, 138, 139
  in callout culture, 56–57
  class and, xviii, 217–218
  Clinton, W., and, 317–318
  CRT and, 312
  double binds and, 127
  Du Bois on, 16–17
  in education, 54
  ethnicity and, 271
  exploitation of, 12
  gender and, xxviii, 148, 240–249, 241, 256
  at HBCUs, 93
  heteropatriarchal hegemony and, 123–128
  heteropatriarchal masculinity and, xxv
  in higher education, 238–240
  longue durée of, 9

neutrality, 197–203
R1 and, 58
racism and, 123–124, 128–135, *129, 135*
reasoning from, 225–232
relations, xxviii, 124, 137–142, *138–139*, 262–263
Supreme Court and, 41–42, 275–276
tenure and, 89–90
in US, 65, 260
at WU, 57–60
racial awareness, 280–282
racial battle fatigue, 71
racial capitalism, xxx
racial despotism, 13–14, 166–168
racial discrimination, 320
racial exclusion, 154, *164*
for Black Africans, 157–160
education and, 164–166, *166*
for people of color, 155–157
politics of, 145–147, 151–153, 161, *162*, 163, 166–169
racial formation, 142–143
racial identity
ethnicity and, 263, 266–270
white, 270–273, 283–286
white identity and, 273–277
whiteness and, 259–265, 286–287
racial justice. See also *specific topics*
with administration, 60
to Biden, 9
campus climate for, 57–58
equity-minded approaches for, 21–22
after George Floyd murder, 10–11, 113
hegemony and, 56
MLK for, 126
protests for, xxvi–xxvii, 97
stakeholders in, 191–192
in US, 319–320

racial politics, 9–13
racialized policy, 196–197
racism. See also *specific topics*
ableism and, 109
anti-Black racism, xxvi
Black, 209
against Blacks, 311–312
in cinema, 142
during COVID-19, 20, 193–197
definitions of, 269–270
to Dyson, 69, 72, 278
education about, 187–188
in Europe, 318
in feminism, 191
gender politics and, xxii
in higher education, 62–63, 188–191
immigration and, 152–153
learned, 56–57
Make America Great Again and, 39, 152
in media, 14–15
after Obama, B., 276
patterns of, 115
policy and, 264–265
at predominantly white institutions, 62
prejudice and, 269
psychology of, 47
race and, 123–124, 128–135, *129, 135*
racial stereotypes, 149, 213
racist jokes, 46–47
racist policy, 284
sexism and, 16–17, 22, 35, 59–60
on social media, 173–174
in sports, 218–224, 233–234
structural, 52
Supreme Court on, 262, 266–267, 278–279
systemic, xv–xvii, xxiii, 53–54, 189, 193–197, 208–213, 234

racism *(continued)*
  of Trump, 13–14, 160–161, 167, 300–303
  in Ubuntu ethics, 292–296
  in US, 9–13, 32–33, 44–45, 100
  violence from, 41
  white privilege and, 265
  white supremacy and, 134, *135*
  whiteness and, 266–270
  WRF for, 43–44
Racist America (Feagin), 177–178
Radical Reconstruction, xxix–xxx, 13
Ramos, Carlos, 219, 223
Rankine, Claudia, 222–223
Reagan, Ronald, 102–103, 134, *135*
Reagon, Bernice, 298
recognition, 98–99, 109–110
reconciliation, 316–323
Reconstruction, xx, xxix, 323
reeducation, 76–77, 115
Regents University of California v. Bakke, 5
Rehnquist, William, 275
religion, 10, 100–101, 157, 164–165, 313
remote learning, 197–203, 205–206
Research 1 (R1), xxiii, 53–54, 58
restorative justice, 303–304, 308–309
Rethinking Columbus (Bigelow & Peterson), 104
rhizomatous racism, 196
Rhodes, Cecil, 292–295
Rich, Adrienne, 47, 79
Riggs, Marlon, 177–178
risk management, xvi, xxiii, 18–22, 51–57, 75–76, 97–99
Roberts John, 275–276
Rochon, Tom, 60, 238
Rockefeller, Nelson, 100–102
Roe v. Wade, 21, 311–312
Roediger, David, 186
Romney, Mitt, 143
Rosaldo, Renato, 79

Ross, Lawrence, 60, 70–71, 185, 190, 295–296
Ross, Loretta, 46
Rost, Joseph C., 82
Rousseau, Jean-Jacques, 250, 290
The Routledge Companion to Inclusive Leadership (Marques), 3
Rufo, Christopher, 297
Russell, Kathy, xviii, 31
Russell-Brown, Katheryn, 225
Ryan, April, 14

Safe OUTside the System, 304–305
safe spaces, 42–43
Saleh-Hannah, Viviane, 221–222, 291–292
San Francisco State University, 40, 98, 184
Savage Inequalities (Kozol), 102, 104
Sawyer, Wendy, 90
Scalia, Antonin, 275
Schaefer, Richard T., 131, 268–269
Schlesinger, Arthur, 136–137
Schneiderman, Eric, 231–232
school shootings, 19
SchwarzRund, 234
Scott, Patricia, 119
Secure Fence Act (2006), 160
segregation, 297–300
Segrest, Mab, 186
self-awareness, 83–84
Selvaratnma, Tanya, 231–232
Semenya, Caster, 225
Seneca Falls Declaration of Sentiments, 227
separatist politics, 297–300
Sertima, Ivan Van, 158
Sessions, Jeff, 157
settler colonialism, xxii, 119, 189, 221, 225, 300, 322
sexism, xxv, 16–17, 22, 35, 59–60, 77, 115. *See also specific topics*

sexual orientation, 10, 32, 85, 126
Shades of Black (Cross, W.), 286
Shakur, Assata, 235
Sharma, Robin, 76
Sierra Leone, 234
Simmons, Ann M., 151
Sinophobia, 153
Sirleaf, Ellen Johnson, 35–36
slavery, xv–xvii, 60, 157–158, 175–176, 183–187. *See also* holocaust of enslavement
Smith, Barbara, 119, 261
social alexithymia, xxii–xxiii, 27
social asphyxiation, 209–210
social change model, 83–84, 254
social identity, 112–113, 124
social justice. *See specific topics*
social media, xxvii, 92, 117–118, 173–174, 225, 235
social trust, 246–247
sociocultural phenomenons, 132
socioeconomics, 9–10, 95–96
sociology, 268–269
sociopolitics, 32–33, 81–82
solipsism
 in society, 70, 220, 290
 white, 179–180, 187–188, 244, 246, 298, 300
somatopolitics, 224–225
Sotomayor, Sonya, 259, 276
South Africa, 290–291. *See also* Ubuntu ethics
sports, 10–13, 218–224, 233–234, 246
standardized tests, 92
Stanford University, 75
Stanton, Elizabeth Cady, xvii, 227
State Department, US, 320
State University of New York (SUNY)
 AAC&U and, 31–32
 administration, 48–49
 campus climate at, 28
 CIDOs at, 238–239
 CUNY and, 99

history of, 100–101
 leadership of, 205–206
 Obama and, 110
 PRODiG at, 4
 whiteness at, 40–41
statues, 292–296, 316
status quo, 315–316
Steck, Henry, 114–115
Steele, Claude M., 94, 96
STEM education, 4, 21, 105
Sterling, Alton, 210
Stimson, Blake, 56
structural racism, 52
students. *See specific topics*
Students for Fair Admission, Inc. v. President & Fellows of Harvard College, 5
Students for Fair Admissions, Inc. v. University of North Carolina, 5
study abroad, 72–75
SUNY. *See* State University of New York
SUNY Cortland
 AAC&U and, 34
 administration, 30–32
 affirmative action at, 42
 antiracism at, 27
 BIPOC students at, 28–29
 Black Student Union at, 184
 Black studies at, 40
 diversity studies at, 34–37, 45–49
 Harvard University and, 246–247
 higher education at, xxii–xxiii
 people of color at, 114–115
 policy at, 33–34
 recruitment by, 108
 remote learning at, 205–206
 research from, 27–28
SUNY New Paltz, 48
SUNY Oneonta, 112, 205–206
Supreme Court, 21, 41–42, 228–230, 262, 266–267, 274–279, 311–312
Syracuse University, 60, 75

Systema naturae (Linnaeus), 130
systemic oppression, xxiv–xxv, 189
systemic racism, xv–xvii, xxiii, 53–54, 189, 193–197, 208–213, 234
Syverud, Kent, 60

Taft, William, 134, *135*
Talbot, Margaret, 228–229
Taney, Roger B., 275
Tatum, Beverly, 271–272, 286
taxation, 167–168
Taylor, Breonna, 210, 234
Taylor, Keeanga-Yamahtta, 263
Tea Party, 102
Teaching to Transgress (hooks), 180, 191
tenure, 89–90, 117–118
terrorism, 160
Texas, 105
Thernstrom, Abigail, 263
Thernstrom, Stephen, 263
This Bridge Called My Back (Moraga & Anzaldúa), 119
Thomas, Clarence, 229–231
Thomas, Jack, 238
Thomas-Greenfield, Linda, 320
Till, Emmett, 174, 177, 211
Title IX, 8, 55, 57, 63, 296, 300–307
Tometi, Opal, 119–120
town hall meetings, 114, 184–185, 190
tradition, 292–296
transactional leadership
  in business, 239–240
  in corporations, 238
  heteropatriarchal leadership and, 255–256
  inclusive leadership and, 2–3
  in institutions, 82–83
  paradigms in, 251–254, *252*
  theory of, 251–254, *252*
  Trump and, 20–21
  in US, 240

transformational leadership, xxvii–xxviii, 186–187, 251–254, *252*
transgender rights, 105
transphobia, xxix, 21
Traub, James, 107–108
Tribal Colleges, 296
triggers, 114
True Colors (documentary), 224
The Truly Diverse Faculty (Fryberg and Martínez), 88–89, 117–119
Trump, Donald
  Biden and, 56–57, 104, 157
  BLM to, 102
  Clinton, H., and, 253
  on COVID-19, 200–201
  Electoral College system and, 7–8
  George Floyd murder and, 276
  impeachment of, 209
  January 6th insurgency and, 48–49
  leadership of, xxii, 153, 156–157, 176–177
  Make America Great Again and, 14–15
  Obama, B., and, 3–4, 39
  police and, 172–173
  public trust with, 274
  racism of, 13–14, 160–161, 167, 300–303
  reputation of, xxv, 2–3, 20–21, 62, 64, 134, 152, 159–160, 165
  transactional leadership and, 20–21
Truth, Sojourner, xvii
Truth and Reconciliation Commission, 292, 295
tuition, 101
Ture, Kwame, 66
Turkey, 233–234
Turkish-Americans, 73–74
Turner, James, 40
Tuskegee study, 214, 307
Tutu, Desmond, 289, 297

typology, of presidents, 134, *135*

Ubuntu ethics, xxviii, 95
  accountability work in, 300–307
  diversity management and, 296–297
  ideology of, 289–292
  racism in, 292–296
United Kingdom, 10–11
United Nations, 234–235, 320
United States (US)
  Africa and, 245, 293
  African diaspora in, 193–194
  Afrophobia in, xxvi, 157–161
  American Dream, 143–144, 156, 179
  BIPOC in, 59
  Black Africans in, 154–155, 161, *162*, 163
  Blacks in, xv–xviii, 266
  Black/white binary model in, 137–142, *138*, *139*
  BLM in, 98
  Canada and, 233
  census data, 25–26, 165–166
  Central America and, 156–157
  class in, 239–240
  Congress, 274
  Constitution, 38, 227
  after COVID-19, xxi–xxii
  cultural imperialism in, xxii, 10–12
  Declaration of Independence, 9
  DEI in, 25–26
  diversity management in, 116
  diversity studies in, 37–40
  East Africa and, 73
  England and, 10–11
  equal opportunity in, 247–248
  ethnicity in, 287
  Europe and, 13, 235
  health insurance in, 204–205
  hegemony in, 80–81
  history of, 151–152
  holocaust of enslavement in, 10, 65–66
  HSS in, 157
  ideology of, 6–7
  immigration in, 123–124
  inclusive leadership in, 2–3, 240–249, *241*, 256
  Indigenous people in, 316–317
  institutional change in, 291–292
  K-12 education in, 110
  Kumbaya sessions in, 203–208
  Latin Americans in, 153
  Latinos in, 143
  media in, 306–307
  Mexico and, 145–146, 152
  Nigeria and, 2, 152, 161, *162*, 165–166, 168–169
  with Obama, B., 123–128, 245
  partisan politics in, 146–148
  politics in, 71
  predominantly white institutions in, 54
  race in, 65, 260
  race relations in, 262–263
  racial exclusion in, 160–161
  racial justice in, 319–320
  racism in, 9–13, 32–33, 44–45, 100
  segregation in, 297–300
  social justice in, 37
  society, 22, 34–35, 163, *164*, 312–315
  State Department, 320
  Title IX in, 300–307
  tolerance in, xx
  tradition in, 292–296
  transactional leadership in, 240
  war on drugs in, 101
university citizens, 84–85
University Life and Living Center, 57–58

University of North Carolina, xxx, 5, 105, 107, 294, 323
University of Umzukulu, 72–74
US. *See* United States

VanDerLinden, Kim E., 255
Vidal, Gore, 59
Vietnam War, 39–40
Virginia Tech, 19–20, 75
Virginia v. Black, 185
Visconti, Luke, 140
Vitter, David, 142
Vollman, Alexandra, 96
Voting Rights Act (1965), 38

Wagner, Peter, 90
war on drugs, 101
Ward, Eric, 18, 21–22
Washington, Booker T., 283
Washington, George, 151, 183
Watts rebellion, 107
Weinstein, Harvey, 217–218, 231–233
Wellman, David, 269, 285
Wells-Barnett, Ida B., 323
West, Cornell, 130, 267
What Doesn't Kill You Makes You Blacker (Young), 171
When They See Us (film), 177
white administrators, 72–75
white feminism, 220, 225–232
white fragility, 185–186, 224–225
white hegemony, 281
white identity, 273–277
White Identity Politics (Jardina), 265, 281–283
white ignorance, 221
white institutional presence, xx, 5, 18, 22, 53
white leadership, 76–77
White Lives Matter Most and Other "Little" White Lies (Meyer), 173

white negativity, 131
white privilege, xxviii, 3, 133, 159, 189–191, 265, 272–273
white racial frame (WRF), 43–44, 168, 188–189, 212–213, 237–240, 244–245
white racial identity, 270–273, 283–286
white solipsism, 179–180, 187–188, 244, 246, 298, 300
white supremacy
  against BIPOC, 194
  against Black women, xvii
  to Blacks, 225
  against CRT, xxix
  DEI and, xx
  education against, xv
  in Europe, 233–234
  history of, xviii
  immigration and, 156
  racism and, 134, *135*
white syllogism, 243–244
white women, xxvii, 5, 103, 108–109
Whitehill University (WU), xxiii, 49, 53–54
  beloved community at, 75–77
  campus politics at, 63–65
  faculty development at, 61–63
  hegemony at, 65–72
  international curriculum at, 72–75
  microinvalidation at, 63–65
  race at, 57–60
  risk management at, 51–57
whiteness
  for BIPOC, 94–95, 195–196, 279
  Blackness and, 172–178, 272
  color neutrality and, 6
  cultural imperialism and, 244, 272
  difficult dialogue and, 188–191
  in discourse, 59
  Dyson on, 58, 64–65

elitism and, 99
gender and, 173–174
hegemonic masculinity and, xxv, 12–13
heteropatriarchal hegemony and, xxv, 12–13, 76, 85–86, 245, 256
higher education and, 22, 57–60
history of, 59–60
Karens and, 173–176
to people of color, xv–xviii
psychology of, 59–60
racial identity and, 259–265, 286–287
racism and, 266–270
social alexithymia and, 27
social justice and, 187–188
at SUNY, 40–41
white privilege and, 159
white racial comfort, 277–283
Whiteview College, 54, 62–63
Whitt, E. J., 27–28
"Who Benefits?" (Harris, J. C.), 4
Why Are All the Black Kids Sitting Together in the Cafeteria (Tatum), 286
Williams, Patricia, 43
Williams, Serena, 219–224
Williams, Venus, 219, 221–222
Wilson, Darren, 125
Wilson, Midge, xviii
Wilson, Woodrow, 134, 182
Winant, Howard, 10, 57, 123, 129–130, 240, 266–270, 318
Winfrey, Oprah, 250
Wise, Tim, 186
wokeness, 3
Wolfe, Tim, 238

women
of color, 119, 323
in higher education, 73
misogyny, 228–232
people of color and, 16, 313–314
white, xxvii, 5, 103, 108–109
Women, Race and Class (Davis), 104, 227
Women's History Month, 299
women's studies, 65–72
women's suffrage movement, 227–228
Woods, Mario, 210
Woodson, Carter G., 299
workshops, 115–116
World Bank, 53
World Cup, 11–12
Wozniacki, Caroline, 223
WRF. *See* white racial frame
WU. *See* Whitehill University
Wu, Frank, 137
Wuerker, Matt, 138, *138*

xenophobia, xxix, 13–14, 77, 142–144

Yale University, 184
Yoffe, Emily, 301–302
Young, Damon, 171
Young, Iris Marion, 12, 86, 98–99, 120
youthification, 163, *164*

Zakaria, Fareed, 194
Zalcman, Daniella, 317
Zimmerman, George, 106, 232
Zimpher, Nancy, 111–113
Zinn, Howard, 104
Zurara, Gomes de, 267

www.ingramcontent.com/pod-product-compliance
Lightning Source LLC
Chambersburg PA
CBHW022032020325
22763CB00019B/425